Exploring social lives

Exploring social lives

Edited by Simon Bromley, John Clarke, Steve Hinchliffe and Stephanie Taylor

The Open University Walton Hall, Milton Keynes MK7 6AA

First published 2009

Edited and designed by The Open University

Typeset in India by Alden Prepress Services, Chennai

Printed in Malta by Gutenberg Press Limited

The paper used in this publication is procured from forests independently certified to the level of Forest Stewardship Council (FSC) principles and criteria. Chain of custody certification allows the tracing of this paper back to specific forest-management units (see www.fsc.org).

ISBN 978 0 7492 1642 9

1.1

Contents

Preface   vii

Introduction: Material lives   1

Chapter 1   The changing UK economy: making a greener and happier society?   9

Chapter 2   Living with risk and risky living   53

Chapter 3   Living in a common world   97

Conclusion: Material lives   143

Introduction: Connected lives   149

Chapter 4   Migration: changing, connecting and making places   155

Chapter 5   Making national identities: Britishness in question   203

Chapter 6   Identity change and identification   247

Conclusion: Connected lives   291

Introduction: Ordered lives   297

Chapter 7   Governing problems   301

Chapter 8   Political ordering   347

Chapter 9   Pirates and predators: authority and
              power in international affairs   391

Conclusion: Ordered lives   437

Acknowledgements   442

Index   447

Preface

Exploring Social Lives is the course textbook for the second part of *Introducing the social sciences* (DD101). As with other Open University texts, *Exploring Social Lives* has been produced by a 'course team' of academic and production staff that included the authors and editors named here but many others besides. This wider course team played a key role in shaping the course, the book and the individual chapters through successive drafts. Professor Alan Warde, our external assessor, was a valued source of critical and supporting advice and we very much appreciate all his careful work on our behalf.

The academic staff at the Open University are unusually lucky in being able to benefit from the expertise and professionalism of the best production and administrative colleagues. Lesley Moore and Annette Portlock, our Course Co-ordinators, were models of efficiency and good humour and provided strong support to the course team. Emma Sadera and Richard Jones, our Editorial Media Developers, did far more than edit and compose the book with care, attention to detail and goodwill: they must take a large share of the credit for the clarity, coherence and accessibility of the text that follows. Thanks are also due to Paul Hillery and Howie Twiner, Graphics Media Developers, for their creative work on the design and artwork of the book. And last, but certainly not least, thanks to Matt Staples, Caitlin Harvey, Lucy Smith and Lucy Morris, and then Eileen Potterton and Meridian, who successively worked as Course Managers on *Introducing the social sciences*. They oversaw the production of this book and the rest of the course with such energy, efficiency and patience that our lives were made much easier than we had any right to expect.

Exploring Social Lives is divided into three strands of content – Material lives; Connected lives; and Ordered lives. While focusing mainly on aspects of UK society, each of these strands is set in an international and global context. The strands are introduced and concluded by the strand editors, respectively, Steve Hinchliffe, Stephanie Taylor, and John Clarke. Along with the rest of the course team, they worked to shape and refine this text and we are very grateful for all their creative efforts.

Georgina Blakeley and Simon Bromley
Co-chairs of the *Introducing the social sciences* course team

Introduction: Material lives

Steve Hinchliffe

Introduction: Material lives

As you make progress within the social sciences you will find it possible to use the tools that you have acquired to address new issues, confront new problems or think about things in different ways. In the process you can build on your current understanding of society and even add new skills to your social science toolkit. This book aims to build on the understandings and knowledge that you gained in *Making Social Lives* in the following ways:

- First, the book is organised into the same three strands that you encountered in *Making Social Lives*. So you will be meeting similar ideas and concerns about material lives, connected lives and ordered lives.

- Second, the same questions will inform your study of these chapters: 'How are differences and inequalities produced?'; 'How is society made and repaired?'; 'How do we (as social scientists) know?'.

- Third, we are concerned again with learning how to *do* social science (hence the 'How do we know?' question and sections animate each chapter). In reading these chapters you will add to the skills and understanding that you have already developed, becoming more experienced in applying those skills to new situations.

Finally, while in *Making Social Lives* the chapters shared a similar starting point – the street – and used this to understand contemporary society in the UK, here chapters tend to take the UK more generally as a starting point. Moreover, many of the chapters move quickly beyond the UK today in order to tease out the interrelations between social lives in one place and time and those in other places and times. So we learn how UK lives are connected to, ordered by and materially shaped by lives that may be many miles away.

In *Making Social Lives*, many of the chapters that used the street as a point of departure quickly took one step off the street, and you encountered department stores, rubbish heaps, gardens and census data as other sites where we could usefully study society in the making. In this book we move even further from the street and start to explore more sites where society is made, broken or repaired, and where the issues of inequalities and differences colour our understanding of society. The chapters have a common reference point – the contemporary UK – but this reference point quickly takes us elsewhere. So, chapters in this book often start with the UK, with its banks, people, health services, atmosphere, but sooner or later you are taken to Bhutan, to the Mediterranean, to international treaties, to India and to a host of other locations.

As in *Making Social Lives*, each of the strands has its own introduction and set of concluding comments. So you will read more about the second and third strands in the introductions that precede each group of chapters. This first strand, 'Material lives', remember, looks at *how* people live, their material existence, and how these ways of life have consequences for their own and other people's welfare, for society and for the environment. In *Making Social Lives* we used one particular social activity, shopping, to open up a set of questions about how people live material lives (where and how they shop, whether or not they have choice, how people's shopping and consumption connect to issues of inequality and to environmental concerns). In this book we take these issues further in the following ways.

In Chapter 1, we take a step back from all that shopping in order to think about how economies are made and repaired. You will learn how an economy is characterised and how, in particular, the UK economy can be understood through its relationship with the global economy and through the interrelationships of the individual economies of Scotland, Wales, Northern Ireland and England. Akin in some ways to the consumer society that you learned about in *Making Social Lives*, the UK economy is often characterised by its relative affluence (it's also what some people call a developed economy), its reliance on services, and, until very recently, on the ascendancy of financial services. However, the author Ian Fribbance wants you to think about at least three issues.

First, when you characterise an economy as developed or increasingly reliant on financial and other services, what does this obscure? Are there regional differences within that economy? Is the Welsh economy the same as the English economy, and within those countries are there areas that are doing more or less well? Similarly, does it make sense to talk of a UK economy in isolation when many of the businesses depend on money from overseas and, as we saw in *Making Social Lives*, many of the goods consumed are made elsewhere? In short, by looking at the facts and figures that relate to an economy, what differences and possible inequalities are left out of the picture?

Second, is this economy, which is largely based on services and so-called knowledge industries better for the environment? On the one hand, it would seem that the closure of a large amount of manufacturing in the UK heralded a less polluting form of economic activity. But, as Fribbance shows, if we look at the bigger picture and think about the environmental costs of the goods that the British import from overseas (and of course the rubbish that they export back again – see *Making Social Lives*, Chapter 3), then the idea that the UK is somehow greener than in the past starts to look questionable.

Finally, even with recent downturns, if we look at the figures then it seems that the UK is a more affluent society than it was in the past and better off than many other nations. Apart from the fact that this measure may hide gross and widening economic inequalities within the UK, does this average growth in prosperity make people, on average, any better off in terms of quality of life and happiness? As Fribbance shows, it is difficult to tell, but there are indications that happiness does not follow from economic growth. The point is an old one – money does not buy happiness – but it, and the realisation that economic growth might be generating huge environmental costs, starts to show how the social sciences are often called upon not only to study society but also to question how it is materially organised.

In Chapter 2, the balance between the benefits of an activity (such as producing material wealth) and its costs (such as a reduction in well-being and increased environmental damage) are considered together under the heading of 'risk'. For some observers, we now live in something called a risk society – a society where we are increasingly faced with the consequences of the ways in which we live. Environmental problems are just one example of such consequences – should we continue to grow our economies at the risk of turning the earth into an uninhabitable planet or are there other ways of organising life? As Simon Carter and Tim Jordan suggest, risk also has a more mundane, everyday part to play in people's lives. Should we eat this food, take this medicine, cycle to school or take a bus, lie in the sun, work this hard? Some of these things we do without a second thought, but we also live, it is argued, in a society where we are increasingly asked to recognise risks. The problem is, as the authors note through detailed examples of growing food on an allotment and holiday makers' attitudes to suntanning, that it is often difficult to know who to believe. Do we avoid the sun when it often makes us feel healthier? If one scientist says something is safe and another says it is risky, how do we judge? How does society carry on despite the fact that the risks that threaten to undo it are becoming more apparent? How is society repaired?

The authors argue that people make sense of risks in complex ways. They certainly don't take 'expert' claims as truth; rather, such claims are judged against other knowledge and used selectively. Indeed, it turns out that this scepticism is highly reasonable, for all knowledge, no matter how expert and sophisticated, is open to being questioned and interpreted as it is used. Rather than this lay form of knowledge being labelled as somehow ignorant or stubborn, it is the case that often people make quite sophisticated judgements on risk. For example, it turns out that many public health campaigns, such as those encouraging us to exercise more or drink less, have by nature to be aimed at a general population, which means that if people decide that the change in lifestyle is not for them then many of them are, partly at least, right. What works at a general level, for a whole population, may not be right for individuals or groups within that population. There is a paradox, then, in living in a risk society that the more people are told to live in a particular way in order to minimise risk, the more they may fail to be motivated by the advice. This issue of how to live with risk, and, indeed, the problem of organising diverse groups, is particularly evident when we consider global issues – something that is taken up in Chapter 3.

One of the key aspects of a risk society, and one of the issues that currently informs our thinking about the economy, is the environment. While environmental issues were once mainly the concern of natural scientists, they are now a key concern for social science. How people live, their material lives, are dependent on a host of connections to the environment. Therefore, if we are to be able to do anything about current environmental problems, then we must look at the ways that societies are materially organised, connected and ordered. In the final chapter of this strand we look at the ways in which social science ideas have, selectively, been used to generate solutions to one of the most pressing social and environmental issues – global climate change. The chapter asks whether we can live in a common world – common, that is, with over 6.5 billion other people, with many nation states and with other non-human inhabitants of the planet. If the atmosphere is imagined as a common, rather like the land that people used to be able freely to graze their sheep and cattle on and which was held in common (meaning people had a right to use it and it was in that sense open access), then can we start to find ways of avoiding the problem of overusing that common by, in this case, using it to absorb all of our exhaust gases from our factories, cars, houses, and so on? Michael Pryke takes you through some of the ways in which global climate change has been addressed and notes how it is the market and the supply and demand mechanisms that you learnt about in *Making Social Lives*, Chapter 3, that are currently in vogue and are seen as the most efficient and effective way of dealing with the external costs of economic growth. But, as Pryke argues, the market that has been created to deal with the overuse of the atmosphere is far from ideal. It seems to be rewarding those who already pollute, is subject to the vagaries of the financial markets (which have been unstable in the last few years), and seems to reimpose divisions between the relatively wealthy in the global North and the impoverished in the global South. In short, as an attempt to repair society's failings, the recent fashion is to turn our backs on a certain style of government and put faith in something called the market to repair things. And yet real markets can reinforce rather than mend divisions. They can, if we are not careful, simply increase the gap between rich and poor, and make overuse of the environment more rather than less prevalent. There is little sign as yet that the new markets that have been made to counter climate change are having the necessary effect in taking us to a low-carbon society, and, more broadly, to a world that can be lived in in common. Rather like the conclusion to Chapter 1, it may be that until there is a realisation that the economies of the global North are part of the problem rather than the solution, we may be no nearer to fixing global social problems.

Each of the chapters you will now read can start to provide answers to our key questions – 'How are differences and inequalities produced?'; 'How is society made and repaired?'; 'How do we (as social scientists) know?'. Moreover, they speak about a world that is complex, interconnected and where there is rarely one right answer. Social scientists need to be wary of simple solutions to complex social issues. We will return to these questions in the brief conclusion to this strand, and focus in particular on how we know.

Chapter 1
The changing UK economy: making a greener and happier society?

Ian Fribbance

Contents

Introduction   13

1   The UK economy: a period of change   15

   1.1   What is an 'economy'?   15

   1.2   An overview of the UK economy   17

   1.3   Inside the UK economy   27

2   An economy that is getting 'greener'?   30

   2.1   Economic growth and environmental change   30

   2.2   A weightless economy?   31

3   The UK: an increasingly well-off economy and happy society?   38

   3.1   Comparing the UK economy more widely   38

   3.2   Are measures of national income enough?   40

   3.3   Economic growth and happiness over time   45

Conclusion   49

References   50

Introduction

A changing economy and a changing society

Activity 1

To start this chapter, I'd like you to take 10 minutes to think about how your life compares with the life someone like you might have led forty or fifty years ago. Think about your shopping, the items you own or consume, perhaps your employment or other forms of work or caring activities, your family, relationships and domestic arrangements. Would you describe yourself as 'better off' than such a person from the past? Are you likely to be 'happier'? And what about your impact on the environment, from shopping, eating, heating and travelling, compared with someone from that time? Jot down some of your thoughts.

We're all likely to have very different answers to the questions. There are data which show that, in fact, the average income of UK citizens is more than twice what it was about forty years ago (ONS, 2008, p. 62). Generally, they also have many more 'luxury' items than they did forty years ago, such as household appliances and electrical consumer items, and a wider choice of relatively cheaper foods, including ready-prepared and exotic foods. People in the UK also have far greater access to all kinds of items from abroad that would have been much rarer forty years ago. And they are living significantly longer on average too. There is data showing, for example, that in 1981 a 21-year-old male would live for another 51 years (to age 72); but by 2008 that figure had risen to almost 58 years, so a 21-year-old male would live to be over 79 (Government Actuary's Department, 2008). Does this help convince you that UK citizens are becoming 'better off' and therefore happier than people used to be in the recent past?

Luxury goods and changes in affluence are discussed in *Making Social Lives*, Chapters 1 and 3.

Perhaps not – and there is some evidence that suggests otherwise. According to quantitative data collected each year since 1973, the proportion of people very or fairly satisfied with their standard of living has remained more or less unchanged at around 85 per cent (ONS, 2008, p. 64). And if UK citizens are only as satisfied with their *economic* well-being as forty years ago, despite their rise in income, perhaps people are 'less happy' overall. For example, a poll conducted for the BBC claimed that, despite all the economic benefits of modern-day life,

UK citizens are actually *less* happy than back in the 1950s, with the proportion of people saying they are 'very happy' having fallen from 52 per cent in 1957 to 36 per cent in 2005 (BBC Online, 2006).

Waste is discussed in *Making Social Lives*, Chapter 3.

And what did you jot down about our impact on the environment? Perhaps you instinctively think that as the UK has got richer so its citizens are consuming more, and engaging in more environmentally damaging actions, such as the creation of waste, using more aeroplanes and cars that put greenhouse gases into the atmosphere, and consuming more domestic energy. Or maybe you instinctively think that UK citizens are more environmentally friendly now – perhaps living in better-insulated houses in cities that are smoke-free, driving more fuel-efficient cars, and not being so reliant on coal and heavy industry as forty years ago. Doubtless, evidence can be found to support both of these points of view too.

The complex relationships between the economy and economic change, and issues of the environment and of well-being, are of great fascination to many social scientists, and these are the kinds of issues that this chapter is going to start to explore. These are necessarily important parts of a course strand that looks at material lives – and important in examining whether our increasingly material lives are better lives too. So, Section 1 introduces you to some recent economic changes, and starts to characterise what the UK economy looked like in the early twenty-first century as a result. In Section 2, we briefly explore the relationship between economic change and the environment. This will start to open up questions such as whether economic changes are helping to make the UK a 'greener' place, and are reducing its contribution to pollution and greenhouse gas emissions. Then, in Section 3, we consider in more detail whether the kinds of economic changes I have described are helping to make the UK a 'happier' society too; for example, does economic growth – the process of us becoming richer – make us truly 'better off'?

1   The UK economy: a period of change

1.1   What is an 'economy'?

To start to address some of these issues, we need to begin by thinking about what exactly we mean when we talk of an 'economy'. On the one hand, there are resources, including natural resources such as land, oil, fish or forests; human-made resources such as machines, offices and roads; and labour resources, namely people and how much and what type of work they can do. On the other hand, there are the many different things that people want to be produced from those resources – these could be goods (such as food, cars, fuel or computers) or services (such as insurance, banking, health care or education). An **economy** is the name given to the range of activities and the social arena that brings about the *production* of those goods and services from the many different economic resources. An economy also somehow organises the *distribution* of those goods and services, thus determining who gets those goods and services and in what proportion – or, to put it more bluntly, who becomes richer and poorer in an economy. The term also covers the processes of the *exchange* of those goods and services, whether that be through buying and selling (through mechanisms such as shops, wholesalers and the internet), through government activity such as raising taxes and spending to provide certain goods and services, or through work done within households, most of which is not bought and sold. Finally, people's *consumption* of goods and services is also economic. So, an economy covers a whole range of human activity and is an inherent part of society.

Economy
The name given to the range of activities that gives rise to the production, distribution, exchange and consumption of goods and services.

One very common way of organising all this production, distribution, exchange and consumption, especially in Western societies like the UK, is through markets and changes in prices. You probably already know that prices change according to changes in demand and supply. The prices charged for all these resources, commodities, goods and services act as a signal to the various buyers and sellers, who are the economic agents that make up the economy. They might respond to price rises for a particular commodity by buying less of it, or to price falls by buying more of it. But economic production, distribution and exchange can also be determined by things that a government decides or does. For example, in the UK the government collects various taxes, and uses these to pay for goods and services such as health care, which is

You first met markets and price changes in *Making Social Lives*, Chapter 3, Section 3.

generally free at the point of use (or has a zero price), and education, which is available free to the recipient (at least at lower levels of education). The extent to which economies are best organised by the market mechanism or by the government, or some mixture of the two, is the subject of often fierce debate between social scientists, as it is between politicians and political commentators.

Goods and services can be traded through markets and prices, or delivered through government taxation

Economies operate at many different *levels* too. So some social scientists will be interested in economies at *household* level – who earns household income; who gets to spend it and on what; how and what financial decisions are made in a household, and the connected gender roles. One interesting point about household-level economics is that, generally, the production of goods and services within a household (such as cleaning or caring) is not given monetary value within measures of the economy. Other social scientists will be interested in the economics of *firms* – such as how firms in particular industries compete with each other. Yet others are particularly interested in *local* or *regional* economies (such as those of, say, South Wales or the valleys of South Wales), considering issues such as what goods and services are produced in a particular locality and why; or perhaps why the levels of unemployment in a particular area are high, and what can be done about that. Others again will be most interested in *national* economies. They will be studying the economies of states such as the UK, France, China or Ghana, and what kinds of production, exchange and distribution take place in those states, and how they trade with one another. Some social scientists will look at the *global* economy, where questions affecting the whole world become most important. At a global level, social scientists might be interested in questions such as how production is distributed and how climate change might affect what is produced in the future, while others will be interested in questions that were brought into sharp relief during 2008/09, such as how economic and financial crises spread between countries and how the global economic system is very interconnected. As we shall see, none of these levels is self-contained. Household economies are closely tied to global markets and vice versa. For example, the collapse in 2006/07 of the American mortgage lending and credit markets impacted directly on household budgets and, in turn, because households had less money to spend, this fed directly back into the downturn in the global economy in 2009.

I am now going to focus on one particular national economy – the UK – in order to draw out some important points about recent economic changes. I will refer to the global economy and sub-national economies too, because – like most economies – the UK is tied into the global economy, and has economic variations within it.

1.2   An overview of the UK economy

There are many ways that I could describe the UK economy and how it is changing, and many sets of statistics I could use to illustrate this. So, to give an overview, I am going to have to make a choice and focus on certain aspects. That might immediately get you thinking about some critical social science questions, such as 'Why is he choosing certain things to present and not others?' and 'What is the significance of particular statistics being included?' Reading this chapter should encourage you to think about these kinds of questions. To start with, I am going to focus on the UK as an economy within the wider global economy.

The UK is a **developed economy**, with its citizens, on average, having very high levels of income in global terms, and large parts of its economy involved in the creation and selling of services, rather than in manufacturing goods or in agricultural production. According to most definitions of a developed economy, there are about thirty such countries, as illustrated on the map in Figure 1 where those countries are coloured blue.

The UK is also often characterised as an increasingly **open economy**; namely, one in which people and businesses trade freely in goods and services with people and businesses in other countries. By contrast, a **closed economy** would be one without international trade. There are few examples of a closed economy in today's world, though countries like North Korea and Bhutan, which have few dealings with other countries, might be categorised like this.

Developed economy
A developed economy or country (sometimes called an advanced economy) is one in which income levels are high, and the economy has a large service sector.

Open economy
An economy is that is open to trade in goods and services with other countries.

Closed economy
An economy that does not trade with other countries.

Figure 1   Locations of the world's developed economies (countries coloured blue; as defined by the International Monetary Fund, 2008)

Activity 2

What would your shopping and consuming be like if the UK was a 'closed' instead of an 'open' economy?

If there were no international trade, many of the items for sale in our high streets would simply not be available. For example, there would be no tropical fruits in food stores, because they cannot be readily grown in the UK. Many other goods would still be available, but they would have to be produced in the UK. This means they might be much more expensive – it would, for example, take a lot of extra resources to grow, say, peaches on a large scale in the UK, so their price would be higher. And while it might be technically possible for the UK to make all its own clothes, the cost would be higher as the wages of workers making them are higher than they are in China, for instance.

The UK has a comparatively high level of international trade as it exports many goods and services (i.e. those sold to other countries) and imports many goods and services (i.e. bought from other countries). For example, in 2006, just over 30 per cent, by value, of everything produced in the UK economy was traded internationally. This was higher than some other similar economies, such as the USA (14 per cent), Japan (15 per cent) and France (28 per cent). And all developed economies have seen increases in their international trade in recent years – for instance, the comparative figures for 1992 were that the UK traded 24 per cent of the value of its economy, the USA only 10 per cent, Japan 8 per cent and France 21 per cent (OECD, 2008).

Supporters of greater international trade argue that being in an increasingly open economy allows UK citizens to benefit from a wider choice of goods and services, many of which are imported more cheaply than they could be produced in the UK, while the UK can produce and sell certain things abroad more efficiently. They argue, therefore, that increasing trade makes all the countries that take part in it better off, by allowing goods and services to be produced where they are cheapest to make. So, buyers (in this case, UK consumers) benefit from cheaper goods and services, and sellers are able to freely sell the goods and services they are most efficient at making. However, there are serious questions about this 'win–win' view of trade.

Making Social Lives, Chapter 2, gives an example of how similar arguments are made by large retailers when they justify their international sourcing and buying strategies, and discusses the problems with this 'win–win' view of trade.

Globalisation and openness

In addition to being increasingly 'open', the UK has also been seen as particularly supportive of the wider process often referred to as **economic globalisation**. In this context, this means that the UK is said to be particularly open to increasing economic activity across international borders – whether that means the trade of goods and services, flows of money, or flows of people. Increased economic globalisation and integration have affected most countries, especially developed economies. But some aspects of the UK's globalisation can be seen as being more pronounced than elsewhere.

Economic globalisation
Economic globalisation is the process of increasing economic integration and interaction between different states, leading to the emergence of increasingly global markets.

For example, in the UK there is relatively little 'protection' of domestic industry, such as special taxes against foreign goods and services, or special subsidies paid from the government to support UK industries against foreign competition. Similarly, there are almost no special measures to defend declining industries in the UK or weaker individual firms against competition or takeover by overseas firms. Alone among major developed economies, the UK Government has been relaxed about the closure of its last volume car maker, MG Rover, in 2005. It has also overseen the takeover of major British utility and transportation firms by foreign companies, such as France's EDF Energy, which is now a major supplier of domestic gas and electricity in the UK.

And the UK Government allows its financial firms to be taken over by international rivals, such as when Abbey Bank became a part of the Spanish Santander Group in 2004, and Alliance & Leicester did the same during the financial crisis in 2008. In contrast, governments in some other major EU economies have fought to protect similar companies in similar sectors in their own countries against takeover by foreign corporations. For example, when, in January 2008, French bank Société Général came under threat of takeover because of severe trading losses, the French prime minister announced that his government would 'defend' the bank against a foreign takeover and encouraged other French banks to develop takeover plans.

A different but related aspect of economic openness is the way the UK was relatively open to foreign workers immigrating in the first part of the twenty-first century – though the openness to people is different from the much greater openness to flows of money and trade. (Flows of people have often been selective and temporary, and the degree of openness, and openness to whom, are the subjects of ongoing debate.)

You will read more about migration debates in Chapter 5 of this book.

In 2007, it was confirmed that of the extra 2.7 million jobs created in the UK since 1997, more than half of the increase was accounted for by foreign or migrant workers (Statistics Commission, 2007). This was a trend that had increased when the UK – unlike other large EU economies – fully opened its labour markets to citizens from countries that joined the EU in 2004, such as Poland and Lithuania – although restrictions were imposed when Romania and Bulgaria joined the EU in 2007.

Openness to international investment

Foreign direct investment (FDI) Investment made by a corporation based in one country to acquire a long-term interest in a corporation in another country.

One particular and important aspect of the UK's openness is that the UK is an economy that has been very open to **foreign direct investment (FDI)**. This is investment made by a firm (or 'corporation') based in one country to acquire a long-term interest in a corporation based in another country. So, for example, 'inward' FDI to the UK could take place when a Chinese car firm or a Japanese electronics firm invests in or acquires a British firm or plant. And an 'outward' FDI flow takes place when a British bank or insurance company acquires an overseas subsidiary in, say, the USA or Germany. The result of this FDI is usually a corporation that is based primarily in one country but which has overseas subsidiaries or affiliates that together form what is known as a **transnational corporation (TNC)**. There are very many examples of such TNCs across the world. For example, the India-based Tata Group

Transnational corporation (TNC) A corporation that is based primarily in one country but has overseas subsidiaries or affiliates, and so produces across more than one country.

now owns such well-known firms as Tetley Tea, Corus Steel, Jaguar and Land Rover – all once typically 'British' brand names. Corus was a firm formed from a merger involving British Steel, so a nationalised industry that was once considered a British staple is now part of a TNC based overseas. Conversely, there are many British-based TNCs, such as household names like Tesco (which has operations in many countries such as the USA, the Czech Republic and Malaysia) and British Petroleum, lesser-known pharmaceutical giants like GlaxoSmithKline, and some financial sector global giants such as Barclays, the banking group, and Aviva, the insurance group. Some people argue that the increasing size and number of such TNCs is a good thing – helping to globalise the economy and increase efficiency because they can easily move production to where it is cheapest. Others worry about the implications for workers in terms of possibly reduced wages or lost jobs when production can easily be 'shipped abroad' to less developed and lower-wage economies, or fear the possible consequences of, say, the UK having strategic industries such as car making and steel making under foreign ownership.

The seemingly 'British' brand names Land Rover, Tetley and Jaguar, are part of an Indian-based transnational corporation

I am now going to introduce the first quantitative data in this chapter to explore this point a little more. The USA has long been both the largest foreign investor in other countries and also the biggest recipient of inward FDI from other countries. However, when comparing what's happening in different economies it is often best to do this taking into account the *relative size* of those economies. I did this earlier when I said that foreign trade accounts for just over 30 per cent of the UK economy, compared with the USA's 14 per cent – in fact, the USA's *total* trade is higher than the UK's, because the *total size* of the American economy is about five times the size of the UK economy. So I am going to look at FDI as a percentage of **gross domestic product (GDP)**. GDP is one particular measure of the size of different national

Gross domestic product (GDP)
An important measure of the national output of a particular state; it is the total value of everything produced in an economy in a time period such as a year.

economies – it measures the total market value of all goods and services produced within a country in a particular year. So, as the UK had a GDP of approximately £1.33 trillion in 2007 (or £1330 billion), this figure refers to the total value of everything produced in the UK in 2007. By contrast, the total size of the American economy was about $13.7 trillion (about £6.85 trillion, or just over five times as big).

Activity 3

Look at Figure 2, a chart on FDI from the Organisation for Economic Co-operation and Development (OECD) and answer the questions that follow.

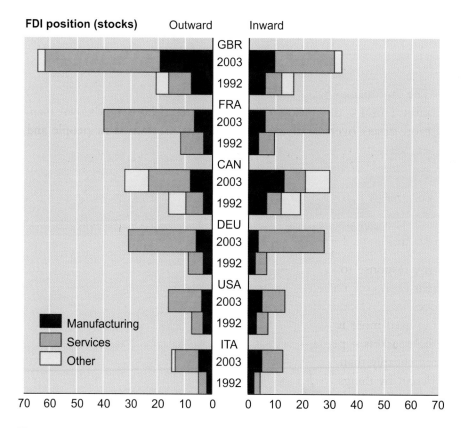

Figure 2   Total FDI in six developed countries, in 1992 and 2003, as a percentage of GDP (Source: OECD, 2007a)

Key: GBR = United Kingdom, FRA = France, CAN = Canada, DEU = Germany, USA = United States, ITA = Italy.

What do you think this graph tells us about the UK's (denoted as GBR) level of economic openness to FDI? Note down three points of interest about the UK position, in comparison with the other major developed economies.

It looks as if the UK is relatively highly open to FDI. By 1992, it already had the largest quantity of outward FDI as a percentage of GDP of all the countries shown, and was second only to Canada in inward FDI. By 2003, it had accumulated both the highest amount of inward FDI (about 34 per cent of its GDP) and the amount of FDI overseas (over 60 per cent).

Three points that I find of interest are as follows:

1   The big increase in both inward and outward FDI between 1992 and 2003 – meaning the UK has become much more open to FDI over that period.

2   The fact that outward FDI is much higher in percentage terms than inward FDI – this means that UK firms and households own many more assets overseas than UK assets that are owned by people and firms aboard.

3   I also notice that a very large proportion of FDI relates to services, rather than manufacturing – an issue to which I will return.

Maybe you can see other interesting points, but check you can see my points in Figure 2 too.

In my response to the activity, I started to highlight another important recent economic change. This is that openness to trade and to the processes of globalisation has resulted in the UK's economic resources being used more in those sectors where the UK can compete well in global markets – perhaps because it can do certain things better or more cheaply than in other countries – and less where it can be undercut by things being produced more cheaply elsewhere. I mentioned earlier that, as a developed economy, the UK has a large services sector, so you perhaps won't be surprised that the manufacture of goods in the UK has shrunk substantially as a proportion of the total economy or GDP, and of total employment, while the services sector has grown substantially. Even by the early 1990s, the UK had one of the largest proportions of employment in services, and one of the lowest in manufacturing, among the major developed economies. And since then this trend has continued, with rapid increases in employment in what are called 'knowledge-intensive' services, such as in information and communication technologies, services to businesses, and banking and insurance.

The UK's welcoming approach to FDI, TNCs and economic globalisation has been argued by some to have contributed to improvements in the UK's **productivity**. This is because the openness of the economy can promote greater competition between firms and the least productive or least profitable firms have to exit the market. Inflows of FDI and the presence of foreign TNCs can also facilitate the transfer of the latest technologies and best practice to UK-based firms. New information and communication technologies (ICT), combined with this openness to the global economy, have also permitted UK firms to cut costs through activities such as 'outsourcing', where firms subcontract a productive process such as ICT functions to an outside company in order to reduce costs, and 'off-shoring', which is the relocation of such a productive process to another country altogether. And prior to the recession that began in 2008/09, UK firms were able to sell the services they specialise in – such as banking, insurance, ICT consultancy and software programming – at profitable prices as these became more in demand across the world.

Productivity
Productivity refers to how much can be made from a particular input into the productive process.

Markets and liberalisation

In Section 1.1, I mentioned how economic decisions about what is produced and how it gets distributed can be decided both by markets through prices and by government action. Another area of major economic change in recent years has been a process of **liberalisation** that has shifted the balance between the two. Governments have followed policies that have increasingly emphasised free markets and competition, with less emphasis on government and public-sector provision. This started under the Conservative Government of Margaret Thatcher (1979–90) when industries such as telecommunications, gas, electricity and water were privatised, and subsequently under John Major's Conservative Government (1990–97) industries such as the railways followed. These privatisations were undertaken partly in an attempt to promote competition between different firms that provide such goods and services. New bodies were then set up to regulate these liberalised markets (e.g. Ofcom for telecoms and Ofwat for water), partly to compensate for the limited extent of actual competition, especially in industries such as rail and domestic water supply. This emphasis on free markets spread throughout other areas of government policy. For instance, there were attempts to make the job market more

Liberalisation
A set of government policies to promote free markets and competition.

competitive by encouraging employment mobility, and by limiting the powers of trade unions. The City and financial services were also heavily deregulated and encouraged to innovate and expand. The process of liberalisation also included the introduction of commercial principles into areas of public-sector activity such as health. The Labour Government that was in power from 1997 did not directly reverse any of the previous privatisations, and indeed embraced the principles of liberalisation in introducing market-type systems into various areas of public provision, such as higher education.

Privatisation began during the Thatcher Government but continued under Major

Comparatively richer

Arguably, by 2008 the UK was also much better off than it was ten or twenty years earlier. In addition to UK citizens on average being better off, they were also better off in *comparative* terms – that is to say, comparing standards of living with people in other countries. In order to make such international comparisons we not only need to look at the size of economies, we also need to take population size into account. Economists often look at how 'well off' individual members of an economy are by looking at the level of **GDP per head** (or **GDP per capita**). To get this, we divide the size of the total economy by the population total, so we can see what, on average, each person's share of the total economy is. Social scientists often use such *per capita* data to take into account the different size of countries (or other units such as regions or localities) – see Table 1.

GDP per head/GDP per capita
A measure of national income per person in a particular country.

Table 1   GDP per capita for the 'Group of 7' major developed economies

GDP per capita (US $), 1997		GDP per capita (US $), 2005	
USA	30 228	USA	41 789
Canada	24 481	Canada	34 058
Japan	24 113	UK	32 860
Germany	23 208	Japan	30 842
Italy	22 846	Germany	30 777
France	22 752	France	30 266
UK	22 312	Italy	28 094

Source: OECD, 2007b

Using this measure, we can see from the data in Table 1 that the UK went from having the lowest ranking in terms of GDP per head in the 'Group of 7' major developed economies in 1997 to the third highest, after the USA and Canada, by 2005.

Whether or not that relative rise in GDP over that period was a *result* of the kind of changes I have described in the UK economy is an important and contentious point for social scientists. For example, by 2009, it was being argued by many that the UK's good economic performance over the previous decade was based not on the embracing of globalisation and improved productivity, but on excess debt and an over-reliance on the expansion of financial services. Increased specialisation in services and increased economic openness, and a relative lack of government regulation over the activities of the financial sector, meant the UK became more subject to turbulence in global markets; this was seen clearly in 2008/09, when the UK's banking sector was particularly affected by global financial turmoil and the government had to fund multibillion pound capital injections and rescue packages. There was thus a danger that the UK's GDP per head might fall faster than some other countries as a result of the recession that began in the second half of 2008.

These points were introduced in the 'Material lives' strand of *Making Social Lives*.

There are other objections to highly globalised, open economies too. For instance, Joseph Stiglitz, himself a former World Bank chief economist, has argued that economic globalisation has helped create 'unfair' trade that has benefited the richer developed countries, hindered the economic prospects of poorer countries, and created societies where the distribution of income and wealth is increasingly unequal (Stiglitz, 2002).

1.3   Inside the UK economy

In this discussion of 'the UK economy' and its characteristics, we mustn't overlook the fact that the UK is made up of its different nations and regions. In Section 1.1, I referred to how an 'economy' can exist at many different levels. For example, do any of the component nations or regions of the UK have economies that are substantially different from that of the UK as a whole? The method of comparing the economies of different sub-national units is to look at their **gross value added (GVA)**. This is a very similar measure to GDP, but is the method used to measure the contribution to the economy of individual producers, industries, sectors or regions within a country. (The only difference is it excludes taxes and subsidies. It has to do this because taxes and subsidies are generally applied at a national level and not at regional or single-industry levels.)

Gross value added (GVA)

A measure of economic output for individual parts of a national economy.

Table 2   GVA per head, and as percentage of UK average, in UK regions and nations

	GVA at current prices by residence (£ per head)	GVA at current prices by residence as percentage of UK average	GVA at current prices by workplace as percentage of UK average
North East	13 433	79.9	80.0
North West	14 940	88.9	89.0
Yorkshire & Humberside	14 928	88.8	89.0
East Midlands	15 368	91.5	91.0
West Midlands	15 325	91.2	91.0
East	18 267	108.7	97.0
London	22 204	132.2	149.0
South East	19 505	116.1	109.0
South West	15 611	92.9	93.0
England	17 188	102.3	102.0
Wales	13 292	79.1	79.0
Scotland	16 157	96.2	96.0
Northern Ireland	13 482	80.2	80.0
UK	**16 802**	**100**	**100**

Source: Adapted from ONS, 2006, pp. 218, 223, Tables 12.1, 12.6

Activity 4

Take 5 minutes or so to look at Table 2 and make sure you understand what it shows. For example, in columns 2 and 3, a figure above 100 would show that that region or nation has a GVA above the UK average (e.g. if the figure is 109, then that is 9 per cent higher than UK average). Take another 5–10 minutes to think about what patterns, if any, stand out for you from Table 2.

London stands out as being *most* different from the UK average, with a much higher level of GVA (over 32 per cent above average in column 2). Wales and the North East of England are the lowest, being over 20 per cent below the UK average in both cases, while Northern Ireland is just under 20 per cent below. Scotland's GVA is quite close to the UK national average.

World city
A city that has a major role in the global economic system of finance and trade.

Much of London's high gross value added stems directly from its particular role as a **world city** (along with a few others, such as New York and Paris). London has an unusual economic role because of its position as a global centre of business and finance, and the increased specialisation in this referred to in Section 1.2 above moved this balance further in London's direction between the 1990s and 2008.

You'll also be interested in the third column. This is measuring almost the same thing as column 2, but if you look carefully at the heading, you'll see that it is now allocating people's productive output according to their *workplace* rather than where they actually reside. Why do you think this column makes London's GVA appear even greater than the average, and why do the figures for the East and the South East (of England) take such a tumble? It's because many people work in London but reside in those neighbouring regions. It's a reminder that social scientists need to look carefully at the *detail* of any data – presenting either column 2 or 3 on its own would tell a significantly different story!

A detailed survey of the Scottish economy suggested that 'the Scottish economy has many more similarities with that of the rest of the UK than differences … [although] some of the differences are substantial' (Peat and Boyle, 1999, p. 1). These differences include an even higher level of openness to trade and investment with other countries outside the UK (including, for example, Scotland developing a significant financial services sector throughout the 1990s and 2000s, which in turn faced serious problems in 2008/09) and a slightly different composition of economic output. For example, Scotland famously specialises in the production of electronics, and food and drink, has a large oil-related sector, and slightly higher levels of public spending and a larger public sector. Wales and Northern Ireland have been marked in terms of difference from the rest of the UK mainly in terms of a slightly lower national income per head than average, as seen in Table 2, along with higher levels of public spending per head, and somewhat less of the increased specialisation in services compared with elsewhere in the UK.

Summary

- An 'economy' exists at many different levels – from household to global – and these levels interact with one another.
- The UK economy has been an increasingly and particularly open economy, with more trade with other economies and more investment in and from other economies.
- The UK economy increasingly specialises in services and has experienced processes such as outsourcing, and a policy of liberalisation.
- The UK's GDP per head rose substantially between the mid 1990s and mid 2000s, both in comparison with the UK before that period and compared with similar developed countries.
- There is some variation between the UK's different regional and national economies.

2   An economy that is getting 'greener'?

2.1   Economic growth and environmental change

Economic growth
The increase in the output of an economy over time, as measured by the rate of increase in GDP (adjusted for inflation).

Developing countries
Often taken to be those that have a lower GDP per head, and are less industrialised, than developed countries.

Waste is discussed in *Making Social Lives*, Chapter 3.

One of the things I noted in Section 1 was the rise in the UK's GDP over time, and especially from the mid 1990s to 2008. This is a process known as **economic growth**. Seeking to achieve growth in the size of the national economy, as measured by GDP, has long been a major policy goal for all the main UK political parties, and in developed countries generally. Indeed, economies and often governments are perceived to be performing badly if GDP falls, as it did in the recession that started in the UK in the second half of 2008. Economic growth is also often seen as the crucial means of improving the standard of living in **developing countries**. For example, the UK's Department for International Development says that 'the central lesson from the past 50 years of development research and policy is that economic growth is the most effective way to pull people out of poverty and deliver on their wider objectives for a better life' (DFID, 2008, p. 3). In Section 1, I implied that economic growth was a good thing because it was making UK citizens richer and 'better off'. Over Sections 2 and 3, I would like to provoke some thoughts about whether that is necessarily the case.

Here, in Section 2, I want to introduce environmental questions into the analysis. One of the common effects of economic growth in developed countries for many years was increased pollution as economic *production* increased – the industrial output of factories, the amount of travel and energy use all consequently increased too. This was broadly the pattern in the UK over many decades until the 1990s, for example. Another effect of economic growth is on *consumption*: as economies and the citizens in them become richer, so they are increasingly likely to consume more, including 'luxury' items, such as high-technology consumer electronics, and to travel more in cars and aeroplanes. Doing this also tends to increase the amount of pollution, as well as the amount of waste. So, in a growing developed economy, it has been the case that pollution increases as GDP grows. This is why many politicians often use the language of a 'trade-off' between the 'needs of a growing economy', on the one hand, and environmental concerns about pollution, on the other, and how it is their job to strike the right 'balance' in this economic growth versus environmental damage trade-off. A typical example was in 2009, when approval was given for a third runway at London Heathrow airport, and the secretary of state referred

to the runway as important because it 'connects us with the growth
markets of the future – essential for every great trading nation …
[so that] Britain remains a place where the world can come to do
business' while simultaneously announcing measures to try to limit
the environmental impact such as stating that 'only the cleanest
planes will be allowed to use the new [take-off and landing] slots'
(BBC Online, 2009).

But the relationship between economic growth and environmental
impacts is very complex. For example, there is an important counter-
argument that economic growth goes hand-in-hand with technological
change, which may in turn facilitate energy efficiency and other types of
innovation that may actually help reduce pollution and environmental
damage. For example, in the case of travel, cars and aeroplanes are
becoming more fuel-efficient, and innovation may produce new kinds
of less polluting vehicle fuels, such as biofuels, solar power or other
alternatives. With domestic energy use, data shows that households in
the UK have not become much more energy-intensive than they used
to be. Energy use per household rose by just 1.5 per cent from 1971
to 2005. However, total domestic energy consumption increased by
32 per cent over the same period – because of a growth in the number
of households, the percentage of households with central heating and
the increased ownership of electrical appliances (ONS, 2008, p. 155).
Another factor that makes the picture very complex is the role of
government regulation and taxation. It may be this rather than
economic growth that is the key to promoting environmentally friendly
innovation. For example, regulation has been particularly important in
the UK in reducing the emission of a number of major air pollutants,
such as carbon monoxide, mainly the result of introducing catalytic
converters into cars, and sulphur dioxide – implicated in 'acid rain' –
which fell by 81 per cent between 1990 and 2005 (ONS, 2008, p. 156).

2.2   A weightless economy?

One idea that has emerged recently is that – contrary to the view that
economic growth goes hand-in-hand with greater pollution – some of
the fundamental changes in the economy described in Section 1 are
creating a new kind of economy with the potential for much lower
levels of pollution. This idea is that the UK, along with some other
developed economies, is moving towards becoming a 'weightless
economy'. In Section 1.2, I noted how a declining number of people are
employed in manufacturing and an increasing number are employed in

knowledge-intensive service industries. These industries are often said to be 'weightless' in that not only do they not produce goods, but the knowledge and service that they generate could be reduced, literally, to a series of 1s and 0s – the binary 'bitstrings' of digital information. The 'weightless economy' is generally held to include such things as information and communication technology, the internet, intellectual property – including advertising and brand names, patents and copyrights – education, broadcasting, biotechnology, medical knowledge, financial services and consulting. This is a large subset of the services sector. (Some services are not knowledge based, because they still include elements of tangible physicality – car washing or beauty treatments would be examples: they could not be reduced to 'digital information'.)

Activity 5

Spend 10–15 minutes thinking about some possible implications of moving towards an increasingly weightless economy. To help, try to contrast a weightless economy with an economy (say the UK fifty years ago) where the predominant mode is the production, transportation and trade of physical goods, often large ones. Consider some general social implications as well as environmental ones.

Some thoughts spring into my mind. For example, it makes the nature of *geography* in economic transactions very different. If you use the internet, you might already be aware of how easy it now is to socialise, play and interact in other ways with people from other countries or continents. Trading across the globe is also becoming increasingly common – whether it is individuals buying and selling in internet markets such as eBay, or companies selling their services globally. Another changing dimension is *time* – consumers can get products of the knowledge-intensive industries very rapidly; there is no waiting for transportation. Think of the speed with which digital media clips can be spread around the globe. And consumers are closer to producers in this digital world, both in the sense that there is more direct trading between them, and also in that the line between them becomes blurred – consumers can also become creators of digital knowledge.

The potential environmental implications of having a 'weightless economy' are significant. If an economy is producing only very little in the way of tangible goods, and most of the output is simply 'digital information', then, intuitively, this could potentially be a much less polluting economy, compared with the one of fifty years earlier where many goods were produced and transported.

But does this idea, that one environmental implication of moving toward a digital 'weightless economy' will be significantly reduced pollution, stand up to scrutiny? One major contemporary environmental issue is global warming. This is the process of climate change in which the earth's average air and water temperatures are increasing over time, said by the UN's Climate Change Panel to be over 90 per cent likely to be caused by human activity, through, in particular, the emission of greenhouse gases, mainly carbon dioxide (CO_2). In turn, this is causing problems such as shrinking glaciers and polar ice caps, species extinction and pressure on agricultural processes. How does moving to a more digital weightless economy affect the UK's emission of such greenhouse gases?

One obvious problem with the idea of a low-polluting 'weightless economy' is that even if the UK is producing a lot less in the way of manufactured goods as a result of its economy changing, the economy grew strongly until 2008 and the average UK citizen became a lot better off, and this went hand-in-hand with the increased *consumption* of goods and services. As we saw in Section 1, an increasing amount of the goods that we consume are being imported. So it could be argued that the UK's greenhouse gas emissions are, in effect, simply being *exported* – those economies that produce the goods for UK consumers have been left to 'do the dirty work' of satisfying increased levels of UK consumption. The following article explores this idea further.

The increased importation of goods is discussed in *Making Social Lives*, Chapter 3.

UK 'exporting emissions' to China

The UK's increasing dependence on Chinese goods is contributing to a rise in carbon emissions, a report suggests. The New Economic Foundation (nef) says such reliance is adding to CO_2 levels because China's factories produce more CO_2 per item than British ones.

The report also says many similar goods are both imported and exported, adding needlessly to CO_2 output in transport. Over the last year, UK imports from China rose by 10% nearing 6.5 million tonnes, nef reports.

This is the second year that the London-based think-tank has produced an 'Interdependence Day' report on the extent to which Britain's economy is tied up with imports from, and impacts on, the developing world. Last year nef found that global consumption levels pushed the world into 'ecological debt' on 9 October; this year, it says, we are in debt three days earlier.

Ecological debt means that our demands exceed the Earth's ability to supply resources and absorb the demands placed upon it.

Polluter pays?

The organisation calculates that Chinese factories produce about one-third more carbon than European ones for making the same product; and more CO_2 will be produced in transporting the goods.

'Every time we hear a government minister talking about climate change, they seem to be drawn towards scapegoating China and its rising emissions,' said nef's policy director Andrew Simms. 'But a big factor in that rise is that China has become the major factory for the western world, so their greenhouse gas emissions are largely driven by higher levels of consumption in the west.'

Two years ago, US researchers calculated that 14% of China's carbon dioxide emissions were accounted for by exports to the US. Nef believes that international negotiations on climate change should move towards a system where emissions are attributed to the end user rather than the country producing the goods.

It points out that rising production of consumer goods in China and other developing countries also contributes to local pollution, depletion of water supplies, and deforestation.

'Wasteful trade'

Nef also said the international trade pattern prompted higher greenhouse gas emissions from transport but had little discernible benefit for the consumer. During 2006, the UK exported 15,845 tonnes of chocolate-covered waffles and wafers, but imported 14,137 tonnes. During the same period, 20 tonnes of mineral water were exported by the UK to Australia, while the UK imported 21 tonnes. And thirty-four tonnes of vacuum cleaners went from the UK to Canada, with 47 tonnes travelling the other way.

'Why would that wasteful trade be more the rule than the
exception?' asked Andrew Simms.

BBC Online, 2007

Activity 6

You should spend about 15 minutes on this activity.

- What do you think is meant by the idea of 'wasteful trade'? How could
  this contradict the arguments for increased free trade and openness
  that we saw in Section 1?
- What might be some of the implications for the UK of limiting trade
  with countries such as China, where factories 'produce more CO_2 per
  item than British ones'?

'Wasteful trade' is used here to describe cases where similar goods – such
as vacuum cleaners – are traded in both directions between two countries.
This idea clashes directly with the arguments for free trade in a globalised
economy outlined in Section 1.2. Supporters of free trade might counter-
argue that the trade in vacuum cleaners between two countries could be
justified on the grounds of cost, efficiency and consumer choice.

One implication of limiting trade is that it is likely that some goods
would become more expensive when they are sold in the UK. For
example, if cheap clothing imports from China were banned and
replaced by UK-produced goods, or they had extra taxation imposed,
then clothing would become more expensive in the UK.

In order to try to address the problems caused by global warming, most
states signed up to the Kyoto Protocol in 1997 (it came into effect
in 2005). This is an international agreement setting targets for most of the
developed countries to cut their combined greenhouse gas emissions to
5 per cent below 1990 levels by 2008–2012. The UK Government set its
own additional target in 1997 of cutting UK CO_2 emissions by 20 per cent
from 1990 levels by 2010, and in 2008 the Climate Change Act targeted
an 80 per cent reduction in greenhouse gas emissions from the 1990
baseline by 2050. We can see how the UK is faring against the Kyoto
Protocol and its own 1997 target in the line graphs shown in Figure 3.

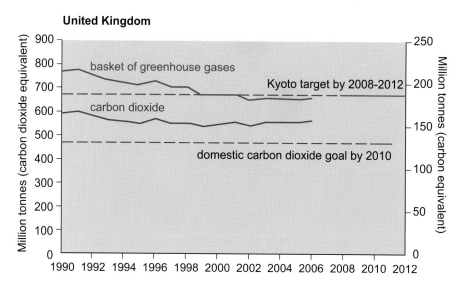

United Kingdom

Figure 3   UK emissions of greenhouse gases: 1990–2006 (Source: Defra, 2007, p. 28)

You will return to issues of global warming and the proposed regulation and limitation of greenhouse gas emissions in Chapter 3 of this book.

As you can see, the UK has already met its Kyoto commitments by reducing its greenhouse gas emissions below the target level. This is largely connected to the move away from manufacturing to services discussed in Section 1, as well as the closure of many coal mines and a shift to natural gas as a means of generating more of the UK's electricity. But it seems to be having more problems in meeting its own 1997 target on CO_2 emissions. The main reason for this is that, while CO_2 emissions from industry fell steadily, emissions from transport have actually been increasing. For example, over the period 1990 to 2005, CO_2 emissions attributable to transport rose by 14 per cent from 134 million tonnes to 153 million tonnes – around 28 per cent of the entire total (Defra, 2007, p. 29). And, as we saw in Section 2.1, emissions from domestic users of energy have also been rising. This has resulted in the almost level amount of CO_2 emissions you can see in the lower line in Figure 3.

What all this illustrates is that the relationship between economic growth, economic change and environmental impacts in terms of pollution and emissions is a complex and changing one. However, I hope that it has started to raise in your mind some questions about the assumed benefits of economic growth. In the next section, we will examine this further, and look at the question of whether economic growth necessarily makes us better off and indeed happier.

Summary

- The UK and other countries have economic growth (i.e. rising GDP) as a key policy objective

- Economic growth is often associated with increased pollution and energy usage, but this is complicated by issues such as technological change and government regulation.

- There is a notion that the UK is becoming a 'weightless economy', with implications for reduced pollution and greenhouse gas emissions.

- The UK's economy may be more 'weightless' than in the past, but it is increasingly importing goods from countries where emissions may be even higher to satisfy the rising demand that comes from economic growth.

3   The UK: an increasingly well-off economy and happy society?

3.1   Comparing the UK economy more widely

As we saw in Section 1, measures of national income such as GDP per head or GVA per head are often used to compare different economies, or to compare different sections of one economy. Economists actually have many different detailed ways to calculate figures to measure the size of an economy, depending on *exactly* what it is they are trying to measure. They also have lots of different ways of comparing figures between countries – this is because it can be difficult to 'translate' the figures into a common yardstick of measurement, given that many countries have different currencies that fluctuate in value against one another over time.

Gross national income (GNI) per head

A measure of national economic output that includes income received from and money paid to other countries.

One reason that social scientists might be interested in data like this is to see if it can help us to understand how 'well off' citizens of a particular country are in comparison with others. Of course, how we might want to measure this partly reflects different views of what makes people 'well off'. I'd like to start introducing these issues by revisiting the kind of data we saw in Table 1 earlier, but this time I am going to add some different measures and also rather more countries so we get a wider spread of comparison across the globe (see Table 3). You might also notice that in the first column I have changed the precise measure of national incomes to that of **gross national income (GNI) per head**. The only difference between this measure and GDP is that it takes into account income received from and money paid to other countries, such as in the form of dividends paid on shareholdings, or interest on deposits, etc. Just making this technical change has altered the UK's position from third to second in the 'rank' order of the G7 countries – we saw in Figure 2 in Activity 3 how much more than other countries the UK had invested overseas, so it isn't surprising that the UK's comparative position benefits from adding money received from overseas investments. This is another example of how social scientists always have to look carefully at the *exact* nature of the data being presented.

Table 3   Some measures of economic development for various countries of the world

	GNI per head, 2006, Purchasing Power Parity (PPP) method ($)	Telephone subscriptions (per 1000 people)	Internet usage (no. of people per 1000), 2005	Life expectancy (years), latest	Infant mortality rate (no. of deaths per 1000 births), 2005
Luxembourg	59 560	2112	690	79.18	4.68
USA	**44 260**	1227	693	77.71	6.37
UK	**35 580**	1616	624	78.95	5.01
Canada	**34 610**	1080	681	80.18	4.63
France	**33 740**	1376	485	80.21	3.41
Japan	**33 150**	1202	675	82.08	2.8
Germany	**31 830**	1628	468	78.93	4.08
Italy	**30 550**	1659	493	80.33	5.72
Greece	24 560	1472	342	78.99	5.34
Poland	14 830	1073	278	75.00	7.07
South Africa	11 710	825	109	47.66	59.44
Russia	11 630	1119	166	65.47	11.06
Brazil	8800	587	139	71.24	27.62
Bhutan	5690	111	39	63.98	96.37
India	3800	128	55	63.50	34.61
Vanuatu	3280	83	36	69 (est.)	52.45
Pakistan	2500	116	67	64.86	68.84
Tanzania	740	56	10	46.30	71.69

Note: The G7 states are in bold type.

Sources: Adapted from WDI from World Bank 14/09/07 (GNI), Nationmaster (telephone subscriptions) and CIA World Factbook, 14 June 2007 (infant mortality rates/life expectancy/internet usage)

Activity 7

Look at Table 3 and take 15–20 minutes to consider the following:

- How has your perspective changed on the UK's standard of living by the addition of countries as diverse as Luxembourg and Tanzania to this larger table?
- Why do you think the data for the 'material' and 'health' measures of well-being don't have exactly the same rank order as the economic data (i.e. with Luxembourg always top, the USA second, etc.).

- Ignoring where you or your family come from, which would be the country that you'd choose to be born into if you could, based on its *set of data*? Would it be the one with the highest life expectancy? Or perhaps you'd prefer to live in the economy with the highest income level? Or maybe you'd prefer a country with the highest access to material goods such as telephones and the internet?

Perhaps you think the UK isn't doing so well economically, now I've introduced Luxembourg. Or maybe, looking at the figures, you put emphasis on what an incredibly high national income UK citizens have on average compared with Tanzanian citizens – UK citizens are almost *fifty times* better off than Tanzanians, who, on average, have to survive on about $2 per day.

There are many factors at work which, as you study more of the social sciences, will become clearer. Some are cultural issues, such as the Japanese diet being connected with their long life expectancy. Others are political and economic, such as the strong health-care system in Russia being associated with lower infant mortality rates than one might expect from Russia's economic 'league table' position.

There will be variation in what people will choose, reflecting their different values and the things they consider to be most important. There are probably many other aspects, not in this table, that you want to consider too – from climate to religious observance. However, I would hazard a guess that you didn't choose the Pacific island of Vanuatu, which comes near the bottom of most of those columns, except that for life expectancy. I shall return to Vanuatu later.

The above activity will have encouraged you to think more about the kind of quantitative data we've seen in this chapter. Such data often gives us important information that can be analysed and interpreted, and useful descriptions of many issues discussed in the social sciences, and thus insight into the matter under consideration. But we also need to consider it carefully – for example, we've now seen that you'll want to think carefully about *with whom or what the data is being compared.* You'll also want to consider *what exactly is being measured.*

3.2   Are measures of national income enough?

Activity 7 might also have suggested why it is not always ideal to rely on simple economic measures of things such as GDP/GNI per head to provide the best **proxy measure** for how 'well off' a particular country is. Indeed, there are well-established criticisms of doing so. First, there are environmental criticisms that relate to some of the material that was introduced in Section 2. For example, it is argued that measures of national income such as GDP/GNI should be reduced to take account of the creation of pollution and rubbish, the production of socially 'bad' things like weapons or cigarettes, and the using up of non-renewable resources. In the absence of such adjustments, environmentally damaging actions such as chopping down a forest and not renewing it would add to a country's national income, which might seem perverse.

Second, we have to remember that GDP/GNI figures are *averages* for members of a particular economy. Such figures can disguise different degrees of inequality. It seems intuitively likely that for two countries with equal national income, one where there are a few people in extreme wealth and most live in serious poverty would have less overall well-being than one where there is less poverty. Do measures of national income need to be adjusted for this?

Third, another important criticism of GDP/GNI figures is that they don't take account of how long people have to work, on average, to produce the economic output that makes up this national income. For example, an American citizen may be better off on average than someone in France, but the French generally work significantly fewer hours per week, with the result that some people feel that the French have a better 'quality of life' in a way that cannot be measured by GDP figures alone.

But there are wider questions too. Do we need to move beyond measures of the economic, however accurate these may or may not be, to try to measure something broader? Are we trying to look at strictly economic measures of 'richness', or is there some wider notion of 'well-being' or indeed 'happiness' that we are seeking to capture? Social scientists interested in questions of 'happiness' sometimes look at another country to raise this difference. The tiny South Asian state of Bhutan has 'happiness' as a central policy objective (rather as developed economies typically have 'economic growth'), and it aims to maximise not GDP/GNI but what it refers to as GNH or 'gross national happiness'. This leads it to make many decisions that are different from those of most other countries, developed and developing, that pursue economic growth. Among decisions that may seem odd to UK residents, the government of Bhutan has banned tobacco, plastic bags, traffic lights, MTV and various other television channels, and

Proxy measure
A measure that acts as a substitute for another value that we are interested in measuring.

advertisements for Coke/Pepsi cola drinks. Instead, it emphasises Bhutanese culture, 'spirituality' and care for the environment, and has strict conservation laws. But it is a country with limited freedom in terms of religious worship and political involvement, as well as consumer choice, and was, until recently, an absolute monarchy.

■   In what sense does the absence of such freedoms really help make people happy or have greater well-being? What about the absence of consumer choice, the inevitable lack of product innovation and the lack of exposure to other cultures – do you think these things would make you 'happy'?

Some measures have been created to address broader questions than the purely economic. For example, the United Nations Development Programme uses a 'human development index' (HDI) to try to give a more rounded picture of well-being. This uses GDP as one-third of its index, but also includes life expectancy at birth (as a proxy measure of health and longevity), the adult literacy rate and a measure of educational enrolment. If you look back at the top of Table 3, you might be interested to know the rank order changes somewhat when the different states' economies are measured by the HDI – Luxembourg is only eighteenth in the world, now *lower* than the UK in sixteenth place and the USA in fourteenth. Canada is right up in fourth place on the HDI, even though it is ranked lower than all three of those states on GNI.

Some have gone much further and suggested that far more comprehensive 'green accounts' of economies are needed. For example, the new economics foundation (nef) and Friends of the Earth argue that we need to find a completely different way to approach measurements of human well-being and happiness in order to foreground environmental concerns. Read the news report below, and then do the activity.

Vanuatu tops wellbeing and environment index

The most deservedly happy place on the planet is the South Pacific island nation of Vanuatu, according to a radical new index published today.

The United Kingdom does not even make it into the top 100, according to the survey, which has been compiled to draw attention to the fact that it is not necessary to use up the earth's resources to achieve long life and happiness.

The innovative global measure of progress, the Happy Planet Index, has been constructed by the new economics foundation (nef) and Friends of the Earth using three factors: life expectancy, human wellbeing and damage done via a country's 'environmental footprint'.

Vanuatu comes top because its people are satisfied with their lot, live to nearly 70 and do little damage to the planet. Zimbabwe takes bottom place in the table. Guatemala, El Salvador, Honduras and Colombia, countries that have experienced recent civil upheavals, all feature in the top 10 on the grounds that they do little environmental harm and manage comparatively high levels of satisfaction with life.

The big industrial nations fare badly. The United Kingdom trails in 108th, below Libya, Gabon and Azerbaijan. The US is 150th and Russia is 172nd, near the bottom of the 178 nations for which statistics are available.

'Don't tell too many people, please,' was the response of Marke Lowen of Vanuatu Online, the country's online newspaper, to the news that Vanuatu had topped the poll. 'People are generally happy here because they are very satisfied with very little. This is not a consumer-driven society. Life here is about community and family and goodwill to other people. It's a place where you don't worry too much.'

The small population of 200,000 and the lack of aggressive marketing in what is essentially a subsistence economy were other factors which might have elevated the country. ...

The Happy Planet Index essentially divides the damage we do environmentally by the payback through life expectancy and satisfaction. No country does well on all three indicators but the survey shows that people can live long, fulfilled lives without using more than their fair share of the earth's resources, says the foundation. ...

The UK's heavy ecological footprint, the 18th biggest worldwide, is to blame for the country's low rating. Life satisfaction varies greatly from country to country: questioned on how satisfied they were with their lives, on a scale of one to 10, 29% of Zimbabweans, who have a life expectancy of 37, rate themselves at one and only 6% rate themselves at 10.

In contrast, 28% of Danes score their life-satisfaction at 10 out of 10 while fewer than 1% rate it at one. At the bottom of the index, above Zimbabwe, were three other African nations, Swaziland, Burundi and Congo. ...

The real message ... that the survey seeks to convey is that the environmental damage being done by the wealthier nations, presumably in the pursuit of happiness and long life, may have the opposite effect.

Campbell, 2006

Activity 8

In Table 3, Vanuatu came third from bottom in GNI per head, second from bottom in the prevalence of telephones, and seventh from bottom in life expectancy. Yet this article reports research claiming that Vanuatu is the happiest place on earth. How do you explain this seeming paradox? What do you think it might tell us about the different sets of figures and what they are trying to measure?

The Happy Planet Index specifically excludes any measure of different economies' national incomes – indeed it marks economies down for environmental damage, which is likely to be most significant in countries with the largest economies. So it's not surprising the rank order is so different. The Happy Planet Index has been produced by people with strong views on the environment so maybe we should think that this is to be expected. On the other hand, one could equally argue that bald economic data such as GDP fails to take any account of environmentally damaging actions – we are back to a question of values, what we consider to be important, and what we are trying to measure. Similarly, one could ask whether it makes sense to claim people in Gabon are 'happier' than people in the UK when their life expectancy is so much less, and their levels of education and health lower. This again raises the question of the value we place on different things.

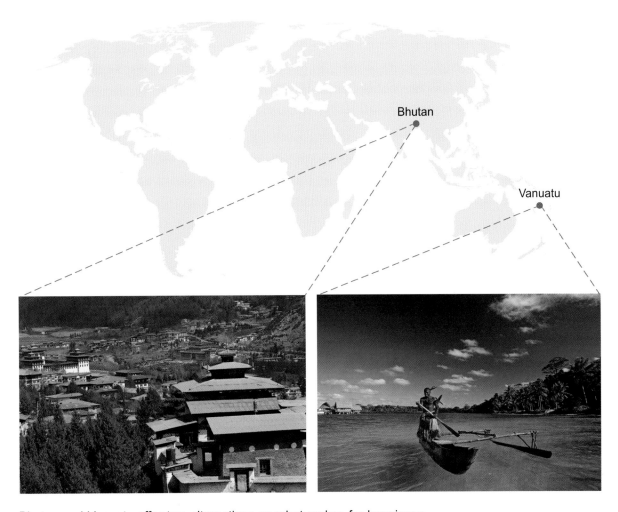

Bhutan and Vanuatu offer two alternatives on what makes for happiness

3.3   Economic growth and happiness over time

If it is hard to make comparisons of economic well-being and what these figures mean across countries, then another interesting and related question is whether the economic growth and rise in national income in *one* country makes its residents feel better off and indeed happier over time. For example, GDP per head in the UK is now over double what it was in the 1960s, consumer goods are far more prevalent and UK citizens live longer, healthier lives. But are they *happier*?

One social scientist called Richard Layard has claimed that, as economies and societies become richer, they don't seem to become happier, and that this is supported by **empirical research** findings. Indeed, he suggests that, on average, people have grown no happier in

Empirical research
Research that is done by careful observation or experiment.

45

the last fifty years, even as average incomes have more than doubled. He argues, therefore, that 'GDP is a hopeless measure of welfare. For since the War that measure has shot up by leaps and bounds, while the happiness of the population has stagnated. To understand how the economy actually affects our well-being, we have to use psychology as well as economics' (Layard, 2003, p. 3). He notes, for example, that alcoholism and depression are more common than they were fifty years ago in the UK, the USA and other European countries. He argues that not only does economic growth not make people happier, but that the pursuit of it is, at best, futile and can actually be responsible for making people more unhappy. This can be through a whole range of mechanisms. For example, there can be excessive pressure on children at school. There can be increased 'status anxiety' about one's relative economic and social position in an increasingly unequal society. This may be accompanied by continual adaptation to increasing income levels so that as people get used to those higher income levels, their idea of what constitutes a *sufficient* income grows in line too, causing them to want ever more, as do changing tastes that reflect the latest trends and cultural norms so the relative worth of one's accumulated possessions effectively falls. These competitive life and work pressures can make people more likely to suffer from mental illness. So, instead, he advocates a move toward a 'happiness economics' in which direct measures of happiness replace economic measures like GDP as markers of how well societies are doing (rather like in Bhutan), and that in order to achieve increases in happiness, societies should refocus on rather different values such as trust, fairness and equality.

This whole area is one where there is a very exciting contemporary debate among a range of social scientists – especially psychologists, economists and environmentalists. Some have argued strongly against Layard's ideas. For example, Indur Goklany emphasises that the world, especially the developed world, is a far better place today than fifty or a hundred years ago, and that, to paraphrase the title of her book, we are all living healthier, longer and more comfortable lives, and even on a cleaner planet – for example, air quality is generally far superior in the developed world compared with fifty years ago. She says that, today, the average Briton, for example, 'has never been richer, better fed, healthier or longer-lived … and is also wealthier [and] freer from hunger and disease' (Goklany, 2007, p. 4). She argues strongly that it's a myth that economic growth and development makes humanity in any way worse off. Similarly, two American economists called Stevenson and Wolfers have argued that *their* empirical research shows that there *is* 'a clear positive link between average levels of subjective well-being and GDP per capita across countries, and [they] find no evidence of a satiation point beyond which wealthier countries have no further increases in subjective well-being' (Stevenson and Wolfers, 2008, p. 1). In other words, these social scientists are all arguing that it is precisely the case that the richer you are, the happier you will be, and that this is true all the way up to the highest income levels, and as economies keep growing – a polar opposite view from Layard's.

Summary

- There are a number of broad questions and challenges about an often assumed link between levels of income in an economy and notions of happiness and well-being.
- In addition to national income figures, there are other ways of measuring levels of material or economic success, such as the prevalence of material goods.
- National income figures are subject to criticism from environmentalists and others as giving only a partial view of how well off an economy is, which also raises broader questions about well-being.
- There are alternative measures that take a broader view of well-being, including aspects such as development and the environment.
- There is a bigger debate about what lies behind concepts such as happiness and well-being – a subject matter for psychologists, economists, environmentalists and other social scientists.

How do we know?

Questioning evidence

We've seen lots of quantitative data in this chapter – data that is measured or identified using *numbers*. Such quantitative data can be analysed using statistics, and it can be displayed in clear and concise ways using, for example, the tables and graphs we've seen here. Quantitative data can provide lots of interesting information, and helps address and inform many social scientific issues and debates, not just economic ones.

You looked at the interpretation of different kinds of evidence in *Making Social Lives*.

Sometimes people instinctively see quantitative data and numbers as being more convincing than other forms of social scientific evidence. But, as with *all* forms of social scientific evidence, quantitative data needs to be examined carefully, looking in detail at exactly what it shows, the kinds of comparisons that can be made with it and the inferences that can be drawn from it. And quantitative data can be *interpreted* differently, just like other kinds of evidence.

Quantitative data also throws up another important aspect of studying social sciences: we need to be clear about what it is we are trying to measure, especially if we are using the data as a proxy measure for some other concept. We saw this when we looked at how measures of national income are not the only way to approach issues of how well off or happy people in different societies might be. We must not allow the presence of the numbers to make us believe something that we may need to consider carefully in the different, informed ways of the social scientist.

Conclusion

In this chapter, we have explored some important questions about economic change, and its relationship with the environment, our well-being and happiness. These are complex but fascinating questions. How changes to our economy – especially the process of becoming richer through economic growth – influence our impact on the environment and our sense of well-being is a crucial part of considering the broader topic of our 'material lives' and the senses in which these are, or are not, becoming better lives.

Economic growth and development is often implicitly assumed to be a good thing, but social scientists need to think critically about whether that is necessarily always the case. Economists, environmentalists, psychologists and others all have contributions to make as this subject area continues to develop – both as social science evolves academically, and as economic and social change continues.

Some of the subject matter of this chapter also poses some fundamental questions about what exactly we mean by concepts such as 'well-being' and 'happiness' – almost timeless questions to which there can be no definitive answer. But the nature of the debate around those topics shows the importance and excitement of the social sciences, and some of the tools that this chapter has helped to develop, such as beginning to look at quantitative data in an informed and critical way, mean that you can develop your engagement with questions about our material lives as we move forward into later chapters of the course.

This chapter has started to question the idea that societies like the UK are always 'making progress' – that is, becoming more affluent, happier and more sustainable. There are, it seems, some serious reasons, supported by social science investigation, to suggest that, while social change means people live longer, have more choice and greater access to goods and services, there are parts of people's lives that become less satisfactory and possibly more challenging. The environment is one area where this is clearly the case, particularly when we take a global view. In the next chapter these issues are investigated further as we turn to look at the risks and hazards of contemporary society – and understand how these are understood and acted upon.

References

BBC Online (2006) 'Britain's happiness in decline' [online], http://news.bbc.co.uk/1/hi/programmes/happiness_formula/4771908.stm (Accessed 17 January 2009).

BBC Online (2007) 'UK "exporting emissions" to China' [online], http://news.bbc.co.uk/1/hi/sci/tech/7028573.stm (Accessed 14 April 2009).

BBC Online (2009) 'Go-ahead for new Heathrow runway' [online], http://news.bbc.co.uk/1/hi/uk_politics/7829676.stm (Accessed 18 January 2009).

Campbell, D. (2006) 'Vanuatu tops wellbeing and environment index', *The Guardian*, 12 July; also available online at http://www.guardian.co.uk/world/2006/jul/12/healthandwellbeing.lifeandhealth (Accessed 14 April 2009).

CIA (2009) *CIA World Factbook* [online], http://www.cia.gov/library/publications/the-world-factbook/index.html (Accessed 20 February 2009).

Department for Environment, Food and Rural Affairs (Defra) (2007) *The Environment in Your Pocket*, London, Defra.

Department for International Development (DFID) (2008) *Growth: Building Jobs and Prosperity in Developing Countries* [online], http://www.dfid.gov.uk/Pubs/files/growth-policy-paper.pdf (Accessed 21 October 2008).

Goklany, I. (2007) *The Improving State of the World: Why We Are Living Longer, Healthier, More Comfortable Lives on a Cleaner Planet*, Washington, DC, Cato Institute.

Government Actuary's Department (2008) [online], http://www.gad.gov.uk?Demography Data/Life Tables/docs/2006wUKperiod06.xls (Accessed 17 January 2009).

International Monetary Fund (2008) *IMF Data Mapper* [online], http://www.imf.org/external/datamapper/index.php (Accessed 7 May 2009).

Layard, R. (2003) *Happiness: Has Social Science a Clue?*, Lionel Robbins Memorial Lectures 2002/3, delivered on 3, 4, 5 March 2003 at the London School of Economics [online], http://cep.lse.ac.uk/events/lectures/layard/RL030303.pdf (Accessed 14 April 2009).

Nationmaster (2009) http://www.nationmaster.com [online] (Accessed 20 February 2009)

Office for National Statistics (ONS) (2006) *Regional Trends*, no. 39 (Accessed 7 May 2009).

Office for National Statistics (ONS) (2008) *Social Trends 38*, Basingstoke, Palgrave Macmillan.

Organisation for Economic Co-operation and Development (OECD) (2007a) *International Direct Investment Statistics and National Accounts of OECD Countries – Online Databases* [online], http://www.oecd.org (Accessed 20 February 2009).

Organisation for Economic Co-operation and Development (OECD) (2007b) *OECD Factbook 2007: Economic, Environmental and Social Statistics* [online], http://oecd.p4.siteinternet.com/publications/doifiles/303007011P1T000.xls (Accessed 20 February 2009).

Organisation for Economic Co-operation and Development (OECD) (2008) *OECD Factbook 2008: Economic, Environmental and Social Statistics* [online], http://oberon.sourceoecd.org/vl=988708/cl=11/nw-1/rpsv/factbook/030101.htm (Accessed 16 January 2009).

Peat, J. and Boyle, S. (1999) *An Illustrated Guide to the Scottish Economy* (ed. Jamieson, B.), London, Duckworth.

Statistics Commission (2007) 'Foreign workers in the UK – Statistics Commission briefing note' [online], http://www.statscom.org.uk/C_1237.aspx (Accessed 16 January 2009).

Stevenson, B. and Wolfers, J. (2008) *Economic Growth and Subjective Well-Being: Reassessing the Easterlin Paradox* [online], http://bpp.wharton.upenn.edu/betseys/papers/happiness.pdf (Accessed 25 October 2008).

Stiglitz, J. (2002) *Globalization and its Discontents*, New York, NY, W.W. Norton.

World Bank (2007) *World Development Indicators* [online], http://web.worldbank.org/WBSITE/EXTERNAL/DATASTATISTICS/0,,contentMDK:21298138~pagePK:64133150~piPK:64133175~theSitePK:239419,00.html (Accessed 20 February 2009).

Chapter 2
Living with risk and risky living

Simon Carter and Tim Jordan

Contents

Introduction 57

1 Food risks 63

 1.1 A transition in the dirt 63

 1.2 Choice and judgement 67

2 Who wants to be 'peely-wally'? Sun exposure,
suntanning and risk 71

 2.1 Negotiating contradictions 72

 2.2 Material risk and symbolic risk 76

3 The risk society 79

4 Epidemiology, 'lay' epidemiology, 'Uncle Norman'
and the 'last person' 83

 4.1 The use of epidemiological knowledge 85

Conclusion 92

References 94

Introduction

The previous chapter ended by raising interesting questions around a seeming paradox. Increasing financial wealth was accompanied by a failure to see a concomitant increase in levels of happiness. Well-being and happiness, though difficult to measure, weren't always closely linked to economic affluence. Moreover, there was recognition that a growth in affluence, even if based on a 'weightless' UK economy dominated by service provision, may have negative environmental consequences. While the UK seemed to be wealthier and greener according to some measures, other measures revealed a heavy reliance on consumer goods made overseas. The broader point might be that something as seemingly 'good' as economic growth involves costs or even dangers as well as benefits. Another way of saying this is that there are risks associated with economic change – these include the dangers of things going wrong (think back to how, in the previous chapter, the UK's economic 'openness' exposed it to the risks of financial breakdowns in the USA and elsewhere) as well as the consequences, intended or otherwise, of our material lives (environmental costs, inequality, and so on).

In this chapter we concentrate on the issue of living with these and other risks; we will focus less on the economic risks alluded to above, and more on the kinds of day-to-day, material risks that we all face as we decide to eat this food or that food, drive a car or cycle, book a holiday, and so on. How do such risks shape people's lives, and how do people make sense of them? In order to start to answer these questions we need to understand not only what risks are, their social and material make-up, but how they are understood and acted upon. Risk, like happiness, is something we are all intuitively familiar with and something that we manage daily, and often automatically, even when we are dealing with major hazards. When crossing a busy road, for example, there is always a risk of death or injury, which we manage by looking carefully for traffic. However, while pedestrians usually move in areas that exclude cars and only have to negotiate the risk of being run over when crossing the street, people riding bicycles operate almost entirely on roads alongside cars, which are, after all, great blocks of metal often moving at fast speeds. Cyclists manage their risk with lights, occasional hand signals (both for direction and remonstration with errant cars, pedestrians and other cyclists) and helmets. The latter, however, cause a controversy.

You looked at the material and social practices involved in ordering traffic, and at different ways of sharing street space, in *Making Social Lives*, Chapter 7. Looking back, you might see that this chapter was also in part talking about different ways of handling risks.

Some cyclists argue it is obvious that helmets can protect against harm. They point to various studies that test for differences between injuries among cyclists with and without helmets. One study found that there was an 85 per cent reduction in the risk of head injury among cyclists who wore helmets (Thompson et al. 1989). That seems a pretty conclusive management of risk! But other research has looked at the relationship between car behaviour and wearing a helmet. This found that, when a car overtakes a cyclist, the car comes significantly closer to a cyclist who wears a helmet (Walker, 2006). On this basis, some argue it is safer not to wear a helmet in order to keep cars further away. Taking both sides into account, and there is a lot more research that an inquisitive cyclist could go and look at, we have a picture of cycling risk and helmets which seems to suggest that if you wear a helmet then you are more likely to have an accident but if you have an accident then you are less likely to have head injuries.

An urban cyclist

The interactions of pedestrians, roads, cars, helmets, cyclists, drivers and pavements exemplify the way risk is both serious and mundane, and how it involves knowledge about hazards and how likely they are to occur. They also make it clear that risk relates to *material* lives, given the tangible nature of the rigidity of helmets, the speed of cars, the bodies of cyclists, the hardness of roads, and so on. However, this raises a question – what do we mean when we speak of risk? One of the problems is that the word 'risk' can mean very different things in different contexts. In many of its uses, 'risk' has now become no more than a technical and rather abstract way of talking about danger or harm. Yet can the word be reduced to anything as unified as the idea of danger or harm? Whereas the word 'danger' calls to mind an unambiguous state of peril, 'risk' alerts us to doubts about whether the future is safe or dangerous – it simultaneously points to the possibilities of safety and danger (Carter, 1997). It may help here to distinguish risk from uncertainty.

Risk refers to the chance of something happening – or, rather, it speaks of a particular and known outcome combined with the consequences of the outcome. In the current example, it is the possibility of a cyclist having an accident combined with the potential physical damage caused to the cyclist that forms the risk. So, if the chance of getting knocked off a bike were high then we could say the risk was high. But, it is also true to say that if the outcome of being knocked off a bike were always nothing more than a scratch and damaged pride, then this would reduce the felt risk. If, however, as is the case today on busy roads with uncompromising vehicles, the outcome can be very serious or even terminal, then the risk might be said to be greater. In addition, in almost all cases when we talk about risk, the consequences are negative or harmful – we might say that cycling is associated with the risk of injury but we would not normally say cycling is associated with the risk of getting healthier. But, one final twist in our understanding of risk is that if the possibility of the 'bad thing' can be avoided then some *benefit* may be gained. For example, riding a bicycle involves knowing an accident might happen, but looking at the risk of riding a bicycle means taking into account not only the physical harm an accident might cause but also the general health benefits of exercise. Many argue that the benefits to general health gained from riding a bicycle outweigh any risk from a crash, but there is always the possibility that bicycling will lead to harm – hence we could say it is a risky activity.

While risk applies to known outcomes and the likelihood of their occurring, in practice it is actually quite rare to know all the outcomes associated with an activity, or even the precise likelihood that they will happen. So, many risks are accompanied by **uncertainties**. In our case, uncertainty might include unforeseen consequences or outcomes (like being struck by lightning while bicycling) and, as in the argument above, the degree to which wearing a helmet can change other road users' behaviour. It may also refer to a general feeling of not knowing.

Risk
A state in which there is a possibility of known danger or harm, which if avoided may lead to benefits.

Uncertainty
Ignorance of, or a lack of precision regarding, the consequences of an activity, or a general feeling of not knowing.

Activity 1

The pictures in Figure 1 are of a football stadium. It is of little significance for this activity which football team, but, as is clear from the photographs, it is Arsenal Football Club in North London. Look at the pictures and, as you examine them, think about pedestrians, cars and risk.

Figure 1   Managing pedestrian flow at Arsenal football club

What did you think? A stadium has to manage intense moments of pedestrian flow – this one holds upwards of 60,000 people for sport and concerts. On a match day all the surrounding streets are heavily policed and are often closed to traffic to allow all those heading to and from the stadium to enter and leave most efficiently. So you may well have been looking at how those flows are directed and managed. But this may have led to some puzzlement when looking at the pictures – don't the large stone letters spelling out 'Arsenal' impede flows? You may also have noticed pillars or bollards on either side of the letters; wouldn't there have been better pedestrian traffic flow if these had been all the way across the entrance, rather than making thousands of people walk around the word 'Arsenal'?

Perhaps that led you to think about the Arsenal sign also being a statue, with an aesthetic dimension – as something pleasing to look at. Or you may have thought about how the baldness of simply stating in ten-foot stone letters the name of the football club is meant to remind all passers-by just who fills the stands behind it.

But there is also a management of risk going on here, for these blocks of letters on the bridge are also an antiterrorist device, and this perhaps best explains why a large obstruction was put right in the middle of a bridge that has to handle sudden flows of thousands of people. Packing a vehicle with explosives is a well-known terrorist tactic and the statue that spells Arsenal is one way of blocking anyone driving a car or van too close to the stadium. In times of heightened security following the 11 September 2001 terrorist attack in New York, the 7 July 2005 bombing in London and other such terrible events, the design of many buildings began to build explicitly in antiterrorist measures. For example, we can think of the attempt to ram a car filled with cans of petrol and gas canisters into the terminal at Glasgow Airport in 2007. This attack is particularly relevant because the car bomb was stopped by bollards, working in just the way those stone letters at the Arsenal stadium are intended to work.

Here we can begin to see how risks of the most extreme kind are managed around Arsenal's stadium through material means. This is done even when it appears to contradict other needs, such as managing sudden flows of large numbers of people who are excited and expecting the pleasure of sport or some other mass event. While we have focused on one of the most dramatic examples of the interlacing of risk and the material world, there is a wide range of examples of social scientific analysis of these connections. It is also, in some ways, the everyday risks that are most helpful because they are so familiar; this chapter will therefore now turn to these more mundane risks.

In Sections 1 and 2, we look at two case studies exploring risk and its integration into our lives. These case studies examine the safety of food grown on an allotment with potentially toxic soil (Section 1) and the way holidaymakers balance a desire for a suntan against the dangers of skin cancer (Section 2). After these case studies, in Section 3, we look at a sociological theory of risk created by Ulrich Beck. Finally, in Section 4, we also begin to see that the management of risk often involves specialist or expert knowledge and discover how the production of this knowledge can lead to disagreement, conflict and the reinterpretation of expert knowledge by 'lay' publics.

Picture taken by a passer-by of a terrorist attempt to crash a car filled with petrol containers into Glasgow Airport. The car was prevented from entering the terminal by metal bollards incorporated into the building design

Summary

- Risk is a key component of all our lives, in both mundane and spectacular moments.
- Examples of bicycling and of antiterrorist urban design have been used to illustrate different kinds of risk and their management.
- Risks are often related to our material environments (from roads to football crowds) but also involve different kinds of knowledge.

1   Food risks

This is the story of an allotment and the risks it posed. It is the story of how some soil was safe then became so poisonous it should not be touched and then became safe again, all without the soil itself being changed one small bit. We will quickly recount the story of this allotment, then we will examine more closely the two moments in which the soil was transformed from safe to poisonous and back again.

In 2003, one of the authors of this chapter (Tim Jordan) and his family received the news that they had been allocated an allotment very near to their house. They had been on the waiting list for nearly four years, which was normal when waiting for an allotment in this specific place. The allotments were located in Hackney, part of urban London, and provided a plot for growing mainly vegetables on land owned by the local government (London Borough of Hackney, LBH). For the first eighteen months things went well, with a lot of digging, weeding and planting. The children each had their own section and a selection of vegetables were grown organically and very happily eaten. Then, without warning, a letter arrived from LBH stating that the allotment soil was poisoned with arsenic and lead, that no food grown on the soil should be eaten and that bare skin should not come into contact with the soil. The lovely organic vegetables suddenly appeared rather risky.

The soil which had been assumed to be safe was now known not to be so. This led to a period of around nine months in which there were consultations about how to remedy the soil, with the favourite option being 'dig and dump', which proposed digging out all the soil on the allotment to a depth of one metre, lining the hole and refilling it with clean soil. However, an alternative arose when LBH staff discovered a different soil test. Whereas the initial scientific test measured the total amount of poison in the soil, this second test measured the amount of poison in soil that a human would take into their body if they ate the soil. This second test then showed that the soil was safe, the levels of poison it measured as able to enter a human's biological system were not dangerous. Most people returned to tending their allotment in the same way as they had before they had been told the soil was poisonous.

1.1   A transition in the dirt

In this short story, we see a remarkable transition in which exactly the same dirt, which it should be emphasised is not changed at all during the story, shifts from being safe to extremely dangerous and back to safe again. The key moments in these transitions are moments of knowledge production because they both hinge on scientific tests. To see how risk and knowledge interact we can look at these two specific moments in turn and ask 'how was knowledge produced in each?'

The first moment was produced because new national legislation required all local governments to check on toxins in soil. LBH in this case decided to test all the allotments and children's nurseries first as these were considered highest risk (because that is where people were most likely to be in close contact with soil and because it is estimated that growing children are most at risk from toxin exposure). LBH proceeded by using a soil test which measured the total amount of poison in the soil. As it is neither sensible nor necessary to take all the soil from allotments and test it, a smaller sample of soil can be taken and this requires, in turn, the definition of what an acceptable or representative sample may be. For this there are various techniques which require a certain number of soil 'plugs' to be taken in a particular pattern across an area of land that is being tested. Each plug consists of a small core of soil dug out of the ground. LBH commissioned tests according to an accepted soil-sampling technique. Soil samples were then sent for laboratory testing.

The laboratory stage is considered by scientists to be standard and straightforward. The soil is taken into a laboratory and broken down into its components using chemicals. It is then measured by various machines that print off results. Methodically, using known and long-agreed methods, the laboratory produces a series of numbers for the levels of various chemicals in each soil sample; these numbers are often expressed as parts per million. This measure of toxin found in the soil was compared to 'soil guidance values' (SGV), which define acceptable levels of poisons in the soil. SGVs are published by the UK Government, through the Environment Agency. Arsenic, a well-known poison, is usually deemed safe in soil if the level is below 20 parts per million. This sounds like a straightforward procedure, but we should note that a series of choices go into the design of the sample, the kinds of tests that are made (and what is being tested for), and the levels of acceptability (acceptable for everyone or only for people who are healthy?). Assumptions are also made over what happens to the poison in the soil when it gets into human bodies. This becomes clear when we look at the different procedures and choices that are taken in the second soil test, the one that labelled the soil as safe.

The change within this story came with the announcement of a second test for the amount of poison in soil, called PBET (physiologically based extraction test). This test was only recently developed and we shall see some of the social processes still at work as the new test struggled to be accepted as authoritative.

PBET begins with a different premise from the standard tests, which measure the total amount of toxin in the soil. PBET aims to measure how much poison in soil is accessible to a human's biology (called bioaccessibility) or, put another way, how much can be absorbed by the human gut. The argument is that it does not matter how much poison there is in soil as long as that poison cannot enter a human's biology and so poison the human. For example, poisons may be made inert by being chemically bound to various elements in the soil and if the chemical bonds in the soil are stronger than those in the human digestive system then the poison will simply pass through a human gut and be expelled in the normal way. The test is therefore designed to mimic a human digestive system. It aims to see what happens when some poisoned soil is eaten by a human without requiring a human actually to eat it. Further, the test tries to mimic a two-year-old infant's digestive system as this is argued to be the most at risk. The picture is of a very young child set down on the ground and eating some dirt; what poison will enter that infant's biology? PBET attempts to measure this by passing soil, or other material that needs testing, through three flasks, each of which holds chemicals meant to mimic the main components of the human digestive system (stomach, small intestine and large intestine). The human is here reduced to a series of three connected flasks through which poisoned material can be passed. By the end, the amount of poison taken in by the fake human digestive system can be measured (Ruby et al., 1996). We can immediately see that a different type of knowledge from that produced by the first test is being created and is likely to define a different risk, though it remains within the general framework of the production of scientific knowledge.

■ Both tests produce numbers that in some way relate to the danger posed by the soil. But which set of numbers would you trust? Both of them, one of them or neither of them? Would you normally want to know how the numbers were generated?

For PBET to be accepted as authoritative and trustworthy it needs to convince other scientists and, later, a concerned public. Consider the definition of the digestive system – how might this gain authority as a legitimate test? It would, of course, have to be tested itself. But this raises a problem, because the test seeks to mimic a human digestive system and it would seem unethical to ask humans to eat poisoned soil so that the results of a PBET and of a human eating the same soil could be compared. In practice, scientists often face this dilemma and have developed methods of overcoming it.

The main method in relation to PBET is to substitute animals for humans. Certain animals, in this case rats, are considered close enough to humans to produce significantly comparable results when tested, but far enough away to minimise ethical concern. This also involves making the ethical decision that it is permissible to poison a rat in the pursuit of human good. If rats suffer poisoning in the way predicted by PBET, then this would confirm the validity of the system of flasks. The animal testing part of the story then fades into the background.

We thus have a test run on a poisoned rat that we are pretending is a poisoned human whose results are compared to a test run on a series of tubes, flasks and chemicals that we are also pretending to be a human, and a comparison of these results tests the validity of PBET. As with any scientific practice there are many choices and assumptions being made here which aren't necessarily clear when the results of that science are published; for example, there are choices about the ethics of poisoning rats and the judgement that rat and human digestive systems are comparable. None of these complications were presented to the allotment holders (nor are such complications usually presented to anyone when a scientific test is used). Instead, PBET was presented as a valid scientific test, which in many ways it is. Defining and managing risk in this way is part of the normal functioning of many societies.

The definition of the risk posed by the soil the allotment holders grew vegetables on was now based on very different knowledge which measured a different object – bioaccessible poison versus total poison in the soil. It turned out that PBET showed much lower levels of poison than the first set of tests. This apparently is normal for PBET, which is at times advertised by laboratories selling the test for this virtue. The PBET results showed quite clearly that the soil was well below the SGV values that determine poison. On this basis, the results were announced to the allotment holders and normal gardening was resumed. LBH provided some extra compost for the affected allotments to be dug in by the gardeners, but this seemed more like a symbolic gesture as the tests were held to have cleared the allotment of danger.

Activity 2

Think about this story and what has been said about the two tests. Reflect on the ways the two tests measure slightly different things even though they are measured against the same definition of what is and is not poisonous (SGV).

Now imagine you are a keen gardener on this allotment who has held their allotment for five years, is settled near to the allotment and has young children. You are expecting to use this allotment for many years to come. Imagine you have been through the events described above.

What would you do next with your allotment?

The choice is fairly simple: to garden or not to garden. Nothing in the sociological account of science given above suggests that anything but good scientific testing has gone on. And many other things we all consume or rely on also require and are dependent on similar scientific testing, from the medicines we routinely use to the safety of food bought in shops. It might help here to remember our earlier brief distinction of uncertainty and risk. While the risks of a known outcome (poisoning) are now available, albeit as a result of two different tests which produced contrasting results, there is uncertainty over the precision of the tests and possibly of other factors that might become important. More scientific testing has led to an increase in uncertainty!

1.2   Choice and judgement

If you are interested, the gardener of the two authors of this chapter chose to stop gardening and gave up the allotment, though he often wistfully walks by his old allotment and enviously looks at the growth there. He, and his family, felt there was something not quite trustworthy in the sudden shift from poisonous to safe, even though they could see no obvious flaw in the science. Their assessment of danger suggested that they were acting somewhat irrationally (or perhaps unscientifically) but the family also felt it could not to go back to the allotment. The presence of serious illnesses among the extended family may have subconsciously contributed to their need for a greater sense of safety.

■   What do you think of this choice? Stop for a few moments and reflect on your own feelings of what risk is here and how it can be judged. Then move on to the final section of this case study in which more information becomes available that alters again the interpretation of risk.

Vegetables growing on allotments

In February 2005, just as the events in the allotment were unfolding, the UK Government's Environment Agency (EA) rejected the use of bioaccessibility tests such as PBET for two reasons. First, the test measures bioaccessibility, which is the fraction of a toxic substance that is available to be absorbed by a human gut, but this does not necessarily mean that this fraction of toxic substances will actually be absorbed (which is known as bioavailability). The relationship between bioaccessibility and bioavailability is complex and still a matter of some debate. Second, there was no single standard PBET, which opened up the possibility of someone shopping around to different laboratories to get the desired test result. The EA, however, also acknowledged that the emerging evidence looked like it supported PBET's applicability and the advice had the flavour more of 'not enough testing' than 'PBET is disproven' (EA, 2005). None of this was known to all allotment holders, which may simply mean that nobody involved in the process was aware of this judgement. It was only found out some time after the allotment was back in action and the author's family had given up their allotment, when the author was researching this story for an Open University course (Jordan, 2008)!

Then, while researching further for the present chapter, it was found that the EA had updated its advice. It acknowledged that, despite its 2005 advice not to use tests like PBET, such tests were regularly being submitted as part of risk assessments on land. This is a significant concern as bioaccessibility tests commonly show lower levels of poison than the standard tests and if bioaccessibility tests are not authoritative then this might lead to poisoned land being passed as safe. The EA therefore decided to test the PBETs. The EA submitted the same soil samples, all with known high levels of poison, to nine laboratories in the UK and Wales, to one in the USA and to one in the Netherlands, and asked for a PBET from each. The results demonstrated enough variation between laboratories for the EA to suggest that such tests may well be underestimating poisons and reasserted its advice that 'the applicability of bioaccessibility tests to risk assessments of contaminated land is limited at this time' (EA, 2007).

- Now, reconsider your previous decision to garden or not to garden. Does this extra information about assessing risk in soil contamination change, reinforce or leave untouched your previous decision? Would you now keep your allotment or let it go?

There are many routes to follow here as PBET searches for final acceptance or clear rejection as a valid approach to measuring the risk soil poses to human health. For our purposes, we can now draw back from the details of scientific testing and reflect on the factors that are at play. First of all, it is important to emphasise that the benefits of a social activity such as gardening were suddenly brought into question by the publication of a scientific test on the soil. What seemed to be benign and healthy turned into something that was risky. The material environment changed from being good into something that was dangerous. Second, the materials that had been brought into question were not straightforward. It was difficult to say exactly how risky something would be. The existence of two soil tests confirms that even within science there are debates over how best to assess risk. For our purposes here it is important to emphasise that risk and knowledge about those risks, and about seemingly straightforward things such as soil, are often contestable and open to debate. The output of risk analyses, the numbers or declarations of safety, are the result of a large number of choices and assumptions, all part of normal scientific practice, and it is these choices and assumptions that are often either explicitly or implicitly challenged by people who have other kinds of understanding of the issues. As we will see, this is a common feature of risk issues. As the next section demonstrates, when it comes to risk there are often different views and knowledges to consider.

Summary

- Whether an activity is healthy or not is often far from straightforward. In the case study, the same soil shifted from being safe, to dangerous and back again solely as a result of different measurement practices.
- Risk is often a contested issue in science and in society. Risk knowledge is difficult to produce and will be plagued by uncertainties.
- Assessing risk often relies on science and expertise. These are practices which involve choices and assumptions that can create debate.

2   Who wants to be 'peely-wally'? Sun exposure, suntanning and risk

Figure 2   Health advice from Cancer Research UK

Let us now turn to a slightly different example of risk that you may have some experience with – the alleged dangers of getting a suntan. Over the last few years concerns about exposure to the sun's rays have been increasing (see Figure 2, for example), yet there remains a strong desire among many people for a suntan. Here we can look at a second case study of risk and risk management concerning holidaymakers and their attitudes to a tan.

2.1   Negotiating contradictions

On the one hand, health advice has warned us that the idea of a 'healthy tan' is a contradiction and that preventable skin cancers, caused by sunlight, are increasing at epidemic rates. We are told that exposure to the sun should be kept to a minimum and always be accompanied by the use of a sunscreen. On the other hand, the international travel and tourism industry has grown to be one of the world's leading export earners, ahead of automotive products, chemicals, petroleum and food (World Tourism Organisation, 2007). A major component of this industry is the movement of people to sunny holiday destinations. Indeed, a number of major travel and tourist companies make reference to the sun in their trading names, logos and advertisements. The sun unproblematically condenses and signifies the essence of modern travel for pleasure, with many tourist leisure activities still focused on the beach and involving exposure of tourist skin to sunlight.

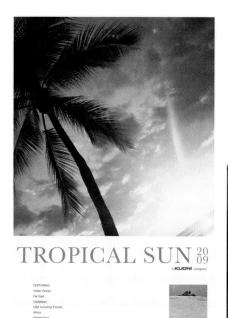

Tourism images are still often focused on sunbathing

This section explores how tourists negotiate and live with these contradictions. It will be argued that to understand the apparently risky practices connected with sun exposure we have to take seriously the ways in which people make sense of expert advice, and measure it against their own knowledge and experiences of the material world in which they live. For this we will draw on some research conducted by one of the authors of this chapter (Simon Carter), which was part of a larger study funded by the Medical Research Council into health and travel. This research used a mixture of interviews and focus groups with tourists aged between 20 and 35 years of age who regularly travelled abroad for their holidays (typical destinations were the Balearic Islands, the Canary Islands and the Spanish Costas). We will reproduce excerpts of what people said in interviews and focus groups to illustrate our arguments.

It is also important to note that this research was carried out in the West of Scotland, with the majority of the respondents living in or near Glasgow – a northern European city surrounded by high ground and facing prevailing westerly winds from the Atlantic. Glaswegians experience long dark winters, relatively short summers and particularly high rainfall throughout the year. While it would not be accurate to say that sunny warm days are unusual in summer, they are not common either. As we shall see, this has a profound effect on Glaswegian attitudes to sun exposure.

There was a discussion of qualitative methods in *Making Social Lives*, Chapter 4. You will learn more about focus groups in the 'How do we know?' section of this chapter.

A postcard from Glasgow

One of the first things that this research found was that people could quite easily recall health education advice about the need to avoid skin exposure to sun by seeking shade, using a sunscreen and/or by covering the body. People knew what the expert advice said about the dangers of exposure to sunlight. However, the research also identified that people did not fully follow this advice partly because they had their own ways of understanding and making sense of the healthy and risky elements of their material lives.

To understand this we can begin by looking at some of the things people do before they go on their holidays. It would be relatively uncontroversial to say that the tourist industry is geared more heavily than other industries towards the provision of goods and services with pleasure as their main aim. One target of such consumption is the body itself, with holidaymakers spending significant amounts of time and money on attaining a specific 'look' for their holiday – through the purchase of fashionable holiday clothes, sunglasses and other services to alter the body's appearance. For example, some people visit gyms to tone their bodies before a holiday. The expectation of having a suntan was also considered as choices about consumption were being made prior to travel. This is obvious in the case of the myriad sun-protection products, such as sunscreens, but other consumption choices are made with sun exposure in mind, such as which clothes to buy to go with a tan. One woman who worked in a clothes shop described how fashion choices changed in the pre-holiday period:

Interviewee   Your clothes look good if you've got a tan ... every summer before people go on their holidays ... everyone buys them in mind of when they've got a tan.

A discussion between two women in one of the focus groups similarly stressed the relationship between fashion choices and having a body colour that complemented these clothes:

Female 1   You can't go out at night unless you're brown because you can't wear any of your clothes unless you're brown.

Female 2   It's not just girls you know ... David used to go away [with his friends] ... they used to buy white vests and jackets for flying home in ... to offset their tans ... complete poseurs!

Another issue that was often mentioned was how tourists compare their own bodies with those of other tourists. Here there was a particular dread of arriving on holiday without a tan and being set apart from other tourists who may already have gained a tan. Tourists from Glasgow felt especially disadvantaged because their local weather could not be relied on to provide a pre-holiday tan. This is highlighted in the following focus group exchange, where arriving on holiday without a suntan was seen as a cause of embarrassment or even shame – it seems that turning up on holiday without a tan is almost akin to arriving at a social function wearing inappropriate dress (please note that the expression 'peely-wally' is Glasgow vernacular for a pale and unhealthy appearance):

Female 1   When you're away and the sunglasses and white legs come out I'm ashamed to be Scottish … it's like if you see a group of peely-wally people then they are Scottish.

Female 2   If you get on holiday and you don't have a tan it's embarrassing … [last year] the English had been getting really good weather and we kept on meeting these English people and they all had tans … and when we walked along together I couldn't bear it.

Female 3   Yeah … it's like … the first few nights when I was peely-wally and everyone else was brown.

Following this exchange, the group was asked whether they ever tried to get suntans before the start of their holidays:

Male 1   Well you don't really get much of a chance in Glasgow!

Everyone   Sunbeds!
shouts

Interviewer   How many people here have used a sunbed before a holiday? [Everyone raises their hands]

Male 1   Sunbeds are different though … they're no use, it's a different ray that blocks out sunlight … and the colour, it's an orange colour!

Female 1   As long as I've got a bit of colour before I go [from a sunbed], I don't mind … but only for a base tan.

Interviewer   Chemical artificial tanning products were unpopular because of their messiness and the difficulty of application – 'they smell … you can't sit down for two hours … they look grim if you get it wrong … it's horrible'.

2.2   Material risk and symbolic risk

We can begin to see that the effects that the sun's rays have on the body are both a source of material risk, from cancers, and of symbolic risk, such as being peely-wally. This symbolic risk is so powerful that people feel that they cannot fully enjoy their holidays unless they can display a tan to other tourists; we can begin to see that the suntan is partially a material sign or **symbol** that is for the visual consumption of other tourists. The modern tourist resort is in many respects organised around the idea of visual consumption and this involves the body itself becoming an object – while on holiday people display their bodies in ways that are quite different from what they might do at home. The suntan has become a significant part of this visual consumption (Urry, 1990).

Symbol
In anthropology and sociology, a material artefact or sign that carries some form of conventional and widely accepted meaning.

A typical crowded beach in Tossa de Mar, Spain

Obviously the visual consumption of the tan does not end with the return from a holiday. A feature of modern tourism is the collection of various symbolic and material objects to take home, either to remind oneself of the holiday or to show others something about the place that has been visited. This category includes drinks, foodstuffs, holiday photos, postcards and locally sold souvenirs. However, the suntan is of crucial importance as a symbolic souvenir to be shown to others on return. It not only gives an immediate signal that someone may have been away but it also gives an indication of the quality of weather experienced; as these focus group participants discuss here:

Female 1   You're under pressure to get a tan ... it's the first thing someone will say to you – 'you've been away, you don't look very brown'.

Female 2   The first day back at work ... everyone says 'WOW, have you been on your holidays?'

Female 3   My first day at work ... I wore this wee white dress ... it was great!

Male 1   You go for a wee kick about ... [and whereas] before you might keep in your track suit ... when you get back and you've got a tan, even if it's raining, you peel them off.

We have seen how, despite warnings known to tourists about exposure to sunlight being a cause of skin cancer, the suntan and sun exposure fit into the structure of a holiday and how the tan is both material and symbolic. Paradoxically, the suntan itself, for many people, also captured feelings of health and beauty. People constantly reported 'feeling' more attractive and healthy with a suntan. What meanings were being attached to these terms? Discussion in one of the focus groups helped illuminate the difference between the health of the suntan and other types of health:

Male 1   If you get a tan you feel good.

Male 2   You're happier going out and at the [night]clubs.

Female 1   Your skin clears up and you look and feel healthier ... You're glowing.

Interviewer   Is it the same type of health that you get from exercise or jogging?

Female 2   No … nine out of ten times if you go out for a run, like one run, you're not going to get anything from it … then if you lie out in the sun for one day you've got something to show for doing that.

Female 3   It's part of the well-being of holiday … being in the sun … it's fantastic … you just bloom …

Female 2   The supermodels they're all brown … they're all tanned.

Getting a suntan is a process in which the tan emerges as a crucial symbol of the material life of a tourist. The suntan is a salient feature in the planning of holidays, in activities undertaken on holiday, and in social expectations on return from holiday. In addition, the suntan is thought to embody certain ideas of health by being an immediate visual symbol that signifies and inspires deep feelings of attractiveness and confidence. This is in opposition to health education where the idea of health is more concerned with the avoidance of distant danger.

As with the example of the allotment, we find that knowledge of risk is contested. People's material experience of the risk seemed to counter the stark warnings of the health experts. The Glaswegians who were part of the research outlined here demonstrated they both knew about the risk of exposing their skin to the sun and they desired a tan for symbolic reasons; and they interpreted a tan as demonstrating some aspect of good health. Here expert knowledge, which almost uniformly tries to persuade people to hide their skin from the sun, confronts lay knowledge of risk.

Summary

- A case study of the risk of skin cancer from exposure to the sun was explored by examining the experiences and behaviours of holidaymakers and their responses to health information.

- People used their material experiences and cultural practices to make sense of and judge the importance or otherwise of expert statements on risk. The knowledge produced by experts was different from that produced by holidaymakers.

- The distinction between expert and lay knowledge meant that expert knowledge was interpreted rather than followed to the letter by the public.

3   The risk society

The examples of sun exposure and of poisoned soil demonstrate how we may have entered into a particular kind of relationship to risk in society today. One key theorist of risk, the German sociologist Ulrich Beck, whose work was first translated into English in the late 1980s and early 1990s, has been particularly influential in social science debates about risk. We will consider his theory as a way of developing our understanding of risk and material lives.

Chernobyl No. 4 reactor after the explosion

Beck's thesis on risk can be best explained by using an example. At 01:23 (Soviet European Time) on Saturday 26 April 1986, reactor number four of the Chernobyl nuclear power complex exploded, causing major structural damage to the plant buildings. The subsequent release of radioactive material caused acute radiation sickness in 200 individuals, 28 of whom subsequently died (Spivak, 1992). The immediate effects of the catastrophe were therefore comparable to a minor air disaster, yet the possible long-term consequences went far beyond that suggested by such a comparison. A plume of dangerous radioactive material spread westwards over Europe, presenting a danger that was invisible and therefore beyond direct human powers of perception. As a result, those living within 'fallout' zones became aware that they may be suffering irreversible and material health damage but, at the same time, they were dependent on the knowledge of 'experts' to find out their risk – a knowledge that was mediated through institutions, argument and causal interpretations and was therefore 'open to a social process of definition' (Beck, 1989, p. 88). In other words, here we have an example of an event that exposed large numbers of people in society to danger, but where the risk was invisible and thus had to be revealed and defined by experts.

Beck uses cases such as Chernobyl to ask what a society may look like in which disputes about new and often invisible risks are increasingly being pushed to the fore. For Beck, we are in a period of transition towards a **risk society**, where political and policy considerations increasingly come to focus on the distribution of risks. Beck argues that this is a move from a previous industrial society in which most political deliberations were around the distribution of wealth, to one where concerns are increasingly focused on the distribution of harm. In the former, one is dealing with 'desirable items in scarcity'; conversely, in the latter, with the 'risk society' one has an 'undesirable abundance' of harms.

Risk society
An account of contemporary society that emphasises the development of the side effects of modernisation and the growth in many people's awareness of risk.

Crucially within risk society, personal experience is no longer adequate for judging danger and harm. Beck argues we have all become dependent on external, usually expert, knowledge in order to define the hazards we face. For instance, within earlier industrial society, threats (i.e. the loss of one's job) could be known without any special measuring procedures or expertise. 'The affliction is clear and in that sense independent of knowledge' (Beck, 1989, p. 53). Yet within risk society the situation is reversed. For example, the allotment holders could not determine the risks contained in their soil by their own means and experiences. Rather, they were told of the potential danger by scientific experts. Similarly, the possible risk from sun exposure has to be made clear to people on the basis of expert evidence. Thus within risk society the extent of people's material exposure to danger and harm is essentially reliant on knowledge created by experts.

Activity 3

Can you think of anything you have noticed recently in the news where there have been disagreements about safety, danger and risk? On the one hand, this may be some individual activity you, your friends or family engage in, or, on the other, it could be some perceived threat or risk at a more global level.

Here are some of the risks that we noticed were current in newspapers on the days we were preparing this chapter:

Levels of alcohol consumption. Apparently drinking some alcohol is healthier than not drinking at all, but it is difficult to find expert agreement about the safe upper limit, and government advice has frequently changed over the last three decades. Pregnant women are in a particularly difficult situation, with UK health education advice currently recommending total abstinence but other medical experts saying that there is no evidence at all that low consumption of alcohol during pregnancy does any damage to mother or child.

Mobile phone use. Mobile phones are very common but some people are concerned about the risks of their use, and the locations of base stations cause particular alarm and dismay for some. This is despite frequent assurances from some experts that the technology is safe.

Suntanning. Recently, controversy among experts has arisen about the dangers of sunlight. After decades of being told that we should avoid the sun, a minority medical opinion that is yet also significant and reputable has arisen that we might, in fact, need to increase our sunlight exposure (Affleck, 2005; Ness et al., 1999). Lack of sunlight has been implicated in negative mood disturbances in winter and also linked with a lack of vitamin D. It has been suggested that reduced exposure to sunlight, while preventing skin cancers, may in fact increase the total burden of disease and mortality (Selby and Mawer, 1999).

No doubt you can think of more, either from your personal experience or from following the news media. One of Beck's central concerns is the role of expert knowledge in defining the risks that go on to cause anxiety for us all, whether that risk is nuclear radiation, arsenic in the soil or the sun in the sky. This argument, however, leaves those who are not regarded as experts helpless in the face of knowledge produced by scientists and other experts, and we have already seen tourists interpreting such advice in their own ways. Beck's claim about the dominance of expert opinion points to our next concern about the ways knowledge circulates between scientists and non-scientists. Our two case studies strongly suggest not only the importance of expert knowledge, as posited by Beck, but also that expert knowledge does not straightforwardly determine public opinion. It is important now to extend Beck's theory by considering the issue of 'lay' interpretations of expert advice. A very useful way of looking at this is to focus on expert and lay epidemiology.

Summary

- A risk society is one in which calculations of risk become increasingly prominent.
- Many modern risks are invisible and need experts to make them visible to the public.
- The process of expert definitions of risk is contested between experts and other interested groups.

4 Epidemiology, 'lay' epidemiology, 'Uncle Norman' and the 'last person'

One science that has contributed greatly to debates about risk is epidemiology. Indeed, epidemiology can rightly claim to be one of the first academic disciplines to adopt and use the concept of risk (Oppenheimer, 2006). Very broadly, epidemiology is the study of the various things that contribute to illness, disease and death in human populations, and it has become the foundation of many public health initiatives. The key here is the combination of studies of illness and health with that of populations. Epidemiology tracks illness across whole nations. Epidemiology, in its modern form, emerged in the middle of the nineteenth century and was initially concerned with tracing the origin of infectious disease, trying to see how a new disease arose in one part of the world and then travelled, while also trying to isolate the causes of such diseases.

While tracing the source of infectious disease is still important in public health (particularly in developing countries), a new type of epidemiological expertise appeared in the latter part of the twentieth century. This was a reflection of changes in patterns of mortality (e.g. rates of death). Simply put, the rate of deaths caused by acute infectious illnesses declined sharply from about 1850 onwards. In the first decades of the twentieth century, in most Western nations, non-infectious chronic illnesses (most notably coronary heart disease and cancers) overtook acute infections as the leading causes of death for the first time. The reasons for this decline of infectious diseases are still under debate but it has been suggested that clean water, sanitary sewage disposal, a suppression of mosquitoes and increasing food safety (e.g. refrigeration and pasteurisation) all played a role (Omran, 1982).

The investigation of the new killers, non-infectious causes of death, led to a new type of epidemiology. Typically, epidemiologists of this type collect a wide variety of data on a large number of individuals, focusing on their material and social lives – this can include individual characteristics, such as blood pressure, height, weight, blood cholesterol levels and lung function, along with social characteristics, such as income level, class position, and psychosocial characteristics. This data is then subjected to a range of statistical tests in order to discover correlations or relationships between factors that may raise the **probability** of the individual or population developing a disease or

The making of populations was discussed in Chapter 9 of *Making Social Lives*.

Probability
The likelihood, or chance, that something is going to happen, expressed mathematically.

illness. The use of probabilities to explain phenomena only emerged when, in the nineteenth century, it became possible to conceive of statistical patterning as an explanation in its own right, rather than thinking of the world as deterministic in character (Hacking, 1990). This is quite a difficult distinction to understand, so let us explain it slightly differently. A deterministic way of thinking about the world would look for the actual causal mechanisms (e.g. detailed practical information about how something works) that lead to something happening; an explanation based on probabilities would attempt to find underlying patterns that may reveal relationships without necessarily saying anything about the actual mechanisms involved. So, a deterministic account of smoking as a cause of lung cancer would need to find the exact process by which smoking tobacco leads to this serious illness. In contrast, a statistical account (Doll and Hill, 1950) would only need to show that there was a very strong pattern among people who both smoked and went on to develop lung cancer (as opposed to those who did not).

We can see that by using a probabilistic approach to health risks there is no need to directly explain or even understand the cause of any particular disease. The main aim in epidemiology is to find a probabilistic relationship between a disease (e.g. coronary heart disease) and the various factors (e.g. diet, environment, habits or genetics) that may play a role in the disease's progression. These probabilistic relationships are then used with existing medical, biological, psychological or sociological theories in order to make informed explanations about why some people get ill and others do not. However, these relationships are not causal. Indeed one of the principles of epidemiology (and of social science!), taught early on to students, is that a correlation or relationship between factors does not imply causation. Thus, to use a common teaching example, there is a strong correlation between sleeping with one's shoes on and waking up with a headache. Hence, it might be concluded that shoes combined with sleep cause headaches. But this ignores the more likely explanation that a third factor was involved – the consumption of large quantities of alcoholic beverages that caused the individual both to fall asleep with shoes on and to wake up with a headache.

Chapter 5 of *Making Social Lives* discussed the correlations that are made between social capital and affluence, and how these shouldn't necessarily be confused with a causal or deterministic relationship.

Epidemiology uses a mixture of indicators to suggest, by using statistical techniques, how illness and health are patterned within society. As such, the science of epidemiology is today incredibly powerful in shaping many aspects of our world. This type of knowledge guides government policies on such things as health education, new drugs and food labelling. It informs decisions about the provision of health services and the types of health specialisms that may be needed in the future. It informs taxation policies on such commodities as alcohol and tobacco. Insurance companies use epidemiological knowledge to calculate the risks of individuals and populations in order to work out premiums. The chances are very high that, if you have ever applied for a mortgage, life insurance or a pension scheme, you will have answered a variety of questions based on epidemiological knowledge in order to determine the risk you pose in case of premature death.

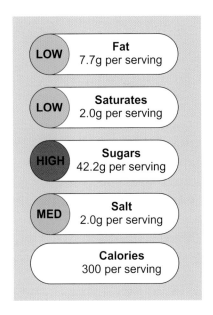

Fat
7.7g per serving — LOW

Saturates
2.0g per serving — LOW

Sugars
42.2g per serving — HIGH

Salt
2.0g per serving — MED

Calories
300 per serving

Epidemiological knowledge has changed the labelling of foods

4.1   The use of epidemiological knowledge

We have already seen some examples of the way epidemiological knowledge is used. The two sides of the argument over cycling helmets in the Introduction drew on epidemiological studies. Further, the suntan example showed how health education campaigns sought to change attitudes to suntanning. These campaigns will have been based on epidemiological knowledge of the risks of sun exposure.

However, as the allotment example suggested, expert knowledge is not a unified body of work and it often becomes the site of, sometimes bitter, disputes. These can occur internally between epidemiologists themselves or between epidemiologists and other 'interest groups', such as journalists, community physicians, civil servants, politicians or drug companies and other industry insiders. For example, by the late 1970s the epidemiological case that smoking led to ill health and premature death was well established in scientific terms. Yet the relationship between smoking and lung cancer was still only a probabilistic one, not a causal or deterministic one. The tobacco industry employed a variety of strategies (and some of their own epidemiologists) to counter the evidence that smoking was harmful. They drew attention to the inevitable uncertainties in epidemiological science in an attempt to show that the case against cigarettes was not proven and that the evidence was merely 'statistical'. They pointed out that no causal mechanism by which tobacco caused harm had ever been identified and that further scientific enquiry was needed (Taylor, 1984). This point connects strongly to Beck's 'risk society' arguments because, although he made expert knowledge central to his theory, he also noted the contested and complex ways in which expert knowledge is generated and challenged.

Another issue is how the public react to epidemiological knowledge. The new insights generated by epidemiology are frequently reported in the media. Often the discipline of epidemiology is not itself mentioned and instead phrases such as 'scientists have shown that …' are employed and reports are also often framed in such a way that the uncertainties of the original investigations are minimised. For example, in 1995 the Committee on Safety of Medicines (CSM) issued a warning, based on epidemiological evidence, which indicated that there was a very slight increased risk of blood clots associated with some forms of the oral contraceptive pill (Department of Health, 1995). The warning from the CSM was widely covered in print and other types of media and generated headlines such as: 'If men had to take the pill my sister would not have died' (Hey and Midgley, *Daily Mirror*, 1995); 'Danger pill: 1½ million women warned' (Hope, *Daily Mail*, 1995); 'Blood clot alert on the pill' (Mihill, *The Guardian*, 1995); and 'Pill alert for a million women: chaos predicted despite official advice not to panic over thrombosis warning' (Hunt, *The Independent*, 1995). There followed much debate about this crisis, particularly on the role of the media and the way the Department of Health handled the release of information. Some even questioned whether the original report should have been released. What is clear, however, is that significant numbers of women immediately, and understandably, stopped taking oral contraceptives. This then led to various material effects on this population (also revealed by epidemiological studies): namely measurable increases in elective terminations and unplanned pregnancies in the months immediately after the crisis (Child et al., 1996; Hope, 1996).

Despite periodic crises such as this one, most of us will encounter epidemiological knowledge through public health and health education advice given out by governments over such issues as diet, alcohol/ tobacco consumption and childhood vaccinations. Such advice has to undergo several transformations between being reported in epidemiological research and its eventual appearance as health advice. The most dramatic is that epidemiological evidence is almost always based on studies of a population or community, often involving very large numbers of people. However, advice to 'the public', if it is going to change behaviour, is often made at the level of the individual. This means that public health campaigns and policies aim to reduce exposure to risk factors for a whole population, which can mean that a whole population (for example, everyone in the UK, or all women, or all cyclists ...) is being asked to change its normal behaviour. The epidemiologist Geoffrey Rose noted that this situation led to something of a paradox, known as the **prevention paradox**, which is that any 'measure that brings large benefits to the community offers little to each participating individual' (Rose, 1981, p. 1850). While a public campaign will have some benefits for a minority of people, most people, Rose argued, will be all right anyway. This can result in a problem – for the health advice might be understood as inaccurate and ultimately demotivating for most of the population, and therefore can have the reverse of the intended effect.

Prevention paradox
Any measure in public health that brings large overall benefits to the community offers little to each participating individual.

For example, vaccinations work best when most of those who can possibly get an infection are vaccinated against the illness. Thus, before mass diphtheria immunisation was introduced into Britain in the 1940s, around 1 in 600 children died of this illness. This meant that, once a successful vaccine was developed, many children who would never have caught diphtheria anyway had to accept the small risk, discomfort and inconvenience of undergoing the vaccination. In other words, 600 children needed to be vaccinated in order to save one child's life, because no one would know in advance who the unlucky child was going to be – '599 "wasted" immunisations for the one that was effective' (Rose, 1981, p. 1850).

The idea of the prevention paradox was further developed by the medical anthropologist Charlie Davison and colleagues. In the late 1980s, they carried out an investigation into lay understandings of the causes of coronary heart disease by a combination of interviews with adult informants and community observations. At this time heart disease accounted for around 25 per cent of all deaths in the UK.

By drawing on simplified versions of epidemiological research it became common knowledge among policymakers and health educators that many of these deaths were preventable. This led to policy initiatives that sought to prevent heart disease by using blanket educational measures aimed at the whole population, who were all deemed to be 'at risk'. This was done in an attempt to instil the idea that heart disease was strongly linked to behaviours (e.g. eating fatty food, drinking and smoking, and lack of exercise) 'which could be changed by the triumph of self-control over self-indulgence' (Davison et al., 1991, p. 3). Particular emphasis was put on a reduction in fatty foods with the dissemination of simple messages like 'saturated fat is bad for you – eat less', 'obesity is dangerous – stay slim', 'exercise is good for you – do more' (Davison et al., 1991, p. 16). In short, this was a classic case of the prevention paradox. Everyone was being asked to change their lifestyle, often quite dramatically, even though these messages were at best a misrepresentation of epidemiological evidence. Indeed, the scientific evidence about heart disease tended to suggest a complex combination of factors, of which lifestyle was only one, lead to illness. Furthermore, there was good evidence to suggest that lifestyle changes would only benefit a few people.

Health education advertisements aimed at the whole population

The study carried out by Davison and his colleagues revealed that the public, rather than being ignorant of health messages, in fact used complex and thoughtful theories that explored the relationships between preventability, inevitability, probability and fate. Indeed, they discovered that the scientific practice of epidemiology had its own lay counterpart, which while not being entirely the same had a 'certain degree of overlap'. In particular, they noticed that in everyday life people take notice of and talk about health and illness, often using humour. As more and more blanket health education messages are released, and as these are aimed at the whole population but pitched at the level of the individual, this has the effect of making people more and more aware of their own behaviours. We saw this in the Glaswegian tourists who were well aware of the risks of suntanning. People who never thought themselves at risk suddenly find themselves moved into new 'at risk' groups. However, health education messages, rather than changing behaviour, had unintended consequences. Because of humorous talk about illness and health, people suddenly become very aware of exceptions. For example, some people who avoided illness had lifestyles that, according to the health education messages, put them at risk of heart disease. On the other hand, there were those who followed health advice but still succumbed to a heart attack. Davison et al., in particular, name two figures that illustrate this process. On the one hand, there were those classified as 'Uncle Normans', as in 'my Uncle Norman smoked and had a fry up every morning and lived to 93'. On the other hand, there were those described as the 'last person', as in 'they used to eat sensibly and exercise all the time – the last person you would expect to have a heart attack'. 'Both types make an appearance in social networks of many individuals, and "the last person" makes regular appearances in the mass media' (Davison et al., 1991, p. 18). The existence of characters such as 'Uncle Norman' and the 'last person' within popular discourse allow many health education messages to be neutralised by the lay public because everyone can recall an example of someone who contradicts the simplified message provided by health education campaigns.

We should note that lay epidemiology does not exist separately from expert or scientific epidemiology. Instead, the lay often takes in, reinterprets and reframes the expert. For example, in the allotment case study, the allotment holders were able to explore the different nature of the two tests (much as you were asked to in reading about them) and to examine the results of the scientific tests. Similarly, the holidaymakers worried about tans were not ignorant of the dangers articulated by public health campaigns, indeed they could all reproduce accurate accounts of the current health education messages. The lay and the expert may seem to be in opposition, and sometimes they are in conflict, but they also engage and refract each other.

In sum, the material risks that we all face are frequently the subject of debate and contest. Different knowledges and experiences are brought to bear on just how risky an activity is likely to be. Expertise may include laboratory knowledge, or may be based on an understanding of risks to a large population. But people rarely take this knowledge as read, or as instantly applicable to their own lives. As the prevention paradox demonstrates, it is difficult to apply epidemiological knowledge to a health campaign or policy, because at the individual level the benefits may be very small indeed. Moreover, people will make sense of a campaign by drawing on their own experiences, and the experiences of others (Uncle Normans and the last person) to question the authority or purchase of public health advice. Risk, in other words, is never clear-cut, and is made more difficult by the diversity of people's lives (their material complexity) and the range of knowledges that are relevant to any assessment of how likely it is that the event will happen.

Summary

- The history of epidemiology involves a shift from tracing mechanisms of disease to assessing probabilities of disease.
- In contrast to Beck, looking at epidemiology reinforced the point made in the suntan case study that public or lay knowledge is active and sometimes opposed to expert knowledge.
- The prevention paradox illustrates the difficulties in reducing the risks a population faces by asking individuals to change the way they behave. Most of the population will be asked to make changes that have no direct benefit to themselves, even though there is an overall benefit to the population.

How do we know?

Public understanding and expert understanding

This chapter explores a style of knowing that revolves around the importance of knowledge in the creation of risk in material lives. In particular, we have touched on the way knowledge produced by experts – epidemiologists, scientists, public policymakers, and so on – is used to create an understanding of risk, but that this understanding is not simply taken as a given by the public it is communicated to. Lay understandings reinterpret and cut across expert understandings. It was important to emphasise that such lay understandings do not equate with ignorance of expert understandings but are a reinterpretation of them combined with a concern for some factors different from those valued by experts.

If we recall our initial definition of risk that separates it from uncertainty, we can see that such knowledge plays a key role, as risk is the probability of an outcome combined with consequences of different outcomes. Knowledge is key in understanding both the uncertainty and the consequences that are integral to a risk. This 'style of knowing' in relation to risk revolves importantly around both expert knowledge, which can be particularly important in relation to 'invisible' risks such as those Beck mentions, and lay knowledges, which are aware of the claims of expert knowledge but develop their own understandings. This leaves those researching risk with an issue of how to get to grips with what it is that lay publics think; whereas expert knowledge deliberately broadcasts itself, lay knowledge tends to reside in daily, ephemeral interactions between people. To get at these daily conversations requires a focus on qualitative research skills, which seek to draw out from people their interpretations. You can think back to the use of research in relation to discourse and using case studies to draw on other qualitative methods. And these research skills are present in this chapter – most clearly, the allotment story is very much a case study style of approach – yet this chapter has introduced the additional research skill of using focus groups.

You read about research using discourse in Chapter 4 and using case studies in Chapter 5 of *Making Social Lives.*

Focus group research normally involves groups of six to eight people who sit together and discuss whatever 'focus' the researcher asks them to discuss. They are called focus groups because the group is normally involved in the exploration of a specific set of related issues (e.g. attitudes to risk associated with sun exposure while on holiday). The focus group should be more than a simple group interview (e.g. with the researcher posing questions and research participants responding to these in turn). Rather, the whole point of focus groups is that they include and explicitly use the group interaction as the main object of research interest and to generate research data. Thus the aim for the researcher is to set up the condition where interactions within the group can take place in order to explore both similarities and differences within a group (Carter and Henderson, 2005).

Conclusion

This chapter began with an account of everyday ways of controlling risks in our lives. We briefly considered the role of the bicycle helmet and the statue spelling ARSENAL. This emphasised the importance of matter in our lives – of the solid and material effects that can be designed to manage harm and promote safety. Having begun to understand the relationship between material lives and risk, we looked at risk in more detail through a case study of an allotment.

The allotment example made clear that risks were not straightforward, and that often there were contrasting accounts of just how risky an activity could be. In other words, defining risk depended on quite complex knowledges. In the allotment example, the risk from the soil shifted dramatically according to the way knowledge was produced about it; from healthy to poisonous and back again. In this case, the knowledge was scientific. We also saw that a question that we would imagine should be easy for scientists to answer – 'Is this soil poisonous or not?' – was in fact more difficult and depended upon a raft of measurements, normal scientific uncertainty and a host of assumptions about the behaviour of soils, rats, people and poisons.

We then turned to look at a related example of knowledge, risk and material lives in campaigns targeted at suntanning and the danger of skin cancer. Here the emphasis shifted from the production of scientific knowledge to its reception. The Glaswegians who used tanning salons and worried about the colour of their skin when they headed off on holiday also knew about the risks of cancer but worked with more complex notions of health and risk.

To understand the implications of these two case studies we first introduced Beck's notion of the risk society. The core of his argument is that our society is becoming ever more defined by the abundance of risks we all have to face; from the risk of the sun, to the risks of food, to risks of distant industrial accidents, we seem to be surrounded by a series of deadly dangers. Furthermore, Beck emphasises the importance of knowledge production in this form of risk, as the risks themselves tend to be invisible to us and need to be defined and exposed by experts. Where a cyclist can see, indeed intimately feel, the danger a car or truck poses, we cannot so easily tell that the sun, a bottle of wine, a carrot or the air contains a deadly risk. Instead, Beck points out how the abundance of risks is defined for us by experts.

To complete our account we introduced epidemiology. In a similar way to the reinterpretation of risk conducted by holidaymakers in relation to suntans and cancer, we can see that not only is epidemiology an expert body of knowledge but it is reinterpreted by the public to produce a lay epidemiology. This lay epidemiology takes up different understandings of risk. Based on personal experience and social networks, and working at the level of the individual rather than the population, these accounts of risk can be quite different from those that inform the public health campaigns. These differences can frustrate efforts to raise population health or reduce risk for an entire population.

We can now see that not only is risk a key component of our lives, something that we negotiate every day, but that it is always intimately tied up with the way that expert and lay people produce knowledge about the world. Not only are we constantly living with risk but we are also doing so in conjunction with the material and social production of knowledge. The latter is not only expert knowledge, as we see with public health campaigns and scientific measurements of dangers, but is also always produced by the public.

In the next chapter, we take this important topic of risk into a slightly different terrain. In recent years a new challenge for social science understandings of risk has become clear – for it is now common to hear people speak of risks not just for people and populations but for a whole planet. Indeed, while Beck had the image of Chernobyl in his mind when he first wrote of the risk society, he'd also witnessed large-scale forest death in western Germany. The latter was caused by acid rain, a result of emissions from power plants in Germany and, importantly, from surrounding countries. It was clear that managing environmental risk was not something that one nation state could do on its own – there needed to be international coordination. More recently, the rise of global climate change has made such coordination even more important. The next chapter considers this issue in some detail and asks how people can respond effectively to these general and common risks. You should keep in mind some of the lessons of this chapter as you read on. Remember that risks are always dependent on different kinds of knowledge, and that what works at the general level may not be meaningful when we try to apply it to people's daily lives (the prevention paradox). If the health of the planet is a common problem, then it will be difficult to find a common solution.

You read about climate change in Chapter 3 of this book.

References

Affleck, P. (2005) 'Sun exposure and health', *Nursing Standard*, vol. 19, pp. 50–4.

Beck, U. (1989) 'On the way to the industrial risk-society? Outline of an argument', *Thesis Eleven*, vol. 23, pp. 86–103.

Carter, S. (1997) 'Who wants to be "peelie wally"? Glaswegian tourists' attitudes to sun tans and sun exposure' in Clift, S. and Grabowski, P. (eds) *Tourism and Health: Risks, Responses and Research*, London, Pinter.

Carter, S. and Henderson, L. (2005) 'Approaches to qualitative data collection in the social sciences' in Bowling, A. and Ebrahim, S. (eds) *Handbook of Research Methods in Health: Investigation, Measurement and Analysis*, Maidenhead, Open University Press.

Child, T., Mackenzie, I. and Rees, M. (1996) 'Terminations of pregnancy, not unplanned deliveries, increased as result of pill scare', *British Medical Journal*, vol. 313, p. 1005.

Davison, C., Davey Smith, G. and Frankel, S. (1991) 'Lay epidemiology and the prevention paradox – the implications of coronary candidacy for health education', *Sociology of Health and Illness*, vol. 13, no. 1, pp. 1–19.

Department of Health (1995) *New Advice on Oral Contraceptives*, London, Department of Health.

Doll, R. and Hill, B. (1950) 'Smoking and carcinoma of the lung. Preliminary report', *British Medical Journal*, vol. 2, pp. 739–48.

Environment Agency (EA) (2005) *Science Update on the Use of Bioaccessibility Testing in Risk Assessment of Land Contamination, February 2005* [online], http://www.environment-agency.gov.uk/commondata/acrobat/bioacc_update_v2_970501.pdf (Accessed 1 February 2008).

Environment Agency (EA) (2007) *Inter-Laboratory Comparison of In Vitro Bioaccessibility Measurements for Arsenic, Lead and Nickel in Soil, June 2007* [online], http://publications.environment-agency.gov.uk/pdf/SCHO0307BMLG-e-e.pdf?lang=_e (Accessed 1 February 2008).

Hacking, I. (1990) *The Taming of Chance*, Cambridge, Cambridge University Press.

Hey, S. and Midgley, C. (1995) 'If men had to take the pill my sister would not have died', *Daily Mirror*, p. 7.

Hope, J. (1995) 'Danger pill: 1½ million women warned', *Daily Mail*, p. 2.

Hope, S. (1996) 'Twelve per cent of women stopped taking their pill immediately they heard CSM's warning', *British Medical Journal*, vol. 312, p. 576.

Hunt, L. (1995) 'Pill alert for a million women: chaos predicted despite official advice not to panic over thrombosis warning', *The Independent*.

Jordan, T. (2008) 'Security in the social world: gardens and Harry Potter' in Carter, S., Jordan, T. and Watson, S. (eds) *Security: Sociology and Social Worlds*, Manchester, Manchester University Press.

Mihill, C. (1995) 'Blood clot alert on the pill', *The Guardian*.

Ness, A., Frankel, S., Gunnell, D. and Smith, G. (1999) 'Are we really dying for a tan?', *British Medical Journal*, vol. 319, pp. 114–16.

Omran, A.R. (1982) 'Epidemiologic transition', *Milbank Memorial Fund Quarterly*, vol. 49, pp. 509–38.

Oppenheimer, G. (2006) 'Profiling risk: the emergence of coronary heart disease epidemiology in the United States (1947–70)', *International Journal of Epidemiology*, vol. 35, pp. 720–30.

Rose, G. (1981) 'Strategy of prevention: lessons from cardiovascular disease', *British Medical Journal*, vol. 282, pp. 1847–53.

Ruby, M., Davis, A., Schoof, R., Eberle, S. and Sellstone, C.M. (1996) 'Estimation of lead and arsenic bioavailability using a physiologically based extraction test', *Environmental Science and Technology*, vol. 30, pp. 422–30.

Selby, P. and Mawer, E. (1999) 'Sunlight and health: exposure to sunlight may reduce cancer risk', *British Medical Journal*, vol. 319, pp. 1067–8.

Spivak, L.I. (1992) 'Psychiatric aspects of the accident at Chernobyl nuclear power station', *European Journal of Psychiatry*, vol. 6, pp. 207–12.

Taylor, P. (1984) *Smoke Ring: The Politics of Tobacco*, London, Bodley Head.

Thompson, D.C., Rivara, F.P. and Thompson, R.S. (1989) 'A case-control study of the effectiveness of bicycle safety helmets', *New England Journal of Medicine*, vol. 320, no. 21 pp. 1361–7.

Urry, J. (1990) *The Tourist Gaze: Leisure and Travel in Contemporary Societies*, London, Sage.

Walker, A. (2006) 'Drivers overtaking bicyclists' [online], http://adrianwalker. com/overtaking/overtakingprobrief.pdf (Accessed 14 April 2009).

World Tourism Organisation (2007) *World Tourism Highlights: 2006 Edition*, Madrid, World Tourism Organisation.

Chapter 3
Living in a common world

Michael Pryke

Contents

Introduction   101

1   Sharing the common duvet: the atmosphere, greenhouse gases and carbon-based economic growth   106

    1.1   Locating emissions, locating a problem   108

    1.2   Repairing the problem   110

2   The atmosphere as a form of commons   112

3   Working towards a market solution: from regulation to permits to market-based approaches to CO_2 119

    3.1   Permits and the retreat of regulation   119

    3.2   Kyoto: a framework for a market-based approach to CO_2 122

4   Markets made for whom?   128

    4.1   Build a power plant in Norway, plant trees in Uganda   129

    4.2   'Efficient boilers' in Yala, Thailand; business as usual in Japan   131

Conclusion   138

References   140

Introduction

As we have learned from the two previous chapters, concern is mounting about the harmful links between the societies we live in and the environmental damage that they may cause. On the one hand, serious questions are being raised about the environmental costs of a carbon-fuelled economic growth, and, on the other hand, the risks associated with human activity are becoming increasingly difficult to estimate and manage. Furthermore, as this chapter makes clear, people are increasingly aware that we live on a small and shared planet; that activities in one place have effects in other places, and for many years to come. In short, we live in a common world, but it is also apparent that we are not particularly good at organising ourselves in ways that respect the need to live together.

Social scientists have an important role to play in trying to solve such problems. As you learn how society is made (through economic growth, for example), you also learn how problems arise and possibly how it is that our social science knowledge can be used to repair those problems. But, as you have also learnt from previous chapters, there are different kinds of knowledge and understanding. There are, for example, different social sciences, and even within one area of social science there are debates over which concept, theory or model is best suited to understanding and acting in the world. This chapter focuses on one particularly pressing issue for society and for social science – global climate change. It will look at some of its causes and the ways in which social science understanding has been used to explain why such change is difficult to halt and to suggest what might be done to repair the damage. You will learn that the main method used for tackling climate change in recent years has been based on markets. I will question how mechanisms geared to combat the emission of carbon into the atmosphere have been chosen, drawn up and implemented. Who has had a say in choosing them? Whose voices have been heard and whose not? Why was one mechanism chosen over others? In seeking some answers to these questions, you will learn that social science doesn't simply study the world, it actively seeks to change it.

Along with the issue of social science understanding and intervention, looking at global climate change also introduces some important concerns about issues of social and material inequality. Should people in countries such as the UK continue to burn fossil fuels when it is becoming increasingly apparent that doing so harms the *world's* – not just the UK's – atmosphere? Similarly, is it equitable for people on this tiny island to rely on carbon-based growth to remake a consumer-driven society, while at the same time others in 'far off lands' seeking to do the same are being told to put their ambitions on hold? Indeed, do people in the **global North** hold all the answers?

The emphasis in this chapter is less on scientific debates that surround carbon emissions and other 'greenhouse gases', although these are of course important parts of the overall jigsaw, and more on the shared issues and questions that the emission of excessive greenhouse gases, such as carbon dioxide (CO_2), generate. Carbon emissions, like rubbish, have a social dimension.

The remainder of this Introduction sets out the issues that later sections will address. Section 1 offers a working definition of the atmosphere as an example of a 'free good' that has been used increasingly by individuals and companies as a convenient dump for carbon emissions. Section 2 introduces the idea of the atmosphere as a form of 'commons' and discusses measures that might be taken to protect it from overuse. Yet, as the section highlights, protecting the commons and dealing with the damaging impact of excessive carbon emissions through measures such as taxes and regulations is not a straightforward task. Thus, Section 3 looks in more detail at one significant measure devised and implemented to deal with the emission of CO_2 into the atmospheric commons: the use of the private market to solve the problem of carbon emissions. Here I question the fairness of market solutions to a global problem (asking who are the winners and losers). Through examples Section 4 considers how the inequalities that result from CO_2 emissions may be made worse by the kinds of market solutions that are being used. The section leads into a brief concluding discussion of the types of issues that any solution to carbon emissions should consider if the delicate balance between living with carbon and living in a global world is to be achieved.

The social organisation of CO_2

Governments in the UK and elsewhere, international organisations and environmental groups are increasingly in agreement that we must reduce the amount of carbon emissions produced in the collective chase to meet the goal of economic growth. Despite this agreement and the frequency of newspaper headlines stating that climate change is accelerating and predicting dire consequences, most people in the

Global North/South Terms used to distinguish between the relatively wealthy and powerful countries and those who tend to be able to wield less power and are, in terms of GDP, less well off. North and South only roughly corresponds to a geographical description (Australia is part of the global North, for example).

Waste and rubbish were discussed in *Making Social Lives*, Chapter 3.

Section 1 contains echoes of the discussion of externalities and the price mechanism which were introduced in Chapter 3 of *Making Social Lives*.

Carbon emissions, climate change and global warming have been discussed in Chapter 3 of *Making Social Lives* and in Chapter 1 of this book.

Is untroubled consumption at the core of life in the global North?

comparatively wealthy countries of the global North trundle along seemingly untroubled by the dire scientific predictions of global warming, its inevitability and why consequently 'we' must radically reorganise the way 'we' go about our lives.

In addition to the fact that quite often the whole issue of climate change and global warming is plagued by uncertainties, and is typical of a risk society issue (it is technical, requires scientific expertise to expose the risks, and there are quite often disagreements – one scientist says this, another that, and so on), the sheer scale of the change demanded to the way we live means that it is tempting to carry on regardless. The trouble is that it is increasingly apparent that we can't carry on this way for ever. On an overcrowded planet, where demand for **finite resources** is growing daily, at some point soon the relationship between

The nature of economies was described in Chapter 1 of this book.

Finite resources
Resources are the materials and means by which societies are made. They include materials such as oil, gas, metal as well as the knowledge used to fashion those materials. Finite resources are those in limited supply that will eventually run out.

economic growth (and its centrality to the way we imagine and design national and international economies) and its impact on the world's climate system will have to be addressed, not just by governments and international institutions, but by all of us. We are all implicated to varying degrees in what is happening to the climate. Recent evidence points to emissions of greenhouse gases as the central cause of rapid climate change. These gases are released from a variety of processes, but most notably it is the burning of fossil fuels (coal, natural gas, oil) in industrial production, electricity generation, space heating and transport, along with emissions from livestock farming and the failure to maintain healthy forest and other ecosystems that can absorb excess carbon, that are to blame. Emissions and the loss of ability to absorb them are, it is often argued, linked inextricably to economic growth, a subject which is very much in the background throughout this chapter.

The loss of ability to absorb emissions has already been introduced in *Making Social Lives*, Chapter 3.

CHRIS MADDEN

WHY CHINA'S CARBON FOOTPRINT IS SO LARGE

Western consumption drives Chinese production

Connections between economies were discussed in Chapter 1 of this book.

The idea of normative issues was introduced in *Making Social Lives*, Chapter 3.

As you have seen previously, it is clear that economic growth in the UK is dependent on a world of connections to other places and economies. Thus the impact of economic growth in the UK has far-reaching implications, all of which are or *should* be taken into account as we think about living in a common world, one where we share an atmosphere and an increasingly small planet with others. In using 'should' it is clear that carbon emissions is a normative issue (just like rubbish). That is, it tends to carry a sense of how people ought to behave and act.

In sum, greenhouse gas emissions are a pressing social issue. Greenhouse gases are produced unevenly and the costs of their production may be felt unevenly, but there is general agreement that action to reduce their emission is important. This chapter will look at how social scientists have understood the issues surrounding climate change and how their understanding has been used to address the problem. In the next section we look in more detail at greenhouse gases, see how they are linked to economic growth and consider how possible solutions to their production may be devised.

1 Sharing the common duvet: the atmosphere, greenhouse gases and carbon-based economic growth

The atmosphere can be thought of as thermal blanket – a big, common duvet – that works to keep 'us' warm by soaking up the heat, initially derived from the sun, that radiates from the earth's surface. Without the so-called natural greenhouse effect, which keeps in some of the sun's heat, most life forms on the planet would not survive. The problem is not the duvet; it's that more recently humans have been overstuffing the duvet. More feathers in the duvet effectively trap more heat. There has been an increase in greenhouse gas emissions since the Industrial Revolution and the economic transformation that this heralded. Figure 1 illustrates some recent statistics on greenhouse gas emissions.

Industrialisation relied, and still relies, heavily on fossil fuels, the burning of which plays a major part in increasing concentrations of CO_2 in the atmosphere. The atmospheric concentration of carbon dioxide has reportedly risen from 315 parts per million (ppm) in the 1950s to over 380 ppm in 2006. The rates of increase are staggering: for CO_2, 200 times faster than at any time in the last 650,000 years. The problem is not just the presence of these gases but their longevity. Some greenhouse gases persist for only a matter of days, but carbon dioxide has a residence time (that is, the average time it stays active in the atmosphere) of anywhere between 5 and 200 years, nitrous oxide 114 years, and methane 12 years (Dow and Downing, 2006, p. 40). These lifetimes of greenhouse gases indicate that the processes under way cannot be quickly reversed; much damage has been done already. The question is, how can we find a means of limiting future damage and stemming the impact of the damage done already?

There are further complications too in dealing with the links between carbon-based economic growth and its impact on the world's climate. For example, the climate is alive – it moves and shifts in unpredictable ways with feedback loops, meaning that one process impacts on another, making the task of intervening with scientific precision and predictability that much more difficult. As the earth heats up by what might seem like very small amounts, a train of effects is set in motion. British Isles.

Cumulative carbon emissions

Share of total emissions of carbon dioxide (CO_2) from fossil fuel burning and cement production 1950–2000

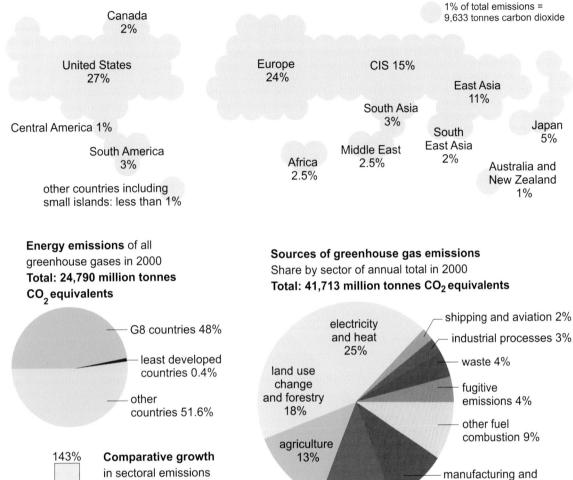

1% of total emissions =
9,633 tonnes carbon dioxide

Canada
2%

United States
27%

Central America 1%

South America
3%

other countries including
small islands: less than 1%

Europe
24%

CIS 15%

East Asia
11%

South Asia
3%

Japan
5%

Africa
2.5%

Middle East
2.5%

South
East Asia
2%

Australia and
New Zealand
1%

Energy emissions of all
greenhouse gases in 2000
**Total: 24,790 million tonnes
CO_2 equivalents**

G8 countries 48%

least developed
countries 0.4%

other
countries 51.6%

Sources of greenhouse gas emissions
Share by sector of annual total in 2000
Total: 41,713 million tonnes CO_2 equivalents

electricity
and heat
25%

shipping and aviation 2%

industrial processes 3%

waste 4%

fugitive
emissions 4%

other fuel
combustion 9%

land use
change
and forestry
18%

agriculture
13%

transportation 12%

manufacturing and
construction 10%

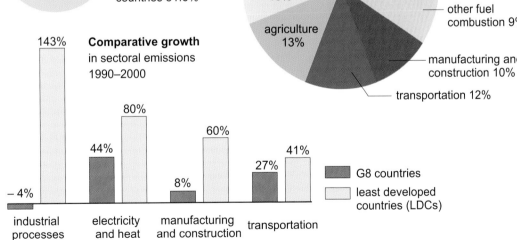

143%

Comparative growth
in sectoral emissions
1990–2000

80%

44%

8%

60%

27%

41%

− 4%

G8 countries

least developed
countries (LDCs)

industrial
processes

electricity
and heat

manufacturing
and construction

transportation

Figure 1   The greenhouse effect

For example, storms, floods, heatwaves and droughts can be triggered with the result that some areas of the earth may be turned to desert; other places may become much wetter. Melting ice caps may alter sea levels. The effects are difficult to predict. For example, one possible effect of the melting of Arctic ice could be a change to ocean currents. This may affect the Gulf Stream system, a system that brings warm water to western Europe and moderates its climate (so that it is warmer in western Europe than otherwise would be the case). If the Gulf Stream is affected, it could mean much colder winters in the UK. So global warming may mean significant cooling for the

Whatever their direction, what these changes have in common is that they don't respect political borders. Pollution and climate do not confine themselves to any one country. Nevertheless, it may not be too difficult to locate the culprits. In other words, who are the major polluters; who is responsible for these global problems?

1.1   Locating emissions, locating a problem

The sources of carbon emissions are not evenly distributed across the planet. There is an uneven geography and history to those emissions. Figure 2 provides an unusual and interesting illustration of the unequal contributions to the present state of global warming between 1900 and 1999. The map, produced by the World Resources Institute, is based on historic data for carbon dioxide emissions from fossil fuel combustion. The areas shown in the map are proportional to these data and illustrate the effect, in terms of carbon dioxide emitted, of decades of industrial output and energy consumption generally in North America, Europe and the countries of the former Soviet Union. The map tells a quite striking tale of just how the production of CO_2 has such an unequal history – let your focus move between the main map and the inset 'equal area world' map – and also confronts us with a question of what such a map will look like if drawn, say, in fifty years' time.

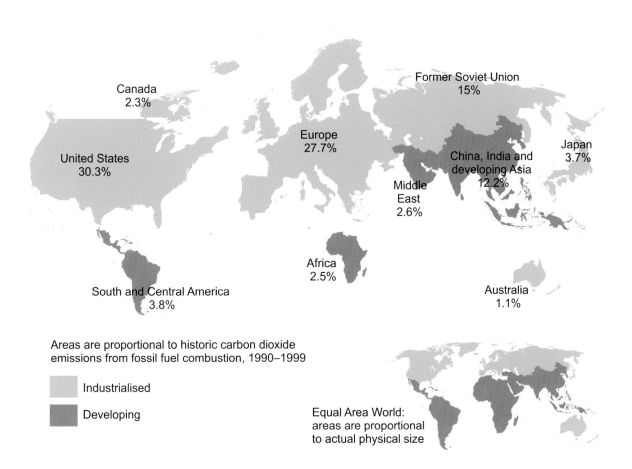

Figure 2   Contributions to global warming, 1900 to 1999

Activity 1

Do you think the map of culprits in Figure 2, or the inset map, or some other map, would best represent who will suffer most from climate changes?

To reflect **vulnerability** to climate change, we would need a third map. The USA and Europe combined may well have contributed significantly to present global warming, but the full impact – drought, failed crops, ill health, and so on – is now being felt throughout much of Africa more than it is in any of the areas shaded green on the map. In other words, the people and states who have benefited from luxury consumption and lifestyles dependent on production processes that lead to the emission of greenhouse gases are not necessarily those who will

Vulnerability
Attributes of people, communities and environments that can increase the risk or likelihood of suffering from a particular danger.

You read about Beck's
risk society in
Chapter 2 of this book.

be most affected by climate change. Contrary to something like Beck's risk society, which tends to suggest that we *all* live with a greater amount of risk, environmental problems often make inequalities greater rather than evening things up. The risk society is riskier for some than it is for others.

1.2   Repairing the problem

■   Given the concerns and this uneven geography of polluters and vulnerabilities, what kinds of action can be taken?

As we will see, transforming concern into action is a little bit trickier. Carbon emissions are all too easily dismissed as someone else's fault, someone else's problem. Part of the reason is that the effects of an accumulation of greenhouse gases have not been fully understood or appreciated, and so have been easy to dismiss or at least conveniently ignore. Until recently, uncertainty surrounding causes and effects has been used as an excuse for inaction. Yet another equally important reason for a limited response to the effect of such gases on climate change is that it has been virtually costless for individuals and firms to pour such gases into the atmosphere. No one owns the atmosphere, so it's all too easy to treat it as a 'free dump'.

The principle of supply
and demand was
introduced in *Making
Social Lives*, Chapter 3.

But although it's free now, why not start to charge people for using it? The conditions would seem ripe for the application of the principle of supply and demand – the greater the demand, the higher the price. If the atmosphere is being overused as a convenient dump for harmful gases, then the price for emitting greenhouse gases should rise until such a point when firms and individuals cut back on emissions because the price of using the dump outweighs the benefits. Simple – or is it?

The failure of markets
to take care of the
effects of mass
consumption was
discussed in *Making
Social Lives*, Chapter 3.

Externalities and the
price mechanism were
introduced in *Making
Social Lives*, Chapter 3.

The question of why prices don't always deal with the environmental impact of mass consumerism, in the form of waste and rubbish or harmful gas emissions, is related to the issue of externalities. An externality is a cost (or benefit) that results from economic activity that does not have a market price associated with it. Activities, such as pollution, that impose costs are known as negative externalities, and those that provide benefits, for example the production of new knowledge, are called positive externalities. In a market system regulated by the principle of supply and demand, activities which do not have prices associated with them cannot be regulated by the price mechanism.

Activity 2

Can you predict what will happen to negative externalities in a market system, as compared with a situation in which their costs have prices attached to them? Think of carbon emissions as a negative externality.

Because the costs are not priced, the supply will be higher than it otherwise would have been: firms produce goods and the costs of the negative externalities for the environment – for example, toxic waste poured into rivers or carbon pumped into the atmosphere – are not borne by the firms themselves but by other people, often very far away. If the costs to the emitter of polluting the atmosphere are low, then the supply of pollutants will be excessive. Conversely, because a firm does not receive the benefits of a positive externality it will tend to supply less of this than it would otherwise do.

In sum, the problem of climate change is a complex one that may be approached with some of the social science tools, and the economic understanding, that you already have. The next section will build on this knowledge by introducing some ideas from social science on managing common resources.

Summary

- Greenhouse gases, and carbon dioxide in particular, are major contributors to climate change.
- The geographies and histories of carbon pollution are very uneven when viewed globally.
- Since the Industrial Revolution the atmosphere has been regarded as a free dumping ground.
- It is important to employ the idea of externalities when thinking about carbon emissions.

2 The atmosphere as a form of commons

One way to begin think about the problem of external costs – which will act as a stepping stone to later sections in the chapter – was provided some time ago by Garrett Hardin, a professor of human ecology at the University of California in a now-famous essay written in the 1960s, 'The tragedy of the commons' (Hardin, 1968). The term 'the **commons**' refers to resources that are shared by a community or population. They can be thought of as either not owned or owned by everyone. Examples include local commons, such as shared grazing areas (from where the term comes), rivers and woodlands, and global commons, such as the oceans, the atmosphere, biodiversity, genetic material and human knowledge.

Commons
Shared resources held by a community or population and often thought of as 'free' to use.

The core of Hardin's argument is captured well in the comic strip in Figure 3. It is an argument that addresses directly the central issue of this chapter: how to live in a common world.

Hardin based his argument on a simplification, or a model. The model he chose was a real common in medieval times, where village people could graze their livestock. As the cartoon depicts, the communal grazing is free for the herders. As there is no charge for using the common, then the temptation exists for individual herders to ask themselves: 'While the commons can provide enough grazing for all of our sheep at present, what would happen if I increased the number of sheep I graze by one?' In short, there is every incentive in this idealised model for herders to increase their herds, and no incentive to limit those increases. But what if in the process of expanding a herd the common starts to be overgrazed, leading to less pasture and environmental decline? All the animals will start to put on less weight and be less productive (of meat, wool, etc.). Will this lead to the individual herders reducing their stock? The answer is 'probably not'. Less productivity may make it even more tempting to add another animal. As the costs of the decline in the common are shared by everyone, but the benefits of adding an extra, even less productive, animal are gained by the individual herder, then there is every incentive to keep adding animals. Until, that is, the common becomes so degraded that an environmental disaster occurs. This is the tragedy, as Hardin termed it. Disaster looms despite everyone doing what they think is in their interests.

Figure 3   The tragedy of the commons

The focus of the example parallels the earlier discussion of private and social costs and the impact of negative externalities. Private costs in the example are those borne by each herder; social costs are those borne by all herders; negative externalities relate to the impact of overgrazing. As the cartoon shows, for an individual herder the addition of one extra sheep can only be a benefit as he gains fully from the price the sheep fetches when taken to market after grazing freely on the common; formally, his positive utility is almost +1. However, the price of overgrazing – that is, the negative externalities relating to the impact of overgrazing – is shared among all four herders. For the one herder who increased his number of sheep from four to five the cost is only a fraction of the social cost (–1), which is spread across all herders. As we have suggested, the problem is that this herder is not alone in his thinking. Not only is he very likely to look at this situation and see only gain – the pluses greatly outweigh the costs of adding one sheep after another – but the other herders are going to realise that they too can benefit from increasing the size of their flocks; after all, why should they share in the costs without seeing any of the benefits? So they too add to the sheep grazing on the common, with overgrazing the result.

Hardin's model is a simplified one, and one that has little basis in history. Most such commons were carefully managed and stocking was highly limited by a landlord, or by the herders themselves (who would have regulated grazing by various rites and rituals associated with the locality). Nevertheless, it is a useful model and can help us to imagine some of the responses to commons problems. Here are three possible responses:

1   **Regulate** *the use of the common.* Devise a policy and a policing system to make sure no one overuses the common, and/or form a community or union of herders to self-regulate use of the common. People rarely behave solely as individuals, they form groups and as soon as the common starts to look endangered or productivity goes down, there may be a good opportunity to agree to reduce stocking rates.

2   *Impose a* **tax**. A second possibility would be to attempt to provide an incentive to reduce stock and at the same time generate some revenue to improve the pasture. This could be achieved by imposing a tax on each animal added. The tax might be based on the external cost generated as each extra animal is added, and could be used to make it less and less attractive for herders to overstock the common.

3   **Privatise** *the resource.* An alternative to taxation and regulation would be to enclose the common (in effect to surrender the idea of it being a common at all) and take it into private ownership. This could be done in the case of our comic strip either by parcelling it up into four plots, or by one herder succeeding in taking over all the

Regulation
Devising and imposing strict rules on the behaviour of people and firms.

Taxation
The practice by which a state both raises revenue and at the same time modifies the prices of goods and services in order indirectly to control their use.

Privatisation
A broad process by which goods and services are taken out of common or state ownership and passed into the hands of private companies and/ or individuals.

land and forcing the others out of business. Privatising the resource means there is now an incentive for any herder who owns all or part of the common to make sure that they don't overuse it. Any added cost of overgrazing will now no longer be an externality, but will be felt by each herder as their land deteriorates.

Hardin's simplified model could, he suggested, be applied to contemporary environmental concerns. The examples range from overfishing in many of the world's oceans to the debates surrounding the use of rainforests. Are fisheries and rainforests part of the 'global commons', or a national resource to exploited, or should they be viewed as a 'local commons' (that is, a resource to be used solely by indigenous people)?

Activity 3

Try to apply Hardin's thinking and each of the solutions proposed above to the problem of pollution. Does pollution present the same core problem as the overgrazing of the common land? Is each solution more or less practical when we are talking about the state of the atmosphere?

Pollution does present similar problems to those discussed above but, as Hardin notes and Figure 3 depicts, in reverse:

> In a reverse way, the tragedy of the commons reappears in problems of pollution. Here it is not a question of taking something out of the commons, but of putting something in – sewage, or chemical, radioactive, and heat wastes into water; noxious and dangerous fumes into the air; and distracting and unpleasant advertising signs into the line of sight. The calculations of utility are much the same as before. The rational man [sic] finds that his share of the cost of the wastes he discharges into the commons is less than the cost of purifying his wastes before releasing them. Since this is true for everyone, we are locked into a system of 'fouling our own nest,' so long as we behave only as independent, rational, free-enterprisers.
>
> (Hardin, 1968, p. 1245)

However, the solutions to such a commons problem may be more difficult to imagine in relation to pollution. First, while it may be possible for a village to agree to *regulate* the use of a piece of common land, policing the use of the global atmosphere would seem a massive and complex issue. Certainly there have been successes – the worldwide phasing out of the use of chlorofluorocarbons (CFCs) in aerosols and refrigerants in the 1980s and 1990s was a notable success. But in that case there were cost-effective alternatives that didn't seem to affect economic growth. Where the issue is not so much an outright ban but a reduction in something that seems closely linked to economic growth, and where the pollutants themselves are more difficult to track and trace back to their source, then worldwide agreement and action is more difficult. Second, *taxation* may be a possibility, though it would involve setting a rate that recognised the global inequality discussed in the Introduction while not providing incentives for industries to locate where tax levels were lowest. It would also face the problem of finding a level that acted as an incentive not to pollute and was sufficient to offset the costs of that pollution. Finally, *privatisation* of the atmosphere is possibly even more difficult to imagine. Certainly air can't be fenced off like a piece of land and few would sanction turning the whole atmosphere over to a single corporate owner. So, privatising the resource may seem the most difficult option. Yet, as we will see, making the pollutant into something that can be owned and traded has been attempted and is a form of privatisation.

In sum, better management of a commons, be it a fishery, a land area or an atmosphere, could be achieved in a number of ways. The classic regulation line would be that government intervention is required to prevent private decision making that fails to acknowledge fully and account for the interest of the public (such as the costs of overgrazing a common). As the price a firm charges for its output fails to incorporate the full costs of pollution involved in the production of a good (the negative externalities associated with overgrazing noted in the above example), then this presents a clear case, some would argue, for government intervention in the form of regulation. Government regulation such as this, aimed at decreasing the negative externalities of pollution linked to carbon-based growth and consumption, will have the same impact as 'scarcity-induced' price increases.

Alternatively, if consumers and pollution sufferers could bargain efficiently among themselves, then they could agree to share optimally the cost of antipollution devices. Yet, for consumers and pollution sufferers to be able to get together, the arrangement would have at least to be practical – it might, for example, work locally or regionally. But when the consequences of pollution are global, things are not so straightforward. This is not to say, though, that this type of regulation is unworkable. Regulation could take the form of setting certain standards for generating fewer emissions or using taxes to give incentives to firms within certain industries to reduce the amount of pollution they generate. Controlling activity through the use of permits is another example of limiting harmful economic activity. The creation of community-based governance, effectively allowing local communities to put together their own policies to deal with pollution, is another possibility. While the 'devil is in the details', and by no means will it be straightforward to manage, for Hardin an 'unmanaged commons' spells deep trouble: 'you can forget about the devil: As overuse of resources reduces carrying capacity, ruin is inevitable' (Hardin, 1998, p. 683).

Although it may be tempting to use regulatory measures such as those highlighted above to deal with CO_2 emissions, in practice things may prove a little more difficult. You may think that, as the commons are so central to life on the planet, there would be agreement that they should be preserved – that the idea of the commons should prevail every time. Yet, despite their importance, there has not always been firm agreement about the benefit of leaving the commons in common ownership. In England in the eighteenth century, for example, the idea of private property began to encroach on the commons. The effective privatisation or 'enclosure' of the commons has been under way ever since, quite often for reasons that employ the language of the market noted above and italicised below. The argument employed to justify the enclosure of the commons is that certain land, for example, will become more *efficient* if it is taken out of common ownership and placed in the hands of the private sector. The market, with its reliance on private **property rights**, the interaction of *supply and demand*, the *price mechanism*, and so on, so the argument runs, is more suited than common ownership to organising the 'best' use of the land and similar resources, indeed the economy as a whole. As this suggests, and as the environmental activist and writer Peter Barnes notes (and he is not alone):

> the economic system as a whole has ... two distinct sectors, the commons and the market. They have different rules and different guiding principles, and the boundaries between these sectors shift over time. For the past three hundred years this shift has been in one direction only: the market has steadily expanded into the commons.
>
> (Barnes, 2003)

Property rights
The title or right of ownership over an object, an area of territory, a piece of knowledge or product, which, within certain limits, allows the owner to dispense with the property in a manner in which they see fit.

The rate of enclosure or privatisation has certainly accelerated greatly over recent decades. It is not just land, but the seas and much of what they contain, the air, DNA, and so on. What we are witnessing, some argue, including the leading environmental attorney Andrew Kimbrell, is the 'corporate enclosure of virtually the entire living commons' (quoted in Barnes, 2003).

Why the market principle has more recently gained the upper hand and why, in particular, market-based practices now form the kernel of measures to deal with the impact of carbon emissions on climate change are issues explored in the following section. As the section discusses, and as Section 4 illustrates through examples, factors such as how such markets are made, how they are pieced together and who gets to be a player in them, and how well they deal with points noted in Section 1 to do with uneven geographies and histories of carbon emissions, for instance, are all critical to judging the consequences of how such a solution works in practice rather than just in theory.

Summary

- The metaphor of the commons helps us to understand better the problems that arise in managing resources.
- The commons metaphor has some limitations when applied to atmospheric pollution.
- There is a variety of ways to manage common resources, from the use of regulation, to taxes, to the price mechanism; these have different degrees of suitability for dealing with the overuse of the atmosphere as a carbon dump.
- There is a struggle of ideas about how best to avoid the 'tragedy of the commons'.
- There has been a rise of market-based solutions to commons-like problems over the past few decades.

3   Working towards a market solution: from regulation to permits to market-based approaches to CO$_2$

As we learnt from an earlier discussion of 'market liberalisation', the push for market-based solutions to climate change has been given added momentum by the broader political drive for the deregulation of economic activities – a political drive that intensified in the USA and the UK in particular from the 1980s. The arguments for deregulation signalled a shift in thinking from supporting the involvement of the public sector in the organisation of the economy to favouring the private sector and the private market as the most efficient coordinators of economic activity. Yet, until fairly recently even those who advocated sweeping deregulation tended to acknowledge that some areas, such as health and the environment, were more suited to organisation through some form of regulatory practice. This could be 'command and control regulation', where a central body (such as government) dictates exactly what should be done (e.g. how much pollution is to be permitted), or less restrictive forms of regulation, such as taxation, which is a form of regulation but effectively allows there to be some choice in how a business runs its operation.

Market liberalisation was discussed in Chapter 1, Section 1 of this book.

More recently, however, there has been a growing tendency, particularly in the USA and the UK, to view almost anything from genetic materials to pollution as accessible to market criteria. For those advocating markets rather than regulation to deal with pollutants, the big breakthrough came in the 1990s in the USA with the establishment of a market in sulphur dioxide (SO$_2$), which is not only a greenhouse gas but is more famously a cause of acid rain and thereby of damage to forests, lakes and buildings. A quick run through the establishment of this market is helpful as it highlights a number of points relevant to the later introduction of market-based approaches to carbon emissions.

3.1   Permits and the retreat of regulation

The sulphur dioxide market was a response to concerns aired mainly by the Canadian government about the effect of acid rain, which was traceable back to the emissions from coal-burning power plants located in the US Midwest. The sulphur dioxide was pumped into the air through tall smoke stacks and was driven towards Canada by prevailing winds, eventually turning to acid rain and causing damage to humans, forests and fisheries in eastern Canada.

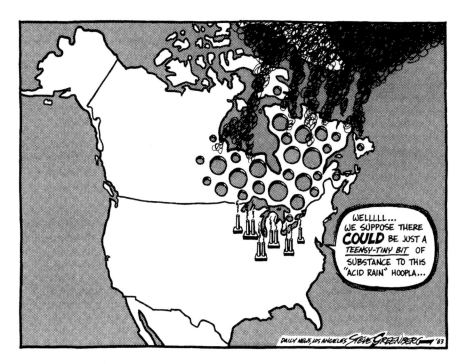

How burning coal in the US leads to acid rain in Canada

Noting the shifting political context and the favourable swing towards liberalisation and away from regulation, the sociologist Donald MacKenzie (2007, p. 29) observes that, while countless attempts to regulate sulphur emissions were put before the US congress, they 'all failed in the face of opposition from the Reagan administration and from Democrats who represented states that might suffer economically from controls, such as the areas of Appalachia and the Midwest in which coal deposits are high in sulphur'. The pro-market liberalisation Republicans didn't like the idea of regulation – they favoured a market solution. What, then, was going to be a politically acceptable way around this problem? The answer lay in the idea of 'sulphur trading'. This involved the establishment of permits to emit sulphur into the atmosphere, which could then be bought and sold in a market for pollution rights (those who had more permits than they could use in a given year could sell them on while those who, for whatever reason, needed to emit more sulphur dioxide could buy up these excess rights at a price dependent on the going market rate). In combining a cap (or limit on the total amount of emissions) along with the ability to trade permits in a market, the policy combined a clear goal that environmentalists could embrace (reducing annual sulphur dioxide emissions from power stations in the USA by ten million tons from their 1980 level, a cut of around a half) with a market mechanism attractive to at least some Republicans (MacKenzie, 2007, p. 29).

Trading in SO_2 permits began in 1995. Yet why were permits viewed as more efficient than straightforward regulation? After all, if government regulation could achieve the same reduction in pollution, why not stick with regulation? The answer, given by those who prefer the market-based solution to that of command and control regulation, is that the supply and demand mechanism is dynamic, it stimulates the production of more efficient technologies and targets those polluters who are best able to adapt their processes and is therefore a more efficient arrangement than a static piece of regulation.

Indeed, one major problem with fixed regulation is that it is difficult to enforce in a uniform way that is seen by all affected parties as fair and not arbitrary. The problems are added to if there is room to contest the evidence, scientific or otherwise, underpinning the effort to regulate. As Donald Kennedy (2006, p. 105) explains, echoing points developed in this and previous chapters, the market-based approach to environmental pollution has been viewed by some as a less contested way to deal with pollution: 'Instead of regarding the polluters as the villains of the piece, it recognised competing interests'. This thinking was based on ideas of a leading economist, Ronald Coase (e.g. 1960, 1988), who published them in the 1960s in the USA. Coase's argument is that if you want to reduce pollution then you look to property rights and the price mechanism and not to government regulation. It's not difficult to see why this idea and the action it suggests to deal with pollution were so appealing for those in the USA who were arguing strongly for market liberalisation rather than tough, restrictive regulation.

Under this type of system:

- The polluters become a set of claimants on a common resource (clean air, for example), and the commons (everyone who uses the air) become the other interest party.
- The government, representing the commons, selects an acceptable level of utilisation by the polluters.

- The government then issues a number of permits, whose total adds up to that level of demand; these can then be auctioned or allocated, and finally traded.

This was the basic idea that helped to give shape to the tradable sulphur dioxide permit market in the USA. The aim of the permits was simple: once allocated, permits could be sold by those producers that had switched to low-sulphur coal or had used 'scrubbers' to cut SO_2 emissions, and bought by those who still needed to pollute at greater levels. This meant that there was incentive enough for companies to change their practices, but those who couldn't were still able to pollute at a rate set by the price mechanism and the market in permits. And, importantly, the total level of pollution is capped and can, over time, be reduced.

For Coase and others who follow his thinking, if pollution is built into the market calculus it can be dealt with optimally. For these social scientists, market criteria rather than broader social thinking inform the calculations about what the correct price for the right to pollute should be. It is worth noting that this belief in the wisdom of the market tends to neglect the social activities, the negotiations, and so on, that set initial acceptable levels of pollution, and seems to regard markets as somehow outside social life. Both of these assumptions are worth questioning. Nevertheless, the basic and simple-sounding idea informed the market, which was established to deal with carbon emissions agreed by a selection of developed countries at a United Nations-sponsored meeting in Kyoto, Japan.

3.2   Kyoto: a framework for a market-based approach to CO_2

In 1992, the United Nations Framework Convention on Climate Change (known as the UNFCCC treaty) agreed a structure for intergovernmental efforts to deal with the problems caused by climate change and in the process recognised that 'the climate system is a *shared resource* whose stability can be affected by industrial and other emissions of carbon dioxide and greenhouse gases' (UNFCCC, 1992; emphasis added).

The Kyoto Protocol was an addition to the UNFCCC treaty (UNFCCC, 1998). The Protocol, in the UN's words, contains 'more powerful and legally binding measures' than the Convention. The main force of the

Protocol was that it set binding targets for thirty-seven industrialised countries and the European Community for reducing greenhouse gas emissions; the target was a 5 per cent reduction in each country's emissions of six greenhouse gases relative to 1990 levels by 2012. The exceptions were the USA and Australia, the only two developed countries not to ratify the Protocol. The USA may not have signed up to the Protocol, but their powerful influence was to show up in the finer details, as we'll soon see. Under the Protocol the principle of *common but differentiated responsibilities* (UNFCCC, 1998; emphasis added) for greenhouse gases was recognised; this was official recognition that over the past 150 or so years developed countries have been particularly responsible for CO_2 emissions. Again, the USA did not agree with this position and thus did not ratify the treaty, arguing that restrictions should not be placed on developed countries alone.

The idea of using the market mechanism to confront the problem of global climate change caused by carbon emissions was not, however, done and dusted. The US delegation may have walked away from signing the protocol, but the idea of a market for pollution had been sown. Soon flesh was to be put on the skeletal form. Markets – rather than other measures, such as government regulation or taxation, or the provision of subsidies for non-carbon technologies – are currently seen as the 'best' way to address the commons problem. As the official documentation put it, with the Protocol 'a new commodity was created in the form of emission reductions or removals'(UNFCCC, 2009). Since carbon dioxide is the principal greenhouse gas, people speak simply of trading in carbon. Carbon is now tracked and traded like any other commodity. This is known as the 'carbon market'. The market works through three complementary market-based mechanisms. The three mechanisms of the Protocol are:

- emissions trading or 'cap-and-trade'
- the Clean Development Mechanism (CDM)
- the Joint Implementation (JI) mechanism.

Here we deal with each briefly in turn.

The Protocol created rights to pollute worth tens of billions of dollars and these went to thirty-seven industrialised countries. The rights allow these countries to make use of the global atmosphere and were limited in supply in order to achieve cuts in emissions. Governments are able to pass these rights to their own companies with no charges attached. In the UK, for example, the rights have been passed to companies responsible for just under 50 per cent of the UK carbon emissions, and this has been done with little or no public consultation. How the carbon-trading or cap-and-trade scheme works is illustrated in the box below.

An outline of carbon trading

Two companies, A and B, each emit 100,000 tonnes (t) of CO_2 per year. The government wishes to reduce emissions by 5 per cent and so gives companies A and B rights or allowances to emit 95,000 t of CO_2 per year. Companies A and B must then decide either to reduce emissions, for example by investing in new technology, or to seek to buy the rights to emit the extra 5000 t of CO_2. The market price for these emissions is US$10 per tonne. Now, Company A finds that it can quite easily reduce its emissions for half this rate per tonne and so reduces its emissions by 10,000 t, selling the extra 5000 t – remember it only needs to meet a 5 per cent reduction – for US$50,000. The company thus recovers its expenditure and saves US$25,000. Company B, however, finds it more expensive to reduce its emissions – it would cost US$75,000 – so decides to buy 5000 t of emissions rights being sold by Company A at a cost of US$50,000 (5000 t × US$10 per tonne) and so it too saves US$25,000.

Assuming that there are only two companies in the country, then the same end – a cut of 5 per cent in emissions – could have been achieved through regulation. However, under the carbon-trading scheme the private sector has benefited to the tune of US$50,000. Moreover, the argument can run that if regulation had been used then one of the firms (A) would have had little incentive to further reduce its emissions by the level achieved through a market mechanism and the other company (B) would probably have been unable to keep operating and would have been forced either to go out of business or to lobby the government to relax its regulation.

based on Lohmann, 2006, p. 47

This cap-and-trade system is then linked to the two other Protocol devices, the Clean Development Mechanism (CDM) and the Joint Implementation (JI) mechanism. Both mechanisms were written into the Protocol at the insistence of the USA and both involve project-based credits to enable global North countries and their corporations to offset their emissions at home by contributing to projects in other countries of the world in ways that would lead to reduced carbon emissions (compared with what would have been the case if they had not become involved). This seems logical as often there are relatively easy gains to be made in countries where industry is old and inefficient, and technology from the relatively rich countries can have beneficial effects in those without the resources to develop or purchase such technologies. However, critics argue that the schemes effectively give corporations and wealthier nations ways of avoiding the restrictions that apply to their use of the existing world carbon dump. Kyoto signatories would now, they argue, be able to meet their commitment by seeking to control emissions either domestically or through the CDM or JI measures. A signatory can use the CDM to pay for its domestic emissions through projects in developing countries; that is, countries that are not signatories to the Protocol. One way to do this is for corporations in the global North to buy land in the global South and plant crops that will sequester carbon (see the box below).

An outline of project-based schemes

The example of how this mechanism works again assumes two companies, A and B. The government's goal once more is to cut emissions by 5 per cent, thus limiting each company to allowances of 95,000 t each. But the government under this scheme tells each company that it wants reductions in emissions to be achieved by these companies investing abroad in projects – anything ranging from investing in biofuel crops, to be used instead of oil or coal, to installing more efficient technology to reduce emissions by the required amount (5000 t) 'below what would have happened otherwise'. For the companies the price of such projects is only US$4 per tonne – labour costs in the countries of the global South are low, subsidies are available from the World Bank for such schemes and there are many 'dirty factories' to choose from. For both companies it makes a lot of sense to buy credits from abroad rather than pay for costly reductions at home. Company A saves US$5000 and Company B makes savings in the region of US$55,000. The private sector in total thus saves US$60,000.

based on Lohmann, 2006, pp. 47–8

In sum, through interlinked stages the market-based approach has the following aims:

- To limit the supply of permits and thereby make the atmosphere a scarce resource. Scarcity is engineered by limiting the use that can be made of it by nation states, the signatories to the Protocol.
- To achieve this by creating *tradable legal rights* to use the carbon dump and by distributing these rights to those countries whose present and past emissions make them the biggest carbon polluters.
- To allow *bargaining* to achieve the right price for use of the carbon dump.
- To allow those emitters who could discover ways of using the dump more *efficiently* to profit by selling their unused rights to pollute to emitters who were not as efficient.
- To allow, in addition, countries to use *project-based schemes* such as those proposed by the CDM to achieve the same ends.

There are some clear problems with these mechanisms. They include, first, giving away tradable rights to companies who are then free to sell these at a profit. This is a problem known as grandfathering and is a kind of 'windfall' or free gift for companies in the global North. Such a gift was not available to those in the global South. Second, the market is not only flexible, it is also highly volatile. The recent economic downturn has meant that companies are producing less and therefore have less need to pollute. The result is that the price for excess pollution rights has collapsed, making it very cheap to buy the right to pollute. Moreover, as financial companies start to trade in pollution rights rather than use them, the market becomes like any other commodity market. It is potentially highly volatile and subject to the vagaries of the financial system. The collapse in world markets in 2008, for example, resulted in pollution rights exchanging for very little money indeed, effectively making the atmosphere free to use again. Third, while the intentions may be good, the CDM and JI effectively make it easy for countries of the global North to carry on pumping CO_2 into the atmosphere at high rates while effectively intervening in developing economies of the global South to offset their pollution. As we will see in the next section, this can have deleterious effects, and is a process that is framed by the different powers available to states of the global North and their companies compared with those of the global South. As we will discover, whether you think this is a good idea or not may depend on whether you see this form of activity as a zero-sum or a positive-sum game.

The concepts of zero-sum game and positive-sum game were introduced in *Making Social Lives*, Chapter 2.

In short, despite the rhetoric of certain pro-market economists, the market is a highly social institution. It is affected by governments (setting limits and then allocating and giving away rights to pollute), social activity (in the form of volatile financial activity), and power and inequality (in reproducing disparities between global North and South). It is the latter to which we will turn in the final section of the chapter.

Summary

- There has been a rise of market-based solutions to commons-like problems.
- The key ideas supporting the case for market rather than regulatory solutions to greenhouse gases have been discussed, using the emergence of the tradable sulphur dioxide permit market in the USA as a vehicle for this discussion.
- The Kyoto Protocol was the key framework for the establishment of a carbon market.
- The key arguments for using market-based approaches to carbon pollution have been presented, noting the chief aims and limitations.
- The making of a carbon market was far from perfect and had social consequences.

4   Markets made for whom?

It might seem that the creation of a market in rights to pollute is uncontroversial. Markets, then, seem efficient – the price mechanism seems to be an almost natural way to regulate supply and demand (after all, the atmosphere, when zero-priced was too much in demand). Rather than a political solution to the problem, or one that depends on government regulation, we have a system that relies on the economic actions of many actors, all of whom are trying to minimise their costs and maximise their income. The market in the rights to send carbon into the atmosphere seems to benefit the atmosphere in ways that allow economies to continue to grow.

The problem, however, is that markets are made. An obvious-sounding point, admittedly, but it is nonetheless important as it draws attention to *how* markets are made and by whom – *whose ideas* they contain, *whose interests* are considered, and so on. When we focus on the making of markets, rather than their supposedly 'natural' qualities, we turn attention to their workings and their outcomes and so make them contestable. So, for example, if the rights upon which a carbon market is based are allocated unequally, then the market is almost sure to produce unequal outcomes in practice. Similarly, if certain voices are heard but not others, if certain ways of life are considered yet not others, then the resulting market is going to be anything but inclusive. There can be little doubt that different powers were at play in drawing up the Kyoto Protocol and in refining the mechanisms. The US Government certainly made sure its voice was heard; it managed to influence the workings of the Protocol – with the introduction of the CDM and the JI mechanisms – without itself ratifying the treaty.

There is a discussion of the use of power, and an account of the influence exercised by some groups over others, in *Making Social Lives*, Chapter 2.

With echoes of the commons question raised earlier we can see how such trading schemes work to:

- deepen inequalities of access to the atmosphere as a commons
- encourage firms and consumers to make more use of the commons as the negative externalities will be paid for by those in the global South.

To illustrate the above points let's consider two examples taken from recent CDM schemes. Both are located in the global South (in Uganda and Thailand) and involve companies from countries in the global North.

4.1   Build a power plant in Norway, plant trees in Uganda

Tree Farms AS, a Norwegian forestry company operating in Uganda, Tanzania and Malawi, leased land in Uganda at 'bargain prices' (Lohmann, 2006) to plant trees to absorb carbon dioxide generated by a conventional gas-fired power plant to be built in Norway. The project gained cross-party support in Norway as it was believed that through the purchase of carbon credits the scheme would be made 'environmentally friendly' (Lohmann, 2006, pp. 237–46). The credits were to be supplied in part by Tree Farms.

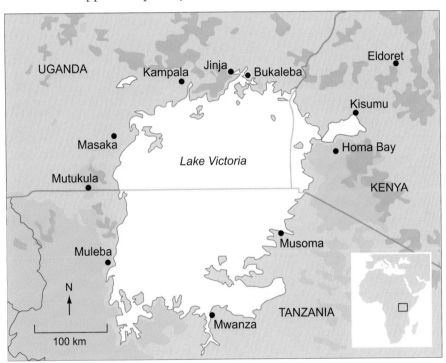

The area of tree planting in Uganda – a long way from Norway

The land acquired in Bukaleba is in one of many state-owned forest reserves on Lake Victoria. The acquisition of the land, however, threatens the livelihoods of an estimated 8000 farmers, people dependent on fishing, and other Ugandans – the people who consider themselves to be the owners of this land. The carbon-offset scheme that would appear at first glance to be a neat means of reducing the impact of a power station located in the global North at the same time as improving conditions in the global South (a win–win situation) fails to acknowledge these people just as it has little to say about the mismatch between the paltry sums paid in rent to the Ugandan Government for the use of this land over a fifty-year period and the very high rates of return in the form of carbon revenues to be earned by the firm about which the Ugandan Government, like many others, knew very little.

There are many interesting aspects to this story, ranging from its impact on the livelihoods of local people to the accusation made by an advisor to the Ugandan forestry authorities that such schemes mean that countries of the global South are being subjected to a 'new form of colonialism' (Lohmann, 2006, p. 243). Our specific interest lies not simply in whether or not this type of scheme is likely to work to reduce the amount of carbon in the atmosphere but also in the wider issues too. Both sets of issues have a lot to do with how the market calculates the effectiveness of the project. The original figures provided by Tree Farms suggested that through their plantations they would be able to generate 500 tonnes of credit per hectare or 2.13 million tonnes of CO_2 in total. Yet was this the true figure, which takes into account the range of issues we've just noted, such as the threat to Ugandan livelihoods? Well, the answer has to be no, not really. What this figure left out, for example, is the carbon that will be generated by those evicted from the lands sold to Tree Farms as they cleared land elsewhere. Arguably, despite the making of several small concessions – the Norwegian firm, for example, gave just under 5 per cent of the land acquired from the Ugandan Government to the local community – the international carbon market works overall to the benefit of the global North rather than people in countries such as Uganda in the global South. For example, the sort of land concessions granted to companies from the global North who seek access to Uganda's forests have not been made available to local communities – the gesture made by the Norwegian firm noted above notwithstanding.

It also seems unlikely, according to local community representatives, that the prospects of higher standards of living for locals as a result of employment generated by schemes such as tree planting will come to anything. Similarly, other issues, such as the carbon generated in clearing the plantation site itself, the ecological effects of the loss in native vegetation and the possible loss of biodiversity and habitat, are also important. So too are issues to do with social dislocation, as families are moved off land to make way for the plantation, and damage to the environment outside the national park as population density rises as a result of evictions to make way for the new plantation. Although important, these are all difficult, if not impossible, to reduce to numbers and thus feed into market thinking. Benefits to locals do occur, but these are relatively small in terms of, say, employment numbers when set alongside the monetary gains to Northern companies and the benefits to those in the global North more generally who may maintain their carbon-emitting lifestyle as usual.

4.2   'Efficient boilers' in Yala, Thailand; business as usual in Japan

A project to build a power plant fuelled by rubber wood waste and sawdust in Yala, a province in southern Thailand, raises a number of issues concerning environmental and social justice (Lohmann, 2006, pp. 280–6). The project is depicted by the companies involved as a means of burning fewer fossil fuels and thereby lowering total CO_2 output (the burning of wood waste is regarded as carbon neutral as the growing trees, eventually used in the new power plant, will have already absorbed carbon from the atmosphere). Interestingly, the companies involved combine national and international interests. The power plant is the project of Gulf Electric, owned by Thailand's Electricity Generating Public Company (EGCO) and Japan's Electric Power Development Company (EPDC). Other firms involved are a local rubber wood processing firm, Asia Plywood, and a Norwegian 'risk management' consultancy Det Norske Veritas (DNV), there to advise parties and mediate discussion between the companies involved and the local people. Nevertheless, there is little opening for local people to have a say and influence the proposed plant.

There are clear benefits for these companies in getting involved in such a project. Each company is participating in the CDM for different reasons but each is set to enjoy the gains of the market-based mechanism designed to reduce the global impact of carbon dioxide, hence the emphasis on switching from fossil fuels to wood waste to power the plant. But how does this all work in practice, in Yala? What does this one example of the CDM in action tell us about geographies of unevenness, of inequality and of knowledge? To begin with, there is the Japanese power company. Geographically distant from Thailand, the company has been drawn to Yala as its involvement and investment in the project enables it to 'earn' Certified Emissions Reductions. These newly minted rights to the atmosphere help both the company and Japan carry on with 'business as usual', allowing them to burn present

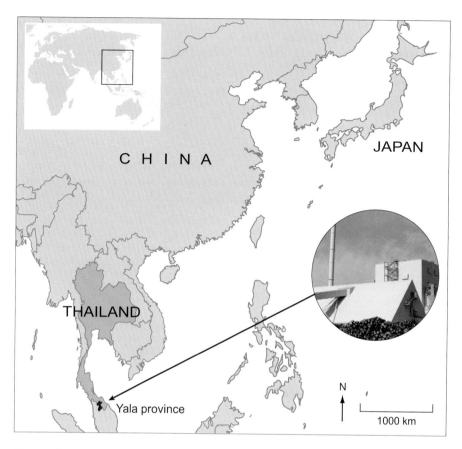

How a Japanese company can earn carbon emissions from operating in Thailand

levels of fossil fuels while assisting countries in the global South to find cleaner forms of development. The positive side of this is that technology is transferred from the relatively wealthy countries to those that, without this help, may have been left to rely on less efficient technologies. However, there are at least two problems. First, through the creation of atmospheric rights and the trading on which these are based, Japan as a society is able to reproduce itself through continued carbon-based consumption and it is able to do so through a scheme that reaffirms, if not strengthens, the geography of economic and social inequality between Japan and Thailand. Second, while it is true on one level that Thailand benefits from the scheme, with its power company, EGCO, benefiting from the carbon-trading scheme underpinning this project, it is also apparent that EGCO's interests and those of the local people of Yala do not necessarily overlap. The local people, who have not been issued with atmospheric rights, were not fully consulted about the project. What is more, although they have been involved in an ongoing dispute with Asia Plywood about smoke and ash pollution of local air, water and land caused by its existing rubber wood processing – a protest acknowledged by the consultants – the reasons for their protest do not comply with market thinking. The locals' concerns revolve not around issues of carbon efficiency but social and broader environmental issues. The consultants' calculations focus only on matters such as better waste disposal, more efficient boilers, and so on – rather than on social and political issues, which are more difficult to deal with through the market mechanism. The market mechanism, from the viewpoint of DNV and the other main firms involved, is a neutral and efficient means of dealing adequately with all of the issues such a project raises. For the local people, a process that leaves aside their interests, and wider social, environmental, cultural and political concerns, is hardly fair-minded.

Activity 4

What do these examples suggest to you about how the market-based approaches to carbon emissions work when viewed from the global South?

These examples suggest a number of issues, for example:

- Local livelihoods are damaged.
- Carbon emissions continue; firms in the global North can continue to contribute to fossil-based pollution; oil extraction and coal mining continue.
- The effect of such pollution falls unequally across the globe. It is the already poor people of countries in the global South who pay in a variety of ways for continued consumption in the global North.
- The same inequalities in effect are written into the future. People in the global North can continue to use the global dump while many of those in the global South are placed in a position where they have to give up the use of their land and also the option of using such land to offset their own carbon emissions.

These points suggest there is a need to think socially about the issue of carbon and other greenhouse gases: about who emits them and how equitable solutions can be found. How society is reproduced requires both scientific and sociological knowledge of the range and interplay of processes involved. On their own, technical fixes are insufficient; the social and political causes of carbon emissions must be addressed too. Significantly, a willingness to embrace and support the type of change needed to combat the impact of carbon emissions is also required. From Colombia, Malaysia and Bolivia to Sweden and St Lucia, communities and governments are acting to address the problems of the commons (see Lohmann, 2001, pp. 10–11). The actions range from protesting and winning the revocation of coal and other fossil fuel mining concessions (thereby keeping carbon in the ground), to moving away from the use of fossil fuels at the municipal level, to wholesale countrywide shifts to investment in renewable energy technology in the case of St Lucia. What these examples suggest is that responsible action in the face of climate change involves a wide range of groups, not just individuals and firms. Property rights and the market tend to focus on and facilitate individuals and firms rather than collective action. We see this in the UK, where the emphasis is very much on the isolated individual consumer, the latter-day lone herder, called upon to act through the market by becoming a 'green consumer'. Such a consumer is placed within a market that skirts over the complicated issues of climate change: the cause of climate change and the part carbon emissions play in this are not tackled head on. The market is framed instead in terms of choice; overindulgence in carbon-related consumption may be offset by planting a few trees. As the campaigner and economist Lohmann (2008, pp. 363–4) puts it, the market response in this case 'conceptualizes global warming primarily through the complex calculations of guilt over individual "carbon footprints" rather than, for example, the study of international oil politics', or for that matter using the knowledge gained by communities whose actions have effectively worked to turn away from carbon-based economic growth.

Activity 5

How effective do you think the idea of a carbon market is in dealing with carbon emissions and their impact on global climate change?

The carbon market is just one response to the problem presented by carbon emissions and their impact on a common resource: the atmosphere. By creating what are, in effect, rights to pollute, and treating these as tradable, greenhouse gases such as carbon dioxide have been blended into market calculations. The market and price signals will, so the argument runs, help society to discover and follow the path to least-cost pollution-reduction supply; in other words, this is a business as usual approach rather than a fundamental shake-up of our obsession with carbon-fuelled economic growth. What is striking is how the Protocol talks in matter of fact terms about the way in which carbon can now be 'tracked and traded like any other commodity'. Through the establishment of private property rights – that is, the tradable permits – the link is then made to a better use of the environment. Without private ownership and markets, the argument runs, climate change will not be effectively addressed. Private title to an environmental good equates with the idea of best stewardship of that good. Yet, as one critic argues:

> By concealing and undermining the knowledge and analysis needed to respond to global warming, by obscuring how needed social and technological changes will take place, by generating new and dangerous equivalences, by participating in neo-colonial mythologies and by befuddling the concerned middle-class public, carbon markets are interfering with effective and democratic approaches to global warming. Calls for pursuing climate justice within a carbon trading framework ... neither help clarify the problems nor provide a useful framework for addressing them. It is time to bring this discussion back down to earth.
>
> (Lohmann, 2008, p. 364)

How do we know?

The power of social science and critical awareness

At the start of this chapter I noted, almost in passing, that social scientists don't just study the world, they contribute to making, repairing and changing it. We have seen how basic models that aid our understanding of the world can be used to offer solutions to its problems. One of these was the price mechanism.

The price mechanism was introduced in *Making Social Lives*, Chapter 3.

Another was the commons model devised by Hardin. Both are effective ways to understand social action but both are also simplifications that need to be handled carefully. This chapter has highlighted the difficulty in using a simple model or theory in order first to predict what happens in the world and second to prescribe what should happen. Hardin's commons model and the tragedy he predicts is a useful device for thinking about how a society made up of individual profit maximisers will, in time, produce the conditions for its own downfall. But, as you have seen throughout this course, society is not simply an aggregation of individuals. People are socialised into families, neighbourhoods, groups, workplaces, classes, and so on. We rarely, if ever, act alone. So, in devising a way out of the tragedy of the commons, we may need to account for the more complex societies that we live in, and therefore be critically aware that our social science knowledge is always partial and in need of careful revision. Likewise, while the price mechanism is a powerful model in terms of predicting how demand and supply for an item will alter given changes to price, and/or changes in demand and supply, it will need to be supplemented by other forms of knowledge and understanding if we are to produce effective and just forms of action. In this case, while the model can be used to generate a market in rights to pollute, we need to be aware that if this market ignores or downplays the huge disparities in wealth and power between global North and South, and neglects to address the assumption that a relatively small reduction in greenhouse gas emissions is all that is needed, then the models that social scientists create will be damaging rather than restorative. It is therefore important for social scientists to recognise not only the power of their theories and models (they are engines, not simply cameras, as the sociologist of finance Donald Mackenzie, 2006, has put it), but also to intervene in the world in order to show their limitations.

Summary

- There are a number of problems with using a market model to address climate change.
- It is important to question who is really served by the market for carbon.

- Livelihoods can be damaged by the carbon market and other environmental, social and political issues can be ignored or downplayed.
- The Clean Development Mechanism and Joint Implementation can be experienced as a form of neocolonialism by countries and peoples of the global South.

Conclusion

Living with CO_2, living in common … what is to be done?

There is now a broad consensus that something must be done and done quickly to cut the rate of greenhouse gas emissions in order to reduce the effects of climate change. How to do this is not straightforward, particularly if carbon-based economic growth remains the central organising principle around which we produce and reproduce our society. Framing the issue in this way is to recognise that climate change is a social problem despite the fact that so often it is talked about almost exclusively in the language of science. Moreover, in addressing the question 'What is to be done?' there is a need, many would argue, to complicate the answer by thinking beyond the imagined bounded space of the UK, Europe and North America so that solutions recognise and address the complex and entangled geographies that describe life in a common world.

If living in a common world is to be taken as a serious goal, then, as this chapter has highlighted, there is a need to question market-based thinking and how markets get made, particularly given the growing tendency to turn to market solutions to help deal with problems such as climate change. There is real battle for ideas between the market, on the one hand, and the language of the commons, on the other.

The solution, though, need not be the end of the market as a policy tool. As we have seen, far from being handed down from above, preformed and set to work only in one way, markets are made and shaped according to particular assumptions and following established geographies of power. If living in a common world is agreed to be a goal worth striving for, then 'markets' provide only one possible solution to the vexed issue of just how highly interconnected societies around the globe should live together equally and fairly in the face of finite resources, such as the atmosphere.

Proponents of market-based approaches to pollution would argue that markets are able to deal with pollutants such as greenhouse gases. The critics would say that markets can only address something like greenhouse gases, including CO_2 emissions, in a superficial way. What the examples in this chapter have highlighted is the need to incorporate concerns presently distanced from 'market thinking' – concerns about equality, concerns for future generations rather than short-term market gains, an idea of ethics that differs greatly from that currently informing private-sector markets. Similarly, market critics would also argue the need to recognise the importance of incorporating a variety of indigenous knowledges into how markets might be made to work so as to remake societies on a much fairer and sustainable basis.

The task is big and not just for scientists to tackle. It involves understanding how social, economic and political powers operate – as the discussion of how establishment of the Kyoto Protocol and the ways in which certain sets of ideas came to dominate thinking demonstrated. The task also involves evaluating a range of knowledges, rather than accepting the one dominant knowledge emanating from key countries of the global North. It also involves understanding what drives us to consume and to carry on consuming in the face of evidence that alerts us to the harm that such consumption and the waste it produces does to the environment. Last, but by no means least, the discussion encourages us to think about the UK – its patterns of consumption and production, the way it organises its economy, and so on – not as bounded but as part of a global geography of relations and to recognise and act upon the responsibilities that attach to these often highly uneven worldly connections.

Are things really changing? The British writer John Lanchester (2007) comments: 'When a government minister goes on television to announce that fewer cars are being sold, that fewer people are flying, that fewer people are buying new stuff, and that this is really good news – that'll be the sign that things are changing.'

References

Barnes, P. (2003) *Capitalism, the Commons, and Divine Right*, 23rd Annual E.F. Schumacher Lectures, October, Stockbridge, Massachusetts, ed. by Hannum, H., Great Barrington, MA, E.F. Schumacher Society; also available online at http://www.schumachersociety.org/publications/barnes_03.html (Accessed 7 May 2009).

Coase, R. (1960) 'The problem of social cost', *Journal of Law and Economics*, vol. 3, pp. 1–44.

Coase, R. (1988) *The Firm, the Market and the Law*, Chicago, IL, University of Chicago Press.

Dow, K. and Downing, T.E. (2006) *The Atlas of Climate Change: Mapping the World's Greatest Challenge*, London, Earthscan.

Hardin, G. (1968) 'The tragedy of the commons', *Science*, vol. 162, pp. 1243–8.

Hardin, G. (1998) 'Extensions of the "tragedy of the commons"', *Science*, vol. 280, pp. 682–3.

Kennedy, D. (2006) 'Managing our common inheritance' in Kennedy, D. and the editors of *Science* (eds) *Science Magazine's State of the Planet 2006–2007*, pp.101–14, London, Island Press.

Lanchester, J. (2007) 'Short cuts', *London Review of Books*, 5 April; also available online at http://www.lrb.co.uk/v31/n07/lanc01_.html (Accessed 18 May 2009).

Lohmann, L. (2001) *Democracy of Carbocracy? Intellectual Corruption and the Future of the Climate Debate*, Briefing 24, Sturminster Newton, Corner House; also available online at www.thecornerhouse.org.uk/item.shtml?x=51982 (Accessed 19 April 2009).

Lohmann, L. (2006) 'Carbon trading: a critical conversation on climate change, privatisation and power', *Development Dialogue*, no. 48, September.

Lohmann, L. (2008) 'Carbon trading, climate justice and the production of ignorance: ten examples', *Development*, vol. 51, pp. 359–65.

MacKenzie, D. (2006) *An Engine, Not a Camera: How Financial Models Shape Markets*, London, MIT Press.

MacKenzie, D. (2007) 'The political economy of carbon trading', *London Review of Books*, 5 April, pp. 29–31.

United Nations Framework Convention on Climate Change (UNFCCC) (1992) *United Nations Framework Convention on Climate Change*, Bonn, United Nations; also available online at http://unfccc.int/essential_background/convention/items/2627.php (Accessed 14 April 2009).

United Nations Framework Convention on Climate Change (UNFCCC) (1998) *Kyoto Protocol to the United Nations Framework on Climate Change*, Bonn,

United Nations; also available online at http://unfccc.int/kyoto_protocol/items/2830.php (Accessed 14 April 2009).

United Nations Framework Convention on Climate Change (UNFCCC) (2009) *Kyoto Protocol to the United Nations Framework on Climate Change: Emissions Trading*, Bonn, United Nations [online], http://unfccc.int/kyoto_protocol/mechanisms/emissions_trading/items/2731.php (Accessed 7 May 2009).

Conclusion: Material lives

Steve Hinchliffe

Conclusion: Material lives

When we concluded the first group of chapters in this strand it was fairly straightforward to provide some clear answers to the key questions that inform this course. In Chapter 1 of *Making Social Lives*, Kevin Hetherington provided some neat answers to the question of who the winners and losers in a consumer society were (the seduced and the repressed). Likewise, asking how society is made and repaired involved us finding out how power was mobilised and how affluence created streams of materials, consumer goods and rubbish. In some ways, after reading the first three chapters of this book, the answers to these questions are even clearer. Certainly there are winners and losers as economies change. Again, we heard about the growth in the gap between rich and poor, on the global as well as the national stage. We heard too about material lives, about how a seemingly 'weightless' economy is underpinned by a flow of materials around the world and how this has impacts on the global environment. So, it could be argued that you have more evidence in this book to support the same kinds of arguments as those contained in *Making Social Lives*.

And yet, some different answers to our questions have also started to emerge in these chapters. For example, rather than there being a world of winners and losers, there may be a sense that there are no longer any real winners. The suggestion that affluence doesn't generate happiness, or economic growth may not be environmentally sustainable, or that we all live with a dazzling variety of risks, means that the old inequalities are being trumped by some generic, generalised problems. This is, at least, one of the conclusions of the sociologist Ulrich Beck, whom you read about in Chapter 2. He distinguished risk society from industrial society on the basis that while some people (the upper classes) could rise above the squalor of an industrial society – think of those who escaped from urban Manchester to the leafy suburbs that Engels wrote about in the 1840s, as you read in Chapter 5 of *Making Social Lives* – no one escapes the risk society completely. Events such as Chernobyl, global climate change, economic collapse, food scares like BSE; they affect everyone.

■   Is this right? Is everyone affected equally?

Beck has been criticised for overplaying the 'everyone is in the same boat' argument and clearly, as Chapter 3 showed, some people and countries can use their power to influence responses in their favour.

However, it is worth bearing in mind that in some ways the kinds of issue that these chapters have been looking at start to reveal not only divisions and inequalities (they certainly do still exist) but also connections and commonalities.

Likewise, while the chapters in this book concur with those of *Making Social Lives*, in that they all emphasise that society is built in highly material ways (they involve material things, they involve transformations of matter, and they include sometimes vast movements of matter over long distances); they also emphasise the complexity of these material lives. The idea of material lives clearly does not refer to something simple or basic (i.e. that we all lead material lives in the sense that we need to breathe, eat and drink to keep going). Just because we emphasise that our lives are material does not mean that there are now some simple, uncontroversial grounds for living in this rather than that way. As the contests over knowledge in Chapter 2 suggest, and as the efforts discussed in Chapters 1 and 3 to change people's dependence on certain forms of economic activity attest, material lives are often controversial and political. Producing a public health campaign on what to eat or how to sunbathe is not straightforward, even though it may be fairly established where the danger lies. Just because the social is also material does not make either society or materiality more straightforward. When we add the material into our understanding of how society is made and repaired, then the resulting complexity requires more social science thinking, not a shift to natural science for all the answers. Ongoing and difficult to solve environmental problems are testament to the need for more rather than less social science work on issues that relate to our material lives.

Finally, as in the chapters in *Making Social Lives*, we have come across a number of skills and approaches to help us to do social science. Some of the skills were somewhat familiar. Ian Fribbance's use of data and his questioning of evidence in Chapter 1 were similar to John Allen's discussion of how evidence gets used in practice (*Making Social Lives*, Chapter 2). But Ian Fribbance also wants you to become critical of how data is constructed and used. He wants you to ask not only what is there and how is it being used, but also what is missing and how the data could have been produced and displayed differently. In Chapter 2, Simon Carter and Tim Jordan talk about a particular methodological approach, focus groups, which can be used to generate public discourse on particular issues. Again, this builds on information you already have from *Making Social Lives*, Chapters 4 and 5. But here the emphasis is not simply on generating data. It is also on developing interactions that give voice to issues and concerns that wouldn't otherwise be available. It is a method, then, which is from the outset partly critical of conventional accounts of knowledge that suggest that only experts speak the truth. It is concerned, in this case, to allow others outside narrow expertise to speak about risks and to have their reasoning and understanding heard. Finally, in Chapter 3, Michael Pryke reintroduced a model that you learnt about in *Making Social Lives* – the supply and demand model, a causal model that was used to suggest that changes in the supply, demand or price of a good or service would have effects on future supply, demand and price. Pryke showed how such a model was used to generate a market in the rights to pollute the atmosphere. However, he also noted that, in practice, the model does not quite predict what happens in something as complex as a market to pollute. The huge disparities between global North and South, the influence of powerful nation states, the vagaries of the financial system – all these and more conspire to make a simple and elegant model into what some might call a dangerous economic device. In short, Pryke warns us that we shouldn't simply ask 'How do we know?' but also 'Is this knowledge the best available for the job at hand?' or 'How do we need to adapt our understanding to the new situation?'. In other words, he wants us to be self-critical. He asks social scientists not only to be critical of others' knowledge but also to be aware that our knowledge often gets used in ways that we should be ready to criticise.

Pryke tells us that some of the models that we have been accustomed to using (the commons model and the supply and demand model) tend to assume that society is made up of an aggregate of individuals. As *Making Social Lives* emphasised, society is messier than this implies – people live through their connections to others, and if they can be thought of as individuals then this can only be a partial story, and one that tends to omit all their relationships and connections. So, we are now ready to return to the 'Connected lives' strand in order to explore this issue.

Introduction: Connected lives

Stephanie Taylor

Introduction: Connected lives

Part of the moving picture of society

The three chapters that form the 'Connected lives' strand in this book look at aspects of 'who' and 'where' in order to understand the identities of people and places, and the relationships that connect, or 'disconnect', people with places and people with each other. Taking the contemporary UK as the starting point, these three rather different chapters consider large topics, including migration, the nation, culture and race. However, to do so they simultaneously discuss life at a more local level. This is because it is through our ordinary, everyday activities that we are connected into bigger processes operating around the globe and over time.

The next three chapters build on ideas you encountered in the 'Connected lives' strand in *Making Social Lives*.

Whether the focus is on a nation, a migrant worker or a woman becoming a mother for the first time, all three chapters are concerned with movement and change, including changes in identity, over lifetimes and across larger histories. This emphasis on activities and processes is part of the moving picture of society. In the next three chapters, you will read about movements of people, the work activities which maintain organisations over time, and the flows of goods and money between different places. You will also read about different kinds of communication as activities, including ongoing political debates about identities in contemporary UK society. (The debates are political even when the debaters are not politicians.) And you will read about less formal communications, such as the everyday chatting and joking which is both private and social.

The view of society as a moving picture was introduced in the 'Connected lives' strand in *Making Social Lives*.

All three chapters show the importance of our ideas and the ways we think about the world, such as our shared 'imagining' of people and places and histories. You will also read about values, such as those attached to aspects of people's bodies, like body shape or skin colour. The chapters emphasise the need to be aware of definitions, of exactly what (and who) we *mean* when we talk about different identities, like 'migrants' or 'the British', and who is included or excluded by those definitions. Such meanings and values are social, because they are shared, debated and challenged in the ongoing communications which are an essential part of social processes.

In the 'Connected lives' strand in *Making Social Lives*, you read about large-scale movements of people within the UK in the nineteenth century, from countryside to city. You also read how people moving from the UK in previous centuries contributed to the making of other national societies and identities, as the Taylor family did when they went to New Zealand.

The first chapter in this strand, 'Migration: changing, connecting and making places', discusses the movements of people. The social geographer Parvati Raghuram points out that in contemporary UK society migration is widely discussed as a problem, and yet in some respects is not seen clearly. For example, there is considerable confusion about *who* is a migrant, and little recognition of the ways in which migrants help to make and remake society. The chapter looks closely at definitions and theories of migration, considering, for example, whether the movements of people from one place to another are less relevant than the resulting connections which are established between places. The chapter introduces two alternative terms, 'diaspora' and 'translocalism', which, it suggests, may provide a better way of understanding relationships between people and places. It discusses a number of examples of the flows of people, money and goods associated with migration, looking in particular at two contemporary cases: a designer fashion business and the National Health Service.

Political discussions of migration generally involve identities of difference, and distinctions between 'us' and 'them'. In Chapter 5, 'Making national identities: Britishness in question', the social policy scholar John Clarke discusses Britishness and other identities associated with 'our' national place. A national identity is a special kind of identity, and the meanings of any particular nation are linked to its distinctive history. The chapter considers different meanings of Britishness which have arisen over time, including its imagined 'other' places of 'America', 'Europe' and 'Empire'. There is a special focus in this chapter on examples of talk and writing about Britain and what it means to be British. These often refer to the shared culture which supposedly connects British people, and these activities of writing and speaking can themselves be seen as cultural practices through which connections are made, remade and sometimes challenged.

The final chapter of the strand, Chapter 6, 'Identity change and identification', is written by a social psychologist, Wendy Hollway. It looks at the identity changes which occur in a person's lifetime, discussing the examples of two people. The first is going through the major life change of becoming a parent for the first time, and the second is moving from school to work. The details of these changes are specific to these people yet the transitions are common ones, shared by many others in society. They are also shaped by society, including by these people's connections, and 'disconnections'. A particular concern of the chapter is the relevance of bodies to identity. It considers both those aspects of the body which change over time and those which do not, and shows that even bodies and biology are 'social'.

As you read, you should again keep in mind the three course questions. The third of these, 'How do we know?', is discussed in a separate box towards the end of each chapter. The first two questions are considered less directly, but as you read you will notice that they come together because differences and inequalities are produced in the same processes through which society is made and repaired. For example, cultural celebrations centred on the appreciation of certain kinds of art, music or literature can unite some people while dividing off or excluding others. Young people may first explore their differences from their parents, and then later recognise similarities of experience and reclaim social identities which are shared within their families. Of course this does not mean that the same differences and divisions in society continue unchanged, or that inequalities are inevitable. There is continuity *and* change over time. You will read, for example, about how

In the 'Connected lives' strand in *Making Social Lives*, you read about Othering, including how the negatively valued, marked identities of 'race' and 'ethnicity' are often connected to (imagined) places and differences.

You may remember from the 'Connected lives' strand in *Making Social Lives* that personal and social identities cannot be neatly separated.

the movements of people which scatter a population around the world also produce a network of connections which can later be used positively – for instance, for business and for the support of new migrants. Old identities can be rejected or redefined, and you will read about how a shared celebration of differences and diversity can itself connect people, becoming the basis of a new social identity.

Chapter 4
Migration: changing, connecting and making places

Parvati Raghuram

Contents

Introduction   159

1   Migration stories   163

    1.1   Who exactly is a migrant?   163

    1.2   Arrival stories: from 'there' to 'here'   166

    1.3   Numbers of migrants   167

    1.4   Categorising and valuing migrants   171

    1.5   Different directions: departure and circulation   175

2   Connecting places   181

    2.1   Business connections   181

    2.2   Diaspora   183

    2.3   Money flows   186

    2.4   Translocalism   187

3   Making an institution   190

    3.1   Theories of migration   190

Conclusion   199

References   200

Introduction

I was driving into the centre of Birmingham on a cold, wet morning in March when I saw a temporary road sign about traffic disruption in the centre of the city. And then I remembered that the St Patrick's Day parade was being held in Birmingham that day. So I abandoned my shopping trip, parked my car, took the train into the city centre and joined the approximately 10,000 people who lined the route of this, the third largest St Patrick's Day parade in the world. We watched and cheered the march of the Irish Guards, the floats assembled by local Irish groups such as the Birmingham Tipperary County Association, by Irish community groups in other parts of the UK and even by some people who had come over from Ireland to take part in the parade. And then there was an Indian troupe performing the bhangra dance who also participated in the parade, expanding this commemoration of the presence of Irish people in the UK to a more general celebration of the city.

The 2008 St Patrick's Day parade in Birmingham, and the Selfridges shop in Birmingham's Bull Ring shopping centre, lit up in green to celebrate St Patrick's Day

Like the Chinese New Year's Day festivities, the Notting Hill Carnival and the Diwali Mela, the St Patrick's Day parade is an event associated with a group in the UK population which has links to a different place, in this case Ireland. The identities of such groups are linked to historical movements of people who are still sometimes described as migrants, although their families may have been settled in the UK (and even in the same part of the UK, such as Birmingham) for several generations. Their experience is obviously different from that of people who 'changed place' more recently. Some migrant communities tend to

As you read in Chapter 4 of *Making Social Lives*, such groups are often defined in racial or ethnic terms.

be less celebrated, although you see them every day, on building sites or farms, in shops and restaurants, care homes and hospitals, and you may also encounter them less directly, through the work they do, and the products and services they have produced which are on offer in the shops. This chapter discusses migration and some of the varied experiences and identities which are evoked by that term.

Even though 'changing places' is a part of everyday life, the presence of migrants in the UK provokes mixed feelings. For instance, there was considerable debate in 2004 after the UK opened its borders to migrants from eight Eastern European countries at the time of their accession to the European Union (the A8 countries as they came to be called). There were news reports about migrants waiting on the streets for the gangmasters who would employ them by the day, and other reports about the migrants' drinking and socialising when they were off work, including complaints about noise and low-level street crime. There have also been news stories about migrant women employed as sex workers on the streets of cities in the UK. Thus, the street is one site where the contradictions of migration are displayed, through, on the one hand, the celebration of the cultural and economic contributions (especially of former generations) and, on the other, the failed hopes and the exploitation of recent migrants.

Migration is also an issue on which people are often asked to take up positions, especially around election time when political parties use their stance on migration to woo voters. Big billboards urge us to consider the government's record on handling immigration while voting; others mock this politicisation of immigration. These views are also cultivated between election times so that migration is a frequent topic in the news. Perhaps it helps to sell newspapers! Newspaper articles range in content from reports on new government regulations on migration, to the results of new studies on how much migrants are worth to the economy, and of course to reports of speeches made by politicians on the whole issue of migration. They discuss the rights and wrongs of migration, whether it is good or bad for the country, how many people would be the right number of migrants for the national economy and which kinds of people are desirable. The views expressed partly depend on the paper you pick up but one thing is certain – there are many people who are interested in migration.

Migration is also important for social scientists. Topics such as identity, citizenship and consumption, which you have already encountered on this course, relate to populations, and in every country mobility and

Election poster from the General Election of 2005 – Conservative Party poster

Election poster from the General Election of 2005 – rival poster by the 'No Borders' campaign

migration are key aspects of who makes up a population. Who has the right to reside in a country? Who belongs to it and who does it belong to? Who is valuable to a country and who is dispensable? These are all questions raised by migration and they may be the reason that feelings about migrants often seem to run high. This chapter cannot provide you with final answers to these questions but it can provide some suggestions and help you to make better sense of the debates around migration as these are currently constructed.

You may find it useful to recall the discussions of imagined origins and places in Chapter 4 of *Making Social Lives*.

Section 1 of this chapter looks at some of the different elements that make up current debates on migration. By the end of this section you will be able to distinguish some of the ways that arguments about migration are often structured. You will see that, underlying migration stories, is a 'here' and 'there' formula which highlights the difference between migrants' places of origin and those of their destination. Sections 2 and 3 then explore some other ways of thinking about migration which don't hold 'here' and 'there' so far apart. Section 2 looks at the ways in which places of origin and destination are connected, and how the UK's migration story can be seen as a story of connections. Section 3 considers the role played by some of these connections in making an institution with a particular importance for UK life, the National Health Service or NHS. By the end of this chapter you will also be introduced to some ways in which migration and nation have been interlinked, a topic which is explored more fully in the next chapter in this 'Connected lives' strand.

1 Migration stories

1.1 Who exactly is a migrant?

For many people, it will seem obvious that the Irish, the Polish and even the Indian bhangra troupe who participated in the St Patrick's Day parade are all migrants. However, as the introduction indicated, this may not be the case. The problem is partly one of definition. Who do we mean by 'a migrant'? If we had the task of sorting people into either 'migrant' or 'non-migrant' categories, what information would we need? The following activity explores this problem.

Activity 1

Look through the list below and decide whether you think each of the people mentioned below should be classified as a migrant or not:

- Person 1 was born in the UK and currently lives there. She holds a British passport. Her ethnicity is Indian.
- Person 2 lived in the UK till she was 2 years old, then she moved with her parents to the USA for twenty years, only moving back to the UK three years ago.
- Person 3 is the child of parents who migrated from Trinidad to the UK in 1952 when that island was still a British colony.

There is no 'right' or 'wrong' answer for each person (and you may perhaps have noticed that these descriptions could even refer to the same person). Your answers will depend on the criteria you used to identify a migrant. You may feel that you simply did not know enough to decide. If so, think about what other information you would have wanted about each case in order to make a decision.

According to the Office for National Statistics (ONS, 2009), a long-term international migrant is someone who changes his or her country of usual residence for a period of at least a year, so that the country of destination becomes the country of usual residence. However, you will find that newspaper stories, government statistics and studies that report the numbers of migrants in the country all use different criteria to define a migrant. Now have a look in the news at some of the different stories about migrants you can find. Here are some of the criteria that might be used to define a migrant:

- *Country of birth:* In this definition, a migrant is someone who lives in a different country from that in which they were born. Studies of population stocks (i.e. of people who already live in a country), such as the census, often use 'foreign born' as a criterion for identifying migrants. Of course this means that those who were born in some other country but came to the UK forty years ago and have taken up citizenship may be considered as migrants alongside those who only arrived in the UK one or two years ago. Children of UK citizens who were born abroad could also be seen as migrants.

- *Movement:* An international long-term migrant is defined as a person who moves to a country other than that of his or her usual residence for a period of at least a year. Studies of such movements or flows often draw on the International Passenger Survey, a survey of 10 per cent of the population who are travelling through ports of entry and exit. Currently, in 2008, this survey of departures and arrivals is the only source of data on both emigration and immigration available in the UK. However, it cannot distinguish people who are moving long-term from those coming or going on short-term visits such as for business or holidays.

- *Citizenship:* In this definition, those who reside in the country but do not have UK citizenship are considered to be migrants. However, as we shall see in the next chapter, the category of citizenship, and accompanying terms like 'nationals' and 'non-nationals', do not provide a sound basis for analysing migration. Migrants who have taken up UK citizenship will not be identifiable through this category while UK citizens who live abroad also get miscounted.

If we apply these definitions to the cases in Activity 1, we can see that neither Person 1 or 3 is a migrant in the terms of the first or second definition. By the third definition, Person 1, as a holder of a British passport, is not a migrant, and to decide about Persons 2 and 3 we would need further information, about their official citizenship. Because of the problems of defining a migrant, some studies combine different definitions. For example, when studying new forms of migration, it can be useful to use 'country of birth' alongside a time frame such as 'resident in the UK for ten years'. Using 'citizenship' alongside 'country of birth' can give us information on how many migrants have taken up citizenship and how many have not. The Labour Force Survey is one dataset that brings these two variables together.

Activity 2

You might now look back to the different ways in which migrants were defined in the news stories you were asked to look at above and compare them with these criteria. Do you think that the term was the most appropriate in the context in which it was used? What other definition would have been more useful?

You may find that it is often not very obvious what makes someone a migrant, yet when we read these stories we do not necessarily stop to think about definitions or whether these are migration stories at all. These definitional issues are often at the heart of different accounts of migration. For example, remember the question raised in the introduction about who is valuable to a country. 'Value' is itself difficult to define, but even if we narrow the issue to economic value, in terms of costs or contributions to the economy, we will find that the answer varies according to the definition of a migrant. In 2006, an anti-immigration group, Migration Watch, reported that migrants 'cost' the UK economy 100 million pounds a year. Yet just a few years earlier a government report had made the opposite claim, that migrants contribute nearly 25 times that much, 2.5 billion pounds a year. What can explain these very different evaluations?

The answer depends, again, on who is defined as a 'migrant'. The main difference was that the report by Migration Watch included more children in its calculations. As non-workers, these children could be seen to cost the economy money, presumably for providing schooling, health care, and so on. Of course, many people would question this way of thinking of children as costs alone – and not as assets, at present or in the future – but the special point of their definition was that Migration Watch included an additional, large group of children, from 'mixed households' where one parent was UK born and one parent

You read about value in Chapter 3 of Making Social Lives.

165

foreign born. According to Migration Watch there were about 750,000 such children. Including the costs of even half of these children in the calculations would have a critical influence in challenging the government's assessment that migrants made a net positive contribution to the economy. Table 1 summarises the two publications about migrants and the economy.

Table 1   Summary of claims made about migrants and the economy

Claim	Source of claim	Definitional differences
Migrants cost the economy 100 million pounds a year	Migration Watch, an anti-immigration group (Migration Watch UK, 2006)	Counts as migrants half of the children born of one UK-born parent and one foreign-born parent (i.e. children of mixed households)
Migrants are worth 2.5 billion pounds per year to the economy	Government report (Gott and Johnson, 2002)	Does not count children of mixed households as migrants

■   Looking at the table, which claim do you find more convincing?

Whatever your answer, you can see that definitions are important. They pop up not only in migration debates but also in the social sciences more generally, and arguments can sometimes hinge just on definitions. How we define something may influence what we think about the topic that is defined. As we saw above, the definition of a migrant can be used to align people on different sides of an argument. Moreover, people can also adapt their definitions to suit their own purpose and to bolster their arguments. The power of migration to evoke strong emotions means that these definitional issues are particularly important.

1.2   Arrival stories: from 'there' to 'here'

You read about this movement of people from the countryside to the city in Chapter 5 of *Making Social Lives*.

The introduction to this chapter referred to 'changing places', and of course there are many people who move from one place to another within national borders. One important example of changing places within national borders is the enormous movement of people from the countryside to the city in the nineteenth century, and the consequences this had for their lives. Why, then, do discussions of migration usually focus on international migration, across national borders? What makes international migrants different? One answer might be simply that they have travelled greater distances, with the practical problems that involves and the possibly greater costs of resettling. Another might be that they speak a different language or have a different culture, although you can probably think of exceptions to most or all of those points. Look now at the quotation below, and notice its source (that is, who wrote, or said this, and where and when).

> We are faced with a situation now where we are getting tidal waves of migration, inward migration into our rural areas from England, and these people are coming here to live to establish themselves here, and to influence our communities and our culture with their own … It makes us even poorer and it is absolutely no use to the community to have retired people from England coming here to live and being a drain on our resources.
>
> (Seimon Glynn, Chairman of Gwynedd County Council's housing committee in an interview in January 2001 on BBC Radio Wales)

This quotation is from someone who works in local (not national) government. He is talking about migration from England to Wales, which would not usually be classified as international, although of course there is considerable debate around that issue as you will read in the next chapter. The first point of interest for us is that internal migration can be made contentious (in fact, following this interview the councillor in question apologised for his remarks). The second point is that many of the issues raised in Seimon Glynn's comments are also used in discussions of international migration to the UK: a concern with numbers, a categorical approach and a value-laden approach, three issues to which I turn below.

1.3   Numbers of migrants

First, let us turn to the issue of *numbers*. In the example above, you can see that the councillor begins with the claim that there are too many migrants. Of course, underlying this notion of too many migrants is the idea that there is a 'right' number and that policymakers can find this, if only they search hard for it. These ideal figures vary. Anti-immigration lobbyists might come up with a figure of zero (i.e. that all in-migration should be stopped); others might choose a higher figure. But how can this right number be decided?

■ Go back to the quotation by the Welsh councillor and see if you can identify some bases for identifying the 'right number' of migrants.

Looking at Seimon Glynn's comments, I found two possible indications of 'the right number' of migrants. The first would be that there are not so many as to 'influence our communities and our culture with their own'. For instance, Glynn argued that there are too many people coming to Wales who only speak English, reducing the importance of Welsh as the spoken language in Wales. Such arguments around culture and language are also used by those advocating a zero immigration policy who suggest that the UK as whole needs to 'adjust' to migrants who are already in the country and that greater numbers 'threaten social cohesion'. Others would argue that the diversity and dynamism resulting from migration are of great value and help to make up the contemporary UK (think back to the example of Birmingham in the introduction).

A different indication of 'the right number' is given by Glynn's comment: 'it makes us even poorer'. This suggests that migrants should not put a strain on the economy, so the right number is the number that the economy can support. One could argue that retired English people who come to Wales may need health care and thus become 'a drain on resources'. In the context of international migrants, the costs of migration may come from those at the other end of the age spectrum, namely, children, as we saw in Section 1.1. Because migrants often tend to be young, and therefore to have young families, local authorities in areas with large numbers of migrants find increasing numbers of children in their schools. These authorities claim that they should be given special dispensation to cope with these numbers and their impact on the costs incurred by local education authorities. Most councils do not argue straightforwardly for a limit to migration but they do want to be recompensed for the effect that increasing population has on their budget. As we saw in Section 1.1, these costs are also calculated at the national level. However, an important point to consider is that the children of today are the workers and taxpayers of tomorrow. It can be argued that the migrant children who consume resources and thus cost the taxpayer today will be needed to contribute to the economy in the future, especially in an 'ageing' population like the UK's in which there is an increasing proportion of older and retired people. They will also contribute to the physical care and maintenance of the wider population and society.

This is one of the points raised by sources which, like the government report which you read about in Section 1.1, argue for higher numbers on the basis that migrants make positive contributions to the UK. Another government study, in 2001, by the Home Office, showed that a 1 per cent growth in number of migrants leads to between 1.25 and 1.5 per cent growth in Gross Domestic Product (GDP) (Glover et al., 2001). A different study showed that total revenue from immigrants grew in real terms from £33.8 billion in 1999–2000 to £41.2 billion in 2003–04 (Sriskandarajah et al., 2005, p. 12). Taxes paid by migrants help to subsidise the non-migrant population. The Confederation of British Industries, one of the main organisations representing independent employers, also claims that the UK needs more migrants to fill gaps in skills, to 'widen the pool of available labour and help develop a more diverse, multicultural workforce' (CBI, 2005, p. 1).

One of the things that it is important for us to note as social scientists is that both sides of the argument deploy the same method: a numerical approach to migration. In other words, they use quantitative data to support their claims. Both those who are in favour of migration and those who are not draw up their evidence by recording, listing and calculating numbers. Numbers sometimes suggest a degree of precision, objectivity and trustworthiness in the arguments being presented. This use of numbers reinforces the idea that migration is a matter for scientific calculation. However, quantitative data can be disputed. As we saw above, numbers will vary according to what is counted – for example, according to who is defined as a migrant. Numbers may also conceal even more difficult judgements, for example about the contributions made by migrants (this point is discussed in more detail below). The same number can also be deployed for different purposes. In short, numbers are not as fixed or reliable as they might seem.

You may have noted that many of those on either side of this argument seem to believe that there is an ideal figure of migrants that is achievable (more or less) if migration regulations are managed properly. Another aspect of calculating the costs of migration is discussed in the box 'The argument for open borders'.

- As you read the text in the box below, make a list of some of the hidden costs of migration that are mentioned. Can you think of other hidden costs that are not mentioned here?

The argument for open borders

In an influential book, *Open Borders: The Case Against Immigration Controls*, Teresa Hayter (2000) argued that migration could never be managed properly because borders will always be porous; there will always be people who arrive and then overstay or become illegal in ways that are difficult to control. Large sums of money have to be spent on rather ineffective border control. She suggests that this money would be better put into more positive action on migration. Given this situation, she argues that the calculations that are made in order to try to regulate migration are about all the wrong things – instead of calculating the costs of migration we should be calculating the costs of controlling migration; that is, of patrolling borders, of surveillance and of the forced return of those who are seen to be illegal. Calculating the costs of migration would also involve recognising the costs paid by migrants themselves for obtaining information and passports, paying for travel and sometimes paying brokers who will help them to get past border controls. Others pay with their lives trying to enter on boats that sink or in overcrowded trucks without adequate ventilation. Hayter argues that if the current expenditure on migration control were instead spent in helping the people and places from which people migrate, migration would become less of an issue. She therefore urges governments to adopt open borders. This is an example of a different form of calculation of the costs of migration, and is one which is often used by those who are proponents of the 'no borders position'. Calculations may be useful sometimes but their usefulness really depends on whether all the calculable issues are properly drawn into the analysis of the costs and benefits of migration.

In addition to the costs mentioned by Teresa Hayter, here are a few of the hidden costs that I noted. You may have thought of others:

- the emotional cost to the family of migrants in being separated from them
- the financial costs of separation, such as phone calls and visits back
- the lost incomes where families have been divided, and possibly the cost of running two households where previously there was one
- the cost to migrants' former communities of taxes that they would have paid if they had not moved
- the cost to the sending countries of trying to manage emigration.

1.4   Categorising and valuing migrants

A second issue raised in Seimon Glynn's comments is that of
different *categories* of people. Glynn distinguishes fairly simply between
those who are already 'here', and those who are coming here: 'retired
people' who will be a 'drain on our resources'. The implication is that
the people who are already 'here' have a right to resources, whereas
those who come here do not. In discussions of international migration,
rights are often related to the categories of legal or illegal migrants. You
have probably noticed that many news stories refer to illegal migrants.
But what makes a migrant legal or illegal? The rights of entry, right to
work, right to stay and right to form relationships are differently
apportioned to people based on their citizenship. For instance, citizens
of the European Economic Area (EEA) have rights to enter, stay,
work and form relationships with UK citizens while Australian citizens
have rights to enter the UK but not to stay beyond a fixed period
without applying for an extension of stay. Pakistani citizens have no
automatic rights of entry to the UK – they have to apply for all
these rights.

However, this has not always been the case. It was only with the
Aliens Act of 1905 that the Immigration Service gained power to refuse
entry to certain groups of people. It was designed at least in part to
reduce immigration of Jews from Russia. Commonwealth citizens had
right of entry to the UK until the passage of the Commonwealth
Immigrants Act in 1962. Thus, immigration rights change over time,
and are modified as political relations with other parts of the world
alter. In the case of migration, one of the most significant changes
we have seen in the last few years arises from the extension of the
EEA to countries in Eastern Europe, with an extension of rights to
stay and work in the UK to many people who historically have not had
that right.

People's own individual situations may also change over time. For
instance, someone may come to the UK to work, then meet and marry
a UK or EEA national. Or a person may come to the UK as a tourist
and then decide to stay on and study. Migrants who have limited
permission to work may change their jobs even though their migration
status does not allow them to do so, or, just before Christmas, they
may be pressed by their employers to work a few more hours than
is legally allowed. The line between legal and illegal migration is,

"Britannia: I can no longer offer shelter to fugitives.
England is not a free country".

The Aliens Act at work.

The Aliens Act 1905 at work: a 1906 cartoon showing Britannia refusing entry to immigrants on the basis of new immigration laws

therefore, easily crossed. It is worth noting that in Australia UK nationals are the second largest overstayers (i.e. those who stay in the Australian community beyond the time period allowed by their temporary visas). Some of them stay a few days or weeks extra without even realising it, but in crossing that time threshold they have moved to 'illegal' status.

Clearly, rights and the categorisation of migrants as legal or illegal follow from regulations. When migrants are discussed in terms of fixed categories (e.g. in news stories about 'illegal migrants'), this does not acknowledge how regulations might change and also how people might move in and out of categories over time. Perhaps we need a less categorical approach to migration and migration control and more recognition of the inevitable complexities of people's lives (Ruhs and Anderson, 2008).

A third issue raised by Seimon Glynn, which is closely linked to the second, is that the categories of migrants are *value-laden*; in other words, they suggest that some types of migrants are more desirable than others. Activity 3 makes this point clearer.

Activity 3

Imagine you are deciding on the value of prospective migrants to the UK (i.e. people who want to migrate here). Rank the following people in order, according to the contributions they could make. Would it be possible to measure those (prospective) contributions in monetary terms, or using some other quantitative measure?

- ballet dancer
- cook
- nurse
- investment banker
- scientist
- student
- business woman
- footballer

You probably found that it is not easy to rank the different occupations. Placing a figure on their value would be even harder. For instance, you might have noted that a ballet dancer has a 'cultural' value which is difficult to count in economic terms.

The right to migrate to the UK often seems to be a kind of reward given to those who are young, have high earnings and are highly educated. The situation is similar in some other countries, including Australia, New Zealand and Canada. The argument may be that young people are desirable migrants because they have a longer working life ahead of them in which to contribute to economic growth and pay taxes, before they draw pensions or make other demands on the state (remember Seimon Glynn's criticisms of retired people). Similarly, people who can earn more will usually be seen as desirable residents because they pay higher taxes, are less likely to depend on state benefits and also contribute to the general economy through their higher spending levels.

The value placed on the education and qualifications of prospective migrants may be less obvious. One way of understanding this is through theories of **human capital**. The economist Adam Smith suggested in his book *The Wealth of Nations*, published in 1776, that the four inputs which produce wealth are land, buildings, machinery and human beings. Human capital theory focuses on that fourth input and suggests that the

Human capital
The economic value of the education, experience and skills of an individual.

173

economic performance of a person increases with their education, experience and skills. It is very difficult to count knowledge, so in effect most countries have taken educational qualifications or skills as a measure of knowledge. They then use that measure as a central criterion in managing migration, filtering out those with less relevant or valuable skills, and encouraging those with skills that (they hope) will drive economic growth. The emphasis on education has also increased in recent years as many social scientists believe that we now live in a 'knowledge economy' in which economic advantage lies in more advanced knowledge.

Over the years the kinds of skills that have been valued in prospective migrants are medical skills, knowledge of particular aspects of information technology (IT), actuarial skills and management skills. Cleaning, caring and cooking are seen as less important to a knowledge economy. (Feminists argue that these kinds of work are not recognised as having economic value because they have conventionally been done by women, within domestic environments.) However, we may want to challenge this neat categorisation.

Activity 4

Imagine once again that you are evaluating prospective migrants, but this time you are deciding between the following pairs of migrant workers. For each pair of migrants, which do you think has skills that are more useful to the economy and why? Are any of their jobs unnecessary?

- A well-paid corporate employee from the USA who will work in the City of London OR a cook who will be employed in their office restaurant.
- A nurse who will work in the National Health Service OR a nurse who will work as a carer in a residential home for the elderly.
- A cook who will work in a restaurant OR a person who will cook in her or his employer's house as a domestic worker.
- A nanny OR a carer who looks after old people.

You read in Chapters 3 and 4 of *Making Social Lives* how value is socially constructed.

You may have decided that the first person in each choice is more likely to get a visa. The investment banker seems to be generating money, there are always nurse shortages in the NHS and restaurants need staffing. However, if you think about it further, you may think that office restaurants are a necessary part of the infrastructure of working places and they too require staffing. In the second example, the formal accreditation of skills, the place where the work is done, the extent to which nurses can take part in curative activities will all influence how we think about the skills that the migrant possesses. In the third example, we find that when the same work is done in the public sphere it is more valued than when it is done within people's homes. Women are also more likely to find employment as domestic workers while the cook in the restaurant is more likely to be a man. Young people are often considered to be more valuable to society than older people so in the fourth example you may find that nannies and au pairs are considered more valuable than carers who look after older people. The value of skills seems thus to depend on the tasks that are done, where they are done, who does them and who they are done for. It is therefore not easy to decide whether one migrant is more necessary than another or what jobs and skills matter, as you may have found.

1.5   Different directions: departure and circulation

You may or may not have noticed that up to now I have concentrated almost exclusively on migrants coming into the country. We are so accustomed to thinking that stories of migration are always stories of arrival, from 'there' to 'here', that we rarely stop to think that the UK is also the site of departure and of circulation. The following activity looks more closely at some of the patterns of immigration (into the UK) and emigration (out). Social scientists who study population (known as demographers) are particularly interested in arrival and also in the rising net emigration among UK nationals (Sriskandarajah and Drew, 2006). Some of these patterns are shown in the graph in Figure 1.

Activity 5

Look at Figure 1, showing UK immigration and emigration, and see if you can work out answers to the following questions:

- In which year did the inflow of migrants first exceed outflow?
- In which year was the outflow highest?
- To what extent do the inflow and outflow patterns mirror each other?
- Can you suggest what categories of people these flows might refer to?

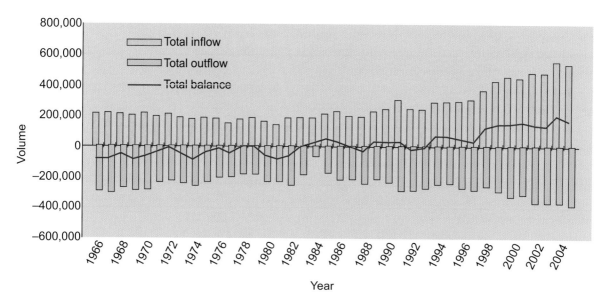

Figure 1   Bar chart and line graph showing annual international migration flows to the UK of all nationalities, 1966–2005 (Source: Sriskandarajah and Drew, 2006, p. 13, Table 3.1)

Broadly, the inflow and outflow do mirror each other. There were higher flows in the late 1960s and early 1970s. Inflows exceeded outflows for the first time in 1983. The lowest flows were around 1980 but after that both emigration and immigration increased, especially after 1991. The outflow was highest in 2005.

The chart shows that between 1966 and 2005, some 2.7 million UK nationals left the country. In other words, on average in each of the thirty-nine years covered by the graph, around 67,500 more UK nationals left the UK than came back to it. In 2005 alone, 198,000 UK nationals left to start new lives abroad, while 91,000 came back to the UK. In 2006, an estimated 5.5 million UK nationals lived permanently overseas (equivalent to 9.2 per cent of the UK's population). Many of these migrants are pensioners who have chosen to settle in places with a warmer climate. Others have found job opportunities abroad or are students. Still others have gone to join family members. The UK thus has one of the largest expatriate populations of any country of the world (see Figure 2). If we include all the historical movements from the UK in the past 200 years, rough estimates suggest that there are about 200 million people outside the UK born into families who at some time have migrated from the UK.

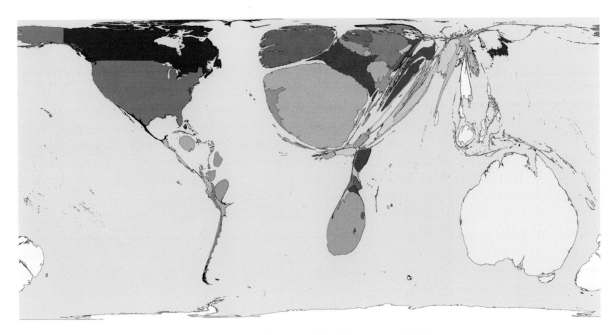

Figure 2   Map of UK expatriate population (Source: Worldmapper, 2006)

The map in Figure 2 shows this expatriate population and its location around the world. The size of each country has been redrawn in proportion to the size of the UK expatriate population resident there. (This type of map is called a cartogram.)

■   Can you see which countries have the highest UK expatriate population?

The five countries with the highest population of formerly British residents (counting those who have lived there for a year or more) are the ones which are largest on the map: Australia, Spain, the USA, Canada and Ireland.

Another aspect of migration that receives little attention is the circulation of migrants as people travel to another country for a few days, perhaps to attend a meeting or close a business deal, or to visit friends and family, or see a few tourist spots, and then return to their base country. (The transit lounges of airports deal with an even faster circulation: the people who land for a few hours between flights, without officially entering the country at all.)

A large number of migrants also come to the UK for one or two years, typically moving into London offices of accountancy, management and consultancy firms before they return to offices in their home countries.

British pensioners in Spain

They provide a layer of border-straddling managerial knowledge for companies with offices in multiple countries. Such inter-company transfers account for a large number of migrants from some countries such as Japan and the USA. In some sectors of the labour market, such as information and communication technology, 80 per cent of migrants come through such arrangements. They provide specialised on-site knowledge and expertise for specific projects for some months and may then return to their home countries and continue working on the project from a distance.

Another system that is based on circulation is the Youth Mobility Scheme. This allows young people from Commonwealth countries, especially those from the 'old' Commonwealth countries such as Australia and New Zealand, to come and work in the UK for up to two years. They are usually employed in low-paid, lesser skilled jobs such as those in the hospitality or tourism sectors. This regulatory framework facilitates movements that in many ways are equivalent to the gap year that some UK students take when they travel abroad.

Processes of transit and circulation are not just an effect of the speeding up and ease of contemporary travel. Even in earlier times, when most travel was by ship and train, the UK was a place of transit

and circulation. At the end of the nineteenth century and during
the early twentieth century, the bustling London Docklands in the Pool
of London were not only places where migrants disembarked from
ships as they came to settle in the UK but also places through
which migrants moved to other parts of the world. For example,
between 1885 and 1905, a number of Eastern Europeans and Russians
moved through these and other ports in the UK on their way to
North America and South Africa. Although large numbers arrived in
the UK at this time, it was still largely a country of emigration. For
example, between 1876 and 1900 about two million adult males left
the UK for North America alone (Green, MacKinnon and
Minns, 2003).

British emigrants on board the steamship *Herald Liverpool* leaving Liverpool,
bound for Australia, in the early 1900s

This information about immigration and emigration might lead you to
think that the whole UK population is constantly moving. However, a
final point to note is that only 9 per cent of the population of the UK
are foreign born and less than 6 per cent are registered as foreign
citizens. Although these proportions are going up, on the whole few
people move internationally. Yet migration is an important and ongoing
event that is continually reshaping place and is still continuously making

the UK. As you have seen in this section, most discussions of migration are a little limited. In particular, they separate the places of origin from the places of destination, treating them as distinctive and unconnected. However, what if we were to think of migration through a different lens, as a way that places become connected? I will turn to this in the next section.

Summary

- Although migration is widely discussed, the exact definition of 'a migrant' is often not specified, and different definitions are possible and in use.

- Different definitions of 'migrant' produce different quantitative evidence.

- Migration is not just about arrival but also about departure and circulation, all of which are important features of past and present UK migration.

2   Connecting places

When people migrate, they change the places where they live. However, whether migrants come for a short or long time, they do not cut off their ties with people in the countries from which they came. Migrants not only make the places in which they stay but they also retain connections to other places, particularly those from which they came last. They often maintain networks of ties with the countries from which they have migrated, bringing and sending money, clothes and food, for instance. This section explores some of the connections established by migration.

2.1   Business connections

In 1996, as part of a project on women entrepreneurs, I interviewed the owner of expensive women's clothing shops in London and the Midlands (Raghuram and Hardill, 1998). The clothes which are sold in the shops are outfits for evening wear and special occasions, designed in Leicester by the owner of the shops, a woman I will call Malini. (Social researchers generally conceal the real names of their participants.) The clothes are made in India, using high-quality fabrics sourced from China. The designs are exclusive to Malini's business but based on Asian styles, such as the salwaar kameez. The clothes are designed for women who, like Malini herself, are young British Asian professionals. They wear 'Western' clothes on a daily basis but prefer Asian styles for special occasions. Malini also sells her clothes to retailers in the USA and South Africa.

■   Think about the connections between places which underlie Malini's business, and also the disconnections. How are these related to migration?

Malini's business activities, her products and her customers have connections to more than one place, as does Malini herself. Her family history is marked by migration. Her grandparents migrated from India to set up a business in Kenya. They were one of the many families who set up shops to serve the indentured workers in East Africa. Indentured workers were migrants who were transported by the British to other parts of the British Empire as contract labour, from the beginning of the twentieth century. Their passage was paid and they received for paltry wages and accommodation for a fixed period. Under British rule

A designer clothing shop established by Malini

in East Africa, the Indian traders were given middle-class jobs, mediating between the white rulers and the Black African rural peasantry. Malini's parents were born in Kenya. After 1963, when Kenya gained independence, there was increasing discrimination and violence against Indians who had settled there and in neighbouring East African countries. Malini's parents were among a number of middle-class Asians who left and came to the UK as refugees. Malini was born and grew up in Leicester. She attended university before starting her business.

Her product biography therefore reflects Malini's own migrant family history. She has set up a multimillion-pound business with a global reach. She utilises her connections with India to produce clothes cheaply in India. But she also uses the locale of production – India – to brand them as somehow authentic, as she is selling 'Indian' clothes, although not conventional ones. She actively uses these connections to produce and sell clothes, becoming a live economic link that connects migrants with places across the world.

2.2   Diaspora

One way to describe the connections underlying Malini's business is through the term **diaspora**, which is derived from Greek and means a dispersed population who share some common cultural elements or heritage arising from their linkages to a home – real or imagined. The term diaspora was originally used to describe the experience of Jews who were expelled from their homeland after the Babylonians' conquest of Judea in the sixth century BCE. As such, diasporic populations were generally defined as forcibly displaced peoples who long to return to their homeland. However, the scope of the term diaspora has been expanded to include the experiences of a variety of migrants whose moves have been sparked by more recent processes such as slavery, colonialism and decolonisation. Social scientists now discuss different categories of diaspora. For example, the Jewish diaspora is often seen as a 'victim diaspora' because of its history of expulsion. The Chinese diaspora is described as 'entrepreneurial', as many Chinese have travelled out to other countries in order to set up businesses while using links with China to help build their enterprises. What is common to these categorisations is the emphasis on a diaspora as a social group who are geographically dispersed but have some collective memory or identity in relation to the place which they left.

There are several reasons for the increasing use of the term 'diaspora' and the expansion of its meaning. One is that, with globalisation, people, ideas, money and goods flow into and out of nations linking and connecting places so that the role of nation states in social processes is changing. National boundaries appear to be more porous and dynamic. The term 'diaspora' is useful because it helps us to understand how people can have continuing attachments to place which can't be explained if we think of populations as static and territorially bound in nations. Another reason why the term 'diaspora' is useful is that it refers not only to the social consequences of migration, such as diasporic networks, but also, at a more personal level, to a form of consciousness and an awareness of home. These personal feelings, and identities, are part of migrants' lived experiences and also affect forms of production and consumption, cultural behaviours and political participation.

Now let us go back to Malini's story as a story of connections between places. Underlying the business are the customers' consumption practices which are similar because of their common diasporic origin.

Diaspora
A geographically dispersed population who share some links to a common home – real or imagined.

The production chains of the business link know-how, production processes and the market, connecting different places across the world. This particular entrepreneur did not personally know those with whom she started working in India, or indeed in the USA, but she used her diasporic affiliation, based on migrant origins, to set up new economic relations. For businesses like this, the 'place of origin' is the diasporic home, the relations between places which make up a network of global connections, even though they are not dependent on existing relations between people. These connections are shown in the **flow map** in Figure 3.

Flow map
A simple graphic style used to show the movement of objects and persons across the globe.

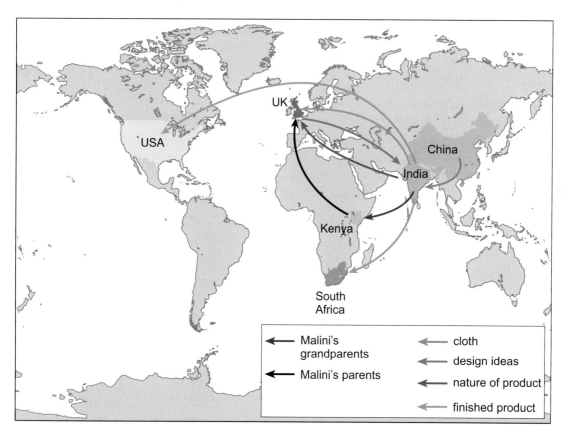

Figure 3   Flow map showing the diasporic connections that underlie Malini's business (Source: author's fieldwork, 1996)

I have emphasised the connections in Malini's business, but we can also see this as a story of disconnections. For instance, you may have noted that not all the people with a similar diasporic affiliation are included in Malini's market. Her clothes are designed largely for women; men of the same background are more likely to wear Western suits even for special occasions. Her market is also marked by class; she is selling expensive designer clothing. Her own family were in middle-class professions in Kenya and, even though as refugees they lost everything and had to start again in the UK, they now form part of an ethnic niche market of well-off people who wear Indian clothes. In designing clothes in the UK, Malini also recognises that what is considered fashionable by well-off 'Asian' women in the UK may be different from the clothes which are liked by the same class in India or Pakistan: she designs the clothes for the diasporic population in the UK. Her business is therefore shaped as much by recognition of class and gender differences within the diaspora as by the connections which it offers. Malini's garments are also purchased by women who do not share this history of migration but want to wear 'Indian' clothes on special occasions. It connects these women to new places through their consumption practices. In sum, Malini's personal biography and product biography are connected but one is not completely derived from or governed by the other.

The concept of the diaspora has been useful for discussing the connections and disconnections in the story of Malini's business. However, the connection of the diaspora to place is not always straightforward. We have noted that there are different kinds of diasporas. The Jewish diaspora is associated with the experience of expulsion from the homeland, but in many contemporary diasporas, a homeland is not so easily identifiable. Malini was born in the UK, her parents were born in Kenya and her grandparents had migrated to Kenya from India to set up a business. It is not clear exactly where the homeland is in this story. More generally, it is not always obvious which places are relevant to a migration story. In this example, the grandparents' migration can be seen to connect India and Kenya, but it was orchestrated and shaped by British policy around indenture so the UK was also involved.

Activity 6

Write down your own 'migration' history. As you have read, there are different definitions of migration. Make a record of your own history of changes of residence. For example, you may have moved up the road with your parents, then moved into some shared accommodation with your friends for two years, then into a flat of your own, perhaps moving to another town when you got that good job.

Now look at your clothes cupboard and your food cupboard. Did you find any items that you think have been influenced by your history of migration?

2.3   Money flows

Another way in which migration connects places is through the flow of money, especially, but not only, between the countries from which migrants leave and those to which they move. For example, we know that many of the older people who have left the UK and gone to live in other countries continue to draw a UK pension. In 2004 the UK Government was estimated to be paying over 2 billion pounds to over a million pensioners who live abroad (Sriskandarajah and Drew, 2006). When these expatriates go shopping in countries like Spain, where many of them have chosen to settle, they use their UK pension money to contribute to Spanish economic growth. Others, who have taken up jobs in Spain, send money back home to their family in the UK, or leave their assets to their family back in the UK on their death. Migrants activate cash flows and in the contemporary world this money may, as this example shows, flow in many directions.

Such cross-border flows can become critical to some countries, forming a very large part of the Gross Domestic Product (GDP). China and India are the largest recipients (see Figure 4), but the impact of such remittances is greatest in small, poor countries, such as Haiti or Lesotho, where they account for over 10 per cent of per capita GDP (World Bank, 2003). In recognition of this contribution, many countries try to help their diasporic populations to send money back cheaply, and to invest in their home countries. A number of countries have also given some political rights to their migrants abroad, including offering them dual citizenship, in the hope that this will increase the flow of money from their diaspora.

Choropleth map
A map in which areas are differently shaded to show numerical variation in a variable.

Some of these flows are shown in the **choropleth map** in Figure 4. In a choropleth map each area is shaded differently to show numerical variation in the variable that the map depicts. For instance, a country with a lower remittance figure might be shaded lightly while a country receiving high amounts of remittances may be shaded in a darker colour, or with a denser pattern.

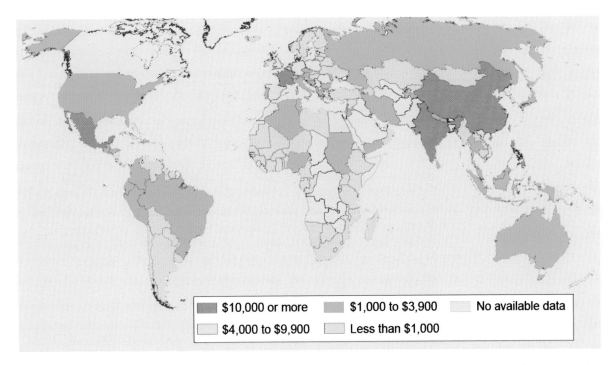

| $10,000 or more | $1,000 to $3,900 | No available data |
| $4,000 to $9,900 | Less than $1,000 | |

Figure 4   Choropleth world map showing amounts of formal remittances (i.e. remittances 'sent through formal channels such as banks and money transfer operators') received by each country, in millions of US dollars, 2006 (Source: Migration Policy Institute, 2007)

2.4   Translocalism

Section 2.2 introduced the concept of diaspora. Another way of understanding people's simultaneous links to more than one locality is through the concept of **translocalism**. This refers to migrants' simultaneous attachment to the places they have left and the places which they move to. It focuses on how the links between these two places are maintained. Translocalism emphasises the many activities that migrants engage in to maintain these relations across space.

Translocalism
A way of understanding people's simultaneous links to more than one locality.

Translocal practices have become more and more common as it has become easier to travel and to keep in touch with people on the phone and on the internet. However, even when communication was more difficult and distances seemed larger, people kept in touch through letters and through networks of friends and relatives who came forwards and backwards. These communication routes also encouraged and assisted newer migrants who would decide where to go, where to stay and what jobs to get. The box on 'Translocalism in the nineteenth century' describes an example of translocalism from the century before last.

Translocalism in the nineteenth century

There is a long history of single women migrating to work. The historian Wendy Gordon studied the lives of migrant women workers who moved to Paisley in Scotland between 1850 and 1881 (Gordon, 2005). She first identified a sample of migrants from the census manuscripts, in order to get a 'snapshot' of migrants in three cities. She then identified more personal information about her sample from qualitative sources including personal letters, Poor Law records, bank records and parliamentary reports. She found that for most of the period she was studying, most of the migrant women in Paisley clustered in two occupations. One of these was domestic work, a major source of employment for women in most places at that time. The second source of jobs for many of the migrant women was the bleachworks outside Paisley.

Gordon found that the women's choice of occupation was related to the region from which they had migrated. Highlanders, particularly from Argyll- and Inverness-shire, had a unique relationship with Paisley's bleachworks because at least one of the bleachworks preferred to employ people who were recommended by their current employees. As women recommended their friends and relatives from the Highlands, a durable set of connections and flows of people (and goods) between the Highlands and Paisley came to be established. This is an early example of translocalism.

The young migrant women who worked at the bleachworks also lived together in boarding houses which were run by the bleachworks companies. Over time, these came to be seen as 'woman houses' and young men were attracted to them. As a result, the houses became disreputable, but also came to be seen as exciting, just like many contemporary streets and city areas with large migrant communities. However, the workers who lived together in these houses were better able to support each other. The women formed a network and helped each other out, so that bleachworkers were far less likely to apply for poor relief than women who had migrated to Paisley to engage in domestic work (Gordon, 2005, p. 65).

Help from other migrants, like that which the Paisley women provided for their fellow workers, can be an important source of support, but it has limits and can even create problems. Some of the migrants who provide help may not really be able to afford it and may be left worse off. Available resources may be shared unequally, so that extra problems are created for the migrants who do not have connections. Help from friends cannot fully replace assistance by the state. Furthermore, connections may become looser over time and even disappear. If we return to Paisley today, the footprints of these women probably won't be visible. We may not see any live links which have survived. There are no clear flows of money or goods between people in Paisley and the Highlands that are attributable to this earlier migration. Like the flows of the people themselves, the connections between places which are established by migration need to be understood over time, as part of an ever-changing, moving picture of society.

Summary

- People who migrated to different parts of the world from the same place form a diasporic population who can maintain some connections with each other and establish new ones, for example through business.
- Migration gives rise to complex global flows of money, from both destination countries and countries of origin.
- Migrants can have 'translocal' connections to more than one place.

3   Making an institution

3.1   Theories of migration

You read in Chapter 5 of *Making Social Lives* about the complex identities of places and how these are made by people's activities.

In this section we will look at how migration can not only connect places but also make the identity of places and institutions. The National Health Service, familiarly called the NHS, is seen as one of the key institutions that make the UK distinctive. In many but not all countries, providing health care is one of the central functions of the state. Since the 1940s, the NHS has provided a comprehensive service to people in the UK, 'from cradle to grave', as Aneurin Bevan, one of its chief architects, said. Health care is free to users because it is paid for from taxes. The NHS is considered by 90 per cent of British people to be a positive symbol of the real UK. Gordon Brown, then Chancellor of the Exchequer, said in 2006, that the principle that access to health care should depend on need, not ability to pay, is part of the core British value of fairness (Brown, 2006). The NHS is a very British institution. Or is it?

Activity 7

What do Table 2 and Figure 5 tell you about the importance of migrants in the NHS, in the past and more recently? Do you notice any limits to the quantitative data, such as associated information that is not provided by these numbers and percentages?

Table 2   Percentage of hospital medical staff in selected grades born outside the British Isles, 1975, England and Wales

Selected medical grades	% born outside the British Isles
Consultant	14.2
Senior Registrar	27.7
Registrar	57.4
Senior House Officer	60.0
All staff	35.2

Source: Kyriakides and Virdee, 2003, p. 292

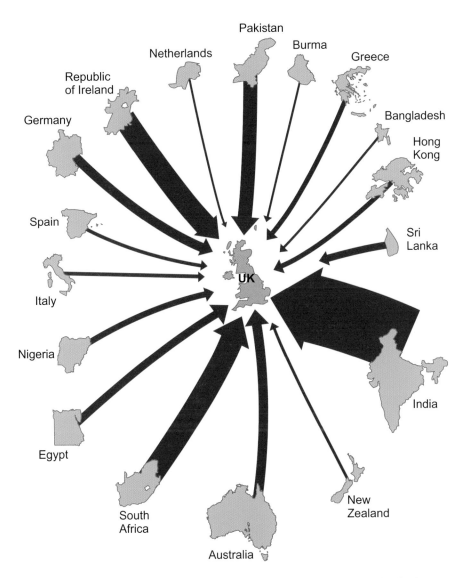

Figure 5   Overseas doctors in the UK: doctors on the General Medical Council register by country of qualification, 2004 (Source: General Medical Council Register)

Note: the data that Figure 5 is based on are as follows:

Country of qualification	Number of doctors in the UK
India	18,006
South Africa	6,208
Republic of Ireland	5,989
Pakistan	3,807
Australia	2,648

Germany	2,577
Egypt	2,152
Sri Lanka	1,903
Nigeria	1,661
Iraq	1,392
Greece	1,384
Hong Kong	1,340
Italy	1,084
Spain	923
Jamaica	763
New Zealand	760
Bangladesh	637
Burma	587
Netherlands	559
Total	**61,551**

Table 2 shows that, in 1975, 35 per cent of NHS staff had been born outside the UK. Figure 5 provides more detailed information, by showing that a significant proportion of the doctors in the UK in 2004 (not necessarily all working in the NHS) had qualified somewhere else, so we could assume that most of them had been educated in another country.

Two points of information which I noticed that the figures do not provide are:

1   How many of the staff are recent migrants: Table 2 might include people who were born elsewhere and came to the UK a number of years ago, even as children. Figure 5 might include people who grew up in the UK but went somewhere else to study.

You read about race and ethnicity in Chapter 4 in *Making Social Lives* and there is further discussion in the next chapter.

2   The race and ethnicity of staff: the important point to note here is that 'migrant' status does not indicate race and ethnicity. For example, both Table 2 and Figure 5 will include people who were white British nationals born in countries which were former British colonies.

These figures raise the question of why doctors migrate. You probably have some ideas of your own, but some possible reasons I thought of are:

*   There are no jobs available for them in their own countries.
*   They can receive better pay in the UK.

- UK hospitals are better to work in than the hospitals in their own countries (e.g. because there is better equipment or there are more staff).
- They prefer to live in the UK (e.g. because it is safer than their own countries).

These factors fit with a **push–pull theory of migration**. The theory explains migration as caused by both the factors which 'push' people away from where they currently live, such as low wages and poorly equipped workplaces, and the factors which 'pull' people to other destinations, such as better hospitals to work in and more opportunities for training.

This theory assumes that migration occurs as a result of the rational economic decisions made by individuals. In other words, people decide to migrate by weighing up the economic costs and benefits of making a move, or staying, and they decide as individuals, rather than larger social units (such as, say, people of the same generation, like the British pensioners going to Spain, or larger population groups like the rural people who moved to British cities during the nineteenth century).

A second and rather different way of theorising medical migration would be to think of migrants as social actors (rather than isolated individuals) who are part of various social groups or networks. For example, some doctors move because other family members have moved – often their spouses, many of whom are also doctors. Existing connections between places can also shape migrations. Just as in the case of the women who followed friends and relations to Paisley to work in the bleachworks there in the nineteenth century, doctors too may move because their friends have moved to the UK. Professional networks can also play an important role.

A third way of theorising migration is to look at movements of people in a longer term historical context. A historical approach to migration shows us that if we go back far enough in time, most people have moved in some way. We can see how the Normans, the Danes and Vikings, the Anglo-Saxons, the Romans and, before that, the Celts were all migrants into the islands which make up the UK. Moreover, the UK as an entity only emerges well after, and in many ways because of, these migrations; it has been made up through political settlements, and by

Push–pull theory of migration
A theory which explains migration as caused both by factors which 'push' people away from where they currently live, and factors which 'pull' them to other destinations.

You read about the migrations from the countryside to UK cities in Chapter 5 of *Making Social Lives*.

people and territory coming together over time. In sum, migration is not a one-off or spectacular event, but one that, over time, may be considered quite commonplace.

A historical approach can therefore show how migrations actually make places and institutions. In the case of medical migration, we know that, since its inception, the National Health Service, the NHS, has been highly dependent on migrant labour. The UK's unified National Health Service was established in 1948. It employs a large number of staff, including doctors. The staffing structure has the shape of a pyramid with more doctors in lower-level, trainee grades (partly to cover the lesser skilled jobs and night and weekend shift working) and a smaller number nearer the top, in senior positions. The number of doctors who are educated in UK medical schools cannot cover all the service requirements, so the difference has always been met by attracting migrant doctors. These migrant doctors, it was planned, would come to the UK to obtain extra training and early career experience but then return to their own countries. Like other trainees, they were to be solely employed in the national health provision (and not in the lucrative private sector or in the more prestigious or permanent jobs within the state sector), and in doing so would help to fill labour market shortages. Their right to stay in the country has been limited in order to create the temporary working population which the NHS requires. The labour of migrant staff is therefore an essential part of this national institution.

It is not just the UK's medical service that has been made through the labour of migrants. The historical links of Commonwealth countries and their education systems to the UK health system meant that migrants from the UK also helped to produce the health services in other countries. For instance, the teachers in the first medical college in India were all from the UK. Migration to India also provided special opportunities for female health professionals from the UK. In 1885, Queen Victoria established the Dufferin Fund to enable women here to train in medicine and then go to India to provide medical care for upper-caste Indian women who supposedly would not accept care from men during childbirth. Medical training for women had only been available in the UK since 1867. The Fund supported British women's demands for the expansion of this training. Travelling to India also enabled women medical workers to gain experience in surgery, which remained a male preserve in the UK, and to run and manage small hospitals by themselves. As a result of the opportunities which India provided, at the turn of the twentieth century as many as a third of the

An Asian doctor working in the NHS in the 1960s or early 1970s; and Dr Suri and his young daughter Sandhya, along with other hospital staff, in a hospital in the late 1960s. Sandhya Suri is the director of the film 'I for India', which records the experiences of both her family in the UK and of the family they left behind in India

graduates of the Royal Free Hospital in London wanted to work there (Guha, 1998). Hence, the UK's medical history also depended on the access and experience that India gave to at least some UK-trained doctors.

Activity 8

Now look back to the three theories of migration that have been discussed. What do you think are the strengths and weaknesses of each?

Table 3 summarises my answers to this question.

Table 3   Strengths and weaknesses of the three theories of migration

Theory of migration	Strengths	Weaknesses
Push–pull	Easy to understand. Gives due importance to economic factors	Doesn't account for the role of social networks such as family or friends, as in the Paisley example. Doesn't really take account of regulatory factors such as immigration control which limit people's ability to move. People's decisions are sometimes made in less rational, more spontaneous or emotional ways than the theory suggests
Social networks	Shifts the analysis away from the focus on individual choices. Explains why a group may move at the same time	Doesn't acknowledge the influence of other factors such as better wages, better environment, etc. (These may affect the movement of the whole social group, although individuals within it will be differently affected.) Doesn't show the larger picture, over time
Historical–structural	Looks at the unequal distribution of economic and political power on a worldwide basis. Takes account of established inequalities which may take a long time to overcome	Leads to an overemphasis on inequalities. Leaves out the people whose movements don't follow these larger patterns

Summary

- Migrants can help to build institutions that are important for national identity although their contributions may be unrecognised or forgotten.
- There are different theoretical explanations that can be used to understand migration.
- However we understand migration, we need to take account of the different factors that affect it, and the ways they operate over time.

How do we know?

Theory as method

In this chapter, you have read about different theories of migration. As a student you will come across theories that are generated within academic institutions, but that is not the only place for them. We all explain, modify explanations and reject explanations as part of our daily life; when these explanations are looked at as rigorous explanatory frameworks, they can be seen as theories.

There are also good theories and less good ones. To move from speculation about all the possible explanations to a plausible theory often requires reading and reflection. It might require a clear line of relationships to be established, perhaps relating cause and effect. It always requires that we look at other competing explanations and take those into account. Some theories can be measured for their usefulness by checking out whether they have some empirical basis (in research evidence) or have been consistently supported by events. We may also use one theory to question and evaluate another. Good, workable theories will not oversimplify complex relationships. Sometimes theories might need boxing in – theories can look as if they apply to all time and the whole world, but few theories in the social sciences will claim to be universal (unlike, say, in the natural sciences): good theories will make their temporal and spatial reach clear. These are judgements that we can all make, in relation to both our own and to other people's theories.

We tend to take some theories for granted because they seem to have stood the test of time. A number of social scientists, especially philosophers, have contributed to helping us understand how theories endure or change. For instance, Thomas Kuhn maintained, in his book *The Structure of Scientific Revolution* (1962), that science progresses through a series of shifts in knowledge. He suggested that an initially simple and comprehensive theory endures with minor modifications and elaborations to accommodate problems and special cases. Eventually, so many changes accumulate that the theory becomes too complex to be workable, at which point a new theory will be proposed which is so radically different that it requires a completely new way of thinking about the world: this is called a new 'paradigm'.

You read about Michel Foucault in Chapter 7 of *Making Social Lives*.

You might find it useful to look back to Chapter 4 of *Making Social Lives*, to the discussion of 'discourse', which is another of Foucault's concepts.

Michel Foucault suggested that we make sense of our lives and the world through our shared knowledge and existing theories. He calls these 'regimes of truth'. It may be difficult to challenge or unsettle established theories because they seem true, but this does not mean that theories should never be challenged. For Foucault, the whole process of theorising is also an arrangement of power. Established knowledge supports social relationships in which people are more or less powerful. Knowledge and power are therefore closely connected. Challenging theories and our knowledge also challenges existing power relations in society.

Conclusion

In this chapter we began by looking at the importance of migration and talk about migration in everyday life, public representations and political discussions. A lot of this talk is 'polarised', presenting migration in extreme for/against, good/bad terms, so it is important for us to get behind the scenes and try to understand the issues better.

Migration clearly matters but current discussions are somewhat limited. Migrants' contributions can be counted, categorised and valued differently, and even the definition of a migrant is unclear. Furthermore, although migration is usually talked of in terms of arrival, departure and circulation also have a role to play in making the UK. Migration does not simply tell us about movement from 'here' to 'there' but is a way of connecting places economically, politically and socially. Moreover, migrants can help to build institutions that are important for national identity and the story of the nation, the topic of the next chapter.

References

Brown, G. (2006) 'The future of Britishness', speech at the Fabian Future of Britishness conference, 14 January 2006 [online], http://www.fabian-society.org.uk/events/speeches/the-future-of-britishness (Accessed 11 May 2009).

Confederation of British Industries (CBI) (2005) *Selective Admission: Making Migration Work for Britain – CBI Official Response* [online], http://www.cbi.org.uk/ndbs/PositionDoc.nsf/88676202a2a63e1e802573d300540d6f/0c956e6541639fdb802570c00052b91e/$FILE/migrationresp1005.pdf (Accessed 3 June 2009).

Glover, S., Gott, C., Loizillon, A., Portes, J., Price, R., Spencer, S., Srinivasan, V. and Willis, C. (2001) *Migration: An Economic and Social Analysis*, RDS Occasional Paper 67, London, Home Office; also available online at http://www.homeoffice.gov.uk/rds/pdfs/occ67-migration.pdf (Accessed 20 July 2007).

Gordon, W. (2005) '"What, I pray you, shall I do with the ballance?": single women's economy of migration', *International Review of Social History*, vol. 50, no. 1, pp. 53–70.

Gott, C. and Johnston, K. (2002) *The Migrant Population in the UK: Fiscal Effects*, RDS Occasional Paper 77, London, Home Office.

Green, A., MacKinnon, C. and Minns, C. (2003) 'Dominion or republic? Migrants to North America from the United Kingdom, 1870–1910', *Economic History Review*, vol. 55, no. 4, pp. 666–96.

Guha, S. (1998) 'From dais to doctors: the medicalisation of childbirth in colonial India' in Lingam, L. (ed.) *Understanding Women's Health Issues: A Reader*, New Delhi, Kali.

Hayter, T. (2000) *Open Borders: The Case Against Immigration Controls*, London, Pluto Press.

Kuhn, T.S. (1962) *The Structure of Scientific Revolution*, Chicago, IL, University of Chicago Press.

Kyriakides, C. and Virdee, S. (2003) 'Migrant labour, racism and the British National Health Service', *Ethnicity and Health*, vol. 8, no. 4, pp. 283–305.

Migration Policy Institute (MPI) (2007) *The Global Remittances Guide* [online], http://www.migrationinformation.org/DataHub/remittances.cfm (Accessed 11 May 2009).

Migration Watch UK (2006) 'The fiscal contribution of migrants', briefing paper [online], http://www.migrationwatchuk.com/Briefingpapers/economic/1_10_Fiscal_Contribution_of_Migrants_Aug_06.asp (Accessed 11 May 2009).

Office for National Statistics (ONS) (2009) *Methodology to Estimate Total International Migration Since 1991* [online], http://www.statistics.gov.uk/downloads/theme_population/

Methodology_for_Revised_International_Migration_Estimates.doc (Accessed 3 June 2009).

Raghuram, P. and Hardill, I. (1998) 'Negotiating a business: case study of an Asian woman in the Midlands', *Women's Studies International Forum*, vol. 21, no. 5, pp. 475–83.

Ruhs, M. and Anderson, B. (2008) 'The origins and functions of illegality in migrant labour markets: an analysis of migrants, employers and the state in the UK', COMPAS Working Paper 30a, University of Oxford.

Smith, A. (1776) *An Inquiry into the Nature and Causes of the Wealth of Nations*, 2 vols, London, W. Strahan and T. Cadell.

Sriskandarajah, D., Cooley, L. and Reed, H. (2005) *Paying Their Way: The Fiscal Contribution of Immigrants in the UK*, London, Institute for Public Policy Research; also available online at http://www.ippr.org/members/download.asp?f=%2Fecomm%2Ffiles%2FPaying+Their+Way%2Epdf (Accessed 11 May 2009).

Sriskandarajah, D. and Drew, C. (2006) *Brits Abroad: Mapping the Scale and Nature of British Emigration*, London, Institute for Public Policy Research.

World Bank (2003) *Global Development Finance*, Washington, DC, World Bank.

Worldmapper (2006) [online], http://www.worldmapper.org (Accessed 22 July 2009).

Chapter 5
Making national identities: Britishness in question

John Clarke

Contents

Introduction   207

1   Britishness as a national identity   209

    1.1   Discovering Britishness   210

    1.2   The consequences of identities   212

2   What makes Britishness?   215

    2.1   The place of Britishness   216

    2.2   A shared culture?   219

    2.3   People and place: a diverse society?   225

    2.4   Imagining communities   229

3   Britain's Others   231

    3.1   Nation, race, ethnicity: what sorts of identities?   231

    3.2   Other places   233

4   Making national identities   237

Conclusion   243

References   245

Introduction

Place and identity are closely connected. Where we live, or where we have come from, can form a crucial element of who we think we are – and of who other people think we are. In this chapter we will consider one specific sort of place – that of the nation – and the sorts of identities that are associated with it: national identities. Of course I could have chosen other sorts of places, such as neighbourhoods, cities or regions. Why then this focus on nations and national identities? Here are three possible reasons.

1   Nations have been an extremely important way of dividing up and organising the world. They have been one powerful way of drawing distinctions between people and between places.

2   National identities have become a way of connecting people and places: to say 'I am British', or 'I am Nigerian', or 'I am Finnish' is to place oneself in several ways – certainly in geographical terms; but also possibly in political and cultural terms. National identities place people – but not always in ways that they find comfortable. We may hold national **stereotypes** about other nations, their people, their politics, their cultures or ways of life. We might, for example, think that Americans (people from the USA) are loud, brash, wealthy and used to getting their own way; or that English people are class-obsessed, repressed and get drunk too easily and too often; or that Spanish people are passionate, exuberant and Catholic. That is to say, people attribute national characteristics to people who come from a particular place and may treat others on the basis of those stereotypes.

A stereotype
An oversimple, exaggerated description or representation of a person, group of people or place. Stereotypes are often used in comedy and political communication.

3   In a world characterised by greater mobility or the movement of people, nations and national identities may have become both less and more significant. You read about mobility and migration in the previous chapter. Some people may have become 'European citizens' or even 'citizens of the world', experiencing a changing relationship between their lives and places as they move around. But people may also feel trapped by their national identity or national origin as their movements become viewed with suspicion or they are treated as being 'out of place'. In these times of greater movement, national identity and its relationship to questions of belonging, attachment and citizenship has become an increasingly important political issue,

as governments – especially those in the global North – invest more effort into controlling who can become a national citizen.

You read about personal and social identity in Chapter 4 of *Making Social Lives*.

National identities, then, have a visible and important role in the way social life is organised. They are part of the 'everyday' stuff of identity in both personal and social terms: Who am I? Who do people think I am? They are a critical point at which such personal and social practices of identity encounter processes of organising or ordering social life. In exploring this issue of national identities, I will be analysing language data as evidence, drawing on spoken and written language from a range of different types of sources – some government documents, some political arguments, some interviews with people about national identity, some analyses presented by social scientists, and even an extract from a play. Encountering such diverse sources makes a lot of demands on the reader – because reading is not just a matter of trying to see what the authors are trying to say, it also involves thinking about how things are being said, by whom, in what form and with what intention. Put so abruptly, that may sound a little daunting, but the aim here is to build on things that you already do, both in everyday life and in studying this course.

This chapter will focus on one particular national identity, Britishness, as a case study, looking at the different attempts to construct and fix its meaning. Section 1 explores some different meanings of Britishness and Section 2 considers what has given rise to them. Section 3 looks at some of the Others (places as well as people) against which Britain and Britishness have been imagined and constructed. Section 4 moves to the more general question of how national identities are made, unmade and remade, drawing on examples from elsewhere. The final section reflects on the chapter's main arguments and approaches.

1 Britishness as a national identity

Activity 1

Stop for a minute and read the following sentence twice:

'British people share a sense of tolerance and fair play.'

There are different things that you can do with the sentence and its meaning. You can accept the assertion it makes about what British people are like or you can deny it, possibly offering evidence of attitudes and behaviour that are not tolerant. Treating this claim as a social observation, and looking for evidence that may support or contradict it, is one thing that social scientists do.

But you can also ask more about who said it, in what context and what effect they were trying to produce when they said or wrote it. Language – in speech or writing – is purposive: that is, we attempt to influence, convince, shape or persuade others in our speech and writing. But there are different types of speech and writing. Think about what difference it might make if the above sentence about British people was:

- part of a government document written for people wanting to become British citizens
- part of a speech by a politician stressing the importance and value of migration to the UK
- part of a pamphlet denouncing the excessive numbers of migrants coming to the UK
- spoken ironically as part of a joke about the experience of being picked out and harassed by immigration officers at a British airport.

You might *read* the claim differently in these different contexts. Where it is used – official document, political speech, comedy routine – can make it mean different things. It may be the same sentence but its use – and its intended effects – may be very different. Reading the extracts quoted in this chapter requires you to think about how they are written and in what context, as well as about what they say. As you encounter different sorts of extracts, I will offer some cues and clues to help you with this approach to reading.

1.1　Discovering Britishness

This chapter will concentrate mostly on Britishness as a national identity. I could have chosen any other one – Finnish, Indian, Australian, Brazilian – since they would give rise to similar social, and social science, issues about relationships between identity, people and place. I have chosen Britishness because it is at the core of this course's concerns with the contemporary UK. It has also been the source of much anxiety, uncertainty and political debate in recent years (although many other national identities share this experience).

So, let's start by reading two very different extracts about Britishness. The first comes from a government booklet written for people wanting to become British citizens (which, since November 2005, involves them taking a 'citizenship test'):

> In the United Kingdom, national identity and citizenship do not always mean the same thing. The Scottish and Welsh will usually say that they have British (or UK) citizenship, but that their nationality is Scottish or Welsh. In Northern Ireland some people say they are British, some people say that they are Irish and some people say they are both. This depends on their political and cultural allegiances. People born in England will more often say that their nationality as well as their citizenship is British … In addition to national diversity, there is a very long tradition of ethnic and religious diversity in the United Kingdom.
>
> Home Office, 2007, p. 1

The second extract forms the introduction to a study about Britishness, conducted by a social scientist (Vron Ware), that was funded by the British Council to explore how people living inside and beyond the UK thought about Britishness:

> Britain is a composite nation, a patchwork of anomalies, mistakes and inconsistencies. It has a standing army but not a football team. It has an anthem, a flag and a queen, but there is no patron saint of the United Kingdom and no founding date of an original

constitution to be celebrated with even token formality. … Its allegiances are split between opposing camps, bound equally to Europe and the United States by history and geography. The country that once boasted an empire is now struggling to find a new role for itself in a vastly unequal global order that it once helped to shape. Welcome to modern Britain.

Ware, 2007, pp. 1–2

The two quotations establish a series of puzzles about national identity that we shall explore in this chapter. Some of these concern the place – the United Kingdom, Britain, the constituent nations of England, Scotland, Wales and Northern Ireland. Others concern its (changing) place in the world. Still others centre on identifications – who do people think they are? Some involve questions of inclusion – who gets to be British (or UK citizens) and under what conditions? Finally, there are matters of culture – the institutions, rituals and practices (flags, anthems, sporting teams) – in which the nation and its identity are reflected.

The Union: national flags and the Union Flag (*Note:* the cross of St Patrick, a red saltire, is also part of the composite Union Flag, but the Welsh flag is not)

Although these extracts point to some common issues, they do so in very different ways. To some extent, they differ in perspective: the Home Office document appears to announce some complicated facts about how UK or British citizenship may be separated from national identity. The extract concludes with an observation about national, ethnic and religious diversity in the UK (not unlike the sentence about Britishness and tolerance in Activity 1 above). The extract from Ware makes rather more of diversity – emphasising inconsistency, anomaly and contradiction – treating Britain as a place whose parts do not fit together easily, and whose history is centred on getting and losing an empire. But these pieces also differ in other ways. The first is a government document – and such documents usually attempt to be authoritative, telling people things that governments wish them to know. They also try to persuade us to act on such authoritative statements. Think about what you as a reader are supposed to do with the information contained in that extract.

In contrast, Ware's extract is from a book written by an individual social scientist. It cannot hope to be authoritative in the manner of a government document. Instead, it must be engaging and persuasive – this opening paragraph tries to establish the ground for the rest of the book in a way that is both interesting and enabling. The emphasis on anomalies and contradictions (an anthem but no patron saint) establishes a puzzle that the author and the reader will explore together in what follows. What are you as a reader supposed to think and do with the analysis being offered in that extract?

■   Before we go any further, you might also want to consider your relationship to Britishness. Is it an identity that means anything to you? Do you identify yourself as British – or with some other national identity? How does the term British relate to other terms that you might use to identify yourself?

1.2 The consequences of identities

Identity as a social sciences concept is discussed in Chapters 4, 5 and 6 of *Making Social Lives*.

The making of census categories is discussed in Chapter 9 of *Making Social Lives*.

Identity is a central concept in the social sciences. National identities are only one among the many identities that people might hold. They might be deeply attached to one particular identity, or they might move fluidly between several depending on the context – and with whom they are interacting. In some contexts, such as filling in official forms or dealing with immigration control, the identity categories are limited – and often very constraining (think about the census categories). Typically I get to identify myself as British (nationality), white (race/ethnicity), male (gender), single (marital status). These certainly describe some things about me – and they are *consequential* things with social, political and policy implications. Being identified as British has consequences at immigration control and for claiming citizenship entitlements (access to welfare benefits, health care, etc.). Being seen as white (in the UK and Europe) means I am less subject to various forms of official scrutiny – from immigration control to stop-and-search processes of policing. I am less likely to be asked to prove my identity – or my entitlements. Being male means I benefit from certain social, economic and cultural norms – for example, employment advantages in job selection, promotion and rewards. The gender gap between men and women's earnings in the UK stands at around 17.1 per cent on average hourly earnings or 21 per cent on average weekly earnings (Office for National Statistics, 2009; Equalities Review, 2007). Being identified as single has less immediate consequences, though it does create legal problems about passing benefits and property to my partner that would not exist if we were a married couple or registered in a civil partnership. But being single has also been a source of disappointment to my extended family – in which all of my twenty plus cousins are, or have been, married.

Such identities are, then, consequential: they matter in social life in a range of ways. But I am not sure that they tell you much about who I think I am. When I tick the 'British' box on a form, does it tell you anything about my ambivalent feelings about Britishness? In the following quotation, Vron Ware reports an interview with Pratap – a film-maker born and brought up in East London – about Britishness:

'What do you say when people ask where you are from?' I asked on the understanding that this was a question that Pratap faced everywhere he went, particularly outside the UK.

'It depends who they are. I usually say I'm a Londoner. If I need to, I explain that my grandparents are of Indian origin – they grew up in East Africa and then took different directions. On my mother's side my grandmother moved the whole family back to Delhi and was involved in the New Delhi Congress and the independence movement and all that. My dad grew up in Zanzibar and got his degree at Durham University.' …

'In my case, for my generation of progressive people, it seemed really important to say that we were British and part of the British landscape. We were involved in a project of reinscribing, reinventing Britishness to make it reflect the realities as a place that is more open, more plural. Why should Britishness be hijacked by patriots, jingoists?' ...

'I don't think I could take a citizenship test now, though,' Pratap continued ...' Apparently you have to swear allegiance to the royal family. I couldn't do it. I don't agree with the hereditary principle and don't see why it has to be defined as Britishness.'

(Ware, 2007, pp. 30–2)

Pratap's comments highlight a number of important issues about Britishness and how it has been made and remade through claims about what it means to be British and who can be British. The extract also points to two more general issues about identity. The first is that people have multiple identities and they are invoked in different contexts – as Pratap puts it, 'it depends who's asking'. The second is that such identities are the subject of more or less conscious reflection on the part of the people who hold them. Pratap (like me and many others) is cautious and ambivalent about identifying himself as British, because it has many meanings that feel troubling or uncomfortable (from identification with the monarchy to the ways in which Britishness is claimed by patriots and jingoists). Identities and the way people relate to them are not simple matters of 'having an identity', but involve negotiations with themselves and with different groups of significant others (from officials to networks of friends to political opponents and more) about who they are.

Summary

- Like other identity categories, national identities have consequences for the organisation of social life, including for what people can and can't do.
- Statements about national identity are often intended to persuade people to think or act in a certain way.
- Many people have both positive and negative feelings about having a British identity. This ambivalence results from the many possible meanings of this identity.

2 What makes Britishness?

Activity 2

What do you think Britishness means?

Make a note of what you think Britishness refers to.

As I thought about this question I came up with several possibilities:

- Is it a matter of place – Britishness being associated with the British Isles?

- Is it a matter of culture – shared values, ideas or ways of life (from William Shakespeare to the Great British Breakfast)?

- Is it a matter of history – for example, of politics and institutions (the Monarchy, Parliament, the British Broadcasting Corporation)?

- Is it a question of race or ethnicity, involving images of the British people?

In this section, I will explore how Britishness has been constructed through several of these ideas, starting with ideas about the relationship between people and place. This is a central issue for thinking about nations and national identities, because nations are spatial or geographical entities with (more or less) clearly defined borders that distinguish them from other nations. This enclosed space is sometimes referred to as a **territory**, identifying the way nations combine a place and a political authority that claims to control that space. The political authority is usually a state. In the case of nations, social scientists usually refer to nation states, although there have been other types of states, such as city states. The idea of a nation refers to both a territory and the people associated with it – but, as you have already seen, it is not quite so simple to identify the associations between the UK, its constituent nations and Britishness.

National territory
The geographical area which belongs to a nation. It usually has clearly defined borders that separate it from other national territories.

2.1   The place of Britishness

Britishness clearly refers to a place – Britain. This place is a geographically distinctive one (it is not France or Norway or China). Like most nations, it is seen as a *special* place, an idea that is conjured in the much quoted Shakespearean imagery of 'this scepter'd isle':

Alec Guinness as Richard II in the 1947 production at the Old Vic theatre, London

> This royal throne of kings, this scepter'd isle,
> This earth of majesty, this seat of Mars,
> This other Eden, demi-paradise,
> This fortress built by Nature for herself
> Against infection and the hand of war,

This happy breed of men, this little world,
This precious stone set in the silver sea,
Which serves it in the office of a wall
Or as a moat defensive to a house,
Against the envy of less happier lands,
This blessed plot, this earth, this realm, this England

Richard II, Act 2, Scene 1

Shakespeare provided potent imagery for thinking about Britain and Britishness, emphasising both the quality of the land and its natural defences against war and invasion. However, the last line poses a familiar geographical and political problem. The place – the isle, even – that Shakespeare refers to is not Britain, but England. He is writing before the Act of Union that formally joined Scotland and England. This is an 'isle' that does not include Scotland, against which England had rarely been inviolable. Wars, trading and border raids formed a long history of encounters. But it is also an isle in which Wales has no independent identity, having been subdued and made into a principality (embodied in the role of the Prince of Wales) long before Shakespeare wrote the play. Ireland, meanwhile, was separate – both geographically and politically. Since Shakespeare wrote *Richard II* in 1597, much has changed, but the place of Britishness has continued to be elusive. Where is included in Britain? The Home Office guide to citizenship tries to explain this geographical and political problem:

There is some confusion about the correct meanings and use of the terms 'United Kingdom', 'British Isles', 'Britain' and 'British'. The United Kingdom consists today of four countries: England, Scotland, Wales and Northern Ireland (the rest of Ireland is an independent country). These four countries came together at different times to form a union called the United Kingdom of Great Britain and Northern Ireland, which is the official name of the country. The name 'Britain' or 'Great Britain' only refers to England, Scotland and Wales, not to Northern Ireland. The adjective 'British', however, usually refers to everyone in the UK, including Northern Ireland. There are also several islands which are closely linked to the United Kingdom but do not form part of it: the Channel Islands and the Isle of Man. These have kept their own institutions of government and are called 'Crown Territories'.

(Home Office, 2007, p. 1)

A United Kingdom?

The unity of the United Kingdom has often appeared strained, as Welsh, Scottish and Irish nationalists have challenged their enrolment into this political union. Indeed, they think that other national identities have been suppressed in the union. They also have a view of the histories of unification that differs from the rather bland statement by the Home Office that 'these four countries came together at different times to form a union'. Instead, they point to more bloody histories of forcible integration and union – from Edward II's suppression of Owain Glyndwr/Owen Glendower's Welsh forces at the beginning of the fifteenth century to the partition of Ireland in 1921–22 following struggles for independence (Williams, 1985; Hennessy, 1998). As I write the United Kingdom involves different forms of government and decision-making bodies that are both alongside, and subordinate to, the United Kingdom Parliament: a power-sharing assembly in the six counties of Northern Ireland, also linked to cross-border arrangements with the government of Eire; a National Assembly in Wales; and a Scottish Parliament.

This unsettled political geography gives rise to problems about where Britain is, and who counts as British. For many people in the other nations of the UK, being British is really about the claimed superiority of England and the English (Kumar, 2001). But the relationship between place and national identity raises other questions:

- Do you have to live in a place to hold its national identity? What about British people living elsewhere – either in colonial trade or government during Empire, or as retired expatriate communities (e.g. in Spain)?

- How long do you have to have lived in a place before you can claim a national identity? Remember that taking a national identity may not be the same as official citizenship.

- How many national identities might a person feel attached to? Is having multiple identities the same as holding multiple passports?

You read about some examples in Chapter 4 of this book.

2.2   A shared culture?

Culture has been an important and difficult concept in discussions of national identities; and 'culture' is a frequently used term. People talk readily about British, French or Japanese culture, and the necessity of valuing it or preserving it. But it is also an elusive term with at least two different sorts of meaning. One connects it with what has been called 'high culture' – the artistic or aesthetic cultural products that are put together to form a national culture: music, literature, theatre, art, and so on. The second meaning involves treating culture as everyday life – the habits, practices and values of a 'way of life' that have been the focus of anthropological studies in many places. For the first meaning, we have seen that Shakespeare is one of the preferred reference points for this sort of view, but other elements of literature and art are associated in the identification of 'British culture': classical music (Elgar, Parry, Vaughan Williams); novels (Dickens, Austen, Hardy, the Brontë sisters); painting (Constable, Turner), and so on.

This view of British culture involves the construction of what the cultural theorist and historian Raymond Williams (1958) described as a *selective tradition*, celebrating some works and excluding others. Different principles guide the selection and constant remaking of such traditions – some are driven by principles of social location (class values or gender,

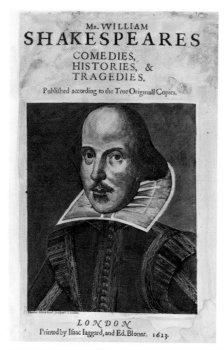

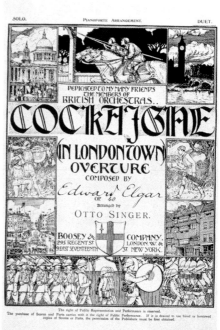

British culture?

for example); sometimes they are shaped by issues of region or
geography (the dominance of English over Scottish, Welsh or Irish – or
colonial – literary or artistic products). For this chapter, the important
point about such cultural products is that they come to symbolise or

stand for 'Britishness'. They provide an *apparently shared* set of reference points, common to all British people. But just like the political geography discussed in Section 2.1, such ideas of British culture can be both a source of unity and a point of trouble, since they are contested in a number of ways.

The high culture view of British culture has been regularly attacked in terms of what is excluded. As noted above, the dominance of English writers, musicians and artists has led to challenges about its geographical and linguistic biases in relation to the other places within the United Kingdom, but also other places tied to Britishness through the legacies of Empire. Is there any reason why literature written in English, but created in India, Africa, Australasia or the Caribbean, should be separate from British culture? Equally, the relationship between 'high culture' and 'popular culture' is also the focus of intense argument – do popular or mass media forms of culture represent Britishness?

Culture is also used to refer to the values, attitudes and habits of behaviour that members of a society share. Sometimes these are ways of acting, sometimes they can be detected in shared rituals or beliefs, and sometimes they are more formally expressed as political, ethical or moral codes about how people (should) live in this society. Here are a couple of statements about Britishness that treat it in terms of common values and practices:

> Britishness is defined not on ethnic or exclusive grounds – but through our shared values, our history of tolerance, of openness and internationalism, our commitment to democracy and liberty, to civic duty and the public space. These values, embodied in our great institutions – such as the NHS, the BBC, The Open University – tell a national story that is open to all citizens.
>
> (Blunkett, 2005, p. 4)

> In spite of its imperial echo, Britishness emerges as a brilliantly coherent civic identity, easily adopted by people of all backgrounds, and laden with unifying value. It is malleable and modern, it is capacious and inclusive. But it is not formless. Critically there is

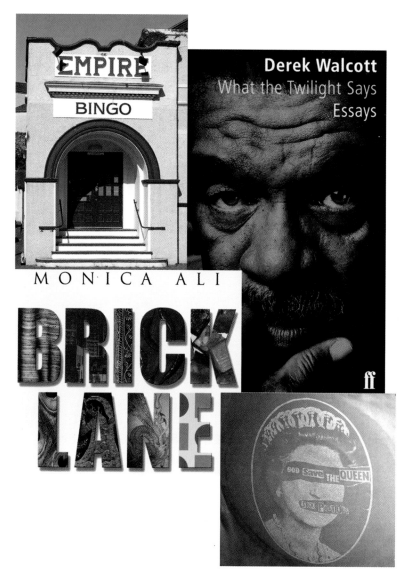

A different British culture?

more to Britishness than just symbols and flags; though these are important, as they stand for underlying values.

In my view the heart of Britishness ... lies in a way of living together characterised by tolerance, egalitarianism, respect for the dignity of the individual and a powerful tradition of dissent. Attempts to create lists of symbols and objects that encapsulate Britishness are wide of the mark; efforts to identify people whose behaviour defines Britishness come closer, because our national identity is essentially about the way we treat each other. In a phrase: British is as British does. It is about what people do, not who they are.

Our national reputation for politeness and reserve is still warranted, even in these days of loutishness in town centres and celebrity vulgarity. But Britishness is not just about etiquette; the rules of behaviour rest on some deeper values. The habits we associate with Britishness are in a complete sense merely the expression of those deeper values of tolerance, egalitarianism and so forth. In a diverse society, the shared values are the fundamental glue that holds us together; and the way we behave towards each other is the outward manifestation of our values.

(Phillips, 2007, p. 42)

What is going on in these two statements? Both are trying to define a common Britishness in terms of shared values. David Blunkett (writing when he was UK Home Secretary) uses public institutions – the NHS, the BBC and the Open University – to symbolise the values of openness, liberty and tolerance. In some respects these overlap with the values singled out by Trevor Phillips (then Chairman of the Commission for Racial Equality) in the second extract: tolerance, egalitarianism, respect for the individual and a tradition of dissent. But Phillips argues that these are symbolised in the ways in which people *behave towards one another*, rather than in institutions.

Both of these views can, of course, be challenged by pointing to other aspects of British life and the experiences of some citizens and non-citizens that contradict these claims about British values. Egalitarianism sits uncomfortably alongside the evidence of deepening inequalities of income and wealth in the UK since the 1980s (Equalities Review, 2007). Tolerance can be set alongside evidence of growing numbers of 'hate crimes' directed against different sorts of minorities (gays and lesbians, ethnic minorities) or evidence of persistent discrimination in the labour market (against women, ethnic minorities, disabled people, and so on). New laws have limited the expression of dissent and offered controls on behaviours and groups seen as anti-social (Burney, 2005). Such laws may be justified in the name of security, civic conduct and social order, but they might also indicate some conflicting or contradictory values in 'British culture'.

The extracts from Blunkett and Phillips were written in a particular context. These are not just reflections on what makes Britishness. Rather they are urgent and anxious political interventions that try to shape a debate about Britishness in the context of what Phillips identifies as 'a diverse society'.

Activity 3

Remember what I said in Section 1 about how to read texts (when comparing the Home Office and Vron Ware extracts). Here, you might wish to reread the two extracts above and think about these questions:

- What question is each of them is trying to answer (rather than just what their answer is)?

- Against what are they (implicitly or explicitly) arguing?

Chapters 7 and 8 of *Making Social Lives* talked about the making of social order.

Both Blunkett and Phillips address the question of what Britishness means. Their answers frame this question in terms of shared values and ways of behaving (a certain sort of social order that guides the way people behave towards one another). Both of them insist on the importance of Britishness being open to 'people of all backgrounds' or 'all citizens', and not being constructed on 'ethnic or exclusive grounds' which exclude some categories of people. This is a reminder about why Britishness was being politically debated in the early twenty-first century. Arguments about Britishness and British citizenship were shaped by controversies about migration, about national security and about social diversity. Both Blunkett and Phillips were arguing against a number of positions: some that argued for a more exclusive definition of Britishness (and of who could be British citizens); some that argued, as you saw in the previous chapter, for a harsher regime of immigration control – whether from the former Empire or from an enlarged Europe; and others that argued for a less repressive approach to both migration and citizenship and for a more expansive or cosmopolitan view of Britishness.

Both Blunkett and Phillips make a case for mutual tolerance in a diverse society – with a view of tolerance as a distinctive British virtue and value that can (and should) inform how people conduct themselves. Both position their arguments in terms of 'diversity', a critical term for thinking about Britain and other contemporary societies (Harzig et al.,

2003; Newman and Clarke, 2009). (Note that I have placed 'diversity' inside quotation marks here because, like many social scientists, I use such quotation marks to emphasise the constructed and symbolic value of a particular word or phrase.)

2.3   People and place: a diverse society?

The extracts from Blunkett and Phillips are contributions to a much larger political debate about national identity in the twenty-first century. One of the crucial points of debate has been the relationship between national identity and **diversity**, or difference. Various individuals, parties and movements have claimed that diversity may have gone 'too far', undermining national identity and the forms of social **solidarity** that 'keep us together'. This view of diversity is in conflict with arguments that Britain has become a multi-ethnic and multicultural society and must develop a more multiple and complex national identity. In the following two lengthy extracts, you can see some of these arguments about 'diversity' and its implications for ideas about Britishness. The first comes from an essay by David Goodhart, the editor of *Prospect*, a magazine devoted to political and cultural questions. Here Goodhart suggests that 'progressives' must choose between the values of diversity and solidarity:

Diversity
This term refers to multiple forms of social difference. For example, it is used in discussions of racial, ethnic and cultural differences as well as gender, sexuality and class differences. It is sometimes linked to arguments about social divisions and inequalities.

Solidarity
The connectedness of different social groups, often involving a sense of mutual support and shared needs or aspirations, in contrast to a situation in which there are major social divisions.

> Britain in the 1950s was a country stratified by class and region. But in most of its cities, suburbs, towns and villages there was a good chance of predicting the attitudes, even the behaviour, of the people living in your immediate neighbourhood.
>
> In many parts of Britain today that is no longer true … To some people this is a cause of regret and disorientation – a change which they associate with the growing incivility of modern urban life. To others it is a sign of the inevitable, and welcome, march of modernity. After three centuries of homogenisation through industrialisation, urbanisation, nation-building and war, the British have become freer and more varied. Fifty years of peace, wealth and mobility have allowed a greater diversity in lifestyles and values. To this 'value diversity' has been added ethnic diversity through two big waves of immigration: first the mainly commonwealth immigration from the West Indies and Asia in the 1950s and 1960s, followed by asylum-driven migrants from Europe, Africa and the greater middle east in the late 1990s.

The diversity, individualism and mobility that characterise developed economies – especially in the era of globalisation – mean that more of our lives is spent among strangers. Ever since the invention of agriculture 10,000 years ago, humans have been used to dealing with people from beyond their own extended kin groups. The difference now in a developed country like Britain is that we not only live among stranger citizens but we must share with them. We share public services and parts of our income in the welfare state, we share public spaces in towns and cities where we are squashed together on buses, trains and tubes, and we share in a democratic conversation – filtered by the media – about the collective choices we wish to make. All such acts of sharing are more smoothly and generously negotiated if we can take for granted a limited set of common values and assumptions. But as Britain becomes more diverse that common culture is being eroded.

And therein lies one of the central dilemmas of political life in developed societies: sharing and solidarity can conflict with diversity. This is an especially acute dilemma for progressives who want plenty of both solidarity – high social cohesion and generous welfare paid out of a progressive tax system – and diversity – equal respect for a wide range of peoples, values and ways of life.

Goodhart, 2004, p. 1

The second extract comes from the report of a commission established by the Runnymede Trust to comment on the future of Britain as a multi-ethnic society. In this extract, the chair of that Commission on the Future of Multi-Ethnic Britain, Bhikhu Parekh (also a sociologist) sets out a different view of the choices facing British society:

England, Scotland and Wales are at a turning point in their history. They could become narrow and inward-looking, with rifts between themselves and among their regions and communities, or they could develop as a community of citizens and communities. Britain as a whole could be such a community, and also each region, city, town and neighbourhood within it. Building and sustaining a community of citizens and communities will involve:

- rethinking the national story and national identity
- understanding that all identities are in a process of transition
- developing a balance between cohesion, difference and equality
- addressing and eliminating all forms of racism
- reducing material inequalities
- building a human rights culture

... Racism is a subtle and complex phenomenon. It may be based on colour and physical features or on culture, nationality and way of life; it may affirm equality of human worth but implicitly deny this by insisting on the superiority of a particular culture; it may admit equality up to a point but impose a glass ceiling higher up. Whatever its subtle disguises and forms, it is deeply divisive, intolerant of differences, a source of much human suffering, and inimical to the common sense of belonging lying at the basis of every stable civilisation. It can have no place in a decent society.

... We believe that it is both possible and vitally necessary to create a society in which all citizens and communities feel valued, enjoy equal opportunities to develop their respective talents, lead fulfilling lives, accept their fair share of collective responsibility, and help create a collective life in which the spirit of civic goodwill, shared identity and common sense of belonging goes hand in hand with love of diversity. Having sketched our vision of a relaxed and self-confident multicultural Britain with which all people can identify, we analyse the obstacles standing in its way and propose policies most likely to overcome them. The obstacles include racial discrimination, racial disadvantage, a racially oriented moral and political culture, an inadequate philosophy of government, a lack of carefully thought-out and properly integrated administrative structures at various levels of government, and a lack of political will. The policies we propose address each of these. They require not only appropriate legislative, administrative and other measures, but also a radical shift in the manner in which British identity and the relations between different groups of citizens are generally defined.

Parekh, 2000, p. 1

Activity 4

Now read these two extracts again. As you do so, try to suspend for a moment your own views and whether you agree or disagree with the points being made. Instead, think about the following questions:

1   How is diversity being understood?

2   What sorts of problems do the two pieces identify – and what are their causes?

3   What does the word 'we' do in each of the pieces?

Here are some of my thoughts about these questions. First, in Goodhart, *the idea of diversity* seems to refer to two different (if related) things. First, there is what he calls 'value diversity'. This seems to refer to cultural diversity in terms of different values or possibly lifestyle choices. Can you think of examples of what Goodhart might mean by this? But the second – and perhaps more significant – meaning of diversity involves 'ethnic diversity', seen as the result of different phases of migration. It is 'ethnic diversity' that produces what Goodhart calls 'stranger citizens' with whom 'we must share'. (I will come back to the question of 'we' in Section 2.4 below.) In contrast, the Parekh quotation implies ethnic diversity but in the context of talking about the valuing of 'all citizens and communities' through a shared 'love of diversity'. This turns diversity from an apparently descriptive term – Britain is a diverse society – into a political value: the 'love of diversity'. In Section 3, I will look in a little more detail about the idea of ethnic difference.

Second, the extract from Goodhart *identifies a problem* about whether social solidarity can be maintained in the face of increasing diversity (primarily ethnic diversity). Goodhart pulls diversity (as ethnic diversity) out of a set of other social changes that might also undermine social solidarity. For example, he talks of greater individualism and mobility as other social changes taking place across the same period as increased migration. But his main focus is on the impact of increased ethnic diversity on the prospects for solidarity. In contrast, Parekh identifies two linked problems – the risk of social fragmentation and conflict and the danger of racism. While recognising that citizens and communities may be divided in many ways, the Commission's concern with multi-ethnic Britain puts ethnic differences in the foreground. It emphasises the way that racism may create or intensify differences between social groups (racism refers to treating groups as if they were different races). It is important to note that for Parekh (and many others) this does not mean there are races (in terms of empirical reliable distinctions of biology, skin colour or other features). Rather, racism is an ideology – a relatively systematic way of thinking – that treats people *as if* they belong to races. It informs social and political action – shaping practices and policies that deal with people differently on the basis of attributed racial identities. You might think, for example, of the apartheid system that ruled in South Africa for most of the twentieth century and distinguished between three different 'racial' categories: Whites, Blacks and Coloureds.

2.4   Imagining communities

In the final part of this section, I want to comment on how the two extracts use the word '*we*'. This may seem a trivial point – giving attention to such a small and commonplace word. But in the construction of national identities, it is often the most mundane or everyday habits and practices that play a vital role. For example, the anthropologist Benedict Anderson (1983) has talked about nations as **'imagined communities'**, that have to be constructed through a variety of symbolic forms (from marking borders to flags, from everyday ceremonies to the little linguistic ways in which a common identity is assumed). Similarly, Michael Billig, a social psychologist, has written about what he calls 'banal nationalism' – the small everyday practices in which the imagined community of the nation is both assumed and reinforced. One example of this is the focus of weather forecasts on the national territory, with an appropriate map (Billig, 1995).

Imagined communities Anderson's view is that nations have to be constructed, involving an imagined set of connections or affinities between the members of the nation, and the invention of a shared history that links them. That is, nations are neither permanent nor eternal.

Here, we can see that the word 'we' performs a different role in the two extracts. In the Parekh extract it refers specifically to the named group of people who were members of the Runnymede Trust's Commission on the Future of Multi-Ethnic Britain. It is a 'we' who can be identified as the authors of a report – like an Open University course team, perhaps. In contrast, Goodhart (in a journalistic essay) uses 'we' to refer to the British people, or, more precisely, *to refer to an idea of the British people*. Perhaps this is most clear in the following sentence: '*The difference now in a developed country like Britain is that we not only live among stranger citizens but we must share with them.*' Goodhart makes a clear distinction between 'we' and 'them', the 'stranger citizens'. This is an important distinction – 'we' have a shared history and culture; 'they' are different.

'We' are obliged to share with 'them' (and are apparently not very happy about it). As you were reading the extract, who did you think you were? Were you part of the 'we', or part of the 'them'? In the construction of national identities (not just Britishness), that little word 'we' performs a central role, constructing an imagined unity against those who are not 'us'. Michael Billig has written about how the little words of nationalism ('we', 'us', 'our' and the opposites 'they', 'them', 'their') are central to the construction of national identities: 'National histories tell of a people passing through time – "our" people, with "our" ways of life, and "our" culture. Stereotypes of character and temperament can be mobilized to tell the tale of "our" uniqueness and "our" common fate' (1995, p. 71).

If nothing else, I hope that this comparison of Parekh and Goodhart's uses of the word 'we' alerts you to its significance. The word 'we' is constantly involved in the construction of imagined communities – whether these are local communities, communities of shared identities or nations as communities. It implies a 'we' that share something in common and makes implicit or explicit distinctions between 'we' (who are members of this community) and 'they' (who are not members; who do not share what we have in common). This is not an argument that such imagined communities are false, or that the use of 'we' should be avoided. Rather, as social scientists, we have an obligation to use the word carefully and to examine what sort of imagined community is being constructed when it is used:

- Who is being included or excluded?
- What is the organising principle for the distinction?
- What are 'we' supposed to have in common?

Summary

- The meaning of Britishness has changed over time and continues to give rise to confusion and debate.
- British culture can be defined selectively, in terms of certain kinds of art, music and literature, or more inclusively, as a way of life and shared values and behaviours.
- The diversity of modern British society is a much debated issue, raising questions about who 'we' are and how 'we' might live together.

3   Britain's Others

In this section I will look at an alternative way of constructing Britishness. Previously I explored different ideas of the unifying principles that made up Britishness, here I consider ways in which Britishness is defined relationally – that is, through its relationships with other people and other places. Such relationships have two aspects: first, they are used to define what Britishness is not; and second, the relations with these others have played a part in shaping Britishness. This double aspect produces feelings of **ambivalence** about these other places and people. In Section 3.1 I look at the identification of Others involved in the construction of racial and ethnic identities. In Section 3.2, I look at how Britain's identity has been defined partly in relation to the imagined character of three Other places, America, Europe and Empire.

You read about 'Othering' in Chapter 4 of *Making Social Lives*.

Ambivalence
A state of uncertainty created by the co-existence of conflicting feelings, orientations and desires. In psychology, it is often used to describe the combination of positive and negative feelings towards something or someone.

3.1   Nation, race, ethnicity: what sorts of identities?

As I noted in Section 2, ideas of nation, race and ethnicity are often blurred together in discussions of national identities. Although being British might imply sharing a place of residence (Britain or the UK), it has sometimes been treated as a racial category: being British means being part of the 'British race' or being white/Caucasian. At other times, it has been treated as an ethnic identity. This blurring can be found in everyday categories, in official documents and in the social sciences. Ideas of race – what some scholars have called 'racial thinking' – have a long history, but are powerfully associated with the period of European colonialism when European nations sought to rule other parts of the world (Gilroy, 2001). Racial thinking provided a way of mapping the world that legitimated European power and rule. White people were able to dominate other groups and other places because, it was claimed, they were the superior race. Other races (and there were extensive arguments among racial thinkers about exactly how many races there were) were at a lower level of development. Colonial rule was thus justified either as a right of superiority or as the responsibility of the superior race to look after, civilise or develop the more 'backward' groups.

Although racial thinking centred on biological questions – body type, colour of skin, and so on – it always constructed connections between *race, place and culture*. So, dominant racial groups lived in the most economically and socially advanced places – the nations of Europe – and possessed the most sophisticated cultures. Other cultures were primitive, tribal or traditional. All these terms marked the differences between the sophisticated and cultured white race and their backward Others. These imagined connections between racial types, places and cultures are important because they make possible the blurring of national, racial and ethnic identities.

In the social sciences, ideas of ethnicity were developed as a way of trying to escape from the crude **biological reductionism** of racial thinking. In 1950, the United Nations issued a statement on 'The race question' in which leading social scientists argued for the replacement of racial categories by ideas of ethnic identity (UNESCO, 1950). They argued that questions of cultural differences – and how people *perceived* themselves to be associated – were more significant than propositions about racial types. This view of ethnicity was developed from ideas of the German sociologist Max Weber (1978 [1922]) who argued that ethnic groups were

> those human groups that entertain a subjective belief in their common descent because of similarities of physical type or of customs or both, or because of memories of colonization and migration; this belief must be important for group formation; furthermore it does not matter whether an objective blood relationship exists.

(Weber, 1978 [1922], p. 389)

Biological reductionism
Explanations which are based on the body or physical characteristics. Reductionist accounts attempt to explain a complicated situation or phenomenon as resulting from a single cause.

You might see some similarities here to the imagined family origins discussed in Chapter 4 of *Making Social Lives*.

Remember the discussion of census categories in Chapter 9 of *Making Social Lives*.

You will see that Weber's stress here is on a shared subjective belief: that is, ethnicity is about who people think they are. He distinguishes this from objective or observable criteria, whether these are biological or cultural characteristics. He allows for a wide range of features that might provide the foundation for such beliefs – similarities of physical type, customs, common experiences or memories, to which we might add religious beliefs and practices. But it is the *shared belief* in 'common descent' that makes ethnicity a social category, and one that might be acted on. In this sense, ethnic groups have to define themselves – and how they define themselves may change over time, or in different social contexts. For example, people in the Indian diaspora in the UK may identify themselves as Indians, Asians, Hindus, Sikhs, Muslims, British, British-Indian and using many more terms, including regional rather than national identifications: Gujarati, Punjabi, and so on. Turning such fluid and potentially contested identifications into apparently solid categories for census and other governmental purposes has some problems (and indeed Weber warned that the whole idea of different ethnicities was so complex and so vague that it might be better to abandon it).

In these processes we can see that place (especially place of origin) and ethnicity are often entangled. Coming from India may make you Indian (as a place of origin) but it may not give you 'Indian ethnicity' (think about all those children of 'British' parents who were born and brought up in India during the colonial period). There are always attempts to fix these shifting and unstable definitions – because governments, social groups and political parties like to 'know who we (and they) are'. Identities – ethnic, cultural or national – are central features of how social life is organised, and that creates political, administrative and social incentives to clarify and solidify them: to make them real and to make them count.

You read about some of the complexities of racial and ethnic identities in Chapter 4 of *Making Social Lives*.

3.2 Other places

Although Britain exists in many relations to other places, there are three that have a particular significance for the construction of the national identity – these are America, Europe and Empire (if you look back at the first extract by Vron Ware, in Section 1.1, you will see that all three terms are there too). You will see that these names refer both to places (though not very precisely – for example, people often refer to America when they specifically mean the United States of America) and to ideas about these places and the people who inhabit them. In the rest of this section, I will put these three words – Empire, Europe and America – inside quotation marks. This is a way of trying to mark the *imagined* character of these places: they are possibly more important as sets of ideas than as identifiable geographical places with which the UK has had specific economic, political and cultural connections. This style of marking the imagined or constructed character of things by using quotation marks can be very irritating for readers – but it may be less irritating in this context than constantly encountering phrases such as 'what people tend to imagine as America' or 'how Europe is conventionally constructed'.

Activity 5

Take a few moments and make a note of what you think are the relationships between:

'Europe'

'Empire'

'America'

and Britishness.

Each of these relationships has involved material flows of objects and subjects, and of power and influence. Each has contributed to some of the key conditions of Britishness: from the colonial wealth (and power) of 'Empire', through 'Europe' as a troubled history of alliances and enmities, to a subordinate, if not subservient, relationship to US global power.

These three relationships have also shaped Britishness in other ways. 'Europe' has been a site of persistent British anxiety, and the focus of shifting alliances and conflicts with other European nations, not least over securing imperial domination during the nineteenth and twentieth centuries. More recently, there has been the stress of remaking 'Europe' as an economic and political space – the European Union (EU) – that links national economies into a regional block with the aim of improving Europe's competitiveness in a global economy. Britain officially joined the EU in 1973 (when it was the European Economic Community or EEC) but much argument still goes on around its possible loss of political authority and cultural distinctiveness through becoming part of 'Europe'. You might want to note here that 'Europe' refers both to a geographical space (whose southern and eastern boundaries are a little imprecise – where does Europe end?) and to the political institutions of the EU. The EU itself has changed size and shape often since its creation – and has a variety of relationships with other nations beyond the current membership (e.g. with what are called 'accession states' who will become members, or with the 'good neighbours' who border the EU).

How does 'Europe' shape Britishness? First, there is a strong sense of antagonism – the British are often imagined as being 'at war' with 'Europe' in some form or another, whether fighting off the Spanish Armada or wrestling with the 'Brussels bureaucracy' of the EU. Second, there is a sense of distinctiveness — Britain stands at a distance (both geographical and cultural) from continental 'Europe'. Such a sense of distinctiveness is sometimes associated with a sense of superiority. Third, there are also some desires to be *more* European. These may range from acquiring second homes in France or Italy (or retiring to Spain); through admiring cultural patterns and practices (better adjusted alcohol consumption; 'cafe society' in towns and cities); to political desires (e.g. for the well-funded and universalist welfare states of Scandinavian countries). I want to suggest that these three elements — antagonism, distinction and desire — produce a certain difficult *ambivalence* towards 'Europe' that shapes what being British means: an ambivalence captured in the idea that the UK is 'in, but not of, Europe'.

The relationship between Britishness and 'Empire' might also be seen in terms of ambivalence. There is often a sense of nostalgia or loss in discussions of 'Empire': what Paul Gilroy (2005), a cultural studies scholar, has described as 'postcolonial melancholia'. Imperial rule undoubtedly fuelled Britain's rise to economic power between the eighteenth and twentieth centuries. It certainly provided a whole vocabulary of cultural superiority (for example, colonists justified their activities using phrases such as the 'civilising mission', 'the white man's burden', and talked about the dangers of 'going native'). Such pride in 'Empire' has always existed in tension with a sense of doubt about the political and moral consequences of imperialism, most notably — though not only — in terms of the slave trade.

'Empire' continues to be represented as a series of other places and other people. In this image, the other people should have remained in those other places — rather than coming to the UK. Popular and political discourse around African, Indian and Caribbean migrants in the UK has been haunted by this sense that 'everyone has their place', so that migrants (and subsequent generations of the children of migrants) should 'go back' to 'where they belong/where they came from'.

In this view, being British is about a combination of place and racial/ethnic identity. This sits alongside — and in tension with — those other British values of openness, tolerance and solidarity: the willingness to cohabit, interact and exchange with people as fellow citizens (Gilroy, 2005). 'Empire' has profoundly shaped economic, political and cultural life within the UK through the exchanges of goods, ideas and people, both British people going to the colonies and people from the colonies coming to the UK (Hall, 2001).

You read in Chapter 4 of this book how movements of people can connect places and how migration has contributed to the making of the contemporary UK.

Finally, there is the persistently problematic relationship with 'America'. This is filled with fantasies of power and images of desirable modernity; for example, the USA stands as the model of the 'consumer society'.

You read about the consumer society in Chapters 1 and 3 of *Making Social Lives*.

Yet it is also the focus of fears about the effects of economic, political and cultural dependency and the anxiety about the risks of choosing the wrong sort of modernity (the USA is dominated by excessive consumerism and individualism, or excessively powerful corporations, and suffers from a 'thin' welfare state). 'America' has had a powerful hold over the economic, cultural and political development of the UK. However, it has always proceeded in tandem with varieties of anti-Americanism: from elite or patrician disdain for the brashness or loudness of American culture to political critiques of US imperialism in its various economic, cultural or military forms.

Each of these relationships involves material and cultural dynamics. In cultural terms, each carries a strong sense of ambivalence, involving poles of attraction and repulsion. 'America', 'Europe' and 'Empire' are the 'imagined' Others of Britishness – bound up in complicated connections of desire, loss, anxiety and fear. These orientations continue to shape ideas about who 'we' (the British) are, who 'we' were – and who 'we' might become.

Summary

- Contemporary Britishness is shaped by how other people and places are imagined.
- Social life continues to be organised around ethnic, cultural and racial identities which arose under colonialism to justify European domination.
- Britain is imagined in relation to 'Europe', 'America' and 'Empire'.

4   Making national identities

In the preceding sections, the processes by which national identities are made (and unmade and remade) have been explored in relation to the example of Britishness. In this section, I will make some more general points about the making of national identities and refer to other examples that can be set alongside Britishness. Britishness may be a unique case, but the other examples will demonstrate that the making, unmaking, and remaking processes are common to the formation of national identities. So too are the problems of constructing a coherent and stable sense of the 'we' of the nation.

Turning first to the way in which national identities are constructed through ambivalent relationships to other people and places, other national identities offer illustrations of this point. Spain offers a very different example of national identity being shaped by different sorts of Others. These include the legacy of Moorish domination and the Mediterranean as an economic, political and cultural region, alongside the history of Spain's own colonial power, especially in creating what we now talk of as 'Latin America'. But Spanish national identity has also been powerfully shaped by the presence of a powerful **transnational** institution (the Roman Catholic Church) which has had a profound effect on both national culture and politics. While there may be many other relationships that shape the construction of Spanishness, such relationships have the same sorts of ambivalence as the 'Others' of Britishness (Boyd, 2007; Herb and Kaplan, 1999).

Transnational
Term used to identify processes, connections and relationships that take place across national boundaries.

National identities are also closely bound up with ideas of place: people think of nations in territorial terms, as areas clearly bounded by borders that separate the nation from neighbouring places. But nations are sometimes invented anew or reinvented, while borders are only ever temporarily fixed: borders between European countries have moved frequently during the last hundred years. For example, Alsace has been French and German at different times as claims to the ownership or inclusion of the region have been contested between France and Germany (and their allies). Alsace is now part of France, although the German language continues to be used extensively and Alsace is exempted from some of the regulations and policies that promote a French national identity through the use of the French language. Equally, the internal coherence of other nations is strained in ways that echo the tensions about Britishness.

Contested places and identities: the Basque country and Catalonia in Spain, and Alsace and the French/German border

Spain, for example, is a national territory within which there exist powerful separatist tendencies – among Basque and Catalan people in the regions that form part of Spain's eastern edge. Such separatist movements are often associated with distinctive cultural forms and practices (language, literature, music, clothes) that mark differences between the group and the nation.

Separatist movements define themselves against the dominant conceptions of the nation – identifying themselves as marked by differences of territorial identity (we belong here; this place belongs to us) and by differences of history, ethnicity and culture. Such movements may move between political and cultural emphases: sometimes campaigning for political autonomy or separation from the larger nation; at other times campaigning to preserve cultural habits or practices (from language use to cultural traditions or habits). Of course, the distinction between the two emphases is not clear-cut (think, for example, about political campaigns for cultural rights – of language use or religious practices). Nevertheless, the continued existence and significance of separatist movements is a reminder that the supposed fit between territory and people that make up a nation is rarely clear-cut. The long history of nation making is full of examples of efforts to tidy up the relationship between the territory and the people that range from expulsion to education, or from extermination to repopulation (importing new people with a better 'fit' to the image of the desired population).

In the late twentieth century, the concept of 'ethnic cleansing' was developed to refer to the more violent methods of remaking the relationship between territory and people in the former Republic of Yugoslavia (although it quickly became applied to many other sorts of nation-making violence). But expelling or killing the 'wrong sort of people', and dividing up territory so that people and places have a better fit are nation-making practices that have a much longer history. The partition of India at the end of British colonial rule created two nations – India and Pakistan – each to be dominated by a particular ethnic–religious–cultural grouping (Hindus predominating in India; Muslims in Pakistan). This nation making built on what had been formalised as 'communal traditions' during British rule and installed these communal differences as one of the central organising principles of the subsequent political life of the two countries, even if they had not been the main features of cultural and political organisation before that (Pandey, 2006a, 2006b).

During the first half of the twentieth century, the occupation of the Baltic states (Latvia, Estonia, Lithuania) by the Soviet Union and Germany, at different times, was accompanied by policies of forced emigration and repopulation, such that the existing population was diminished and then supplemented by Russian- or German-speaking immigrants. The consequences for Latvia have been summarised as follows:

Ethnic engineering of the population

Partly because of huge population losses – estimated at up to ⅓ of the pre-war population of 2,000,000 – but also because the remaining ethnic Latvians had to be subdued and controlled and because Communist ideology foresaw the creation of a new classless homogenised Russian-speaking society, immigration and settlement of migrants from other areas of the Soviet Union became the policy until the very end of Soviet rule. Latvia's Russian minority, which before the war had been about 10% of the population, grew into a majority in the largest Latvian cities and reached 34% of total population, while ethnic Latvians by 1989 decreased from 75% to 52%.

(Museum of the Occupation of Latvia, 2005, p. 35)

These places – and the people within them – were remade (and did not become independent nation states until the collapse of the Soviet Union in 1989). My purpose here is not to say that there are some places where bad things happened and the rest of the world is made up of nice relationships between people and places. Rather, I want to stress that nation making is always a process that involves tensions around how people and places are organised. Whether that involves the enforcement of a single national language (English in the UK; French in France) against other languages; whether it involves the forced movement of 'wrong' people or the repression of regional, religious, ethnic or cultural differences: the 'unity' of nations is the result of intensive processes of making. As you have seen, questions of national identity – who forms the 'we' of the nation – remain troubled and contested issues. Of course, these issues are not only troubled and contested in the UK: one leading US conservative thinker (Samuel P. Huntington) wrote a book with the title *Who are We? Challenges to America's National Identity* (2004) that reflects on the dilution or fragmentation of the national identity in the face of migration (especially by Spanish-speaking people from Latin America). Other European countries have had their own public debates about how to sustain national identity in an increasingly globalised world – and often these debates come to centre on the question of migration. It may be worth reflecting that, despite such debates centring on migration, many other processes have also called nations and national identities into question.

Migration was discussed in Chapter 4 of this book.

Activity 6

Stop for a moment and think about your work on the course so far. Can you think of any other processes that might make either nations or national identities seem less secure or stable?

Here are a few processes that struck me as possibly contributing to a less secure sense of nation and national identity:

- Increased consumption, especially where this involves goods imported from elsewhere. This may weaken a sense of nation in several ways – the decline in production of such goods in the home economy; the greater diversity of goods on sale; the importance of other cultures or cultural values in consumption (sometimes called 'Americanisation').

  See Chapter 1 of *Making Social Lives.*

- Greater economic interdependence, which might be in terms of production, consumption, the mobility of rubbish, or the ownership of national companies or businesses by investors elsewhere.

  See Chapter 3 of *Making Social Lives.*

- Greater environmental interdependence, such that national spaces are not closed or immune to the consequences of actions elsewhere.

  See Chapter 3 of this book.

- People are more mobile (not just migrants) so may have attachments to, or even homes and families in, different places.

  See Chapter 4 of this book.

- People may identify with people or places other than nations (e.g. neighbourhoods, communities, religions, and so on).

  See Chapter 6 of *Making Social Lives.*

I'm sure there are plenty more examples, but these are ones that struck me as potentially unsettling ideas of nation and national identity.

This is a reminder that many social processes go on simultaneously, and identifying or concentrating on a single cause or issue may conceal other dynamics. I mentioned this in the context of the discussion of the extract by Goodhart in Section 2.3, but it has more general relevance: certainly the apparent instability of nations and national identities emerges at the intersection of different economic, social and political changes.

Summary

- Like Britishness, other national identities are also constructed through ambivalent relationships to other people and places.
- Nation making is always an ongoing and troubled process.

How do we know?

Speaking and writing as qualitative data

In this chapter, you have encountered diverse sources of data: social science and other studies, political speeches, official government statements, articles and reports. Some of these have been contributions to the analysis of making national identities offered by this chapter (Michael Billig's comments about 'banal nationalism', for example). Others, however, have been used as sorts of *evidence* – evidence about how people think, speak and write about 'Britishness'. In this chapter, extracts used in this way – as evidence – are styled with a blue shaded background.

In the course so far, you will have mainly seen people referring to evidence in the form of quantitative data, like statistics, and qualitative data, including interviews and observations. But how people write and speak also provides us with sorts of evidence, evidence that is particularly important if we are interested in ideas about social life (how these ideas are made, how they are used, how they change). This sort of qualitative data makes reading a distinctive skill for social scientists interested in how ideas (sometimes talked about as language, or rhetoric, or discourse) shape social life. In the work on the extracts in this chapter, I have tried to indicate some of the cues and clues that might be useful in helping us read carefully or systematically. These include questions such as:

- What's the context?
- What's the purpose?
- What's the question?
- What's the opposition?
- Who are 'we'?

Conclusion

This chapter has explored several ways of thinking about Britishness. Sections 1 and 2 considered some versions of Britishness that offered a *unifying* image of Britishness and the British (linking people, place, culture). Section 3 examined questions of race and ethnicity in relation to national identity, not least in the context of debates about 'diversity'. Section 3.2 considered an alternative to the emphasis on unifying images – exploring how Britishness might be constructed in relation to other places (America, Empire and Europe). Section 4 moved from looking at Britishness to the more general question of how national identities are made, unmade and remade, drawing on examples from elsewhere. While Britishness has distinctive features, the same *processes* of making national identities are visible in other places. In each of these sections, I have tried to stress the existence of tensions between the attempt to construct stable, unified nations and national identities and conflicts over inclusion, belonging and integration. People and places are difficult to assemble into coherent and stable 'imagined communities'.

So is there a social science lesson from this exploration? If so, it is not the demonstration that social scientists can pick holes in anything. Rather, it is that major social categories – like national identities – *are always in process of being constructed*. They are 'made up' in both senses of that phrase. Nations are 'imagined communities' (in Anderson's phrase) – they have to be invented or imagined, conceptualised as a grouping of people (a population, perhaps) that shares a space and other characteristics. They also have to be made up in terms of the work that goes into constructing them, bringing them into being as a social group. The idea of 'imagined communities' may sound a bit lightweight – imagination tends to sound not very solid or material. But just think about all of the social and political work that is necessary to produce and sustain this imagined community – from defining and controlling its national borders to teaching its national anthem; from ensuring that people follow its laws to issuing passports so that its members can leave the country; or from trying to provide a shared language through to issuing honours to deserving figures on the occasion of the Queen's official birthday (the day on which I am writing this chapter).

This view of national identity as always being constructed is a reminder that such identities are always vulnerable to being deconstructed, challenged or changed. Much of the debate about Britishness since the late twentieth century derives from nationalist challenges in the other nations of the United Kingdom – and the unwillingness to be subordinated within a British identity (Perryman, 2009). It also emerges from migration, from decolonisation and from the recurring question of 'how can we live together?' The 'we' is always a problem – as attempts to define who is included and excluded are always contested.

In the process, you have considered some central issues in the way that social scientists study identity:

- who people think they are
- the production of inclusions and exclusions through national identities
- how identities are attributed to people
- the ways in which national identities are constructed
- some the resources that are used in constructing national identities
- why national identities are always vulnerable to change, challenge and contestation.

In the course of this chapter, you have also encountered particular issues of evidence and argument in studying national identities.

References

Anderson, B. (1983) *Imagined Communities*, London, Verso.

Billig, M. (1995) *Banal Nationalism*, London, Sage.

Blunkett, D. (2005) *A New England: An English Identity within Britain: Speech to the Institute for Public Policy Research, 14 March 2005*, London, Institute for Public Policy Research; also available online at http://www.ippr.org.uk/members/download.asp?f=%2Fecomm%2Ffiles%2Fa+new+england%2Epdf (Accessed 15 May 2009).

Boyd, C. (2007) *Historia Patria: Politics, History and National Identity in Spain, 1875–1975*, Princeton, NJ, Princeton University Press.

Burney, E. (2005) *Making People Behave: Anti-social Behaviour, Politics and Policy*, Cullompton, Willan.

Equalities Review (2007) *Fairness and Freedom: The Final Report of the Equalities Review*, Wetherby, Communities and Local Government Publications.

Gilroy, P. (2001) *Between Camps: Nations, Cultures and the Allure of Race*, London, Penguin.

Gilroy, P. (2005) *Postcolonial Melancholia*, New York, Columbia University Press.

Goodhart, D. (2004) 'Too diverse?', *Prospect Magazine*, no. 95 [online], http://www.prospect-magazine.co.uk/article_details.php?id=5835 (Accessed 15 May 2009).

Hall, C. (2001) 'British cultural identities and the legacy of the Empire' in Morley, D. and Robins, K. (eds) *British Cultural Studies*, Oxford, Oxford University Press.

Harzig, C. and Juteau, D. with Schmitt, I. (eds) (2003) *The Social Construction of Diversity: Recasting the Master Narrative of Industrial Nations*, Oxford, Berghahn Books.

Hennessy, T. (1998) *Dividing Ireland: World War I and Partition*, London, Routledge.

Herb, G. and Kaplan, D. (eds) (1999) *Nested Identities: Nationalism, Territory, Scale*, Lanham, MD, Rowman and Littlefield.

Home Office (2007) *Life in the United Kingdom: A Journey to Citizenship* (2nd edn), London, The Stationery Office.

Huntington, S.P. (2004) *Who are We? The Challenges to America's National Identity*, New York, Simon & Schuster.

Kumar, K. (2001) 'Englishness and English national identity' in Morley, D. and Robins, K. (eds) *British Cultural Studies*, Oxford, Oxford University Press.

Museum of the Occupation of Latvia (2005) *The Three Occupations of Latvia, 1940–1991: Soviet and Nazi Take-overs and their Consequences*, Riga, Occupational

Museum Foundation; also available online at http://www.occupationmuseum.lv/lat/services/gramatu%20faili/3_okupacijas.pdf (Accessed 15 May 2009).

Newman, J. and Clarke, J. (2009) *Publics, Politics and Power: Remaking the Public in Public Services*, London, Sage.

Office for National Statistics (ONS) (2009) 'Gender pay gap' [online], http://www.statistics.gov.uk/cci/nugget.asp?id=167 (Accessed 12 May 2009).

Pandey, G. (2006a) *The Construction of Communalism in North India* (2nd edn), Oxford, Oxford University Press.

Pandey, G. (2006b) 'The politics of community: some notes from India' in Creed, G.W. (ed.) *The Seductions of Community: Emancipations, Oppressions, Quandaries*, Santa Fe, NM, SAR Press; Oxford, James Currey.

Parekh, B. (2000) *Introduction to the Report of the Commission on the Future of Multi-Ethnic Britain*, London, The Runnymede Trust [online], http://www.runnymedetrust.org/reportIntroduction.html (Accessed 15 May 2009).

Perryman, M. (ed.) (2009) *Breaking Up Britain: Four Nations after a Union*, London, Lawrence and Wishart.

Phillips, T. (2007) 'Britishness and integration' in Johnson, N. (ed.) *Britishness: Towards a Progressive Citizenship*, London, The Smith Institute.

Schwarz, B. (2001) 'Britain, America and Europe' in Morley, D. and Robins, K. (eds) *British Cultural Studies*, Oxford, Oxford University Press.

United Nations Educational, Scientific and Cultural Organization (UNESCO) (1950) 'The race question', 18 July, Paris, UNESCO; also available online at http://unesdoc.unesco.org/images/0012/001282/128291eo.pdf (Accessed 13 May 2009).

Ware, V. (2007) *Who Cares about Britishness? A Global View of the National Identity Debate*, London, Arcadia.

Weber, M. (1978 [1922]) *Economy and Society, Volume 2* (ed. G. Roth and C. Wittich; trans. E. Fischof), Berkeley, CA, University of California Press.

Williams, G. (1985) *When Was Wales? A History of the Welsh*, London, Penguin.

Williams, R. (1958) *Culture and Society*, London, Chatto and Windus.

Chapter 6
Identity change and identification

Wendy Hollway

Contents

Introduction   251

1   Identity change   252

    1.1   Identity change through the life course   252

    1.2   The uneven pace of identity change   253

    1.3   Identification   255

2   Doing empirical research on identities   258

    2.1   Researching identities in the UK   258

    2.2   Designing the project   259

3   Analysing data to understand identity changes   267

    3.1   Silma's case   267

    3.2   Analysing identification   269

    3.3   Interpreting connections   270

    3.4   Theories of identification   274

4   Bodies and identity: black skin and social meaning   277

    4.1   Racism and black identity   278

    4.2   Researching racial difference   279

    4.3   Researcher reflexivity   280

    4.4   An interpretation of the data   282

Conclusion   286

References   289

Introduction

This final chapter in the 'Connected lives' strand turns to the topic of identity change. There has been a renewed interest in this aspect of identity recently, perhaps because social scientists see the pace of social change increasing and want to explore how this is reflected in identity change. To investigate this, I will move 'down' a level from the larger scale discussions of migration and national identity in the preceding chapters in this strand. These big topics are still relevant of course, because of the inseparability of the social and the personal. In this chapter, however, 1 look at how the connections and 'disconnections' between people operate at the level of individual lives. I also look in more detail at empirical work on identity, and at social change in the lives of two young people.

Section 1 discusses different ways of understanding how people's identities change over their lives. Section 2 looks in detail at a research project on the identity changes associated with becoming a mother, showing how and why the project was organised and the decisions which the researchers had to make. Section 3 analyses data from the project to investigate the processes of identity change. Section 4 discusses a different example of identity and the body – the meanings of black skin for identity. This section also presents another example of data analysis. The final section reflects on the theories and empirical work on identity change which have been covered in the chapter.

This topic of identity provided the focus for Chapter 4 of *Making Social Lives* and has been discussed in all the chapters in the 'Connected lives' strand in this book.

1   Identity change

1.1   Identity change through the life course

Erik Erikson, a psychologist writing in the 1950s, was interested in how identity change is accomplished over the whole of the life course. Developmental psychologists study changes over time (as the term 'development' suggests) but they had largely restricted their focus to studying children, as if changes stopped after childhood. Erikson (1980 [1959]) extended the idea of development to apply throughout life (including old age). He studied how a person's identity is influenced by past experiences, as well as how it changes in the face of the new tasks that confront people as they live their lives.

Activity 1

Look back on your life so far and identify one life task that was new at the time, something that you did that seems to mark out your movement from one life phase to another. How smooth was the change for you? What difficulty or conflict was involved?

Erikson defined identity as a sense of one's continuity over time as a being or entity that is different from others. This emphasis on continuity over time was complemented by his conviction of the importance of change in understanding identity. Erikson defined eight stages of life through which, he claimed, identity was inevitably transformed, but in unique ways. Movement from one to another was not smooth and forward development was not inevitable. It involved what he called a series of 'identity crises'. For example, he looked at the passage from adolescence to early adulthood in terms of the pressing changes that have to be faced in this transition.

The idea of conflict is important in this emphasis on identity transition: ordinary conflict – brought about by inevitable changes in life circumstances – is seen as the motor for identity change. Conflicts need not be huge or insoluble to qualify for this label; they refer to any tension between wishes or between events that makes the flow of life less smooth, less even, less effortless. According to Erikson, the principle of conflict as something that propels identity transition can be applied to identity over time for everyone, even though there will be

differences in the extent of conflict at different times of life and some
people will experience greater changes than others.

1.2   The uneven pace of identity change

Erikson focused on change over the life course, but this is only one way
to look at identity change. It is also interesting to consider in what ways
our identities change in the moment-by-moment activities and
relationships that make up daily life. Different influences on identity
change also suggest different paces of change. Here are three examples
I thought of.

First, bodies change. They change more quickly or more slowly at
different times of life and in health and illness, but the changes
associated with ageing are quite slow and our bodies largely remain a
source of familiarity and continuity.

You read about
identities and everyday
practices in Chapters 4
and 6 of *Making Social
Lives*.

Three photos of my mother from young adult to old age

For these reasons, change over the life course is relevant to this aspect
of our identity. However, people also change their bodies by choice –
through bodybuilding, cosmetic surgery or more simply by means of a
change in hairstyle, hair colour, make-up and clothes.

Activity 2

Think of your own body five years ago and now. How has it changed? To what extent are these changes due to the life course and to what extent are they a consequence of choices you have made?

You read about the connections between identities and practices in Chapter 4 of *Making Social Lives*.

Second, practices change. Most aspects of life involve repetition of familiar activities, such as those involved in domestic life like washing, shopping and preparing food, and those involved in working. When aspects of life change force us to adjust routines and habits, these have effects on who we are, which are sometimes subtle and taken for granted, and sometimes momentous, such as the changes involved for parents looking after a new baby. Considering changes in practices shifts the focus in the formation and changing of identity from being to doing. Over days, months and years, new practices can become habits and the associated new identities probably become established or embedded.

Third, relationships change. Social psychology has emphasised how our experience of our identities (who we are) is influenced by other people's views of us (who they think we are). For this reason, our continuing relationships with other people are likely to afford continuity in our own identities (assuming that their views of us do not change drastically). On the other hand, new relationships, especially in new settings, are likely to push us in the direction of identity change.

The idea that we each have multiple identity positions was introduced of Chapter 4 in *Making Social Lives*.

Moreover, it is often the case that different relationships in the various spheres of our lives push us in different directions. Think of a teenager whose parents and friends may be exercising influence in uncomfortably different directions. In circumstances like that, our identities may change as we move from one relationship setting to another, and the pace of such a change will be so fast that it is almost immediate. This fits with the idea that we each have multiple identity positions, depending on the situation we are in and who we are with. If we move quickly to and fro (or 'oscillate') between identity positions, it seems less likely that changes in identity can become sufficiently embedded for us to recognise them. How, then, and under what circumstances do changes in identity become embedded?

1.3   Identification

Another way of thinking about changes or movement of identity is through the act of **identification**. This involves imagining oneself in another person's place. An example of this occurred in the research project I will discuss in this chapter, when one of the participants was looking at a photograph. I will call this young woman 'Liyanna'.

Liyanna had prepared some family photos to show the researcher. One photo was of Liyanna's mother with her older sister as a baby. Talking about this photograph, Liyanna says:

> It's this picture, it's so strange. ((baby cries)). I was showing it to my sister the other day, and I said to her that when I used to look at this before it was like 'oh there's Mum and Amina' (her sister) … and you just sort of flick through it, you know, and I never really stopped to analyse it. But I said to her, since I've had Maryam, I look at that picture and I know exactly what my Mum was feeling when she was looking down at my sister. (Interviewer: Really?) 'Cos I know how I feel when I look down at her, and when I play with her, and it's just taken on a whole new meaning, you know, it's like there's my Mum and that's her first-born child, it's a little girl, same as me, you know, and I can just see the love and the emotion that she's feeling when she – when she – when that picture was taken.

Identification
The act, conscious or not, of accurately imagining oneself in another's place.

As you read in Chapter 4 of this book, social researchers usually give a false name or 'pseudonym' to each of their participants.

A mother and her new baby

The picture that Liyanna is looking at is an ordinary family photo that she has looked at many times ('when I used to look …') but something has changed (it has become 'so strange'). Liyanna explains (by reporting to the interviewer what she said to her sister) that the change is since she has had her baby daughter. She is quite precise about it: 'I look at that picture and know exactly what my Mum was feeling' when (as in the photo) her mum as a new mother looked down at her firstborn daughter. She is seeing her mother in a new way, and she is also explicit about the reason she knows what her mum was feeling. She can *put herself in her mother's position* through her own experience of 'the love and the emotion that she's feeling'. In other words, she is identifying with her mother. The route for the identification is the parallel of the new baby, the firstborn child, a daughter, in both cases. Liyanna is describing the experience of being in a new pivotal generational position which includes both mother and daughter, based on being able to identify with both her mother and daughter at the same time.

Four generations of women in my family, taken in 1947. The baby in the picture is my older sister

The example of new mothers shows some of the complexity within the concept of identification for multiplicity and identity change. Their identifications with their babies necessarily put new mothers in pivotal positions in the middle of three generations since they have been babies to their own mothers. They are thus simultaneously 'self-as-mother', 'self-as-child' and, therefore, 'mother-of-self-as-child' (Gous, 2004). This enables them to access identifications with their mothers and with their babies, The fact that, in her mother's case, the baby daughter was Liyanna's sister, not herself, does not provide an obstacle to the identification; indeed, perhaps because she is so close to her older sister, an identification with her same-sexed sibling is accessible as well: 'a little girl, same as me'. Through this new series of identifications occasioned by a family photograph, Liyanna acquires an emotional understanding that was not accessible before she became a mother herself.

Summary

- Erik Erikson suggested that a person's identity changes over the course of a lifetime because of the conflict produced by ordinary life circumstances.
- Our identities may also change with changes to our bodies, and relationships, and the practices of everyday life.
- Another way to understand a movement in identity is through the act of identification, when a person imagines her- or himself into another person's position.

2 Doing empirical research on identities

During the course, you have read a considerable amount about identity research, especially in the 'Connected lives' strand in *Making Social Lives*.

In this section we look more closely at how social scientists research identity. I begin by describing a large, government-funded programme of empirical identities research, including the kinds of questions it focused on, the topics it included and the social science disciplines which contributed to it. I then look in detail at one project from the programme, about identity change. I focus on some of the key questions which the researchers had to consider, including which participants to use and how many, where to conduct the project, what research methods to use and the potential relevance of the project to government policy. Finally, I discuss some of the limits of the project, or what was not included in the research.

2.1 Researching identities in the UK

Doing research on identity is not a simple matter because this is such a broad idea and can refer to so many different things, as you have seen in previous chapters. Nonetheless, in 2003 the government-funded organisation that sponsors social science research in the UK (The Economic and Social Research Council) decided to invest over £4 million in a programme of research entitled 'Identities and Social Action'. Research into identities was a government priority because identity issues were seen as relevant for government policy and professional practice and also as a live issue of debate among citizens. The aim of the programme was to fund high-quality research on identity and related issues, including marginalised identities and social conflict, and the links between identity and political and civic involvement.

After a large-scale competition between researchers from UK universities, twenty-five research projects were chosen for funding within the Identities and Social Action programme. These brought together researchers from different social science disciplines, including psychology, sociology, geography, political science and anthropology. On some projects researchers worked together in multidisciplinary teams so as to benefit from the many different perspectives these afforded.

The projects covered a wide range of topics, including 'transsexual identity, the settlement of migrant children, community relations in

Northern Ireland, the identity conflicts of persons with a learning disability, mothering under pressure, and identity and community regeneration in areas such as South Wales, the former coal-fields of East Durham and Norwich housing estates' (Identities and Social Action brochure). The project in which I was involved investigated the identity changes in becoming a mother for the first time. We wanted to know how such women experience this important transition in their lives.

Designing our project required us to make choices which could be explained and justified, and also which were practical within the programme limits of time and financial resources. Eventually we decided to use twenty new mothers as research participants. They varied in age, class, living situation, partnership status and ethnicity, but they all lived in a part of East London with high levels of poverty and social deprivation as well as expanding pockets of economic advantage. This area, Tower Hamlets, has been home to many different migrant groups over several hundred years. We interviewed each participant three times, starting late in their pregnancies and ending around the time of their child's first birthday. The interviews were recorded and transcribed. Six of these women also had observers to visit in their homes every week for the first year of their child's life. Detailed notes were written after each visit.

You saw some examples of transcripts in earlier chapters, including Chapters 4 and 6 of *Making Social Lives*.

Activity 3

I have not specified whether this research project was using qualitative or quantitative methods. Read the paragraph above again and see if you can work out which approach would suit the research question better.

HINT: What were the two methods of data collection used in the project? What forms of data did they produce? Is it likely that these forms of data and this number of participants could usefully be converted into numbers?

2.2   Designing the project

Let me examine some of these decisions about the design of our research project, starting with why one would choose first-time mothers to explore the wider question of identity change. This will give you an idea of how a social scientist (in my case a social psychologist) approaches the business of creating an empirical research project.

Why first-time mothers?

Although there has been a huge amount of research into motherhood, it hasn't explored deeply the life-changing nature of becoming a mother. We wanted to look at this transition because it was interesting in itself, and also because it is appropriate for more general questions about changes in identities over the life course. Becoming a mother is more life-changing than most other events because becoming responsible for a life that is completely dependent, that you were responsible for bringing into being, demands of a mother that she ceases to prioritise her own needs. Instead (as so many of the mothers told us) she has to 'put the baby first'. This is likely to involve her in the kinds of ordinary conflict talked about by Erikson as people move through different phases of their lives. For example, one of the participants in our project commented, several months after becoming a mother: 'I like being a Mum, I love it, um especially when we're on our own. ... I've noticed my whole persona slowly started to change. I have to be a lot more – funnier, more creative or just – basically to impress her. Everything I do has to impress her, so it's weird. I feel a bit topsy-turvy.' Feeling a bit topsy-turvy suggests that the change has affected her identity (her 'whole persona'), rather than just changed the way she has to live. The example of feeling the need to be 'funnier, more creative' to 'impress' the new baby ('her') illustrates two of the forms of change discussed above: changing practices and changing relationships. This participant does different things (funnier, more creative *practices*) and she does these because she needs to see, reflected in this new relationship, herself as a more impressive person.

You read in Chapter 4 of *Making Social Lives* about the importance for identity of practices in everyday life.

Practices and relationships are two areas that have been highlighted in recent research and theorising on identities. Regarding relationships, it is argued that other people are like a mirror in which we find out who we are. We become who we are, and modify who we are, because of how we experience ourselves through the ways that others treat us and respond to us. When a woman becomes a mother, she is in a very intense relationship with her baby. However, she is also treated differently by others; for example, as a result moving from being a daughter of her parents to being also a parent herself.

You read in Chapter 4 of *Making Social Lives* about how people are positioned by others, and position themselves.

Regarding practices – the ongoing activities of our daily life through which we get things done – there is recent emphasis on how these forge an identity for us over time. This is especially so when practices turn into routines that we don't need to think about any more. New mothers have to learn and repeat a great array of practices (feeding, bathing, nappy changing, winding, putting to sleep) through which their new identities as mothers become established.

I commented in Section 1.2 on changes in our bodies as one possible cause of identity change. (Of course, the aspects of bodies which do not change are also important, as I will discuss in Section 4.) Most bodily changes are gradual, except in serious illness, but the bodily changes that accompany pregnancy, childbirth and lactation are quite fast and momentous. Given the media and consumer attention paid to women's body image in Western societies – including the emphasis on slimness – it is not surprising that women's bodily changes during pregnancy and after birth matter to most of them. Our first research interview (conducted before the women gave birth) therefore included a theme based on the question 'Can you tell me how your body has been changing during your pregnancy?', and we followed this up at subsequent interviews. Our data suggested that women differed considerably in their enjoyment of feeling and looking pregnant. After giving birth, the majority of them were intent on regaining their former size and muscle tone: 'getting my body back' was a common phrase. So, where their bodies were concerned, they were keen to get their old identities back.

What practical use does the research have?

Post-natal depression (i.e. after childbirth) is a common occurrence in the Western world. It can vary from passing 'baby blues' to a serious and prolonged state of mental distress. If a new mother's depression continues, this is likely to affect her baby's well-being too.

There is little agreement on what causes post-natal depression and therefore how best it can be alleviated. Feeling 'topsy-turvy' (as the participant above described it) suggests a psychological upheaval, which is perhaps not surprising as new mothers often make quite profound adjustments in their priorities and sense of self. Therefore, understanding the identity transition involved in becoming a mother could have practical implications for government policy to support new mothers. In fact, after a period when the Labour Government emphasised getting mothers into employment to alleviate poverty, and put the emphasis on 'parenting', 2008 saw maternity services being made a government policy priority for the National Health Service and

Bodily changes during pregnancy

an increase in funding from £1 billion to £1.6 billion, as well as the planned recruitment of 4000 new midwives. The Conservative Party policy to increase the numbers of health visitors reflected and intensified debates about the need for a universal health visitor service (Gimson, 2007). Research into the identity transition involved in becoming a mother is also relevant in the training of professionals such as health visitors, midwives and GPs.

Why East London?

We wanted to find participants who were diverse in terms of ethnicity, class, living arrangements and partner status and who lived in the same area so that they shared common ground in terms of the local services available to them. For example, all participants gave birth in the same hospital. This shared geographical location meant that we could explore how the place these women lived in (in its many variations) affected their changing identities.

We chose the Tower Hamlets area of East London partly because there were already government programmes there: the 'Sure Start' programmes, started to support children under 5 years old and parents from deprived communities. This meant that there was a community of interested professionals locally who could help us with our own project.

The Tower Hamlets area of East London

What research methods?

Research methods in social science can broadly be divided into qualitative and quantitative, with some projects combining these (usually called 'mixed methods'). The methods chosen for a particular project depend on what is appropriate for addressing the major questions the researchers are asking. For our project, we decided to interview participants.

You read about the difference between qualitative and quantitative research in Chapter 4 of *Making Social Lives*.

Activity 4

A research interview is a structured conversation. Types of interview range from very structured (the same questions for every participant, permitting simple answers, perhaps even limited to 'yes' or 'no') to very unstructured (in which the questions do not attempt to 'shape' the answers and participants can say as much or little as they choose).

1   What type of interview would lend itself to producing quantitative data?

2   What type would lend itself to producing qualitative data?

3   Which would be most appropriate for this project?

---

1   To produce quantitative data, researchers generally use a highly structured interview format. For example, if answers are limited to 'yes' or 'no', these can be turned into 'scores' (such as 1 for yes, 0 for no). Alternatively, there could be a limited choice of answers framed so that each answer receives a score to indicate its strength. For example, for the question 'How much do you think you have changed since you became a mother for the first time?' the possible answers could be 'It has changed me totally/quite a lot/a bit/hardly/not at all'. These alternatives could, in principle, then be scored as 4, 3, 2, 1 and 0 respectively to represent the amount of change. (I have given this example as an illustration, but I would not see it as an appropriate way to investigate this particular question.)

2   To produce qualitative data, researchers generally use questions which encourage people to talk at some length; for example, to give an account of their experiences related to a chosen topic or to tell stories about a relevant selection of events. Our interviews were of the latter, unstructured, kind. The questions we asked were sometimes similar to the one discussed above (for example, 'Can you tell me how your body has been changing during your pregnancy?' and 'Can you tell me about the birth of your baby?'), but participants' answers were not limited and in order to move beyond generalisations, such questions would be followed up with requests for stories about particular incidents and experiences.

3   As the above answer indicates, we chose to use unstructured interviews which produced qualitative data because we wanted to find out about how the participants themselves experienced this life change.

As I have described, interviewing was not the only research method used in the project. We were also interested in the aspects of becoming a mother that are unlikely to be talked about, perhaps because they are taken for granted. For this reason, we decided to use observation as a second method. For instance, we observed how a mother holds her baby, and how this changes over time. This example raises the interesting question of why a researcher would be interested in a specific detail like holding the baby. 'What has that got to do with a mother's identity?', you might be asking. For empirical research, it is important to get to specifics (rather than staying with a very general idea like 'identity'), and it is often theoretical ideas that guide the research into specifics. The idea of holding is from the psychoanalyst and paediatrician Donald Winnicott, who concluded that bodily holding also contained important elements of holding in a wider, psychological sense, such as being reliable and providing security. It can therefore say a lot about the relationship that a mother was able to establish with her infant.

How many participants?

Why twenty mothers? Why not two or 200? The number of research participants depends on the methods used. A quantitative research method like a survey would require high numbers in order to be representative of all mothers in a particular location. At the other extreme, it would be possible to conduct a piece of research based on a single individual as an 'individual case study'. The choice of a single case would be inappropriate if one of the research questions was about, for example, if and how the changes happening in a woman's identity when she becomes a mother differ depending on her ethnic and class background and other features of her living situation. To answer that question, it is obviously necessary to have participants from a number of different identity categories.

You read about case studies in Chapter 5 of *Making Social Lives*.

In our project, we wanted big enough numbers to be able to include more than one example from various social categories (middle or working class; Bangladeshi origin; white English or African Caribbean). We also wanted to have as much variety as possible in terms of participants' living situations; for example, living alone with the baby, living with a partner or husband as well, living with one's family of origin or parents-in-law, or with these nearby. This was because different living situations provide different amounts and styles of support.

However, we did not want so many participants that we would produce an unmanageable amount of data. Qualitative data is very time-consuming to analyse; it can't be 'crunched' by computer but must be looked at in detail by the researchers. Spending too much time doing the interviews would not leave us enough time for making sense of the findings. For the observations, this consideration meant even smaller

You read about the analysis of transcripts and other qualitative data in Chapters 4 and 6 of *Making Social Lives*.

numbers, because the amount of data was huge (detailed observation notes every week for a year), as was the time commitment of the six trained observers who each carried out one of the year-long observations.

What was left out of the project?

Every research project has its limits. For practical reasons, the researchers have to decide what not to include. One major aspect of mothering which was excluded from our empirical project was social mothering. This takes numerous forms, such as mothering by adoptive, step- and foster mothers, and more extended forms such as the kinds of mothering that are performed by a wide circle of adults including fathers, grandparents, siblings and friends. The decision to omit it was not a comment on its importance but simply a practical choice. However, although the project focused on biological mothering, it was still a social research project because, even for biological mothers, the role of bodies in the formation of identity, and in identity change, is never a direct or determined one. Social and personal meanings always play a part in how bodies are experienced, as I will discuss in later sections.

Summary

- An empirical research project asks specific questions, establishes an appropriate location for finding relevant information, gathers that information (known as 'data') and uses it to address the questions it started out with.
- To design a research project, the researchers had to make practical decisions about the best locality, participants, methods and data for their topic (the identity changes in becoming a mother).

3 Analysing data to understand identity changes

Once the mothers had been recruited into the sample, once the consent and ethical framework had been worked out and approved, once the interviews and observations had been conducted, the notes taken, the audio recordings transcribed and pseudonyms substituted for real names … then we qualitative social science researchers had a vast amount of data and the challenge, which in the early stages felt pretty overwhelming, of putting it to good use. This stage is called doing the data analysis.

The focus of data analysis has to be on addressing the research questions. We wanted to know not how new mothers' lives change but how their identities change. A data analysis has a focus (in this case how to understand identity change through the example of becoming a mother for the first time) and needs a set of concepts through which to make links between the general concept (here, the concept of identity) and the data. The specific concepts I will use here are those we have already discussed in the chapter: ordinary conflict, identification, and practices and relationships as processes of identity change. These key concepts will appear in italics in the rest of this section, to draw your attention to how they are used in the data analysis.

In this section I will illustrate these four key concepts using data from the research project. (Of course the data did not relate exclusively to becoming a mother, as you will see in Section 4.) From a set of interview transcripts and field notes, extracts were selected which were the subject of some detailed interpretations. I will show how this kind of analysis can be conducted at the very specific level of the grammar of a phrase and also at the level of knowledge about the case as a whole.

3.1 Silma's case

'I always wanted to be a mother. I wanted to be a young mother', Silma says, and she becomes a mother just a few days before her twenty-fifth birthday. At the time of our interviews, Silma was living with her husband and her in-laws in her in-laws' council house. The three interviews take place in Silma's bedroom and the field notes describe how the first interview felt 'overwhelmed by Silma's in-laws' and how the interviewer felt that the baby, Abeedah, was 'wanted quite hungrily' by the whole family.

Soon after giving birth, Silma talks about her close relationship with her baby daughter Abeedah. She has worked out her needs and preferences by being close to her '24/7'; for example, she knows that 'she won't drink as well' when her nappy needs changing. This full-time preoccupation with her new baby entails learning a whole new set of practices, such as the feeding and nappy changing one referred to here. One way for her new identity to develop is through this set of *practices* that will become routine and also will have to adapt to Abeedah as the baby becomes able to do more for herself. Silma's new relationship with her baby is a preoccupying one, which affects the way she experiences herself, but it is only one relationship out of a whole set of relationships (with family, friends and ex-colleagues) that change as a result of Silma having her first baby.

Silma's local community is predominantly of Bangladeshi origin. Bangladeshi people constitute the largest ethnic group in Tower Hamlets (33 per cent of the population according to the 2001 Census, in comparison with 0.5 per cent of the population in England and Wales). Most are Muslim by religious background (with 36 per cent of the Tower Hamlets population enumerated as Muslim; ONS, 2001). For Silma, whose parents and in-laws moved from Bangladesh to the UK, the community is also an extended one.

You read in Chapter 4 of this book how migration can create an extended, diasporic community.

Phone calls, digital photos and visits 'home' are routine ways to maintain connections with extended families and thus put into *practice* her new identity within and beyond her family. In addition, the neighbours act towards Silma's new – maternal – identity by positioning her as a new mother. A group of people who surround her in her daily life therefore 'recognise' her as changed and by their talk and behaviour position her differently. This is exemplified when Silma says: 'I was like so proud that people can look at me and say "hey I've got a baby" (laughs).' That is how she describes her feelings when she returned from hospital during the first few days which were full of visitors (relatives and neighbours) calling to welcome the new baby.

■   Do you notice anything odd about what Silma said? Look at her use of 'I' in the words she attributes to people in the community where she lives.

In this short extract, the double-ness of identity (I and me) is expressed: Silma is 'me' ('people can look at me'), positioned by others recognising that she now has a baby. She is also 'I' ('hey I've got a baby'). The flow between these is conveyed especially strongly by the confused grammar of her sentence, as she talks to the interviewer. Using reported speech to convey what other people say, she would in principle have said 'hey, Silma's got a baby', but the 'I' takes over, despite the illogical grammar. This slip of wording suggests a powerful connection between her experience of herself with a new baby as the object of others' recognition and her experience of her own (new) identity in her claim: 'I've got a baby'. Her meaning is effectively communicated in this way. This movement between 'me' and 'I' demonstrates the idea that our identity is continuously positioned and repositioned by other people's responses to us, as well as by what we imagine these to be. Another way of putting this is that she *identifies* with the identity that others offer her in their *relationships* with her. This is an example of relational identity being renegotiated in the flow of everyday life.

3.2 Analysing identification

Getting home from hospital is one early transitional moment in Silma's identity positioning. She tells the interviewer of many other instances; for example, how after a while she feels she is treated with more 'respect' by her aunts. Before they used to tell her to call in any time but now they invite her and her husband and baby formally for a meal: 'official phone calls, dates being fixed and the food being cooked.' Before she wouldn't stay around in the room listening but now finds 'it's quite interesting how they talk'. Her young sister now gives her 'dirty looks' and says:

> 'oh my God, you're talking like Mum … you're not my Mum. You used to be like this. You used to be worse than me' (laughs). But now … because I've changed, and I don't want my little sister to be in that state [for example, staying out late in case she gets hurt] … she goes 'oh what about when you used to stay out late, did anyone hurt you?' And I was like, 'Yeah that was *me*' (laughs).

This is a good example of the way that *practices* and *relationships* change together in response to her new situation. Silma starts by noticing her different treatment by the women of her mother's generation. It is not just their positioning of her (for example, the formal invitations), but how her own preferred practices have started changing too: she now likes to stay around with these aunts, listening to 'how they talk'. The ordinary conflict between her new identity as a mother and her old one is drawn through how she experiences her sister who still tries to position her as she used to be – giving her dirty looks because she prefers the aunts' company and because she is now talking just like their mum. Her little sister accuses her with the charge 'you used to be worse than me' and it becomes clear that she is referring to Silma's old practices of staying out late. It looks as if Silma has started to *identify* as a mother when she worries about her little sister doing just the kind of thing she did until not so long ago herself. Silma recognises her inconsistency but puts it down to being 'because I've changed'.

The roles of the aunts and the little sister in this account suggest that Silma is undergoing a change in generational *identification* that involves occupying a maternal position not only with her new baby: she is finding more in common with her aunts and less in common with her younger sister (and may well be oscillating between these identifications). These aunts are simultaneously carriers of a gendered identity, a generational identity, to which she now has access as a mother, and an ethnic identity that derives from one part of the Indian subcontinent.

In the same section of the interview, Silma reflects on some other features of her current changes. She describes her old self as 'so wild', out with friends all the time, staying out late. Now, she says, 'I've gone a bit mature, more understanding, like a more motherly type'. She is 'around family more'. 'Strangely', she says, this has affected her clothes-wise: from being a 'jeans maniac', she feels less comfortable in them ('my bum would stick out'). Now she refers to salwaar kameez as 'normal clothes' and 'the ones I really like' (she received four as birthday gifts). That she finds this change 'strange' suggests that it is not something that she has consciously chosen but rather that she has discovered her preferences have changed.

3.3   Interpreting connections

When analysing interview data it is often revealing to look at the connections between ideas, rather than just each bit of the content. Silma moves from talking about turning into a 'motherly type' directly to her new discomfort in wearing jeans. This must mean that she experiences a meaningful association between them, since one came into

Women wearing salwaar kameez

her mind as a consequence of the other. The reason, she implies – suggested by a further association to the idea that her bum stuck out in tight jeans – is that she is not so comfortable with exposing her body in tight clothes, despite still being 'petite' (as she called her body size, before and since). The clothes 'I really like', she says, now referred to as 'normal', are salwaar kameez. The many birthday gifts of salwaar kameez show that this was not simply an individual choice but encouraged by family members.

What is the status of the above example of data analysis? It involves interpretation: what an interviewee means by what she says is unlikely to be self-evident. Interpretation involves a difficult balance between using the evidence in the data and using the insights that the researcher brings to the analysis (for example, as a result of the focus on a specific research question, knowledge of the relevant literature, cultural knowledge and wider familiarity with the participant and sample). Drawing on cultural knowledge appropriately is always tricky, partly because people are not fully aware of all the culturally specific assumptions they are making. If the interviewee's cultural meanings are not shared with the researcher – here, for example, the significances of salwaar kameez in Silma's changing experience – then interpretation has to proceed with particular caution. Caution involves not overgeneralising. Silma might choose a different style of dress in

Twin sisters choosing different clothes

different contexts. For example, in the final interview, Silma talks of meeting up with her old friends in McDonald's and it is an open question what she wears on such occasions (at home she was wearing salwaar kameez on each interview occasion). Hence, from one interview we cannot claim that Silma will continue to move in the direction that is suggested here. That would be to assume smooth, 'forward-moving' development. Rather, *conflict* can mean oscillation – moving back and forth.

Nonetheless, the example of Silma's changing clothes preference (which may vary over time and situation) provides a way of showing how data analysis uses links between the raw data (extracts from the transcript) and the four concepts that I have used to pin down the abstract and general idea of identity. In this way I have provided an example of an identity *practice* that is in the process of changing in tandem with her new *identifications* with an older generation of women in her family whose primary identities are defined by being mothers. The *practices* and the positioning in her *relationships* with significant others are bound up together in the same experience. The example also illustrates how the dynamics involved in identity – the forces that propel the identity change – are based on *ordinary conflict*. (Remember that by ordinary conflict here I do not mean aggression between two people, nor anything very intense. I mean that there are different dynamics that rub up against each other and compete for influence within a person.) We saw this kind of *conflict* in the differing influences of Silma's aunts and her little sister. At the time of this (the second) interview, the aunts represent a new feature of her identity and the sister an old feature, associated with the freedom of her youth before motherhood. But in this period of transition, she is not either one or the other, but a mobile mixture of both as she re-experiences herself from moment to moment in the course of different events and *practices*.

Erikson's idea of stages in the life course, through which people pass, contained both an idea of development (with its connotation of smooth flow in a forward direction) and of *ordinary conflict* as the motor of identity changes. In my analysis of Silma's identity change, I have focused on the conflict, rather than on the developmental phases. I find it convincing that becoming a mother can be powerfully experienced as a move from youth to adulthood. But one does not obliterate the other. There was evidence that Silma regretted the loss of her position as the indulged eldest daughter, with the freedom to live an independent life in which she could largely please herself. The conflict between pleasing yourself and putting the baby first does not simply dissolve away but continues to provide the material for identity changes. Out of such material, every individual forges their own, never fixed, identity. This is likely to be a general principle of identity change, not confined to becoming a mother.

This discussion shows how Erikson's theory of the life course and identity conflict provides one way of understanding Silma's case in relation to the big question of identity on which the empirical project was based. This is, of course, not the only theory of identity available and it is not the only theory we used in this project. In the next section, I will outline two theories of *identification* used by social scientists and, particularly, by social psychologists.

You read about some other examples of identity theories in Chapter 4 of *Making Social Lives*.

3.4 Theories of identification

In commenting on Silma's identity transition, I used the term 'identification', which I first introduced through the example of Liyanna and the family photo in Section 1.3. It is a term that I find useful in explaining the changing nature or dynamics of identity. As well as having everyday meanings, identification is a technical concept in social psychological and psychoanalytic theories of identity.

One way of understanding identification comes from social psychologists who suggest that individuals get their identities through belonging to a set of social groups. In the 1970s, the social psychologist Michael Billig (1976, p. 322), in an influential book about people's group identifications, defined social identification as 'the process by which any individual is bound to his [*sic*] social group and by which he realises his social self'. He stresses that identification is 'a process rather than an act' (p. 322). This raises the question of how this process occurs, how something external – a social group – affects something internal – identity. Billig sees people identifying with whole groups of others because of recognising a common quality among them. We could apply this to Silma with her aunts: they are all mothers, as well as being members of the same family, Muslim women and Bangladeshis living in the UK. However, not everyone identifies with all the social categories that would fit them; indeed, some might actively *disidentify*, as Silma used to (and as her younger sister still does) in relation to her aunts' generation. So we need to ask some more questions about how identification works under what psychological circumstances.

A second way of understanding identification comes from **psychoanalysis**. This is a body of theory that started with the writings of Sigmund Freud in the nineteenth century. It is based on the therapeutic treatment of people who wish to accomplish changes in themselves that they hope will help to improve their lives. The idea of internal conflict is central to psychoanalysis, which is also famous for being based on the principle that much of what motivates people's actions is not available to conscious thought. Put these two ideas together and you will see that psychoanalysis is likely to regard identity as always in motion, powered by ordinary conflict and not always under conscious control. The psychoanalytic concept of identification addresses the question of how identification works at a psychological level. Freud (1921, p. 105) said that 'identification is known to psychoanalysis as the earliest expression of an emotional tie with

Psychoanalysis
A set of theories and therapies based on the work of Sigmund Freud and subsequently developed by many other writers, including Donald Winnicott. It is based on the idea that many of our motives are not available to conscious thought or control.

The psychoanalyst Sigmund Freud

another person'. In my own work, like the research project, I find the concept particularly useful when it focuses on psychological dynamics that work between people. For example, an aspect of someone's identity can imaginatively be borrowed from someone else and 'tried on', as we saw in the case of Liyanna looking at her mother in the photograph.

Psychoanalytic theory suggests that identifications are of two kinds: the feelings and ideas that are projected (sent out, unintentionally), to be received by others, and the ones that are taken in (introjected), also unconsciously, to furnish one's own identity. Silma can be seen as trying on – introjecting – aspects of her aunts' identities by joining in their talk. She has become more open to this (unlike her younger sister) because she now objectively shares something important with them – having a child. But this objective new status does not automatically bring with it a psychological identity and so Silma borrows aspects of her aunts' maternal identities, which in a sense they are offering by their new way of including her. Over time, such relational practices – and the omission of others – will help enable her to fill out her new identity. For example, Silma tells the interviewer that she now tends to meet up only with the friends who also have babies, and that now they 'sound like old ladies'. Presumably, some aspects will fit better than others and these identifications will become a taken-for-granted part of who Silma feels herself to be as a mother.

The principle of inevitable ordinary conflict between different identity potentials can also be seen in the example of Silma and her sister. The sister is *disidentifying* with the new maternal aspect of Silma and resisting it; she is sending out this unwanted stuff, lodging it in Silma and attacking it (verbally) there. This is an example of what I referred to (above) as projection.

Summary

- The data analysed by the researchers included participants' everyday behaviour, such as their talk and the ways they dressed.
- The data analysis focused on the four concepts of ordinary conflict, identification, practices and relationships as processes of identity change.
- The meaning of 'identification' varies according to different theories, such as psychoanalysis or the social psychology of groups.

4   Bodies and identity: black skin and social meaning

The social scientific study of identities has often been criticised for giving too little attention to the importance of bodies and biology for identity, at least until recently. Of course the research on becoming a mother, described in the previous sections, could not 'leave out' bodies. Reproductive biology was central to its focus, although the importance for identity of all of the associated bodily processes (including egg production and fertilisation, cell division, the labour of childbirth, milk production) is inextricable from their social and personal meanings. Throughout the 'Connected lives' strand you have read about other identities which are implicated with the body, such as gender identities, family identities (including generational identities), and racial and ethnic identities. Again, none of these identities is exclusively about bodies (remember the arguments against 'biological reductionism' which you encountered in the previous chapter). In each case, however, a social identity refers to some aspect of biology or the body: its 'femaleness' or 'maleness'; relationships like those of the biological family; and the marked 'racial' and 'ethnic' identities associated with Others who are often (wrongly) assumed to be neatly categorisable according to features of the body.

This section will centre on a feature of bodies that is biologically given – skin colour – and examine how black skin constructs identity, not directly but through dominant social meanings and power relations. Section 4.1 introduces the work of the psychiatrist and social theorist, Frantz Fanon. He examined how a long history of racism was behind the meanings of black skin and showed how people's experience of being black was influenced by how white people related to them via their skin colour. Section 4.2 returns to the topic of identity change, looking at the common but important life transition from school to work. It looks at the example of how being black (in East London) is experienced by one school student as he faces the challenge of finding a job. To do this, I present data taken from a set of observation notes from a young man's joking 'role play' after receiving his exam results. Section 4.3 discusses a particular issue in social research, especially qualitative research: the extent to which the researcher's own social identity (or identities) affect the interpretation. Section 4.4 presents my analysis of the 'role play' data from Section 4.2.

4.1   Racism and black identity

You read about race in Chapter 4 of *Making Social Lives* and in Chapter 5 of this book.

Skin colour and its evaluation has played a defining role in the categorisation of groups according to 'race', even though this term has been shown to be genetically meaningless by biologists. Frantz Fanon, born in 1925 in the Caribbean island of Martinique, moved to France (the colonial power of that island) to study medicine and psychiatry. In a book entitled *Black Skin, White Mask*s, powerfully drawing on his own experience of living in France (and later, as a qualified psychiatrist in Algeria), he wrote about the effects of racism on black people's identities. It was one of the earliest such explorations (published first in French in the 1950s).

The psychiatrist Frantz Fanon

Fanon (1970 [1952], p. 78) describes the time when he moved from the Caribbean island, where he was among other black people, to Europe: 'and then the occasion arose when I had to meet the white man's eyes.' In these eyes, he found that his overriding and inescapable identity was as a black man. It was, he said, as if 'I was responsible at the same time for my body, for my race, for my ancestors' (p. 79). He felt imprisoned in this identity, unable to escape from it, when 'all I wanted was to be a man among other men' (pp. 79–80).

You might see some similarities to the negative positioning of the Street People which was discussed in Chapter 4 of *Making Social Lives.*

Through the description of his experience of white people's reactions to his skin colour, Fanon showed that there was a powerful 'racialisation' being accomplished in ordinary interchanges. His account shows how the significance of skin colour is not about biology but about how this aspect of biology is treated and experienced in social relationships. It is not biology that is the cause of the problem, not black skin, but the whole history of the way that race has been constructed to produce a 'schema' in which black people are treated as inferior to white people. Fanon illustrated, using his own experience, how this penetrated into black people's identities.

4.2   Researching racial difference

The history of racial difference has moved on since the 1950s, although it is debatable how much it is characterised by change and how much by continuity. I want to look at a current example of how racial difference may be experienced by one young black teenager, faced with the transition from school to work that Erikson explored (Section 1) as part of moving into adulthood. This example is extracted from a set of observation notes that were part of the 'Becoming a mother' study described in Sections 2 and 3 above. (The six case studies based on observations of new mothers in their own homes were subsequently published, and this one is referenced at the end of the following quotation.) The observers were trained in writing up detailed descriptive notes of their hour-long observations and the extract that follows is an example. The research observer was there when Calise, a 17-year-old mother of African Caribbean origin, had a friend Anthony – also black – round at her family home where she lived with her parents, two brothers and her baby Davy. The focus in this extract is on Anthony.

Calise and Anthony had recently got news of their GCSE examination results and together had been scouring the London newspapers, trying to find employment. Anthony is role playing an imaginary conversation with a potential employer, as if he were phoning to see if they had vacancies:

'Yes, em, good afternoon. My name is David Harding and I wonder if you have any vacancies. Oh you want people of a very high standard, more than one GCSE, better than a D grade? Yes, well I think I can meet that, I've got eight'. [Pause.] 'Yes, well there's twenty of us and we're all hoodies, that okay?' Anthony then calls to Calise's brother to 'turn down that black music, yar. How can you have that stuff on so loud? Turn it down!'

(Watt, 2007, p. 286)

Activity 5

What does this extract say about Anthony's identity changes as he faces the transition from school to work?

It is worth remembering the precautionary note I struck when discussing data analysis in Silma's case (Section 3.3). Interpretations should be treated as provisional and open to others' perspectives. As you read the following, keep in mind the question 'What do I think this extract suggests about Anthony's identity as it is played out in the presence of the observer?' Bear in mind the four concepts used earlier to help pin down identity: ordinary conflict, identification, relationships and practices.

Before discussing Activity 5 and proceeding with my example of an interpretation in Section 4.4, I want to raise an issue in Section 4.3 which may have occurred to you: namely, the importance of the researcher's own identity in an analysis of this kind.

4.3   Researcher reflexivity

An extract like the one above does not speak for itself and different analysts could well come up with different accounts of what is going on here. The extract and what is known of its context afford evidence but what that means is not set in stone. In this case, my interpretation is being made across ethnic as well as gender, class and age differences. There was a time when it was believed that the researcher, through exercising a form of objectivity, could be so neutral as to have no effect on the data produced. However, it is now widely acknowledged amongst social science researchers that the social identity of the researcher affects what is said and what is done in the research relationship and this is therefore reflected in the data. So how do researchers take into account their effects on the research situation? Looking at the example above, how should the observer think about her own position as she observes this scene?

Social science researchers talk about this under the label of **researcher reflexivity**. Before I comment in detail on what I concluded this extract says about Anthony's identity changes, it is important to look at the effects of the observer on this data extract and how she documented them so that they were made visible in the research process.

The observer (attached to the research team, but not one of the researchers) was a white professional woman in her forties and this was the first time she had been in Calise's home when Anthony came round to visit. The fact that an observer is present in a 'natural' setting such as Calise's home produces a new relationship within which identity is negotiated. This relationship is like any other (although fleeting, in this case) to the extent that we experience ourselves as if through the eyes of those we meet and respond to this experience in how we behave in their presence. Fanon makes the same argument, also applied to the situation of black people negotiating their identities within a set of unequal power relations.

The observer quoted above carefully noted the details of her interactions with those she met during the observations. She also reflected on how these made her feel and noted this down (an example of researcher reflexivity). In recorded interviews, this is an important part of field notes. In observations, it is a feature of the notes that are written up afterwards. This observer noted that Calise had forgotten that she was visiting that day. She described how the TV was on, showing the Wimbledon tennis championships, and how Anthony asked her if she would like to watch too. When she explained what she had come for (to see the baby Davy and Calise), he turned the TV to a music station playing a mixture of reggae and hip hop. Shortly after, Calise's brother emerged from his bedroom. The observer noted 'my feeling in relation to him is that I am an intruder, an older woman and white; as though he is thinking "What is she doing here?"'. With this prompt, it is not difficult to put oneself in the position of the group of young people not expecting a visit, especially not one from a white, middle-aged, middle-class professional woman. Despite behaving respectfully and politely, they would probably feel resentful of the intrusion.

In this context, the enactment of a job-seeking scene that stages relations between a white employer and a young black job-seeker takes on further meanings. Anthony behaved politely towards this visitor, who belonged to similar group categories as the imagined boss on the phone. The observer's feelings about how she was being seen by Calise's

Researcher reflexivity
The principle that a researcher should reflect on what effect their identity, presence and actions have on the information that is produced in the research setting.

brother indirectly suggest the significance of these identity categories for Anthony's role play.

In my view, the imaginary employment scenario would not have happened in the precise form it did if the researcher had not been present. If so, this is an example of the idea that no research scene is ever completely 'natural' in the sense that it is never just the same as if it were not the subject of research. This does not invalidate the data. It does require researchers to take into account the effects they are having. Some of these effects are to do with the social identity categories they embody: in this observer's case, these were the categories of being a white, middle-aged and middle-class professional, rather like the kind of people who have the power to give or withhold employment for Anthony.

4.4   An interpretation of the data

In Activity 5 I asked what the data extract of Anthony's 'phone conversation' tells us about the identity changes in his transition from school to work. My interpretation of the data is that in the first half of the extract Anthony is role playing being white.

- Anthony does not say explicitly that the two characters in his imagined phone conversation are white. Do you agree that they are? If so, what evidence in the text would you use to support the claim that the two characters on the phone – employer and job-seeker – are both white?

To gather evidence in the text in this way is an example of how interpretation of people's meanings is a central activity in data analysis. I identify two bits of evidence to support this interpretation. First, Anthony starts 'Yes, em, good afternoon'. If you read this out loud (or listen to the sounds in your head) it is likely that you will not hear the accents of a young black Londoner, but of a white middle-class person. To me, this is particularly caricatured in the 'em'. Second, Anthony chooses a white English name that sounds 'proper' ('David Harding'). He does not use his own name, even though on the phone it would probably not mark him out as a member of a minority ethnic group. The fact that he is imagining pretending to be white implies to me that he is also imagining a white employer. Otherwise, the game – of playing out a racialised relationship – doesn't make sense.

The following section of the extract is about the qualifications the employer expects. Anthony demonstrates his pride at having achieved such good results. What is going on for Anthony as he contrasts his eight GCSEs with the one subject at D grade cited by the imaginary employer? After I had read this part a few times, I began to wonder why Anthony used 'more than 1 GCSE at D grade' as the definition of a high standard. This could represent his experience of the criteria he has encountered in job-hunting so far. In any case, the contrast does allow him to express his pride in having passed eight subjects. The implication is that his qualifications should guarantee him the job. But he is not David Harding.

In the last section of the extract, Anthony invokes a commonplace stereotype that contrasts with the well-qualified, well-spoken 'David Harding' of his role play: the gang of 'hoodies' (young men in groups who supposedly wear jackets with hoods in order to conceal their identities from surveillance cameras while they carry out anti-social or criminal activities).

A group of young people in hoodies

This stereotype is one that disadvantages white as well as black working-class youths (usually male). The observation took place at a time when hoodies were being publicised in the British media in terms of the way they were perceived as threats to law and order. Anthony is not just identifying as a black youth here, but also as a working-class youth who is unjustifiably stereotyped in this way. Racial difference is joined here by age and class difference (and also sex difference) in the image of the hoodie. His question 'that okay?' (twenty hoodies wanting employment) is sarcastic in imagining the impossibility of this scenario. The social identity categories combined in the hoodie stereotype create a powerfully negative image, as a result of which an employer – different in respect of all these categories – might well ignore his qualifications and reject his application for a job. Anthony's scenario here suggests his cynicism and pessimism about the chances of being treated fairly by the average employer, as he imagines such a person to be.

The role-played phone conversation ends abruptly here: it had achieved its point. But his performance of an identity carries on as he calls to Calise's brother in his bedroom 'turn down that black music, yar'. Anthony has chosen to play black music too (reggae and hip hop on the MTV channel) and in this regard at this time is therefore in the same (young, black) identity position as Calise's brother. So he is still performing a different role as he calls to the brother (probably that of an older person, since it is someone who calls black music 'stuff', who finds it too loud and has the authority to order it to be turned down).

■   How could you use the idea of projection to explain Anthony's relation to Calise's brother in the moment of telling him to 'turn down that black music'?

In saying this, Anthony could be projecting a young black part of his own identity into this other black youth and momentarily identifying it there while he performs being someone different.

In this data analysis, I have tried to show how, in an ordinary everyday encounter, Anthony is performing salient aspects of his identity. The term 'perform' is particularly appropriate here, because he is creatively enacting the role of someone other than himself, different according to a number of significant social categories. However, it was a serious, realistic performance because, in my view, it came directly out of the challenge he was facing in trying to find employment that reflected his hard work, intelligence and successful qualifications. Any young person would be faced with the ordinary conflict involved in this transition: how to leave behind the familiarity and structure of school to earn one's own living. Anthony was faced with this challenge in a situation where the odds were stacked against him, despite his achievements. According to his imagined scenario, he experienced this in terms of being black, being young, and being working class – a cluster of social categories associated with discrimination in employment.

Anthony's skin colour has important consequences for his identity and the realities that he is encountering as part of the life course changes in his identity. But as Fanon remarked, it is not the biology of skin colour that is the cause, it is the social meanings built up historically that have effects, in this example, on black identity.

Summary

- Social scientists are interested in the social (and personal) meanings of the body and biology, including the importance of these meanings for identity.
- Frantz Fanon suggested that the importance of skin colour for identity is given by white people's reactions to black skin.
- Qualitative data analysis often includes the researcher's reflections on her own identities within the research process.
- The interpretation of the participant's 'role play' refers to the social meanings of skin colour and the reactions of an imagined person (a prospective employer).

How do we know?

One research project and its data

Throughout the 'Connected lives' strand you have read about research on identities, movements of people, and the connections, and 'disconnections' between them. This chapter has presented a more detailed account of one example, a three-year social research project on the topic of identity change. I described the decisions which were involved in the design of the project, the different theories and concepts on which it was based, and the methods which were used to collect data. I presented two examples of data analysis. The first addressed the identity changes in becoming a mother, the second the transition from school to work. Both analyses referred not only to changes in identity but also to multiple identities. Each analysis introduced further issues for research, including the nature of interpretation, the possible problem of overgeneralising and the importance of reflexivity in research.

Conclusion

This chapter is about understanding how identities change. It asks how life changes change identity. Identity change is about flow and about ordinary conflict. Flow is about being and doing and experiencing oneself in the process and through the eyes of others over time. Ordinary conflict is about two or more pressures or possibilities colliding and creating the pressure for some resolution in action. This emphasis on action – doing, being, experiencing oneself through others' reactions, identifying, resolving tension – is central to how identity changes over time.

Section 1 of the chapter discussed various ways of approaching the theme of identity change. It tried to be specific about an idea that can mean very different things, from moment-by-moment change to gradual changes over the life course – and paces of change in-between these two extremes. I specified three sites of identity change – bodies, practices and relationships – and returned to these in the examples I used in Sections 3 and 4. The idea of identification was introduced because it too provides a focus on movement, not fixity.

In social science, the main tool for finding out about issues such as identity change is empirical research. Section 2 was about how to turn a rather abstract and elusive question concerning how identities change into a researchable topic. To this end, I gave details about a project on identity change in first-time mothers which was part of a large recent programme of identities research. I described the various stages of research design, from choosing a topic and methods to defining a sample. Section 3 showed how results from that study can be analysed. I used the idea of identification across generations to show how Silma actively engaged in practices and relationships that linked her in to her own mother's generation as a mother, not any longer just as a daughter or a niece.

Section 4 centred on a feature of bodies that is biologically given – skin colour – and examined how black skin constructs identity, not directly but through dominant social meanings and power relations. The section had a double aim. The first was to think about an aspect of bodies, namely skin colour, and why its effect on identity can benefit from a social psychological exploration. The second was to illustrate a particular identity transition.

I cited Frantz Fanon's work which examined how a long history of racism was behind the meanings of black skin and showed how this influenced black people's experience of being black through how white people related to them via their skin colour.

I then used a short extract taken from a set of observation notes to illustrate a similar theme. Anthony's job-seeking role play dramatised the conflict he was experiencing as he faced the life course challenge of finding a job after getting his school exam results. This example drew on two basic ideas from the work of Erik Erikson introduced in the first section of the chapter. The first is the idea of life course transition. In this case, Anthony was poised in the transition from school to employment. The second idea is that of ordinary conflict being the motor for identity change.

I interpreted the extract as showing how Anthony enacted the conflict he was experiencing between an aspect of his newly achieved identity as an educationally successful school leaver and the stereotype of the hoodie through which his imagined white employer might see him. I showed how Anthony's experience of his social context – being a young black man in London where many employers are liable to act on prejudices and stereotypes – imposed on him a particular set of dilemmas about finding a job that recognised his educational achievements. To this extent the social categories that describe his identity – young, black, male and working class – are highly relevant to the conflict he faces in the life course transition involved in getting a job.

When we take all these ideas and put them together, we have an understanding of identity that includes things that stay the same and things that change. It is not *either* one *or* the other that characterises identity, but both. Total change with no continuity would be very destabilising for the psychologically necessary experience of having a reliably continuous identity over time. Fixity would make it impossible to adapt to a changing world or to the inevitable ageing that we all undergo across the life course.

In addressing the question of how identity change takes place, I focused on three sites: bodies, practices and relationships. These are not separate influences. In the example of Silma, we saw them all working together in her identity transition to becoming a mother. I showed how the process of identification could explain how people actively achieve the changes that they experience as impinging on them from the outside. By identifying with aspects of other people's identity and taking on similar practices it is possible to internalise social influences that might otherwise remain optional identities not taken on board for ourselves. This explains the active element in identity change. It means that people are not just a product of surrounding social influences. Identifying with something or someone may not be consciously intended but it involves personal agency nonetheless.

References

Billig, M. (1976) *Social Psychology and Intergroup Relations*, London, Academic Press.

Erikson, E.H. (1980 [1959]) *Identity and the Life Cycle*, New York, W. W. Norton.

Fanon, F. (1970 [1952]) *Black Skin, White Masks*, Harmondsworth, Penguin.

Freud, S. (1921) 'Group psychology and the analysis of the ego' in *Standard Edition*, vol. 18, pp. 69–143, London, Hogarth Press.

Gimson, S. (2007) *Health Visitors: An Endangered Species*, London, Family and Parenting Institute.

Gous, A.M. (2004) *The Ghosts in the Nursery: The Maternal Representation of a Woman Who Killed Her Baby*, University of Pretoria PhD thesis.

Identities and Social Action, leaflet, Milton Keynes, The Open University.

Office for National Statistics (ONS) (2001) 'Census 2001 – Ethnicity and religion in England and Wales' [online], http://www.statistics.gov.uk/census2001/profiles/commentaries/ethnicity.asp (Accessed 26 May 2009).

Watt, F. (2007) 'Mixed feeds and multiple transitions – a teenager becomes a mother', *Infant Observation*, vol. 10, no. 3, pp. 281–94.

Conclusion: Connected lives

Stephanie Taylor

Conclusion: Connected lives

The 'Connected lives' strand in this book has included a number of examples of empirical research. Each chapter has presented and discussed quantitative or qualitative data, as part of the ongoing focus of the course question 'How do we know?', addressed in the box at the end of each chapter.

Discussions of migration often focus on numbers and in Chapter 4 Parvati Raghuram discussed quantitative data from several sources, some of it presented in tables, graphs and maps. However, as she made clear, numbers do not 'speak for themselves' as evidence. It is necessary to know *what* is being counted and this raises issues of definition. Definitions are often related to theories and in Chapter 4 you read about different theories of migration. Each had both strengths and weaknesses, making it appropriate to some purposes but not others.

As one example of definition, you may remember the question about whether migrants represent a cost or a contribution to the economy, and how different answers have been given depending on whether certain children were counted as migrants or non-migrants. Of course a further issue is whether children should be regarded as a current cost to the economy or as future contributors (through their work and the taxes they will pay as adults, for example). This requires a decision about the appropriate time period for research (months? years? decades?). An additional problem concerns the numerical (i.e. quantitative) *measure* of value. How can 'human capital' be measured, if at all? For example, is the work of an unpaid or low-paid carer worth less than the same care given for a higher salary?

As well as the quantitative evidence, this chapter also included examples of qualitative evidence, such as election posters, a cartoon and a transcribed extract from a radio programme (Seimon Glynn's speech). The account of Malini's design business came from an ethnographic study which had probably drawn on both qualitative and quantitative data (such as details from her financial accounts) although you read only a summary of the main findings: academic research often uses more data than can be published in full. Similarly, Wendy Gordon's historical study had built up a detailed picture of the women workers in Paisley by combining quantitative data, including numbers from the census, with qualitative material, like personal letters.

In the 'Connected lives' strand in *Making Social Lives* you were introduced to different approaches to the collection or analysis of data, and sometimes both together. You read about interviewing, observation, participant observation or ethnography, experiments, and interpretive or discursive analyses of photos, interview transcripts and television programmes.

Researchers often use quantitative data which already exists for other purposes, like records of bank transactions, or the number of people crossing borders, or the citizenship of NHS employees. However this will still need to be selected and interpreted by the researcher. There may also be legal obstacles to obtaining access to the data: for example, banks are unlikely to make their records freely available. Researchers may also find that the numbers which already exist are not really the ones which will be useful for their purposes (remember the International Passenger Survey which records how many people arrive and leave but not how long they stay).

Existing quantitative data can sometimes be re-presented in order to show something new. For example, the choropleth map in Chapter 4 is a summary of a huge amount of financial information which probably needed to be assembled from different sources. The map is not only a way of making the data easier to read, but is a method of presentation which shows new connections and comparisons.

The UK Census is discussed in Chapter 9 of Making Social Lives.

Although researchers often use existing data, some forms of data are produced especially for research purposes. Many forms of quantitative data will be expensive to produce because of the scale involved: for instance, think of the cost of the UK Census.

Qualitative data may also already be in existence, needing only to be found and selected by the researcher though that in itself can be a very big job. The electioneering posters and cartoon in Chapter 4 would be examples. Chapter 5 discussed short pieces of writing taken from a range of existing sources including government booklets, special reports, speeches and academic publications. It's easy to see that in this case there is an almost limitless amount of possible material: part of the researcher's job is therefore to know which material is relevant. For example, a writer or speaker may have a special role (like Home Secretary or Chairman of the Commission for Racial Equality) which gives her or his words particular significance.

Other qualitative data, like Malini's story, can be collected by the researcher; for example, through interviews or observation. This requires further decisions; for instance, about 'who', 'what', 'how' and 'how much'. The final chapter of the strand, Chapter 6, looked in more detail at the research process which produces new data, by describing one particular academic research project. The chapter outlined how the project came about and the decisions which the researchers had to make. It presented some of the new data generated. (It also drew on some existing, quantitative data referred to by the researchers, about the population of the area from which they recruited their participants.)

The moving picture of society becomes more complex

Finally, the chapter illustrated one approach to analysing qualitative data, discussing two examples in detail. The analysis is not a straightforward 'reading off' of meaning. The analyst thinks about possible interpretations, coming back again and again to check them against the data, and possibly against the interpretations of other researchers. She links the data to concepts which are suggested by theories. She thinks too about the researcher's role in the research process, considering how what is found depends partly on who does the investigating. Research itself is therefore another social process, contributing, if it is successful, to the ideas shared across a society and the ways in which we think about ourselves and our lives.

Introduction: Ordered lives

Simon Bromley and John Clarke

Introduction: Ordered lives

The final three chapters of the book turn to the theme of 'Ordered lives'. They are concerned with some of the fundamental questions of social science:

- How is social order produced, maintained and remade?
- What sorts of processes and authorities are involved in the making and remaking of order?
- How are threats to order – or the dangers of disorder – identified and governed?

The following three chapters explore these core questions in different settings. While you are working on these chapters, you should – as always – keep the key course questions in mind:

- How is society made and repaired?
- How are differences and inequalities produced?
- How do we (as social scientists) know?

These three chapters point especially to questions of how society – or at least forms of social and political order – is made and repaired. But they also have important links to the other two questions.

In Chapter 7, Simon Bromley and John Clarke take up the idea of governing social order. They begin by asking what sorts of things need to be governed and what sorts of actors or agencies are expected to govern them? There are many reasons why people think that things need to be governed: to maintain social order, to improve society, to deal with social problems, or to address controversial issues or political conflicts. In such circumstances, there is often a claim that 'something must be done' to create order or to manage problems. Governing public issues usually implies that specific sorts of people or social institutions have the authority to do something about them. Such authority might be based on particular types of knowledge or expertise (e.g. that of scientists, or of professionals responsible for some areas of policy); it might be based on democratic or representative claims (to speak on behalf of the public or specific groups of people); it might be based on the power of the law (the authority exercised by police officers, judges, and so on).

Chapter 7 ends by pointing to what social scientists call 'the state' as one distinctive and significant agency in these processes of governing.

The state is a focus of authority, and this becomes the central issue for Chapter 8, by Georgina Blakeley and Michael Saward. They ask important questions about what states are and how they are involved in the processes of governing and ordering social life. Beginning from an awareness of just how much of everyday life involves the state, they ask how states have this authority to govern. They also ask about situations in which states may not be able to command such authority – where their governing role is not accepted as legitimate. In this way, we see how individuals and the communities in which they live have different experiences of the state. The state, in other words, is experienced unequally and in different ways. The chapter explores how states can be seen as a type of political order (a set of institutional arrangements) and as a set of processes and practices that tries to produce political order – stabilising social and political arrangements to create a sense of order.

Chapter 8 ends with a question about whether states are necessary for the organisation of social order. Chapter 9, by Simon Bromley, takes up this issue to raise questions about the limits of state authority – particularly in relation to the forms of order and disorder that arise in the international arena. International disorder can take many different forms – from piracy to the international flow of diseases such as swine flu or SARS; from the demand for humanitarian intervention in conflict zones to the deterioration of the global climate. This chapter asks how international order is possible and how it can be governed. Can states collaborate in an international system of order? What sorts of authority are at stake in such processes?

Across these three chapters, you will see how the concern with ordered lives leads us to questions of authority, power and political institutions. Each of these chapters explores the intertwining of everyday life and the social and political institutions of government, states, and organised power and authority. For the authors, this is the core promise of doing the social sciences – to connect the apparently mundane and micro-level stuff of everyday lives with larger scale processes, relationships and arrangements. The stress on authority in these chapters indicates its centrality to the processes by which order is made, challenged, repaired and even remade in new ways.

Chapter 7
Governing problems

Simon Bromley and John Clarke

Contents

Introduction   305

1   The most severe problem?   307

    1.1   Making threats   308

    1.2   Evaluating threats   311

    1.3   Identifying threats   315

    1.4   Making public issues   319

2   Governing public issues   322

    2.1   How are public matters governed? 325

3   Whose problem? The issue of social inequality   331

    3.1   Inequality in the UK   335

    3.2   What sort of problem is this?   337

    3.3   Governing inequality   340

Conclusion   343

References   345

Introduction

In this chapter, we return to questions of order and ordering – and the processes by which order is made, maintained, broken and changed. In Section 1, we examine how some issues come to be seen as issues of public concern. In particular, we concentrate on how some issues come to be seen as *things that need to be governed*. That is to say, some issues command public or political attention and create the demand or expectation that 'something must be done'. In Section 2, we examine how such issues are governed. You have encountered many such issues – from risk to climate change, and from migration to the economy. Here we focus on the view that some issues require coordinated action to manage, direct or control them. In Section 3, we take up one specific issue – social inequality – and consider the ways in which it is governed. Although the word 'governing' is usually associated with governments or states, you will see that other social institutions may also be involved in the processes of governing problems. During this chapter, we examine the following key questions about governing problems:

1   What issues need to be governed?

2   How do people know about them?

3   How are the dangers, threats and problems of such issues evaluated?

4   Who is expected to govern these problems?

We examine these questions through two issues that have been the focus of recent discussion in the UK: climate change and social inequality. We begin with climate change; you have already encountered discussions about the environment and climate change in previous chapters. We are returning to it here to pose some different questions. You have also looked at some aspects of social inequality before, but here we look at some of the ways in which this issue poses some important questions about how it might – or might not – be governed.

Activity 1

Before we begin, we would like you to think about and make some brief notes on both climate change and social inequality.

What, if anything, do you think should be done about (a) climate change, and (b) social inequality?

If you think something should be done, who should do it?

We will not comment on these issues here, since they form the substance of this chapter. However, you might want to return to your notes when you finish the chapter and reflect on what the chapter has added to your understanding.

1 The most severe problem?

What sorts of issues need to be governed? The issues that command public and political attention often seem to be disruptions or breakdowns of order – or anticipated breakdowns of order. We begin by looking at a specific argument about what issues need to be governed. Read the following quotation from Sir David King, who at the time was chief scientific advisor to the UK Government, and consider what questions it raises for you:

> climate change is the most severe problem that we are facing today – more serious even than the threat of terrorism. …
>
> [An international solution to the problem of climate change] requires a political decision based on sound scientific evidence and the UK government firmly believes the time to make that decision is now.

(King, 2004, pp. 176, 177)

Sir David King

King was arguing that the threat we face from climate change is greater than that from terrorism. But you might have wondered how one can tell if one threat is more severe or serious than another. You might also

You looked at questions about who is included in the word 'we' in Chapter 5 of this book.

have asked, what does it mean to base a political decision on sound scientific evidence? Finally, you might have asked who are the 'we' that face these problems? We will take up these questions in what follows, but first let us say why they matter. Although the quoted text was published in a scholarly scientific journal, King's argument was also a piece of advocacy: he was arguing for governments, in the UK and especially in the USA, to take the problem of climate change as seriously as terrorism. 'We' referred in part to the political leaders – including, specifically, President George W. Bush of the USA – who had political choices to make. 'We' might also refer to the residents of those countries – those who were governed by these political leaders. For King, it was evident that climate change was at least as serious a challenge as terrorism and he was urging the US and British governments to act accordingly. So, here is one example of making an issue a matter of public concern and demanding that 'something must be done' (by governments) to govern the threat posed by climate change.

1.1   Making threats

We start by taking a closer look at some of the details and structure of King's argument. He began by stating that: 'Climate change is real, and the causal link to increased greenhouse emissions is now well established' (King, 2004, p. 176). Next, he presented some evidence for his claim about the threat of climate change, giving data on patterns of flooding and storms, on changing patterns of land use, and on the potential loss of life and property arising from these and the economic costs of repairing damage or adapting to the possible consequences. For example, he noted that:

- 'usage of the Thames Barrier, which protects London from flooding down the Thames Estuary, has increased from less than once a year in the 1980s to an average of more than six times a year' (p. 176)
- rising sea levels and an increased severity of storms in the UK 'have the potential to increase risk of floods in 2080 by up to 30 times present levels' (p. 176)
- 'in the worst-case scenario, the number of people at "high" risk of flooding in Britain will more than double to nearly 3.5 million. Potential economic damage to properties runs into tens of billions of pounds per annum' (p. 176)

- in 2003, 'Europe experienced an unprecedented heat wave, France alone bearing around 15,000 excess or premature fatalities as a consequence' (p. 176)
- 'by 2080, if we assume continuing growth rates in consumption of fossil fuels, the numbers of additional people exposed to frequent flooding in the river delta areas such as the Nile, the Mekong, and Bangladesh, and from coastline cities and villages of India, Japan, and the Philippines, would be counted in hundreds of millions assuming no adaptation measures were implemented' (p. 176).

Flooding in India

So it seems that the 'we' that King had in mind, when he talked about climate change as 'the most severe problem that we are facing today', also referred to people all over the world – London, the UK, Europe, the Middle East, Asia and the Pacific are all mentioned – both now and in the future. King emphasised not only the harms induced by climate change but also the increased frequency and likelihood of their occurrence. While he recognised that projections like these – as far ahead as 2080 – were necessarily uncertain, King presented them as objective, and to some extent quantifiable, outcomes that his readers could presumably observe or verify for themselves. So, several different features of the environmental threat can be identified in King's argument: first, the threat of environmental harm was to some degree caused by human activities; second, the harms were being felt by many people across the world, and would continue to be in the future; and third, these harms were becoming both more severe and more frequent.

In short, King presented environmental harms as something that social activity had played a role in causing. He argued that they were objectively measurable and quantifiable, and that public policy should treat the threat of climate change with at least as high a priority as the threat of terrorism. At the time, King was chief scientific adviser to the UK Government and so it was perhaps not surprising that he argued for 'sound scientific evidence' as a basis for public policy. But King also implied that we (the public?) can appeal to 'experts' to inform us about the threats we face, and he invoked the authority of science in support of his argument. In King's view, we could and should trust the scientific community to deliver knowledge and understanding of threats and we should expect our political decision makers to act appropriately on the basis of such knowledge. King was not being naive: he recognised that some things were, and would likely remain, uncertain and that scientific experts disagreed about some things. Nevertheless, he clearly believed that there was a sufficiently established body of scientific evidence and understanding to support his claims. It is not only eminent scientists who argue that governments should act on the basis of the findings of science. Politicians often invoke scientific evidence (sometimes provided by their scientific advisers) to explain policy choices. Equally, popular pressure from individuals and groups in society often draws on representations of scientific evidence to justify support for a particular policy or course of action.

Activity 2

What do you think is the relationship between the different sorts of 'we' identified in David King's argument – we as people in general; we as politicians or political actors; we as experts or scientists?

The conventional view is that the people (often identified as the public) have anxieties or aspirations; scientists collect evidence about the risks and threats and inform the public and politicians; politicians then act on public aspirations or anxieties by making policies that are informed by scientific evidence.

Why might social scientists be sceptical about this conventional view? What have you encountered in your study so far that might lead you to think differently about these relationships?

We – the authors – can think of several ways in which this set of relationships might not work like the conventional story, some of which you have already come across:

- Science does not give a singular view. There may be disagreements between scientists about particular tests, sources of evidence or explanatory mechanisms; or expert definitions of problems and solutions may change over time.

- Expert knowledge is not simply absorbed by the public. It is mediated by other knowledge and ways of thinking: for example, lay theories of health and probability.

- Politicians or political actors may not base policies on scientific evidence or advice. They may have other pressing concerns or sets of beliefs, or may have to deal with a public who want more than one thing.

- The public may not hold a singular view of such issues. They may be divided in many ways and even have different aspirations and anxieties. They may not trust scientific advice. They may not trust politicians.

You have read about expert evidence, and how it may change, and about other ways of thinking, such as lay theories of health and probability, in Chapter 2 of this book.

In this chapter, we explore the different ways in which these relationships – between sorts of knowledge (especially scientific or expert knowledge), politics and the public – may influence how governing happens.

1.2   Evaluating threats

But let's step back a moment and ask a different question: why did King need to make this argument at all? Who could possibly be against basing public policy on sound scientific evidence? Part of the answer is that there was some disagreement within the scientific community about the causes and likely consequences of climate change. Another part of the answer is that some experts argued that it was better to adapt to, rather than seek to mitigate, climate change. But a much bigger issue was that many people, especially but not only in the USA, simply did not believe it was true that climate change represented a bigger threat than terrorism. Whatever the science may have said (and King did not mention what science had to say about terrorism), it is a social fact that different people, groups of people and even whole societies perceive problems such as climate change and terrorism differently. This might make arriving at a sufficient consensus to support political action difficult.

This is not to say that scientific findings have no bearing on what people think, or that some people – for instance, those who agree with King – are more rational than others. Rather, there are differences between the ways in which scientists make and represent judgements of risk and the ways in which ordinary people (including scientists in their lives outside work) perceive risks. The rest of this section takes a look at some scientific research, social scientific work, on processes of risk perception.

Risk assessment and features of a 'risk society' were examined in Chapter 2 of this book.

David King's discussion of threats reflects approaches that are widely used in the activity of risk assessment. One of the features of a 'risk society' is an increasing number of individuals, groups and organisations of all kinds engaging in activities of risk analysis or risk assessment: from soil quality to hospital infections; from the risk of harm to children evaluated by child protection agencies to investment planning (whether for an individual's pension or in organisational developments). The most basic idea is that a threat has two independent components that have to be estimated: first, there are the consequences of the harmful event; second, there is the likelihood or probability of the event happening. The harms and probabilities are then measured or estimated in some way – perhaps from past data, by extrapolating present trends or by inputting the data into a model designed to generate forecasts. Consequences, for King, are things like lives lost, coastlines destroyed, loss of property, increased disease, and so on. Likelihoods are similarly quantifiable: the use of the Thames Barrier has gone up from less than once a year in the 1980s to more than six times per year in 2002/03; the risk of flooding could increase thirtyfold by 2080; etc. If we multiply a measure of the consequences of a given threat by the frequency of its occurrence, we get a summary measure of how severe it is. In this way, by measuring consequences and probabilities we can measure and thus compare threats.

One simple way of approaching risk assessment is to make a binary distinction between consequences that are or are not very severe and events that are or are not very frequent – as in Table 1. Another way of representing this, which recognises perhaps more realistically that consequences and frequencies are distributed along a continuum, is on a graph such as Figure 1.

Table 1   Consequences and frequencies of threats

	Consequences are not very severe	Consequences are very severe
The event is not very frequent		
The event is very frequent		

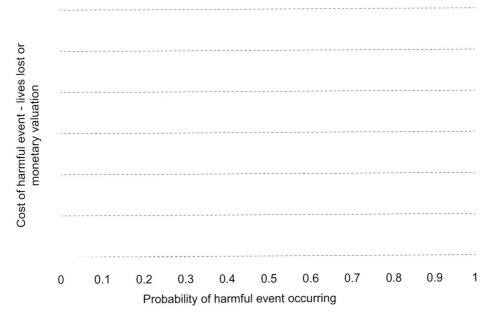

Figure 1   The probability and extent of potential harms

Activity 3

Consider the following potential threats:

1   Substantial flooding of towns and cities in the UK in the next ten years.
2   A collision between the earth and a large meteor in your lifetime.
3   A terrorist attack in the UK in the next five years.
4   Significant erosion of much of the UK coastline over the next century.
5   Malfunction of a nuclear power station resulting in a release of radioactivity in the next fifty years.
6   Violent international conflict as a result of countries competing for scarce natural resources in your lifetime.
7   Your death in a road traffic accident in the next ten years.

Where would you place each of these either in Table 1 or in Figure 1?

Why is it a difficult activity to complete?

We confess that we found this very difficult to complete with any confidence. Partly this reflects our lack of knowledge and understanding of the evidence and models that might be needed to form a judgement about some of the items in the list. In these cases we could presumably become better informed and improve our confidence in our judgements. That is to say, there are things that we know we don't know but about which we could in principle find out more, perhaps by consulting an expert. But some of the items on the list don't seem to fall into this category; for example, what is the likelihood of a terrorist attack in the UK in the next five years? That seems to be something that we don't know, and we are not very clear about what additional information would make us any better informed. Are there any experts who we could trust in this area? Would they tell us, if we asked – or would their calculations of the probability of a terrorist attack be concealed behind the demands of 'national security'? Interestingly, David King presented no evidence about either the consequences or the likelihood of terrorist acts.

In any case, how severe might the consequences of a terrorist attack be were one to take place? Would we measure it in lives lost and property destroyed? This last question raises a further point: doesn't any assessment of the severity of consequences involve more than an objective measurement of effects? Would you distinguish between a death resulting from a terrorist act and one arising from the flooding of a city centre? Does it matter that in the former case the death is intended and someone or some group of people can be said to be directly responsible for the act, whereas flooding seems to be unintended and the issue of responsibility is less clear? We will return to these questions but we hope that they are enough to suggest that how people perceive threats may be more complicated than the picture given to us in King's argument.

1.3   Identifying threats

Studies of people's perception of risks tend to show that, while their perception of potential harms is informed by expert knowledge about consequences and probabilities, it is also shaped by many other considerations. In particular, people's perception of risk is heightened – often very substantially – if the harm is:

* one that applies to groups of people rather than to individuals
* faced by future rather than present generations
* one that people could not expect, or where they did not voluntarily put themselves 'at risk'
* uncontrollable rather than controllable
* delayed in its effects rather than immediate
* associated with feelings of fear, outrage and other strong negative emotions.

This kind of research is important because it tells us that when people perceive and respond to potential harms they do not do so by surveying the available evidence and making a careful, deliberative judgement about the scale of the potential consequences and the likely frequency or probability of the event. In this light, exercises like those in Table 1 and Figure 1 capture only a limited part of how people identify and evaluate threats. Even in cases where the potential harms are quantifiable and where the probabilities are known for the relevant population, people often employ mental shortcuts to make their judgements and decisions. As you have seen, there are 'lay knowledges' and models that shape people's understanding of, and responses to, potential risks.

'Lay knowledges' and models that shape people's understanding of risk were examined in Chapter 2 of this book.

This is not to say that these mental shortcuts are 'irrational'. On the contrary, Tversky and Kahneman (1973) have argued that when making judgements and decisions in conditions of uncertainty people rely on

Availability heuristic
A common mental shortcut through which people deal with a general question by substituting a more particular and more familiar example. That is, they use ideas and images that are available to them.

'heuristics'; that is, principles that simplify a complex question into a simpler one. One such heuristic is what they call the **'availability heuristic'** (an example of social scientists coining an abstruse term for a well-known, if not well-understood, phenomenon). This refers to people answering a general question (say, how big a threat is global warming?) by substituting a more particular example with which they are familiar and which is salient to them – perhaps they live in a town that has recently been flooded, or they have read that the north face of the Eiger can no longer be climbed in the summer because of melting ice and rock fall, or they have seen images of melting ice caps on the television.

Melting ice in the Arctic

But availability is not a given – the ideas and images available to people to use in performing such shortcuts are varied. So, what produces availability? One answer is imagery – what can be clearly and easily imagined, as well as the ways in which images are mediated and circulated through society, including (but not only) by the mass media. Ideas or images that are familiar and salient to people can serve as availability heuristics. Such ideas may derive from a variety of sources – personal experience, reports or stories of other people's experiences, media sources (fictional as well as news or documentary programmes), and social networks (either face-to-face or virtual through the internet). For example, the internet site Mumsnet (www.mumsnet.com) links many mothers (it claims 350,000 hits per month), enabling them to share anxieties, ideas, problems and solutions. Interestingly, Mumsnet makes a virtue out of this process of sharing experience and advice between mothers, arguing that the website gives people the chance to get advice from 'the real experts' (Gambles, 2010). 'Ordinary people' (mothers in this case) – rather than scientists, professionals or other authorities – can claim to be experts too.

Because of the socially mediated and circulated character of knowledge (images and ideas as well as information), many individuals can come to focus on the same example, experience or image in forming their judgements, such that some ways of thinking about harm become part of a *shared culture* of reference and understanding. To the extent that people form judgements on the basis of their interaction with those they know and trust, whether those interactions are face-to-face or mediated in some way, shared beliefs might be to some extent self-confirming and groups might come to adopt a common belief just because others in the group do. For example, relatively closed communities may maintain beliefs about particular risks or threats (e.g. Armageddon, or the end of the world) because they share a strongly defined and mutually reinforcing frame of reference. This shared frame of reference provides an availability heuristic that they hold in common. A different example is provided by some forms of mediated knowledge – and the availability heuristic it creates – about levels or crime and the risk of being a victim of crime. Popular perceptions speak of rising crime – and increasing risk of becoming a victim of crime – sometimes even when official figures of both recorded crimes and reported experiences of crimes are falling.

■   To what extent do mass-mediated images and information about the scale and probability of crime help to shape a particular availability heuristic?

One reason why people's *perceptions* of threats are important is because they influence what action people are prepared to take, both individually and collectively through the political process, in order to reduce or combat such threats. Clearly, people draw upon expert testimony on the consequences and likelihoods of harms in forming their own judgements. However, it is important to note that expert judgement may also be shaped by the psychological, social and cultural contexts we have discussed. Such contexts may shape the sorts of issues that scientists (social or natural scientists) examine (e.g. a recent increasing interest in health risks and their variation between social groups), or how they assess and evaluate such risks (think back to Figure 1: how do experts choose between an evaluation in terms of loss of life and one in terms of loss of property?). Such contexts may also influence how they inform politicians and the public about their knowledge. (Do scientists just write learned articles for publication? Do they provide evidence to governmental commissions? Do they provide exciting or entertaining stories for the mass media? Do they lend their authority and knowledge to campaigning organisations?) Nevertheless, there can be a tension between the ways in which threats are known and made public in scientific work and in the social life and culture of society. In some cases, the divergence between expert and lay opinion can be quite dramatic and might give rise to the kinds of scenarios illustrated in Table 2.

Table 2   Expert and lay assessments of action needed to combat or reduce threat

	Experts believe action is necessary	Experts do not believe action is necessary
Lay public believes action is necessary	**A**	**B**
Lay public does not believe action is necessary	**C**	**D**

Activity 4

Can you think of examples that might fit scenarios A, B, C and D?

Which of A, B, C and D are more likely to cause problems for political decision makers?

A and D are unlikely to cause any problems as they represent a consensus that something or nothing, respectively, needs to be done. There may be other problems associated with A and D: for example, whether reliable or agreed solutions exist, or whether there is the political will to overcome powerful obstacles to the implementation of such solutions. But in scenarios B and C there are immediate political problems because of the conflict between expert and lay judgements. What might political decision makers do in cases B and C? After all, just as it is important that political decision making is informed by sound scientific evidence, it is also desirable that public policy meets the test of public acceptability – at least if we wish to continue to be governed and govern ourselves in reasonably liberal and democratic ways. In the process, of course, issues might be moved from one category to another by the emergence of either new scientific knowledge or new popular concerns. Examples of the former might include emerging evidence about the effects of 'passive smoking' leading to a wider public concern (followed by legislation about smoking in public places). Examples of the latter might include lay/public anxiety about paedophilia producing changes in legislation about public access to information about convicted paedophiles.

1.4   Making public issues

It is time to take stock. We have seen that people perceive threats differently according to criteria that are unrelated to both consequences and likelihoods, and that there are psychological, social, cultural and political processes by which particular understandings of risks get taken up and made public. There are, therefore, no guarantees that the biggest risks (even assuming they are known) will have the highest importance in the culture and politics of society. People may worry unduly about threats that are not very risky and may be relatively unconcerned about things that are likely to cause them considerable harm. The ways in which 'we' perceive threats in our political culture – that is, how they come to be made public – are not the same as the scientific practice of risk assessment. Part of political life involves attempts by social groups and organisations such as political parties, professional bodies, non-governmental organisations, etc., to create issues of concern and availability heuristics through which the public might think about them. For example, when we were finishing writing this chapter in May 2009, we could find examples of:

- political parties addressing the public about the importance of political and constitutional reform (to restore 'public trust' in politics, politicians and government)

- professional bodies identifying problems that needed to be governed better (teachers' and head teachers' organisations campaigning against 'over-testing' children in school, with the object of improving pupils' health and well-being by reducing levels of stress and anxiety)

- non-governmental organisations (NGOs) identifying rising inequality both within the UK and globally as a result of the global financial crisis that began in 2008, with demands that government spending be directed to reduce such growing inequalities.

Public knowledge is socially mediated in many ways. People tend to 'know' many things through mediated forms – whether through the mass media of press, radio and television, through online networks and virtual communities or through everyday networks and interactions in which conversations identify and explore 'common concerns'. In particular, we have seen that an availability heuristic that is clearly and easily imagined, extensively mediated throughout society, identified with a responsible perpetrator, able to mobilise powerful emotional responses and articulated in the dominant languages of politics, is likely to have a powerful impact on how people respond to different threats.

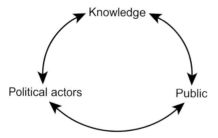

Figure 2   Mediated relationships

Figure 2 summarises the mediating relationships at stake here: political actors and the public are socially mediated by mass and other media. Politicians rarely speak directly to their publics, but address them through broadcasts, reports of speeches and events, interviews and appearances, and online reportage and networks. Such mediation is always selective and often involves 'framing' devices – ways of representing politics, politicians or political issues that shape our approach to them. Such framing devices may be positive (enthusiastic or endorsing the person, party or programme); they may be negative (treating the person, party or programme as wrong or problematic); they may also be sceptical (calling the person, party or programme into question, casting doubts on their value or validity).

Knowledge is also mediated: scientific or expert knowledge is often presented in popular forms (campaigns, education programmes or reports of the latest 'scientific breakthroughs'). Experts may be approved (phrases such as 'leading scientist') or they may be challenged (experts who are talked about as being detached from reality, as 'ivory tower' academics, and as partisan or, even worse, 'political' rather than independent).

If both knowledge and politics are mediated to the public – so the public are also mediated in several ways. They are mediated to political actors and organisations, through such techniques as online public opinion polling ('should the government resign?'), surveys ('what's the most important problem today?'), interviews with the 'man – or woman – in the street' and focus groups, all designed to reveal 'what the people think'. As a result 'we' (the public) often come to hear about what 'we' think through the media. The results of such investigations are also framed. Lay knowledge or public attitudes can be presented in very different ways. Sometimes such knowledge or attitudes are framed approvingly – 'the public expects X or Y'; sometimes they are presented disparagingly as 'old wives' tales', popular stereotypes, urban myths or 'common sense'.

Summary

- Issues such as climate change have to be identified as public matters in order to be seen as threats or risks that need to be governed.
- Threats or risks may be defined and understood differently by expert and lay constituencies.
- Central to making things public are processes of mediation, through which knowledge, information, ideas and images circulate to provide frames of reference or interpretation (including availability heuristics) that may be widely shared.

2 Governing public issues

So far we have used the issue of threats to draw attention to some of the ways in which things get made public and to how they might become issues of political concern for people and governments. We want now to look a little bit more closely at what it means to make something 'public' and what it might mean to govern it. Consider, first, the following definition of private life as 'the things that matter most to us as social beings: home, family, friends, sex and love ... the rhythms of leisure and relaxation, comfort, sadness and happiness' (Weeks, 1995, p. 131). Jeffrey Weeks relates the 'private' to things that engage our emotions, to things that relate us to particular others, to specific activities and to certain spaces. The private is usually viewed as the opposite of public. But what, then, is public?

Activity 5

Consider the following and decide whether they are private or public acts:

- a local council ban on the hunting of animals on land that it owns
- a landowner banning hunting on his or her land
- sexual relations between consenting adults
- relations between parents and children
- childcare.

The first two examples were the subject of a study by the legal scholar Davina Cooper (1998) of how governments seek to govern activities in which different groups in society have opposing or differing views. Somerset council introduced a ban on deer hunting on public land (the Quantock Hills) for which the council was responsible. The ban was overturned in the courts. Here Cooper explains the legal reasoning that refuted the council's ban:

> in the case of Somerset's hunting ban, the court perceived the ban as motivated not only by opposition to hunting, but also by an antipathy towards hunters. While a private landowner could legitimately restrict access on this basis, local government as a public body could not. Bodies like local government are expected

to reach decisions on grounds deemed 'rational' rather than arbitrary (affective equals arbitrary in this context). If a decision is perceived as, or can be constructed as, affective – based on likes and dislikes rather than more acceptable criteria – it may move outside statutory discretion.

(Cooper, 1998, p. 20)

Cooper suggests that certain constructions of a divide between the emotional or affective, on the one side, and the rational, on the other, are mapped onto the distinction between public and private, such that public action (by public bodies) is supposed to be reasonable, rather than motivated by passions or enthusiasms. In this case, the court ruled that the decision of the council was *ultra vires* – that is, outside its constitutional remit – because it was made on the basis of criteria which were in effect 'private' in that the court saw them as motivated by likes and dislikes. In contrast, individual landowners – acting as private individuals – could ban hunting on their land (because private individuals are entitled to express their passions, likes or whims in relation to their own property).

Let's briefly consider the other examples. Sexual relations between consenting adults and relations between parents and children are part of personal lives (or family life) and perhaps therefore private – at least on Weeks's definition quoted above. But these relations are not unregulated by law; indeed, state regulations govern many aspects of private life. Regulations determine at what age we can engage (legally) in some activities (from sexual relations to getting married); they determine with whom we can engage in such activities (barring sexual relationships with close blood relatives – incest); or enabling heterosexual couples to marry while same-sex couples can enter into civil partnerships (as the law stands in the UK at the moment). The *public authority* – the state – regulates, and sometimes intervenes in, private spaces and private lives; for example, do you think that the state (in the form of police or child protection workers) should have the power to remove children from places where they are at risk of violence, cruelty or neglect? Should it have the power to remove vulnerable adults facing the same risks?

The final example in Activity 5 was childcare. Insofar as it takes place within a family, it might similarly be said to be private, but the same activities carried out in a nursery school are public (even if the nursery is a private rather than a public organisation). But even the 'private' realm of the family is subject to various forms of public intervention and regulation: from midwife or health visitor inspections and assessments in infancy through to the scrutiny by social workers, police or teachers of carers who are thought to be putting children 'at risk' of physical, sexual or emotional abuse. Between these private/familial and public/nursery institutions there are a number of other forms of childcare; so, would you say that a paid childminder is public or private? If a child is looked after by a grandparent, is that private? Does it make any difference if the grandparent is paid to look after the child? These examples show that *making something public* is no simple matter; issues or activities have to be made visible, constructed and located in particular ways for them to become matters of acceptable public concern.

Childcare carried out in a nursery setting is public – but what about a paid childminder?

There are always disagreements about where to draw the boundaries between public and private, and things move between being private matters and public issues at different times. But how and where the line is drawn is always a public and political process, and political choices always involve some construction of this public/private divide. Politics is the activity of arriving at collective choices, policies, regulations, and the like, in circumstances where there is always the possibility of doing things differently. Without some degree of cooperation, there is no collective choice and no politics; but without some conflict or competition over alternative ways of drawing the distinction, there is no need for a political choice at all. Thus, those who want politically to contest the way what is public and what is private is distinguished in a given case must do so by invoking an alternative distinction based on an alternative framing and representation of the issues. For example, since the late nineteenth century, various campaigns have demanded that forms of child abuse and domestic violence should not remain 'private' matters (kept within the home or the family). Instead, they argued that abuse and violence needed to be seen as matters of public concern and subject to intervention by public agencies (police, social workers, and so on). Issues have to be *made* public or private – they have to named, defined and constructed in particular ways. This is one reason why the languages and images used in politics matter alongside the material interests that may also be at stake. Questions of who speaks for whom and how issues are represented are central to political activity. This is especially the case where the issue cannot 'speak' for itself – for example, the protection of the non-human environment – and where considerable cultural and political work is needed to make it public, to make it a suitable subject for political consideration, and thus a potential target of attempts to govern.

2.1   How are public matters governed?

You will have noticed that in this chapter – and indeed in the course more generally – we have used some key words in ways that suggest overlaps and a lack of clear distinctions. Ideas of governing are particularly entangled in this way; our list of connected and overlapping words about governing includes:

> govern, government, state, politics, political actors, politicians, parties, public, authority, political authority.

It would, of course, be easier for everyone if there was one simple and agreed definition of each of these terms that allowed clear differences to be drawn out. But that is not true in everyday speech where meanings shift, overlap and are contested. It is unreasonable to expect it to be true in social science writing (not least because social scientists use many of the same words as everyday speech, even if they then call them concepts). Nevertheless, it may be worth trying to draw out some of the differences and connections a little more, as all of these words are important for this chapter and the two that follow it. In particular, we want to indicate some of the ways in which such words are important for social scientists: what do such concepts allow social scientists to see and think about?

So, *governing* might be described as the process of trying to shape, direct or rule some areas of life. The process of governing – usually governing others – is undertaken by many sorts of agencies and groups who combine two things: a commitment to make things, or people, better (or to keep them the same in the face of threats that might make things worse) and a claim that they have the *authority* to bring this improvement about. This double aspect of governing – improvement and authority – can be found in many practices of governing. For example, officially constituted governments claim authority (from elections or other expressions of popular support) to improve the well-being of the population. Equally, religious organisations claim authority over their membership (or the faithful) and seek to guide or direct their actions for their spiritual or material well-being. Schools are given temporary and conditional authority over children to shape their personal and social development. This authority, which is typically licensed by the state, is expressed in the Latin phrase *in loco parentis* (in the place of the parent), a reminder that parents have authority over children. In exercising authority over their children, parents are expected to take proper care of them. Where parents fail to meet that expectation, their children may be removed from their authority and taken into public care.

Governments govern but they are not the only agencies and institutions that attempt to steer and shape the course of collective choices and decisions. Social groups (both formal and informal) campaign on social issues such as poverty, migration, human rights and neighbourhood crime. Organisations such as churches, firms, trade unions, professional bodies and charities, institutions at a sub-UK level such as local, regional and national governments, as well as institutions beyond the nation state such as the European Union or the United Nations – all of these attempt to govern social life by giving it a direction and momentum in one way or another. Nevertheless, *the government of a state* has sources of authority and legitimacy that are highly distinctive. It has a control of territory and population that is not generally given to other organisations and institutions, and ultimately it has coercive powers that are also not generally given to others. The government governs in the name of 'the people' – the population of a given territory. Often, this population is a nation; and we generally associate governments with nation states, although identifying the nation is not always easy.

You looked at some of the difficulties of identifying the nation in Chapter 5 of this book.

Governments claim *political authority*; that is, they claim to be the legitimate leaders, rulers or representatives of the people. Sometimes, this legitimacy derives from democratic processes (elections that are decided by popular vote), sometimes from hereditary descent (monarchies) and sometimes by force or by seizing power (dictatorships). We are not going to examine these different routes to becoming a government here, but it is important that each of them lays claim to legitimacy – ruling in the name of the people. As a result, governments claim the authority to protect, develop or improve the people and the country that they govern.

Governments form one part of the *state*, but states always contain more than governments. They include other parts of the 'machinery of government'. Governments govern through this 'machinery', using it to protect, develop or improve the nation (both the people and the country). This machinery usually includes:

- laws (and the means of putting them into practice – courts, police, and so on)
- military force (to defend the country against external – and internal – enemies)
- Tax-collecting systems (to pay for the machinery of government and to invest in protection, development and improvement)
- improvement systems (from road building to education; from water supplies to controlling additives in food).

The *authority* to govern, like any other kind of authority, is justified in terms of the purpose it is intended to serve and the sources of its authorisation, and there is a delicate relationship between the exercise of authority and its ongoing need for authorisation. Governmental authority is no different in this respect from, say, medical authority, parental authority or the authority of an employer: if it is misused, or if it oversteps its agreed boundary, it is called into question and may need to re-establish itself, perhaps on a new basis. In fact, it can be argued that authority is the single biggest tool that governments have; after all, why do most people, most of the time, pay their taxes and provide the state with the information it seeks, if not because they recognise its authority to ask for these things? One might suppose that, since states generally maintain a monopoly over the organised means of violence, a government could fall back on coercive measures. However, even the most coercive regimes need to maintain the loyalty of their means of coercion: the armed forces and police services.

Authority, even in coercive regimes, relies on consent

Authority, then, relies on consent from those over whom it is exercised. It is this feature that distinguishes authority from the direct exercise of power through force or coercion. Sometimes, and in some places, governments do govern through the use or threat of force, and all states have some machinery of coercion (armed forces, police, prisons, and so on). But it appears to be more economical and effective to govern through consent. By consent, we do not necessarily mean enthusiastic endorsement of the government or its policies. Consent can be passive, grudging or merely a matter of compliance. It may be consent to the 'rules of the game' in political terms, rather than consent to a specific government. But such varieties of consent contribute to, or enable, the exercise of authority.

Nevertheless, authority has to be earned and thus has to be created and sustained, and sometimes repaired and reinvented, on a continuous basis. Perhaps the most important question to ask of any political proposal is, therefore, where or from whom and on what basis would the authority to carry the proposal through come from? Governments certainly have a role to play in creating authority for their actions; they are not simply passive recipients of authority that is bestowed by others. But if they seek to enlist the agency of others, whether individuals or groups, organisations or institutions, and to avoid governing coercively, they have to work to create consent, or at least acquiescence, among those they seek to govern.

Faced with a desire to govern in a particular way, on an issue that does not command public support, what might a government do to seek authority? One possibility, represented by David King's text, is to seek to persuade people by providing information about possible courses of action and the likely costs and benefits of the government's preferred alternative. This enrols 'scientific authority' in the service of governing, either to shape decisions or to give legitimacy to political choices. An alternative is to align political choices with 'lay expertise' – to present a policy as responding to popular desires. For example, in political debates about choice in public policy in the UK, Tony Blair, who was then prime minister, argued that:

> In reality, I believe people do want choice, in public services as in other services. But anyway, choice isn't an end in itself. It is one important mechanism to ensure that citizens can indeed secure good schools and health services in their communities. … Choice puts the levers in the hands of parents and patients so that they as citizens and consumers can be a driving force for improvement in their public services. … We are proposing to put an entirely different dynamic in place to drive our public services: one where the service will be driven not by the government or by the managers but by the user – the patient, the parent, the pupil and the law-abiding citizen.

> (Blair, quoted in White and Wintour, 2004, p. 1)

But if there are so many types of authority, why do we (and other social scientists) see states – what we called political or public authority – as so important? We want to suggest that states do more than 'connect' many other sorts of authority. *States order, organise and authorise types of authority.* They establish who might legitimately claim to exercise authority over particular aspects of society; for example: what authority parents can exercise over their children; where the professions of medicine can exercise their authority (and what the limits are); over what aspects of personal and social life churches can claim to exercise authority. To take the last example, societies vary considerably in the role that religions play in processes of governing. In some societies, religion has been wholly excluded from public and political life in favour of secular policy-making; in others, religions have been tolerated as private rather than public matters; elsewhere, religions have been officially part of the state (the Church of England as a national church; bishops holding places in government, and so on) or engaged in the business of improvement (providing schools or social services, for example). So, states tend to establish the legitimate reach or scope of many other types of authority.

Summary

- Key words in relation to governing include: government, state, politics and authority. The question of authority is particularly important as it enables organisations and actors to shape or direct aspects of social life and to intervene to direct particular sorts of people or improve particular conditions.

- Authority is an important resource for governments, states and other social actors and organisations (from parents to churches) that seek to govern people's conduct. It needs to be legitimate (it can only be exercised with the consent of those being governed), and such legitimacy needs to be renewed, repaired or restored regularly.

- States have a unique role, being both sites of authority and institutions that distribute or license different social actors and organisations to exercise authority in specific relationships.

3   Whose problem? The issue of social inequality

In this section, we explore the issue of social inequality, putting some of the ideas from the previous sections to work in relation to a new example. For instance, we will ask what sort of problem social inequality represents (is it a public issue?) and what it might mean to govern social inequality (who should be responsible for governing inequality?). Inequality is one of the very long-running focal points of social science research and theorising. Studies have explored the forms that inequality might take, and how it persists or changes, and there are intense debates about what causes inequality and what its social consequences are. Within this chapter, we do not intend to cover all of these – but while you work through this section you might want to reflect on why inequality is such a vital issue for the social sciences and why it has links to issues of social order and practices of governing.

Let us begin with a preliminary definition of **inequality** from a social science standpoint: social scientists are interested in the unequal distribution of valued social resources within a society (and between societies). As you will see shortly, most studies of social inequality focus on the distribution of income or wealth, but it is important to recognise that income and wealth are particular sorts of valued resources. There may be others: for example, power can be viewed as a social resource and may be unequally distributed; alternatively, happiness may be socially valued and it may also be unequally distributed. So, too, may life expectancy or good health. The point about stressing valued social resources is that different societies may value different sorts of resources (think about the significance of access to or control of land, for example). But in most contemporary societies, organised around market economies, income and wealth command most social science attention – because income and wealth enable people to achieve desired goals, and may also be taken as a marker of social standing, value or worth.

Inequality
The unequal distribution of valued social resources within a society or between societies.

You looked at how happiness may be socially valued in Chapter 1 of this book.

Activity 6

You should now read the following article taken from *The Guardian* in May 2009. It discusses income inequality over the last thirty years in the UK. As you read the article, make a note of three things:

1 What do you know about income inequality from the article?

2 In what ways do the article and the people quoted within it see inequality as a public issue?

3 Who is responsible for governing inequality?

UK's income gap widest since 60s

- Labour admits child poverty failure
- Incomes of poorest fall

Britain under Gordon Brown is a more unequal country than at any time since modern records began in the early 1960s, after the incomes of the poor fell and those of the rich rose in the three years after the 2005 general election.

Deprivation and inequality in the UK rose for a third successive year in 2007–08, according to data from the Department for Work and Pensions that prompted strong criticism from campaign groups for the government's backsliding on its anti-poverty goals.

In a further blow, the government failed to make a dent in the number of children or pensioners living in poverty after big increases the previous year. Almost 17,000 more children in England are on free school meals this year compared with last, according to government data also published yesterday.

About 15% of pupils in state schools are now entitled to free school meals because their parents receive welfare payments or earn below £15,575 a year, the figures show. Last year, 14.5% of pupils were eligible.

Even before the onset of the UK's deepest recession in a generation, official figures showed that only the better-off families were spared from a squeeze on living standards that saw median income virtually unchanged and fresh cuts in real pay for those on the lowest salaries.

Since Tony Blair's third election victory, the poorest 10% of households have seen weekly incomes fall by £9 a week to £147 once inflation is accounted for, while those in the richest 10% of homes have enjoyed a £45 a week increase to £1,033.

The data shows that the second poorest 10% of households has also had to make do with less since 2005. Overall, the poorest 20% saw real income fall by 2.6% in the three years to 2007–08, while those in the top fifth of the income distribution enjoyed a rise of 3.3%. As a result, income inequality at the end of Labour's 11th year in power was higher than at any time during Margaret Thatcher's premiership.

The Institute for Fiscal Studies, Britain's leading thinktank on tax and benefits, said the increase in poverty in 2007–08 was due to weak income growth for the low paid. Rising inflation had also eroded the real value of state benefits and tax credits. Meanwhile, the number of working adults living below the official breadline rose by 300,000 to 11 million, with childless adults the worst affected. With financial help from the state concentrated on pensioners and the young, one in seven working-age adults without dependent children are now living in poverty – the highest ever level.

Ministers all but admitted that Labour had abandoned the 2010 goal of halving child deprivation from the 3.4m total at the turn of the millennium but insisted that the party was committed to abolishing it entirely by 2020.

Children's minister, Beverley Hughes, said that in the current economic climate 'meeting the 2010 target is very difficult. It is very difficult to model the impact of the recession on child poverty.'

She said that government action since 2007 would cut child poverty by 500,000 but had yet to show up in the DWP data.

After steady progress in the first half of the decade, which saw the number of children in households with income less than 60% of the median fall to 2.7m, there has been a 200,000 rise in this parliament.

The IFS said the government had reduced child poverty by 16% and would need to spend £4.2bn a year to hit its 2010 target, but had allocated only £200m in last month's budget. 'Given the state of the public finances, it seems unlikely that the government will find the remaining £4bn needed in the 2009 pre-budget report' it said.

The shadow work and pensions secretary, Theresa May, said: 'Gordon Brown's pledge to halve child poverty by 2010 is just one of countless Labour promises that lies in tatters. It is a tragedy that the number of children falling into the poverty cycle is continuing to rise.'

Martin Narey, chief executive of Barnardo's, said: 'Today's figures provide confirmation that Labour have abandoned their bravest commitment – to halve child poverty by 2010. For the families left to languish in the misery and debt that poverty inflicts, that is a tragedy.'

Colette Marshall, UK director of Save the Children, said: 'It is outrageous that so many children continue to miss out on the basic necessities most take for granted. Today's figures show the government will fall well short of its 2010 target. In 2001 Gordon Brown referred to child poverty as a "scar on Britain's soul". [It] is taking a very long time to heal.'

Steve Webb, the Liberal Democrats' work and pensions spokesman, said: 'Labour is losing the fight against poverty. What chance has it got of abolishing child poverty if it can't even get halfway?'

'This government's promise to make Britain a fairer place, where income does not affect a child's life chances, rings hollow. Gordon Brown's means-tested benefits have failed to lift children and pensioners out of poverty.'

Elliott and Curtis, 2009

We think that the critical information about income inequality that can be gathered from this article is that the poorest 10 per cent of households' income had fallen (after inflation) since 2005, and longer term since 1997 (the date of Tony Blair's first election victory). The poorest 20 per cent of households were 2.6 per cent less well off than in 2005. In contrast, the richest 20 per cent had seen their incomes grow (by 3.3 per cent since 2005).

Everyone quoted in the piece thinks that income inequality is a public issue, although they have different reasons for arguing that. Some point to the problem of inequality itself; others point to its implications for child poverty. People from other political parties emphasise the issue of government policy failures. But no one says income inequality is not a public issue. Interestingly, they all seem to agree that it is a responsibility of government to govern this problem.

3.1 Inequality in the UK

Recent studies in the UK (including the Equalities Review set up by the government, which reported in 2007) point to a set of patterns and trends. By patterns, we mean the shape of the distribution of income and wealth and the relationship between different groups. By trends, we mean the ways in which those patterns change or stay the same over time. Let us begin by expanding on the issues raised in *The Guardian* article that you read. The data referred to there was about *income* inequality (how much money a household receives from employment or public transfers – benefits, pensions, etc. each week). But income is not the only form of resource inequality: households also differ in the amount of *wealth* that they own. In both cases, data suggests that the country has become more unequal during the last thirty years.

Activity 7

We have included two sets of data from the UK Office for National Statistics (ONS). These deal with changes in income and wealth distribution. As you look at Figure 3 and Table 3, and the quotes associated with each of them, see if you can identify trends as well as patterns.

The extent of inequality in the income distribution has changed considerably over the last three decades. However, between 1994/95 and 2002/03 the income distribution was broadly stable. Disposable income (adjusted for inflation) grew by over a fifth for both those on incomes at the top of the distribution (90th percentile) and those at the lower end (10th percentile).

Between 1979 and 1983 inequality gradually decreased, but this was more than reversed in the 1980s. Between 1981 and 1989 disposable income in real terms grew by 38 per cent for those at the 90th percentile. This was more than five times the rate of growth of 7 per cent for those at the 10th percentile. During the economic downturn of the first half of the 1990s there was little real growth anywhere in the income distribution.

(ONS, 2009a)

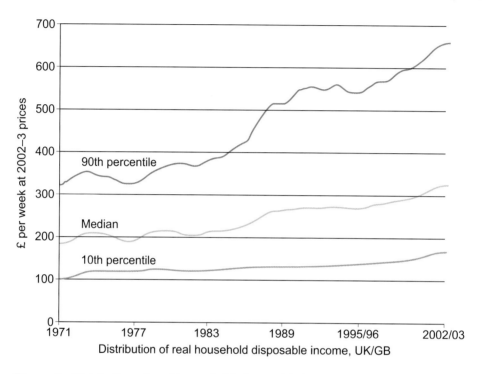

Distribution of real household disposable income, UK/GB

Figure 3   Distribution of real household disposable income, UK/GB (Source: ONS, 2009a)

Table 3   Distribution of marketable wealth

Percentage of wealth owned by:	1976	2003
Most wealthy 1%	21	21
Most wealthy 5%	38	40
Most wealthy 10%	50	53
Most wealthy 25%	71	72
Most wealthy 50%	92	93
Total marketable wealth (£billion)	280	3783

Source: ONS, 2009b

The wealthiest 1 per cent owned approximately a fifth of the UK's marketable wealth in 2003. In contrast, half the population shared only 7 per cent of total wealth. The results are even more skewed if housing is excluded from the estimates, suggesting this form of wealth is more evenly distributed.

(Office for National Statistics, 2009b)

The trends visible in the official data indicate that the gap between richest and poorest income groups has widened, even as overall incomes have grown. The richest 10 per cent earned just over three times the lowest 10 per cent in 1971; by 2002/03 their weekly earnings were over 5 times those of the lowest. They also increased the gap between their earnings and the median (the middle point of earnings).

The data on wealth reveals that the UK became a much wealthier society – but the wealthiest 1, 10, 25 and 50 per cent maintained or increased their share of this wealth. The lowest 50 per cent saw their share decrease by 1 per cent.

3.2   What sort of problem is this?

We think there may be (at least) three different views of inequality as a problem for governing. The first claims that it is not a problem at all: the view that *inequalities are both normal and necessary*. They are normal because people are naturally unequal and all societies have some forms of inequality (see, for example, Gilder, 1985). They are necessary because unequal rewards create incentives and aspirations for people to work harder and to be more innovative or entrepreneurial. This view – often associated with theorists of, and enthusiasts for, social organisation based on 'free-market' principles – has had a strong presence during the last thirty years or more. It has shaped approaches to the economic, taxation and social policies of many governments – towards combinations of lower taxes (individual and corporate), the privatisation of public services and industries, and the deregulation of economic activity, especially in the field of financial services. From this point of view, inequality is only a problem if politicians or governments think they should do something about it and engage in 'social engineering' (a term used to condemn political interference with the 'natural order of things' or the workings of the 'free market').

The second view treats social inequality as a problem of inefficiency. Society is largely fair, but either processes of *social exclusion* leave some people outside normal life or the failings of some people mean that they are unable to participate or compete effectively. Sometimes the focus is on social processes that produce exclusion (discrimination, neglect, and so on), but more often the emphasis has been on the failings of the socially excluded. As a result, government interventions have tended to focus on changing the people – training, creating new skills or providing new incentives. As Ruth Lister (2004) has argued, this is a flat view of society – its centre works well, but around its edges, there are people who need to be drawn back in. She contrasts this flat view with a hierarchical view of social inequality, with tiers of wealth and poverty (see Figure 4). For the sociologist Zygmunt Bauman (1998), this idea of social exclusion has the effect of making the poor responsible for their own poverty: it implies that since society is full of opportunities, it must be their own flaws that prevent them being integrated.

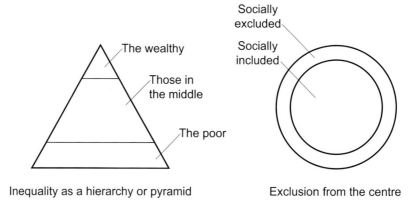

Inequality as a hierarchy or pyramid   Exclusion from the centre

Figure 4   (a) Inequality as a hierarchy or pyramid (hierarchical view)
(b) Exclusion from the centre (flat view)

Finally, there is a view of social inequality as *systemic*: an integral feature of how this society works. A society that values wealth and has means for distributing it unequally necessarily produces 'winners and losers'. Only by changing how the society works can the problem of social inequality be overcome. It is important to stress that this systemic view includes both the *causes* and the *consequences* of inequality. Where the previous two views tend to assume that the consequences of inequality are a problem for the poorest, the systemic view sees a variety of social consequences that affect all members of society (even if they are affected differently). For example, a recent study for the Joseph Rowntree Foundation (2008) estimated that child poverty costs the UK £25 billion per year when direct public spending costs are combined with lost economic productivity. A series of studies by Richard Wilkinson and his colleagues have demonstrated that the greater the spread of inequality in a society, the higher overall levels of sickness will be. That is, greater inequality does not just make poor people sick (although it certainly does that), but it makes all members of the society more prone to illness (Wilkinson and Pickett, 2009). A recent report for the World Health Organization makes similar claims about inequality and mental health (Friedli, 2009). It is worth remembering that a century ago many societies were embarking on social welfare programmes to reduce or at least mitigate the effects of social inequality. One recurrent reason given by politicians was the danger of social unrest or political rebellion; introducing plans for unemployment insurance and old-age pensions, the British politician Joseph Chamberlain claimed that welfare was 'the ransom property must pay' to ensure its continued security (quoted in Saville, 1957).

Joseph Chamberlain

Of course, these are very crude statements of different perspectives on social inequality, but they do indicate something of the range of social science views (and some of their echoes in politics). We have no space within this chapter to explore them in any greater detail. Rather, we want to think about the issues that these conflicting views raise for thinking about *governing* inequality.

3.3   Governing inequality

In this final section, we want to draw out some implications of the above discussion for the processes of governing that we discussed earlier in the chapter. Clearly, one of the critical questions is 'what sort of problem is this?' If inequality is either natural or necessary, then it is not a public problem: it does not require governing. But if inequality is a matter of public concern, people may still argue that the governing processes that can deal with it should be private ones, rather than involve states or government agencies. Many anti-poverty policies and social inclusion strategies have taken this position: such problems of inequality are best overcome by individuals, families or communities improving their own position in life (rather than becoming dependent on the state). The systemic view tends be associated with the view that social inequalities can only be reduced by purposive collective action, usually involving governments using public or social policies to reduce or redress inequality. Here a public problem is to be governed by public means. So we could develop a simple typology in which views of the causes of inequality match with views about how it is to be governed (see Table 4).

Table 4   Governing inequality

View of inequality	Approach to governing inequality
Natural/necessary inequalities	No governing (no 'social engineering')
Failings in poor or excluded people	Private means (help them to help themselves; 'a hand up not a hand out')
Systemic production of inequality	Collective/public action to reduce or redress inequalities

But governing inequality might also involve managing the *consequences* of inequality, rather than having policies for its reduction. In the past, governing strategies have ranged from what – in Roman times – was called 'bread and circuses': providing a mixture of subsistence and engaging entertainment to distract people from thinking about inequality. In the USA in recent decades, forms of spatial segregation have developed that keep rich and poor apart – for example, in the growth of 'gated communities' that insulate the wealthy from the presence of poor (and potentially dangerous) people (Low, 2003).

Gated communities are a form of spatial segregation

A third alternative involves the intense policing or control of poor neighbourhoods to contain inequality and the social or political risks that it may represent. Over the centuries, societies have found many innovative ways of governing inequality that try to avoid the need for greater equality. Making and maintaining social order certainly requires inequality to be governed – but it may be governed in very different ways. Often the desire to preserve the social order means finding ways to legitimate (rather than change) inequalities and finding ways of managing or containing their potential consequences.

Summary

- Inequality can be studied in terms of data that describe the patterns of inequality and data that describe the trends in inequality over time.
- Inequality is framed as a public issue in different ways, and this section has considered three of these: inequality as normal and necessary; inequality as inefficient because it excludes some people

from society; inequality as part of the way the social system is structured and organised.

- Different ways of framing inequality, especially different ways of understanding its causes, are related to different perspectives on how it might be governed.

How do we know?

Evidence and the framing of evidence

This chapter has explored some different types of evidence: it has dealt with quantitative data about forms of social inequality and about some of the risks of climate change. It has also reported evidence of other kinds – studies of the effects of inequality on health and mental health; studies of how ordinary people frame their evaluations of risks, threats and dangers. These also contain or involve quantitative data, but the chapter has simply reported what such studies argue, rather than the data they use.

The chapter has also invited you to think about how things are 'framed' – the ways of looking and thinking about things through which people make sense of issues, information, ideas and images.

Conclusion

In this chapter, we have returned to questions of social order – and the processes by which it is made, maintained, broken and changed. In particular, we have focused on how dangers, threats or problems are governed. Although the word 'governing' is usually associated with governments or states, you have seen that other social actors and agencies may be involved in the processes of governing problems. During this chapter, we have examined the following key questions about governing problems, and we add some very brief thoughts about what the chapter has contributed to answering them:

1   *What issues need to be governed?* Which issues need to be governed is a matter of public or political debate. At different times and in different places, the same issue may be defined as irrelevant, a merely private matter, a necessary consequence of the way 'we' want to live, a source of concern and anxiety, a matter of pressing urgency, or even the 'most serious threat' that people face.

2   *How do people know about them?* People know about issues through various forms of mediated knowledge: ideas that circulate among the communities or networks of which they are part; ideas and images acquired through mass media sources; information, ideas and images that are announced by variously authoritative sources (experts, scientists, politicians and others).

3   *How are dangers, threats and problems evaluated?* Formal methods of assessing or evaluating threats and dangers are associated with quantifying two aspects of the threat: the scale of its impact (loss of life, value of property destroyed, and so on) and the probability of its occurrence. But other orientations may complicate popular or lay assessments of threats and problems. Lay knowledge does not always fit with expert or scientific knowledge, creating political problems about how to deal with particular problems or dangers.

4   *Who is expected to govern these problems?* As with other questions, the answer is 'it varies'. For climate change, there is now increasing pressure on governments to act to control the threat it poses. But in earlier periods, climate change was not thought to be a major problem, or it was a problem that could be left to the actions of individuals and companies to put right. Similarly, domestic violence and child abuse were for a long time treated as 'private matters'

rather than things that needed government intervention. But governments have a dual role. Sometimes they are the agency that acts (making policy, changing rules, etc.). At other times, they authorise other actors and organisations to act (parents, schools, churches, markets, etc.).

References

Bauman, Z. (1998) *Work, Consumerism and the New Poor*, Buckingham, Open University Press.

Cooper, D. (1998) *Governing Out of Order: Space, Law and the Politics of Belonging*, London, Rivers Oram Press.

Elliott, L. and Curtis, P. (2009) 'UK's income gap widest since 60s', *The Guardian*, 8 May [online], http://www.guardian.co.uk/society/2009/may/08/poverty-equality-britain-incomes-poor/ (Accessed 31 May 2009).

Friedli, L. (2009) *Mental Health, Resilience and Inequalities*, Copenhagen, World Health Organization Regional Office for Europe.

Gambles, R. (2010) 'Exploring relationships between the public, private and personal through the phenomenon of Mumsnet.com' in Mahony, N., Newman, J. and Barnett, C. (eds) *Rethinking the Public*, Bristol, Policy Press.

Gilder, G. (1985) *Wealth and Poverty*, New York, Basic Books.

Joseph Rowntree Foundation (2008) 'Child poverty is costing the UK billions', October [online], http://www.jrf.org.uk/media-centre/child-poverty-costing-uk-billions (Accessed 26 June 2008).

King, D.A. (2004) 'Climate change science: adapt, mitigate, or ignore?', *Science*, vol. 303, no. 5655, pp. 176–7.

Lister, R. (2004) *Poverty*, Cambridge, Polity Press.

Low, S. (2003) *Behind the Gates: Life, Security and the Pursuit of Happiness in Fortress America*, New York, Routledge.

Office for National Statistics (ONS) (2009a) 'Income: gaps in income and wealth remain large' [online], http://www.statistics.gov.uk/cci/nugget.asp?id=1005 (Accessed 26 June 2009).

Office for National Statistics (ONS) (2009b) 'Share of the wealth: 1% of population owns 21% of wealth' [online], http://www.statistics.gov.uk/cci/nugget.asp?id=2 (Accessed 26 June 2009).

Saville, J. (1957) 'The welfare state: an historical introduction', *The New Reasoner*, vol. 3 (winter), pp. 5–24.

Tversky, A. and Kahneman, D. (1973) 'Availability: a heuristic for judging frequency and probability', *Cognitive Psychology*, vol. 5, pp. 207–32.

Weeks, J. (1995) *Invented Moralities. Sexual Values in an Age of Uncertainty*, Cambridge, Polity Press.

White, M. and Wintour, P. (2004) 'Public services: the choice', *The Guardian*, 24 June, p.1; also available online at http://www.guardian.co.uk/politics/2004/jun/24/uk.schools (Accessed 26 June 2009).

Wilkinson, R. and Pickett, K. (2009) *The Spirit Level: Why More Equal Societies Almost Always Do Better*, London, Allen Lane.

Chapter 8
Political ordering

Georgina Blakeley and Michael Saward

Contents

Introduction   351

1   Encounters with the state   351

    1.1   Political order in everyday life   351

    1.2   So, what is the state?   354

2   Making and remaking the state   361

3   Legitimising the state   366

4   Repairing the state   371

    4.1   State renewal and repair in Northern Ireland   374

Conclusion   386

References   390

Introduction

In this chapter we explore the significance of the state as a governing authority. Section 1 explores the significance of political order in everyday life, while Section 2 considers the processes through which states are made and remade. Section 3 focuses on one critical issue in the making of political order: the question of legitimacy. Section 4 examines how one particular state and its authority have been repaired – using the example of Northern Ireland to examine contested views of the state and its legitimacy.

1 Encounters with the state

1.1 Political order in everyday life

Jill's story

Jill lay awake in bed waiting for the alarm to ring, worrying about the day ahead. She already had a mental list of things to be done: renew the car's MOT; make an appointment with the health visitor for her toddler's two-year check-up. And there was the inspection they were facing at the school where Jill worked as a receptionist.

The sound of the alarm forced her out of bed and into the shower. Jill managed to leave the house on time, bundling her toddler into the car seat to take her to nursery. Just as she was leaving, the post arrived. Jill ignored the pile of envelopes; probably just more bills and tax demands. She drove the short distance to the nursery, taking care to avoid the potholes and the speed cameras, and left her toddler in the care of her favourite nursery nurse, Vicky.

On her journey to the school, a police car and two ambulances rushed past with their sirens blasting. The noise momentarily drowned out the politician on the radio who was droning on about the next local election. Waving at the lollipop lady, Joan, as she drove through the school gates, Jill braced herself for work. Mercifully, the busy morning passed quickly.

Jill gulped down a quick lunch at her desk while scanning the headlines of the newspaper that one of the inspectors had left behind. One headline declaring the arrival of the 'Big Brother state' turned out, rather disappointingly, to be about the possible introduction of identity cards rather than the reality TV show. Another headline, 'Nanny state bans your chip butty', reminded Jill too late that she had meant to choose the healthy option from the canteen rather than the bacon butty she had plumped for. One headline, however, held her attention: 'More state help for parents: how to save money on childcare'. That's something I really could do with, she thought.

Jill left her desk to dash to the local shops. She needed stamps from the post office; she wanted to join the new DVD rental club (she had remembered to bring proof of identity) and she had to buy a card and present for one of the teachers who was retiring after over thirty years at the school. They were all going to the local pub after work to celebrate. Roll on half-past three, Jill thought, as she headed out into the rain, cursing the weather forecast for being wrong yet again.

Jill's story is in many ways a typical one. You might have had similar mornings yourself or, at the very least, you may recognise some of Jill's experiences as familiar. What any of this has to do with 'political ordering' or 'the state' is perhaps less obvious. After all, this is just a simple account of someone's (hectic) morning. And yet, during this account our protagonist encounters and experiences the state in numerous ways. Moreover, her experience is not unusual. As individuals, most of us will bump up against the state on a daily basis in many areas of our lives, although we might not always notice that we do so. This is because state actors, institutions, practices and discourses order (or try to order) our lives in various ways. The state is not the only mechanism that contributes to social order. Social order is produced and reinforced in various ways, but the state does provide an institutional **political order** that is one important part of the social order it (ideally) produces. In fact, we could argue that there are two types of political order:

1 the avoidance of chaos or disorder generally in society

2 institutions that regulate our lives in many small and large ways.

The two are closely linked. The state is, among other things, an institutional order that aims to prevent social chaos and make social order. But where is the state in Jill's everyday story?

Political order
Both a condition in which there is an absence of conflict and disorder, especially an absence of violent disorder, and a set of organisations that seek to shape or regulate social life.

First, there are the people who are employed by the state to carry out certain functions, such as the health visitor, the lollipop lady, the school inspectors and the teachers. The nursery nurse may be a state employee or she may be employed by a private nursery. Even if she is employed by a private nursery, however, she will still be providing childcare, an activity that is regulated by the state. Though they are not mentioned directly, there are state agents – people employed by a state institution, or in the public sector – behind some of the material objects mentioned, such as the speed camera, the police car and the ambulances. There are also state agents behind some of the practices referred to, such as the arrival of the post.

Some of the state's institutions are also visible, or at least hinted at, in this narrative. By 'institution' we mean organisations (the post office, a government department or ministry, a school or a hospital), but also sometimes regular or patterned 'ways of doing things'. The most visible examples are the school where Jill works and the post office where she buys her stamps. The nursery might well be a state institution. It is also possible to imagine the state institutions behind the police car, the health visitor and the ambulances. Listening to the politician on the radio might conjure up images of the House of Commons, just as listening to the weather forecast might conjure up an image of the Met. Office – although many people may be surprised to know that this is a state institution which operates under the Ministry of Defence.

The state also appears in this narrative through the bureaucratic procedures – that is, established procedures through which state institutions and their employees regulate and order many everyday activities. Jill's office timetable, the length of her working day and the time allocated for her lunch break are regulated by state health and safety procedures. Even the very time that appears on Jill's alarm clock is regulated by the state – an Act of Parliament in 1916 established that people in Britain would get up an hour earlier in summer (from the last Sunday in March to the last Sunday in October to be precise). The requirement to use a car seat, for the car to have its MOT certificate, for Jill to have a valid driving licence in order to be able to drive, all point to the existence of the state through its laws and regulations and the people who work in the state institutions and agencies that make and implement them.

What Joe Painter, the political geographer, calls 'the everyday discourses of state actors' (2006, p. 761) also feature in Jill's story. Most obviously there is the politician talking on the radio, but there is also the labelling that probably appears on Jill's sandwich telling her what ingredients it contains, the road signs on Jill's way to school, the tax demands which may have come in the post and even the fine she might have incurred driving past the speed camera. The state also presents itself to individuals, not just through official correspondence in the form of tax demands or speeding fines, but through the mass media. Newspaper headlines referring to the 'Big Brother state' or to the 'nanny state' do so because these terms have meaning – they reflect ideas about the state that circulate in society. These particular headlines imply a state that is overbearing and intrusive in everyday life, and they are used precisely because this is one image of the state that has resonance for many people. There is, however, a headline that talks about state help, and this suggests another idea of the state that supports its citizens with childcare or retirement; in other words, what is generally defined as the welfare state. We can see here an interesting tension between state provision of security and protection on the one hand, and unfair state intrusion into people's lives on the other. Many political debates focus on disagreements about how to define the point at which protection and support turn into intrusion or interference.

1.2   So, what is the state?

The kind of everyday practices and representations of the state in Jill's story shape, for the anthropologists Aradhana Sharma and Akhil Gupta (2006), the ways in which people experience and learn about the state. But what is the state, exactly, and where is it? From Jill's story, it seems that the state is everywhere, enmeshed in our daily lives through a complex assemblage of institutions, practices, people and discourses.

■   It is worth saying that we could have given more examples of state presence drawing on Jill's story; you might want to have a go at listing more examples yourself.

So, there are many and varied practices through which the state orders – or attempts to order – our lives. Or, to put it another way, there is a lot of political ordering going on in ordinary, everyday life. This fact tells us something about what the state is – it is the thing that does all this complex ordering. But the state remains a rather elusive thing. One might say that it lacks 'thingness'. For example, I can visit a government department, see my NHS doctor, phone the police, write an email to my local council representative and correspond with the tax office. But **the state** is always more than each of these things – perhaps it is not so much a thing as a rather abstract idea which, in a sense, 'sits behind' all of these organisations. The state as such does not appear – it seems to be everywhere and nowhere at the same time. This is one reason why the emphasis on practices is important. But there is a sense in which the state is less abstract, or more concrete. We could say that the state is all the organisations and agents through which and by which these practices are made and remade. So, in that sense, the state is also a set of organisations.

Taking the state as a set of organisations, we can see that the state today is a much larger, more complex, and more numerous set of organisations and practices than it was two hundred, one hundred or even fifty years ago. The English historian A.J.P. Taylor argued that, until August 1914, the state left the adult citizen alone and 'a sensible, law-abiding Englishman could pass through life and hardly notice the existence of the state, beyond the post office and the policeman' (1975, p. 25) (Taylor was writing specifically about England, but what he says applies more generally across the UK). This is certainly no longer the case today. For Taylor, it was the First World War, and then the Second World War, that increased the reach of the state into the daily lives of both men and women, as all aspects of the economy and society were drawn into the war effort on an unprecedented scale:

> The mass of the people became, for the first time, active citizens. Their lives were shaped by orders from above; they were required to serve the state instead of pursuing exclusively their own affairs. Five million men entered the armed forces, many of them (though a minority) under compulsion. The Englishman's food was limited, and its quality changed, by government order. His freedom of movement was restricted; his conditions of work prescribed. Some industries were reduced or closed, others artificially fostered. The publication of news was fettered. Street lights were dimmed. The sacred freedom of drinking was tampered with: licensed hours were cut down, and the beer watered by order. The very time on the clocks was changed. From 1916 onwards, every Englishman got up an hour earlier in summer than he would otherwise have done, thanks to an act of parliament. The state established a hold

The state
The state is: an idea based on shared expectations about the ordering of social life; a set of organisations; and a set of practices.

over it citizens which, though relaxed in peacetime, was never to be removed and which the Second World War was again to increase.

(Taylor, 1975, p. 26)

States today do more, and they need more people and more organisations (departments, agencies, advisory and regulatory bodies) to do so. States are now so large and complex in terms of both their structures and their functions that Christopher Hood (1982), a political scientist, has argued that the bodies that now make up the state are 'a formless mass'. One hundred years ago, even basic ideas of the welfare state, with its structures and operations around health, education and social services, barely existed. Today, along with defence, these are the largest areas of state policy and provision, even after privatisations (the transfer of state bodies and functions to the private sector) and the rise of the market principle from the mid 1980s across Western and a number of other democracies. The economic and social role of the state increased again as a consequence of the financial crisis and downturn beginning in 2008. The large array of things that the state now does requires not only more state employees and agencies, but also more complex patterns of interaction and interdependence between different state bodies, as well as between state bodies and non-state bodies. In short, contemporary states not only consist of enormous numbers of agencies, but they perform an enormous variety of functions.

The size of the state, its organisational complexity and its variety of functions all combine to make the state a difficult thing to grasp (we noted above how it seems to have this 'abstract' quality). Have you ever tried to grasp 'a formless mass'? But there is another reason why the state is difficult to define. In some ways, it appears to be something more than its personnel, its institutions, its practices and its discourses. What is this 'more' that we are talking about here? To try to understand this we will use The Open University as an example. To start with, The Open University consists of all the people who work there in various capacities and of all the people who study with the University. It is also made up of material things, such as its buildings, its computers and all of the course materials generated there, and it is made up of countless practices and daily activities, such as carrying out research, producing courses and marking exam papers. The Open University also presents itself to its employees, its students and the wider society through its official brand, which appears on internal and external communications, and through its advertising in various media. But The Open University also gives the impression that it is more than the sum of all these parts. It appears to have an existence independent of the people, institutions and practices that compose it, akin perhaps to the fictional Unseen University in Terry Pratchett's *Discworld* novels. The Unseen University, which some believe is inspired by The Open University, has an official motto 'Nunc Id Vides, Nunc Ne Vides', loosely translated as 'Now you see it, now you don't'.

We can see this same effect when we try to pinpoint what it is we are talking about when it comes to the state. It is reflected in the distinction that some political scientists make between governments and the state. Government is generally understood as the group of ministers (about 100 people in the UK, led by the Prime Minister) who are collectively responsible to Parliament for making and implementing policy on national issues. While particular governments come and go, mostly as a result of victories and defeats in national elections, the state is 'a continuing, even permanent, entity' (Heywood, 1994, p. 38). More accurately, there is a continuous attempt to create an impression that the state is a permanent thing, even if, in reality, some states also come and go (think of Yugoslavia, for example, a state that no longer exists, having been broken up in recent years into a number of new states – Serbia, Croatia, Bosnia-Herzegovina, Slovenia, Montenegro, FYR Macedonia and Kosovo). But, how is this quality of permanence and

The Unseen University coat of arms invented by the novelist Terry Pratchett

continuity created? Sharma and Gupta (2006) argue that the everyday bureaucratic practices and the representations of the state (of the kind encountered in Jill's morning) contribute to building up an image of the state that is coherent, unified and dominant across time and space. As a result of the seemingly endless repetition of everyday practices and the images the state presents to us, perhaps (for example) through the uniforms state agents wear, the buildings they work in or discourses in the media, the state comes to assume a dominant and permanent position in our lives as something with a ring of solidity to it. This is reflected in Benjamin Franklin's famous adage that 'In this world nothing can be said to be certain, except death and taxes'. This idea of permanence and solidity is what the political scientist Timothy Mitchell (1999) terms 'the state effect'. For Mitchell (1999, p. 180), the mundane activities and state discourses that we talked about in Jill's story all help to give the impression that the state is more than just the sum of its parts.

From the above, you might have the impression that the state is overpowering and all-pervasive. Certainly this is one image of the state that many have held, past and present. As Figure 1 shows, the frontispiece of one of the most famous books on the state, *Leviathan*, written by the English philosopher Thomas Hobbes in 1651, a time of widespread and dangerous religious strife, certainly appears at first glance to offer us this image.

Hobbes's leviathan state, portrayed by the giant body of the king or ruler, towers over the people and territory it rules. And yet, on closer inspection, we can see that Hobbes's leviathan state is composed of countless individuals. The state appears to dominate those individuals (and in Hobbes's account, the state is certainly there to keep its citizens in awe), but the state also depends on those same citizens for its very existence. Today, we can see that the mundane, repetitive practices that build up an image of the state as coherent and unified depend precisely on the activity of citizens, whether or not they work for the state.

The census, which you came across in Chapter 9 of *Making Social Lives*, provides a clear example of how individuals experience the state.

For example, the census illustrates one way in which individuals experience the state. Through the census, the state literally comes through a person's front door in an official envelope, and individuals are asked to fill in the form following the categories the state has chosen to employ. And yet, a significant proportion of the British population chose to subvert the process by ignoring the classifications

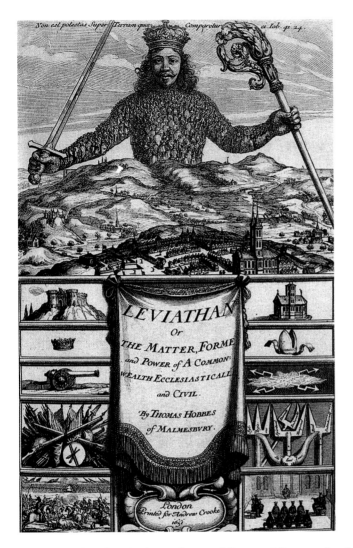

Figure 1 The frontispiece of one of the most famous books on the state, *Leviathan*, by Thomas Hobbes

delineated by the state and identifying their religion as Jedi. Others may well have subverted the process by refusing to fill in the census or by filling it in incorrectly. Thus, there is 'nothing straightforward or obvious about the production and reproduction of the state effect' (Sharma and Gupta, 2006, pp. 17–18).

Summary

- Creating and maintaining political order is largely the job of the state, which we can define as a set of practices, a set of institutions and as a rather abstract idea.

- The state is visible in everyday life through a complex assemblage of institutions, practices, people and discourses which provide social order.

- Most states today are large and complex, and they require more people and more organisations to carry out their functions.

- The repetition of everyday practices and discourses creates the impression of states as permanent and continuous institutions.

2 Making and remaking the state

All individuals, to a lesser or greater extent, are involved in making and remaking the state, as the example of the census above suggests. This happens in numerous and complex ways. To return to her story for a moment, Jill may well have contributed to making and remaking the state by paying her taxes, by not speeding, by renewing her MOT and by taking her toddler to the health visitor for a check-up. On the other hand, she may well have contributed to 'unmaking' the state by doing none of these things or by doing them in ways that go against established processes and procedures.

Activity 1

Figure 2 is a picture of a citizenship ceremony, which is an interesting example of one of the ways in which individuals might be called upon to accept or to reinforce the state. Have a look at the image and jot down a few notes on what the symbols in the picture suggest to you about the state.

Since 1 January 2004, under the Nationality, Immigration and Asylum Act 2002, all successful adult applicants for British citizenship have been required to attend a citizenship ceremony. While they are quite a recent innovation in the UK, citizenship ceremonies have a longer history in other countries, such as Australia. These ceremonies are an example of a performance carried out by individual citizens that contributes to producing and reproducing the state and to creating a particular idea of the state. A key element of this idea is the link between the state and a nation defined by its territory and people. One of the most famous definitions of the state, which is regularly used in political argument today, depends on this symmetrical relationship between a state, its territory and its people. The German sociologist Max Weber, in a lecture given in 1918, defined **the state** as 'a human community that (successfully) claims the *monopoly of the legitimate use of physical force* within a given territory' (Weber, 1991 [1921], p. 78). While other elements are key to Weber's definition, and we shall explore some of these below, territory is clearly central to it – the state claims to be dominant (it claims to say what goes) within a defined territory, or within a country's borders.

The state (as defined by Max Weber)
An organisation that successfully claims a monopoly of the legitimate use of force in a given territory.

Figure 2   A citizenship ceremony for immigrants who become British citizens

The relationship between state and nation was discussed in Chapter 5 of this book.

And yet, the relationship between state and nation, or nations, is not a given – it is constructed rather than natural. The suggestion of a citizenship ceremony for all school leavers in the UK sparked off intense debate because it raises key questions about the relationship between the state, its territory and its people. In part, this is because the borders of a state do not necessarily coincide with the borders of a nation, as in the case of the United Kingdom of Great Britain and Northern Ireland (the official title of the country since 1927) where one state houses three nations – England, Scotland and Wales. Northern Ireland is an interesting example, and one to which we will return below. For now we can say that it is part of the state of the United Kingdom of Great Britain and Northern Ireland, but only some would consider it a nation or would describe their nationality as Northern Irish. Some refer to it as a state-within-a-state, others as the Province, others as the Six Counties, others as Ulster.

Activity 2

In 2008, a report, authored by government minister Lord Goldsmith, and commissioned by Prime Minister Gordon Brown, suggested that all school leavers should be encouraged to take part in a citizenship ceremony, which could contain an oath of allegiance to the Queen. Below is a selection of personal pledges that members of the public invented in response to this suggestion. Read the pledges and try to draw out what they say about the relationship between the people who wrote these pledges and the state they are pledging allegiance to.

> I make a personal pledge to respect my fellow citizens, regardless of race, gender, or religion, and to uphold the laws of Great Britain. In so doing, I acknowledge my personal responsibility to contribute to the country I have chosen to call my own.
>
> Lynne Killeen, from Brentwood, Tennessee, USA

> I pledge my oath of allegiance to my Queen and my country. I promise to watch all reality TV and to emulate those that are put before us as examples of fine citizens. I will honour all sporting figures and raise them upon pedestals until such times as they make an error where upon I will pillory them and mock them to the ends of the earth. As an upstanding member of British society I vow to claim as much social benefit as possible to ensure that my binge drinking does not sink to sub-standard levels. But most importantly, and over everything else, I swear that I will not take myself, or my country, too seriously because I am proud to be British and that is how we do it.
>
> Kiltie Jackson, Staffs, UK

> I swear to be true to the Queen (or King) of England (even though I'm Welsh) and to never watch her speech on Christmas Day because there's always a good film on the other channel. I promise to moan constantly about the weather, the price of fuel, Americans and how much better things were 10/20/30 years ago. I will not leave my bag unattended on a railway station. I pledge allegiance to the flag of Ikea and can't wait for the next series of Dr Who which is

very British and also made in Wales. I will not accept foreign currencies nor will I weigh items in grams when pounds are perfectly adequate.

Wags, Tywyn Gwynedd

I swear allegiance to humanity, to the values expressed by the UN Charter and vow to uphold the Human Rights of all people in accordance with its precepts.

Lorna McAllister, Cumbernauld, North Lanarkshire

(BBC News, 2008)

These pledges of allegiance point to a number of interesting questions about the relationship between state, nation and territoriality, and about issues of identity and belonging.

The pledges suggest that there is a relationship between a state and a territory but that this relationship is not a neat one. The idea of 'my country' is expressed frequently but exactly what this means varies between the pledges: we have references to Great Britain, England and Wales. The last pledge also refers to a wider 'humanity' beyond the confines of nation states or countries. Although none of the pledges cited here refer to the European Union, they could have done so given that all UK citizens now also have European citizenship.

The pledges also hint at a set of common ideas, values and cultural references, often expressed here in terms of humorous stereotypes, which give people a sense of belonging and a sense of identification with a particular state and its territory, even though these ideas and values might not be uniformly or universally shared.

Finally, there is a sense that being a citizen of a state carries with it certain responsibilities, even if these are often expressed ironically, such as promising to moan constantly about the weather. The first pledge, in particular, stresses the responsibility that arises because this person has chosen to be a citizen of a particular state whereas the other pledges assume, to some degree, a pre-given relationship between a person and the nation state in which they happen to be born.

From the above, we can see how the relationship between people, territory and the state is not pre-given but is made and remade through the practices of citizens and the practices and discourses of the state's agents and institutions. In this sense, the state cannot just assume its territoriality, but must constantly lay claim to it.

Summary

- All individuals are involved in making and remaking the state through everyday activities, such as paying tax, or through special events, such as citizenship ceremonies.
- There is a relationship between the state, its territory and its people. This relationship is not pre-given or natural but rather is a product of constant claims.

3   Legitimising the state

We used the example of citizenship ceremonies to open up the issue of the links between state, nation and people. Citizenship ceremonies are just one way in which citizens are requested by the state to legitimise their relationship with the state. 'Legitimacy' refers to a belief in the state's 'rightness', its right to rule, or the idea that its authority is proper. A state that is (believed to be or accepted as) legitimate is more likely to succeed in its constant tasks of political ordering than a state that is perceived as illegitimate. The majority of citizens in the UK, however, are unlikely to be called upon to participate in one of these ceremonies. So, in what other ways does the state seek to claim legitimacy from its citizens? We have already seen from Jill's story that many of the everyday practices and discourses of the state, its symbols and the ways in which state actors and institutions represent themselves to the people, are involved in this process of legitimation; that is to say, the state's claiming of legitimacy from its citizens.

In addition to these everyday practices and discourses, one of the main ways in which individuals express their acceptance or rejection of the state is through the ballot box. By and large, of course, elections do not tend to question the state's overall legitimacy: they provide a means for people to question and reflect on this or that government policy, the adequacy of this or that government agency, or the talents and policies (or lack of them) of this or that party, candidate or official. Nevertheless, in the contemporary world, legitimacy – the sense that the state is in some way rightful – is closely associated with democratic principles. One prominent democratic theorist, David Beetham (1992), suggests that **political legitimacy** can arise from:

Political legitimacy
Political legitimacy arises in political orders that are rule governed, where the basic constitutional rules accord with the values of those who are governed and where the governed have opportunities to express their consent as to how they are governed.

1   legal validity (the government is formed, and state agencies operate, according to the rules of the constitution)

2   the justifiability of those rules in terms of local values (the constitutional rules are themselves acceptable to the people who are ruled by them)

3   evidence of express consent (the people have regular opportunities to give or withhold their agreement with government and policies, especially, though not solely, through democratic voting).

Today, we would see free and fair democratic elections as the main, if not the only, reasonable indicator of whether people have given 'express consent' to those who hold state-derived power over them.

This is a key point. 'Democracy' is the word that, in the early twenty-first century, names the form of political order that few dare to oppose. To oppose democracy is to put oneself beyond the pale in most political discourse in most countries and cultures today. As the Nobel Prize-winning economist and philosopher Amartya Sen has written:

> In any age and social climate, there are some sweeping beliefs that seem to command respect as a kind of general rule – like a 'default' setting on a computer program; they are considered right unless their claim is somehow precisely negated. While democracy is not yet universally practised, nor indeed uniformly accepted, in the general climate of world opinion, democratic governance has now achieved the status of being taken to be generally right. The ball is very much in the court of those who want to rubbish democracy to provide justification for that rejection.
>
> (Sen, 1999, p. 5)

Democracy, it seems, is virtually the only game in town. Beyond groups of ideological and religious extremists, plus the rulers and defenders of isolated regimes such as that of North Korea, few would explicitly oppose democracy, even if (as we shall see) they disagree on what democracy is. 'Democracy' is the word that describes the early twenty-first century's political good thing, its must-have political system. There is irony in democracy's popularity. Only just over 200 years ago, to be a 'democrat' was to be on the political fringe, perhaps a dangerous radical. At the time of the American and French revolutions – often taken to be the twin birthplaces of modern democracy – 'democracy' still largely meant what we would call 'direct democracy'. Direct democracy is a system in which citizens make community decisions in face-to-face assemblies, as in the famous ancient Athenian democracy, or, in the more modern version, a system in which key (or even all) community decisions are made by direct votes of the people (in referendums).

Arguably, and to tell a complex story in simple terms, what those two great revolutions of the late 1700s invented was not 'democracy', but rather *representative* government. Over time, that system of representation based on elections, establishing a system of indirect rather than direct rule by the people, came to be known as 'representative democracy', and then simply as 'democracy'. The foundations of what we call democracy today were laid by constitutional designers such as James

The Athenian Agora, where citizens used to meet in the open air to discuss political issues

Madison, one of the founding fathers of the US Constitution, who sought to restrain rather than to unleash the forces of democracy. The historical advance to today's democratic systems was halting, dangerous and often bloody. Working-class men, then women, had to struggle to get the vote. Extensions of democracy were opposed strongly by conservative factions and parties at almost every step, in most European countries at least.

Setting the history largely to one side, the pressing question remains – how can we define democracy? If it is so crucial to state legitimation, just what is it? The first point to make is that democracy is not so much a 'thing' as a project; not so much something that is already built as something that is always still under construction. Arguably, there is no non-democracy that cannot be a democracy, and no democracy that cannot be more democratic. And democracy will always be built and run differently in different places, depending on local histories and cultures; Senegalese democracy is real, but it does not operate just like Indian or American democracy. A big part of what democracy is, is the continuing debate about what democracy is.

We can take each of those points on board and still be a little more precise, however. Many commentators refer to 'minimalist' and 'maximalist' approaches to **democracy**. Minimalists define democracy as competition in elections for the right to govern. Maximalists accept this as a minimal core, but go further – democracy also requires local and direct participation, or special forums for deliberation, or elements of direct democracy such as policy referendums, and so on. The democratic theorist Giovanni Sartori (1987) has argued that there are two key questions we need to ask: (1) Is this a democracy? (2) How democratic is it? In other words, there is a threshold and a continuum – the threshold specifies the minimum requirements of a democracy, and the continuum a range of further democratising institutions and practices on top of those requirements. That is one route to compromise between minimalists and maximalists. But throughout the twentieth century and up to today, there has been lively debate between the two camps as to who knows best the soul of democracy. Minimalists have claimed variously that they are realists, that they base their views on what works in the real world, and that they do empirical research (e.g. on elections and electoral systems) that backs up their views. Maximalists – variously known as 'participative democrats' or 'direct democrats', or more recently 'deliberative democrats' – claim that minimalists do not take seriously the genuinely radical call, as well as the real practical potential, of democracy as 'rule by the people'. Nevertheless, the grounds for a compromise built on Sartori's notions are strong. There is little point trying to extend democracy in terms, say, of citizens' juries and policy referendums if a system of free and fair elections for parliamentary representatives is not in place. And there is equally little point in establishing free and fair elections and then saying to citizens 'that's it, just turn up to vote every four or five years and there's nothing more you can or should do'.

There are other ways to look at democracy too. Of course, people's lived *experience* of democracy will vary a great deal, within one place or country and between countries. Men and women, younger people and older people, members of different ethnic groups, rich and poor, working-class and middle-class people will experience democracy in divergent ways. Ideals associated with democracy, such as freedom and equality, are just abstract principles; how and to what extent people can understand them and act upon them puts flesh on the bones of these abstractions, and produces complex and mixed stories. There are different cultures of democracy. Further, critics have argued that there is a lot of window dressing involved in the popularity of 'democracy';

Democracy
Democracy can be defined minimally, in terms of procedures such as competitive elections, and maximally, in terms of ideas of participation, deliberation and the direct involvement of citizens in government.

political leaders and others may construct images of themselves as good democrats, but how far in specific cases does the image match people's lived realities? In short, for all its rhetorical popularity today, democracy remains a set of practices and ideas that is subject to complexity and controversy.

Summary

- In the contemporary world, state legitimacy is closely associated with democracy.
- Democracy has developed from a direct form of rule in which the people took the decisions themselves to an indirect form of rule in which people elect representatives to take decisions on behalf of the people.
- Minimalist approaches to democracy define democracy as competition in elections for the right to govern. Maximalist approaches go further in requiring forms of citizen participation beyond voting.

4   Repairing the state

We have seen that democracy is one of the foremost mechanisms through which states today claim their legitimacy to rule over a certain territory and its people. We have not yet asked, however, why states constantly seek to legitimise their rule. As political theorist Rodney Barker (2001, p. 2) has put it, what characterises government generally 'is not the possession of a quality defined as legitimacy, but the claiming, the activity of legitimation'. The contemporary state is in a continuous process of legitimation – a claim that is never fully fulfilled and never uncontested. Again, this is where seeing the state in terms of its constant, everyday practices is important. There is a close overlapping relationship between these practices, political ordering and seeking legitimation.

A number of factors can help to explain this constant search for legitimacy. First, states are human constructions and not pre-given entities. They are artificially created and need to be reinforced in numerous, regular ways. This can be seen by examining historical maps which show how nation states have evolved. The idea of the United Kingdom would have been unintelligible from examining, for example, a map of Europe around 1000 CE (see Figure 3).

This is because the United Kingdom is an artificial political unit that houses competing allegiances and identities. As suggested above, it is possible that few citizens are aware that the official title of the country in which they live is, and has been since 1927, the United Kingdom of Great Britain and Northern Ireland, and few are likely to use this rather unwieldy title in response to the question of where they are from. Wales, Scotland and Ireland all had their own independent parliaments in the fourteenth, seventeenth and eighteenth centuries, respectively, before they were gradually brought under the political control of the parliament in Westminster in a process that was often violently resisted by those territories forced to give up their independent institutions.

Second, this ongoing process of creation and re-creation denotes that states are only ever partially and temporarily successful in promoting social order (and maintaining an institutional order), despite the impression of solidity and permanence that they carefully cultivate. All states succeed and fail to some extent. The artificial and temporary nature of social order means that states constantly seek legitimacy from their citizens through regular elections, for example, or through new

Figure 3   Europe around 1000 CE

innovations such as citizenship ceremonies. As a result, change is a constant factor in the life of states, even in those that appear to be more-or-less stable. The UK is generally seen as an example of a political system in which change has been gradual and evolutionary and it has retained pretty much the same institutional political order over time. But, in fact, even in the UK, the state has tended to be much more fluid and changeable than might appear at first glance. New institutions have been created, and existing ones revised. Malfunctioning institutions are repaired or replaced. The process of devolution in the contemporary UK in 1998, which resulted in a Scottish Parliament, a National Assembly for Wales and an Assembly in Northern Ireland, can be seen as part of this process of state renewal and repair.

Finally, it is curious that, in an important sense, states base their claim to rule on something they can never have. We can see this paradox clearly if we return to Weber's definition of the state. We have seen how territory is crucial to Weber's definition, but there is also another key element. Weber argued that there was no point defining states by what they do – they do lots of different things. Better, he said, to define it by its means – to ask 'how does it do things?' Weber knew that states did things in various ways, but there was one way, one key characteristic of the state, that was unique: *force*. Institutions of coercion are crucial, as Weber suggests, and closely related to the defining idea of the state being the authoritative rule maker in the territory and among the people over which it rules. The idea here is that, in the end, it is only the state that can make and enforce laws legitimately; corporations, trade unions, universities and private citizens, for example, do not have that authority. It is important to note that Weber says that the state *claims* a monopoly of force – he does not say that a state automatically *has* this monopoly. But here is the paradox: as political theorist John Hoffman (2007, p. 45) argues, 'The state is an institution which claims something that it cannot possibly have.' For Hoffman:

> A state claims a monopoly of legitimate force, but ironically it is only because 'competitors' (that is, criminals, terrorists, etc.) contest the state's claim to have a monopoly of legitimate force that the state exists at all. A state that really did have a monopoly of legitimate force would have no reason to exist. Think of a state in which everyone acted peacefully and regarded all laws as legitimate. It would be wholly redundant!
>
> (Hoffman, 2007, p. 45)

We are now going to look at one historical case to help illustrate the range of issues discussed so far. Focusing on Northern Ireland helps to bring alive a series of linked issues – contested claims to legitimacy, disputes about competing modes of political ordering, and the contingent and always unfinished nature of state claims. And by looking more specifically at political murals in Northern Ireland, we can also focus on the important visual and symbolic elements of such issues. As with all the visual evidence you have come across so far in this course, it is important to remember that the murals in Northern Ireland can be interpreted in numerous ways, depending on their intended and unintended audience, and that they are selective in what they represent and what they omit.

4.1   State renewal and repair in Northern Ireland

The creation of Northern Ireland in 1921 demonstrates that the link between a state, its territory and the people within these territorial boundaries is not pre-given. Following the War of Independence with Britain from 1919 to 1921, the partition of Ireland in 1921, as a result of the Government of Ireland Act in 1920, led to the creation of an independent Irish Republic in the south and a British-controlled Northern Ireland (see Figure 4). Northern Ireland's territorial boundaries were drawn by the British Government in order to incorporate as much as possible of the large Protestant population of Ulster who had opposed Home Rule in the wake of partition in favour of union with Britain.

At the heart of the politics of Northern Ireland is a divided population that experiences the state in quite different ways. In simplified terms, a majority in Northern Ireland, although they represent only a minority in Ireland as a whole, regard themselves as British and want Northern Ireland to remain a part of the United Kingdom. This majority of Unionists, and their radical form, the Loyalists, are also predominantly Protestant. A sizeable minority within Northern Ireland, 44 per cent according to the 2001 Census, define themselves as Irish and Catholic, although an increasing number of people do not see themselves as belonging to either category. The Catholic Nationalists, and their radical form, the Republicans, would prefer to be ruled by a single, Irish authority. For the Catholic minority within Northern Ireland, the creation of Northern Ireland in 1921 established 'an artificial state, devoid of geographical, historical or political logic' (Tonge, 2001, p. 634). Both the Protestant majority and the Catholic minority, however, are not static. The size of the majority and minority fluctuates over time. Moreover, both within and outside this majority and minority, other majorities and minorities based on gender, age, sexual orientation, disability, 'race' and ethnicity, for example, coexist.

The ideas of zero-sum and positive-sum power were discussed in *Making Social Lives*, Chapter 2.

The tradition of mural painting in Northern Ireland provides an insight into the political dynamics of these changing communities. When and where murals appear, what they express and what they don't express, how they are renewed and repaired or how they are forgotten and left to fade provide insights into the political process and the ways in which power is expressed and contested in Northern Ireland. As you read this section, think about the ideas of zero-sum and positive-sum power and

Figure 4   Map of Ireland depicting the partition of Ireland in 1921 between an independent Republic in the south and a British-controlled Northern Ireland

try to decide how they apply to the changing community relationships in Northern Ireland.

For cultural historian and museum exhibition designer Judy Vannais (2001), there are two separate traditions of mural painting in Northern Ireland which are indicative of two different relationships to the state. On the one hand, the Unionist/Loyalist tradition of mural painting has been going on for more than a century. This long tradition denoted a community at ease and confident in its relationship with the state. Mural painting was an expression of this confidence and it literally represented a claiming of public space and territory, and an assertion of identity and belonging, that was evidence of the Protestant domination of politics and society in Northern Ireland. Prior to the 1970s, the majority of Unionist/Loyalist murals were linked to the annual commemoration of the Battle of the Boyne on 12 July 1690, when Protestant Prince William of Orange defeated Catholic King James II in the struggle for the English throne. The dominant image in these murals was of 'King Billy' astride his white horse crossing the River Boyne (see Figure 5).

Figure 5 Protestant Prince William of Orange – King Billy – crossing the River Boyne

The Nationalist/Republican tradition of mural paintings, on the other hand, dates only from the beginning of the 1980s, though attempts to claim territory through painting slogans, for example, pre-dated mural paintings. The late development of mural painting as an expression of the Nationalist/Republican community, in comparison with the early development of Unionist/Loyalist painting, is indicative of a very different relationship to the state. Nationalists and Republicans in Northern Ireland generally rejected the idea of Northern Ireland as a separate state and did not feel that the state belonged to them. The state's laws and daily practices were a constant reminder that the Nationalist/Republican community was a minority in a state that belonged to the majority Unionist/Loyalist community. Nowhere was this exclusion felt more strongly than in the policing of Northern Ireland. Jon Tonge notes that the Special Powers Act of 1922 gave the predominantly Protestant security forces in Northern Ireland vast and arbitrary powers. The Royal Ulster Constabulary averaged only 10 per cent Catholic membership while the auxiliary police force, the B Specials, was exclusively Protestant (Tonge, 2001, p. 634). For Catholics, there was nothing legitimate about the state's claim to a monopoly of force in Northern Ireland.

The late development of Nationalist/Republican mural painting, therefore, denoted a community which felt excluded from the state and feared showing its identity in public. Events in the 1970s, however, forced a change in the politics of Northern Ireland and in community relations, and these changes were reflected in changes in the two communities' mural painting traditions. Influenced by similar movements in the USA, in the 1960s the Nationalist/Republican communities began a series of civil rights marches demanding an end to discrimination against Catholics in the political, economic and social spheres. Specifically, Catholics demanded police reform and a fairer voting system to end Unionist domination of the political system in Northern Ireland, where Unionist Party control of the parliament at Stormont from 1922 to 1972 was matched by Unionist control of 85 per cent of local councils (Tonge, 2001, p. 634). Political discrimination was reinforced by discrimination in education, housing provision and employment.

The increasingly harsh response by the police, and ultimately the British military forces, to the civil rights movement led to a spiral of violence that marked the beginning of the 'Troubles'. The last big civil rights march, on 30 January 1972, became known as Bloody Sunday following the killing of fourteen civilians by British soldiers. Later in 1972, the Northern Ireland parliament was dissolved and direct rule was imposed from Westminster. The state's claim to its monopoly of legitimate force was challenged directly, on the one hand by the Provisional Irish Republican Army (IRA), a left-wing paramilitary organisation that sought to bring about a united Ireland, and on the other hand by various Loyalist paramilitary groupings, such as the Ulster Volunteer Force, the Ulster Defence Association and the Ulster Protestant

Volunteers, which fought to maintain Northern Ireland's status within the UK.

Although the onset of the 'Troubles' curtailed the civil rights movement's reclaiming of public space through protest marches, the Nationalist/Republican community began to assert its control of public space visually through an explosion of mural painting. The main catalyst for change was the hunger strike of 1981 by Republican prisoners demanding the reinstatement of their prisoner-of-war status which had been revoked by the British authorities in 1976. From this moment onwards, the Nationalist/Republican community began to use mural painting in much the same way that it had long been used by Unionists and Loyalists, namely, to demarcate territory and affirm their identity. Murals were a means of communication which aimed to get across a message that was often suppressed and denied in the media. Murals honouring the hunger strikers, especially Bobby Sands (Figure 6), proliferated.

Figure 6   Mural of Bobby Sands, one of the hunger strikers

At the same time, political scientist Jean Abshire (2003, p. 152) argues that these early Nationalist/Republican murals also reflected the changing strategy of the Republican political party Sinn Féin, whose new slogan 'Not everyone can plant a bomb, but everyone can plant a vote' aimed to combine the armed struggle of the IRA with increased political engagement, particularly following the election of Bobby Sands to the House of Commons while on hunger strike.

The long peace

For Vannais (2001, p. 138), the 1994 ceasefires by both Republican and Loyalist paramilitary groupings not only represented a new beginning, which would eventually culminate in the signing of the Good Friday Agreement in 1998, they also marked a new phase in mural painting. She argues that most Nationalist/Republican mural paintings seemed to anticipate the ceasefire signed by Republican paramilitaries on 31 August 1994, while most Unionist/Loyalist paintings seemed to struggle to acknowledge the ceasefire had taken place long after it had been signed on the 13 October 1994.

By 1994, British troops had been in Northern Ireland for twenty-five years. This anniversary was signalled by the appearance in Nationalist/ Republican murals of a circular stencilled emblem which read 'Time for Peace – Time to Go' with the number 25 painted in the centre. Vannais (2001, p. 139) argues that this emblem, which became ubiquitous in Republican areas in the months leading up to the 1994 ceasefire, was a message directed not only at British troops but also at fellow Republicans. Vannais describes one Republican mural painted by Danny Devenny several months before the IRA ceasefire that appeared on gable walls throughout Belfast. The image is of a line of British soldiers marching down a road signposted to England. A banner above the soldiers, decorated with green, white and orange balloons, wishes the troops *Slán Abhaile* ('safe home' in Irish) and below this is the message: 'Time for Peace, Time to Go' (see Figure 7). Vannais (2001, p. 140) argues that what is remarkable about this image is how magnanimous the message is, given the levels of hostility against the British Army at that time.

According to Vannais (2001, p. 142), the optimism and magnanimity that characterised the Republican/Nationalist murals in the period leading up to the 1994 ceasefire were not present in the Unionist/ Loyalist paintings. As Nationalists and Republicans became increasingly assertive and confident in their public identity, Unionists and Loyalists were beset by uncertainty and a lack of confidence. Loyalist murals reflected this changing political landscape as the King Billy theme,

Figure 7   Republican mural marking the 25th year of the presence of British troops in Northern Ireland

which had predominated until the 1970s, began to be replaced by paramilitary themes (see Figure 8).

This uncertainty continued up until and after the 1994 ceasefires, when the message in loyalist murals became more militaristic and demonstrated none of the sense of impending change that could be found in the Nationalist/Republican paintings. It could be argued that this represents an example of zero-sum power, where gains by one side are perceived as losses by the other.

From the 1970s onwards, therefore, mural painting developed in each community in diametrically opposed ways. This trajectory continued through the ceasefires of 1994, into the political negotiations that followed and beyond the Good Friday Agreement of 1998, which was the culmination of this process. Following the 1998 Agreement, Nationalist/Republican murals engaged with the process. Some were genuinely supportive of the new political structures put in place by the

Figure 8   Loyalist paramilitary murals

Good Friday Agreement, while others were critical of the way in which some aspects of the agreement were implemented (see Figure 9).

Figure 9   Nationalist/Republican murals engaging with the Good Friday Agreement of 1998

Loyalist paintings, on the other hand, were much more hesitant in engaging with the political process. This reflected the difficulties that the peace process posed for Unionists and Loyalists. Given that this community desired continued union with the UK, it is perhaps not surprising that the murals did not depict the same sense of change that the Nationalist/Republican murals did. On the contrary, they continued to depict Loyalist paramilitary gunmen, often with the slogan 'No Surrender'. These militant murals served as a warning message both to Nationalists/Republicans and to their own politicians who were engaged in the negotiations. This is indicative of the ambivalence felt by many in the Unionist/Loyalist communities towards the peace process as well as the tensions between various paramilitary factions within the community.

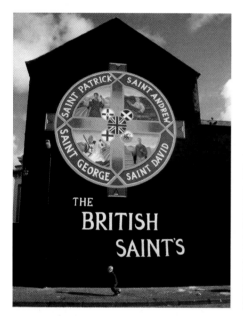

Figure 10   Post-1998 Unionist/Loyalist murals

These different developments in the murals of each community demonstrate the changing relationship of each to the state. They also express changes in the balance of power as murals are created or removed in attempts to demonstrate control over space and place. This case study of mural painting clearly reveals a distinctive and localised way in which disputes over ordering and legitimation claims manifest themselves and change over time, and the important role that symbols and images can play in such processes. As Republicans and Nationalists became more confident and secure in their relationship with the state, the murals began to demonstrate a more commemorative attitude, in much the same way that the early Unionist/Loyalist murals demonstrated their confidence through murals commemorating 12 July. Conversely, new murals by Loyalists and Unionists (see Figure 10) seek to move beyond paramilitary themes to depict new and broader cultural and historical themes, often borrowing icons used by Nationalist/Republican murals in much the same way that Nationalist/Republican murals sought legitimacy for their struggle when they began painting murals in the 1980s (Vannais, 2001, p. 156).

Figure 11 *Painting from the Same Palette* was unveiled at the University of Massachusetts Amherst in the USA

It is still too early to say how politics will develop in Northern Ireland as the power-sharing arrangements established by the Good Friday Agreement continue to evolve. Similarly, it is still too early to say what the fate of Northern Ireland's murals will be, but there are indications that the tradition may evolve rather than disappear, not the least because they are an increasingly popular tourist attraction. In 2008, ten years after the implementation of the Good Friday Agreement and only one year after the historic power sharing in government that began in May 2007, a mural *Painting from the Same Palette* was unveiled at the University of Massachusetts Amherst in the USA (Figure 11).

What was unusual about this mural was that it was painted by Danny Devenny, a former IRA prisoner and famous Republican muralist, and Mark Ervine, a famous Loyalist muralist. According to Danny Devenny: 'During the war, the murals told the story of injustices we experienced. Now they show hope for the future' (quoted in UMassAmherst College of Social and Behavioural Sciences, 2008). Mark Ervine commented that while previous murals reflected the communities' concerns about the conflict: 'Now hopefully this is the beginning of ones that will reflect the peace' (quoted in UMassAmherst College of Social and Behavioural Sciences, 2008). The two artists have continued to work together, most recently on a series of murals depicting the Beatles to celebrate Liverpool's term as Capital of Culture in 2008.

Summary

- There are two traditions of mural painting in Northern Ireland, which are indicative of two different relationships to the state.
- Mural painting is a visible way of claiming territory and affirming identity and a sense of belonging.
- Changes in mural paintings have denoted changes in each community's relationship to the state as the peace process has progressed.

How do we know?

Looking for legitimacy

You have looked at a range of agents, institutions, practices and procedures through which states attempt to order aspects of our social lives. And you have seen that the idea of the state involves a constant work of claiming and receiving legitimacy. That is to say, you have been studying the state through its effects on our daily lives and through the routine, often taken-for-granted, ways in which it seeks to shape and regulate society.

You have also seen that the degree to which people acknowledge that state as legitimate is varied. In the examples of the citizenship ceremony and the ways in which different groups in Northern

Ireland have sought to mark and claim public space, to represent their political identities in visual form, you have seen that the legitimacy of the state is contested, sometimes violently.

In Chapter 5 of this book you were introduced to the idea of reading texts as evidence with a range of questions in mind. Here you have been 'reading' evidence about the legitimacy of the state through a study of its agents, institutions and practices as well as though the ways in which its subjects or citizens represent their vision of the state and their political identities. In particular, the murals of Northern Ireland can be seen as expressing ideas, views or orientations – and need to be 'read' as a source of evidence.

Conclusion

We have seen how the legitimacy of the state was deeply contested in Northern Ireland, primarily by those in the Nationalist/Republican community but also by those in the Unionist/Loyalist community. Moreover, throughout Northern Ireland there are some who were, and still are, critical about the way in which the new power-sharing political structures and institutions of Northern Ireland are developing. It would be a mistake, however, to fall into the trap of seeing Northern Ireland as an exceptional case. Instead it may be located at one point on a continuum that embraces numerous degrees of acceptance felt by individuals and groups towards the state in which they live.

Returning to Jill for a last time, is it possible to argue that her everyday story is a narrative that would be the same whoever she was and wherever she was within the UK? On a general level, the answer is affirmative. It is the case that much of the story would be similar for anyone anywhere in the UK but, on a more detailed level, there would be differences depending on who Jill was and where she lived. This is because individuals, and the communities they live in and belong to, experience the state differently depending on a range of variables, which could include not only territorial location but also nationality, age, gender, class, race, disability, religion and sexual orientation. You might want to think about what kind of narrative you would write about yourself and what kind of experiences of the state would feature in your own story.

Although Wales and Scotland have not, in recent times at least, sought to defend their national identities with force as in Northern Ireland, they have maintained distinct national identities despite being ruled from Westminster on losing their independent parliaments. Most recently, these national identities have gained expression through a Parliament in Scotland and a National Assembly in Wales. It is not just national groups, however, that may feel ambivalence towards the state which governs them. Black people may feel separated from a state that is still run predominantly by white people. Women may question the authority claims of a state still run predominantly by men. Working-class people may at times feel alienated from a state run predominantly by individuals from the middle and upper classes.

Different people might feel different degrees of acceptance in their relationship to the state. Shared experiences of ambivalence or alienation that are articulated and expressed sometimes lead to more-or-less enduring critical perspectives on the state. A number of critical perspectives have grown and declined over the years and decades. Many of these are reformist – advocating relatively minor changes to state structures or practices – and others are radical demands for fundamental change.

Activity 3

Read the extract below. What sort of person do you think it was written by? When do you think it was written? Is it a view of the state that has resonance for you?

> To be GOVERNED is to be kept in sight, inspected, spied upon, directed, law-driven, numbered, enrolled, indoctrinated, preached at, controlled, estimated, valued, censured, commanded, by creatures who have neither the right, nor the wisdom, nor the virtue to do so ... To be GOVERNED is to be at every operation, at every transaction, noted, registered, enrolled, taxed, stamped, measured, numbered, assessed, licensed, authorized, admonished, forbidden, reformed, corrected, punished. It is, under the pretext of public utility, and in the name of the general interest, to be placed under contribution, trained, ransomed, exploited, monopolized, extorted, squeezed, mystified, robbed; then, at the slightest resistance, the first word of complaint, to be repressed, fined, despised, harassed, tracked, abused, clubbed, disarmed, choked, imprisoned, judged, condemned, shot, deported, sacrificed, sold, betrayed; and, to crown all, mocked, ridiculed, outraged, dishonored. That is government; that is its justice; that is its morality.

Now, returning to the thread which opened this chapter, Jill apparently did not take a radically critical view like this (as opposed to being moderately irritated perhaps). But we could just about imagine how the ubiquitous presence of the state in Jill's life might lead to more radical views. The uncompromising words above were written by the classical anarchist writer and political activist J.-P. Proudhon in 1851 in the epilogue to a book entitled *General Idea of the Revolution in the Nineteenth*

Century (Proudhon, 1923 [1851], pp. 293–4). Anarchists are opposed to the state as a matter of principle. The state, for them, is purely an oppressive, exploitative entity. Today, the term 'anarchy' is almost always used as a synonym for something like 'chaos'. The critical perspective Proudhon articulates is associated with the view that individuals can, more-or-less spontaneously, regulate their own behaviour, and that collective rules can arise from the people themselves rather than being devised or imposed by a single sovereign entity, or state. Anarchists argue, therefore, that we can have political order in the sense of avoiding basic social chaos if we do not have institutional political order like the state. Some other form of institutional political order might be fine – a more spontaneously generated, bottom-up, fluid and decentralised set of institutions and practices perhaps. According to this view, Jill, you, me, our friends, family and compatriots could together find ways to organise rules and institutions for ourselves, beyond the state, and doing so would make us freer.

As citizens we experience annoyance with, express support for and criticise aspects of the state's activities and structures in our daily lives. Often we are simply unaware of the many and detailed ways in which the state *orders* our daily routines. Some widely shared critical perspectives on the state, including anarchism, have endured, even as they change over time. Many of these critiques have, to some extent, been taken on by state actors and institutions, for instance in policies on equal pay for women and environmental protection.

We have seen that the work of political ordering is continuous, and that as part of this states are engaged in a constant process of claiming and repairing a sense of their legitimacy. A good deal of this activity involves everyday processes, which order (and in many ways regulate) people's daily lives. In this sense, political order is linked intimately to social order. In this chapter we have explored key ways in which the state acts out its claim to be the ultimate source of legitimate authority over the population and land in a particular territory (or country). Citizens are positioned very differently in terms of race, gender, class, religion and region; individual and group experiences of political ordering, or encounters with the state, will be detailed and varied. There are recognisable ways in which states and their attempts at legitimation are disputed. The specific dynamics of ordering can be highly distinctive in different (often contested) societies, as we saw in the case of Northern Ireland. The state remains a diverse, enigmatic and complex force in all our lives. To sum up, in this chapter you have considered:

- the degree to which states' claims to legitimacy are recognised and acknowledged by individuals and groups varies in time and space

- how a shared experience of ambivalence to or alienation from the state may produce critical political perspectives on the state, both reformist and radical

- how one critical tradition, the tradition of political anarchism, contends that it is possible and desirable to have an ordered society without the institutions of the state.

References

Abshire, J. (2003) 'Northern Ireland's politics in paint', *Peace Review*, vol. 15, no. 2, pp. 149–61.

Barker, R. (2001) *Legitimating Identities*, Cambridge, Cambridge University Press.

BBC News (2008) 'I pledge allegiance to … (add your own)', 12 March [online], http://news.bbc.co.uk/1/hi/magazine/7292172.stm (Accessed 21 July 2009).

Beetham, D. (1992) *The Legitimation of Power*, Basingstoke, Macmillan.

Heywood, A. (1994) *Political Ideas and Concepts*, Basingstoke, Macmillan.

Hoffman, J. (2007) 'Sovereignty' in Blakeley, G. and Bryson, V. (eds) *The Impact of Feminism on Political Concepts and Debates*, Manchester, Manchester University Press.

Hood, C. (1982) 'Governmental bodies and government growth' in Barker, A. (ed.) *Quangos in Britain*, London, Macmillan.

Mitchell, T. (1999) 'Society, economy, and the state effect' in Steinmetz, G. (ed.) *State/Culture: State-Formation after the Cultural Turn*, Ithaca, NY, Cornell University Press.

Painter, J. (2006) 'Prosaic geographies of stateness', *Political Geography*, vol. 25, pp. 752–74.

Proudhon, J.-P. (1923 [1851]) *General Idea of the Revolution in the Nineteenth Century* (trans. J.B. Robinson), London, Freedom Press.

Sartori, G. (1987) *The Theory of Democracy Revisited* (2 vols), Chatham, NJ, Chatham House.

Sen, A. (1999) 'Democracy as a universal value', *Journal of Democracy*, vol. 10, no. 3, pp. 3–17.

Sharma, A. and Gupta, A. (eds) (2006) *The Anthropology of the State*, Oxford, Blackwell.

Taylor, A.J.P. (1975) *English History 1914–1945*, Harmondsworth, Penguin.

Tonge, J. (2001) 'Northern Ireland' in Jones, B. (ed.) *Politics UK* (4th edn), Harlow, Pearson Education.

UMassAmherst College of Social and Behavioural Sciences (2008) 'News' [online], http://www.umass.edu/sbs/news_events/news_stories/mural_unveiling.htm (Accessed 1 July 2009).

Vannais, J. (2001) 'Postcards from the edge: reading political murals in the North of Ireland', *Irish Political Studies*, vol. 16, pp. 133–60.

Weber, M. (1991 [1921]) *From Max Weber* (ed. H.H. Gerth and C. Wright Mills), London, Routledge.

Chapter 9
Pirates and predators: authority and power in international affairs

Simon Bromley

Contents

Introduction   395

1   Pirates   398

     1.1   Pirates – ancient   399

     1.2   Pirates – modern   402

     1.3   Universal jurisdiction   405

2   The United Nations and the international
     community   408

     2.1   The idea of an international community   408

     2.2   Who speaks for the international community?   411

     2.3   The UK and the international community   415

3   Predators, authority and power   418

     3.1   Privateers turned pirates?   419

     3.2   International authority – a tale of two wars   423

     3.3   Power and fear   426

Conclusion   434

References   435

Introduction

In the early years of the twenty-first century, pirates returned to the centre of attention in many cinemas across the world. Johnny Depp's portrayal of Captain Jack Sparrow in *The Pirates of the Caribbean* trilogy – *The Curse of the Black Pearl* (2003), *Dead Man's Chest* (2006) and *At World's End* (2007) – was surely the most successful cinematic rendition of piracy since the Hollywood films of the 1920s and 1950s. Pirates have had a distinguished career in literature: Byron's poem *The Corsair* (1814) and Sir Walter Scott's novel *The Pirate* (1821) are early examples, portraying pirates as romantic heroes and rebels against authority; but the key texts are probably Robert Louis Stevenson's *Treasure Island* (1883) and James Barrie's *Peter Pan* (first performed in London in 1904), which depict pirates as villainous and comic, respectively. Then the Anglo-Italian author, Rafael Sabatini (1875–1950), created a series of stories (*Captain Blood, The Sea Hawk* and *The Black Swan*) which were turned into successful films starring Douglas Fairbanks – the first screen hero to stick a knife in a sail and slide down to the deck – in the 1920s and Burt Lancaster in the 1950s.

Johnny Depp as Captain Jack Sparrow in *The Pirates of the Caribbean: Dead Man's Chest*

Though countless children have known *Treasure Island* and *Peter Pan*, perhaps none of the films and novels mentioned above were as successful in achieving a mass audience as *The Pirates of the Caribbean*;

and Johnny Depp's performance, based in part on the persona of Keith Richards (guitarist of the Rolling Stones), was inspired by the idea that pirates were the 'rock stars of their time'. The pirate world in popular representations is both illicit and attractive: pirates live outside the settled, ordered world of states and government laws and regulations, and yet piracy is an organised activity with its own identities, places and norms. Piracy, for example, cannot function without bases and refuges on land; pirate fraternities have always had their own rules and expectations about how people should act towards one another; pirate captains were generally elected by their crews; pirates divided the spoils of their activities according to widely accepted norms; and piracy worked according to known and acknowledged codes of behaviour. So, although pirates put themselves outside the framework of order and law maintained by states, they had (and have) their own sources of order.

Activity 1

Before reading any further, stop and make a note of whether you think piracy is any longer an issue for international affairs and, if you think it is, what states should do about it. Keep this with you as you study this chapter and see if your ideas change.

I want to start by asking these questions:

- Why did piracy and statehood come to be seen by the rulers of states as inconsistent with one another?
- Why did piracy come to be something that all states sought to suppress, irrespective of the nationality of the pirates or the territory from which they operated?

Universal jurisdiction
The legal idea that perpetrators can be tried in the legal system of any country, no matter what their nationality or the location of their alleged crimes. Examples of crimes subject to international jurisdiction include piracy and international terrorism.

Piracy is a particularly interesting issue from the point of view of studying how relations between countries are ordered and governed because it is the oldest practice that is subject to what is called **universal jurisdiction**. Universal jurisdiction is a legal idea – in this case, a doctrine in the international law subscribed to by all the member states of the United Nations – that says that perpetrators can be tried in any court, no matter what their nationality or the location of their alleged crimes.

Section 1 considers the role of piracy historically and looks at why it was outlawed and subject to the principle of universal jurisdiction, and it contrasts universal jurisdiction with territorial and national principles. Section 2 then considers how far agreement between states is possible, and specifically the idea that there is an international community, embodied in the United Nations, based on agreed rules and norms of international conduct. Drawing on examples of international terrorism and war, Section 3 questions how far international order is legitimate and considers the role of fear and power in international affairs. A brief conclusion considers some implications of the chapter for how to think about international order.

1   Pirates

Consider the following extract from *The Times* newspaper in 2009:

> The number of attacks by pirates in trouble spots around the
> world more than doubled in the first six months of this year
> compared with the same period last year as a direct result of the
> surge in activity among Somalia's pirate gangs. According to a
> report by the International Maritime Bureau (IMB), the total
> number reached 240 by the end of [June] ... This means that 2009
> is already a record year for piracy. The previous highest annual
> tally was 182 attacks, in 2004. ... An international armada of
> warships has been patrolling the most dangerous areas – yesterday
> there were 27 warships from 16 nations in the waters around the
> country – but this has not been enough to stem the hijackings as
> the pirates simply roam farther afield. ... Sleepy fishing villages
> such as Eyl, in the semi-autonomous region of Puntland, have
> been turned into pirate dens where new villas and gleaming 4×4
> vehicles stand out amid the poverty – and the lure of ransoms of
> as much as $3 million in some cases attracts more and more young
> men to the seas. ... Lieutenant Nathan Christensen, of the US
> Navy's Fifth Fleet in Bahrain, said it was impossible to protect
> shipping spread over more than a million square miles. 'Piracy will
> continue to be a problem where there remains no support for law
> or government on land,' he said.
>
> (Crilly, 2009, p. 39)

This report is just one example of the resurgence of piracy as an issue
in the early years of the twenty-first century. Since the collapse of the
state in 1991, Somalia has been a key site of piracy. In 2008, 111 pirate
attacks were launched from the region and 42 of these resulted in the
seizure of a ship, and in the first half of 2009 there were 78 incidents
and 31 hijackings. A major catch in 2008 was an oil tanker, the *Sirius
Star*, carrying $100 million of crude oil, which was hijacked some 450
nautical miles off the Kenyan coast – it was released in January 2009
after a $3 million ransom was paid. Then, in April 2009, Captain
Richard Phillips, a US citizen, of the merchant ship *Maersk Alabama* was
kidnapped 300 miles off Somalia's coast before being dramatically
rescued shortly after by US special forces in an operation launched by
the US navy, in which three of his abductors were killed.

1.1   Pirates – ancient

As its place in popular culture attests, piracy is not a new phenomenon. In the Roman Empire, for example, Pompey the Great, Julius Caesar's rival during the Roman Civil War (49–45 BCE), was known as the 'First Man of Rome', its leading general and defender of the Republic, in part because of his suppression of piracy in the Mediterranean. Rome was seeking to impose its political and military rule across the Mediterranean world and, in particular, to ensure that the ships that carried the seaborne trade of the empire would not be subject to predatory attacks. In roughly three months, according to Pompey's report, his campaign resulted in the destruction of some 120 pirate bases, the deaths of 10,000 pirates and the destruction of 500 ships. Around this time, the Roman statesman and political philosopher Cicero (106–43 BCE), in his *De Officiis* (*On Duties*), said that a pirate 'is not counted as an enemy proper, but is the common foe of all. There ought to be no faith with him, nor the sharing of any sworn oaths' (Cicero, 1991, 3.107).

The point that Cicero was making is an important one about the status of pirates and piracy. He used the term to cover people who threaten the normal social order – in this case, seaborne trade – by violence but who were regarded neither as criminals to be dealt with by the normal process of criminal law nor as legitimate enemies against whom war could be waged. Interestingly, Cicero's phrase has stood the test of time. In the seventeenth century, the English lawyer and politician Sir Edward Coke stated that pirates were 'the common enemy of the human race' and the Latin term for this – *hostes humani generis* – is the phrase used in international law to define pirates and to make the offence of piracy subject to universal jurisdiction. Piracy was the first category of universal jurisdiction because states declared that the activities and livelihoods of pirates were not just illegal but outside the legal framework of any given state.

However, when Sir Edward Coke offered his famous definition, the status of piracy was liable to shift. For in England at the time of Queen Elizabeth I (reigned 1558–1603), the dividing line between a pirate and a **privateer** was far from clear. A privateer was a private individual or group who was charged by the state to commit violence and economic warfare against the interests of another state. That is to say, a privateer was a pirate authorised by the state. As Angus Konstam writes in his history of piracy,

Privateer
A pirate licensed by one state to wage economic and military warfare against another state.

by using privateers such as Drake, Frobisher, Raleigh, Grenville and Hawkins as her naval commanders, [Queen Elizabeth] blurred the line between private enterprise and public service. This was further exacerbated by her tendency to run these expeditions as financial ventures, even though they were ostensibly conducted as official naval operations.

(Konstam, 2008, p. 68)

The statue of Sir Francis Drake in Plymouth, England

Writing about those people taken into captivity during the making of the British Empire, the historian Linda Colley notes that:

> Between the 1610s and '30s, Cornwall and Devon, both sea-going counties heavily involved in trade with southern Europe, lost a fifth of their shipping to North African corsairs [privateers licensed by North African states]. In just one year, 1625, nearly a thousand sailors and fishermen from the major West Country port of Plymouth were seized, most within thirty miles of its shore.
>
> (Colley, 2002, p. 49)

There are many other examples of states authorising private groups to use violence on their behalf, both on land and sea. Indeed, in Europe rulers began authorising private violence in the thirteenth century – a practice that continued at least to the eighteenth century. Very often pirates would be authorised to act on behalf of a ruler, thus becoming privateers; when the conflict was over their licenses would be withdrawn and many returned to piracy pure and simple; and then when a new conflict arose a pirate amnesty would be declared so that some could become privateers again; and so the cycle went on. Organised piracy, in particular, was to a considerable extent produced by the widespread practice of European states adopting privateering as a key means of naval warfare.

In the nineteenth century, by contrast, powerful states increasingly came to the view that private forms of violence were counterproductive and were contrary to their claims to control a monopoly of legitimate violence within their territories (see Thomson, 1994). Accordingly, in a declaration attached to the Treaty of Paris of 1856, France, Britain, Russia, Prussia, Austria, Sardinia and Turkey declared that 'privateering is, and remains abolished'. The USA, at the time a weak naval power, did not accede to this Treaty and indeed during the nineteenth century, at least until the 1860s, the practice of 'filibustering' emanated from US society. A filibuster – derived from the Spanish *filibustero* – referred to pirates, buccaneers or freebooters who organised violent expeditions from the USA, in violation of international law, against territories in Central and South America. Partly this was a simple result of opportunity: the USA was a powerful, expanding society bordered by, or proximate to, weaker territories around it. But this piracy also reflected the relatively weak hold that the state in the USA had over its citizens and their access to the means of violence.

Still, throughout the nineteenth century there was a steady process by which private forms of violence were suppressed by sovereign states. States gradually acted against mercenaries and pirates, and eventually brought non-state forms of trans-border violence under a substantial degree of control as the other side of their efforts to establish monopolies of control within their own borders. Since the late nineteenth century, international law and diplomatic custom and practice have only recognised the rights of states to make war and conclude peace. This has meant that nation states have claimed for themselves – rather than, say, firms, religious organisations or pirates – the right to deploy force internationally. It also means that states hold one another accountable and responsible for acts of violence conducted by each other's citizens abroad.

As part of the general suppression of piracy by states, international law came to define pirates as *hostes humani generis* (enemies of all humanity) who were to be subject to universal rather than territorial or national jurisdiction. Pirates sought to live beyond a world ordered according to principles of territorial rule and national identity. This meant that as states sought to strengthen their grip on territories and populations (that is, as they claimed and enforced principles of jurisdiction based on territoriality and nationality), those who sought to operate outside this framework of control and identification were – literally and metaphorically – *outsiders* not only to any given society but to all societies operating according to these newly emerging rules and norms. For this reason, all states claimed the right to prosecute piracy wherever and by whomever it was committed and without any reference to principles of territorial or national authority. This was the origin of what has subsequently come to be accepted – among states – as the principle of universal jurisdiction.

1.2   Pirates – modern

For a long time this policy was successful. Piracy moved from the world of reality to that of fiction, and the myths and fables of pirates' lives abounded. So why has piracy again become a real rather than a fictional issue in the early years of the twenty-first century, and why are the navies of the most powerful military states involved in suppressing it? Piracy is potentially big business. Some 22,000 vessels pass through the waters off the Somali coast each year, carrying around 8 per cent of world trade and 12 per cent of the total volume of oil transported by sea. Another important site of piracy in recent years,

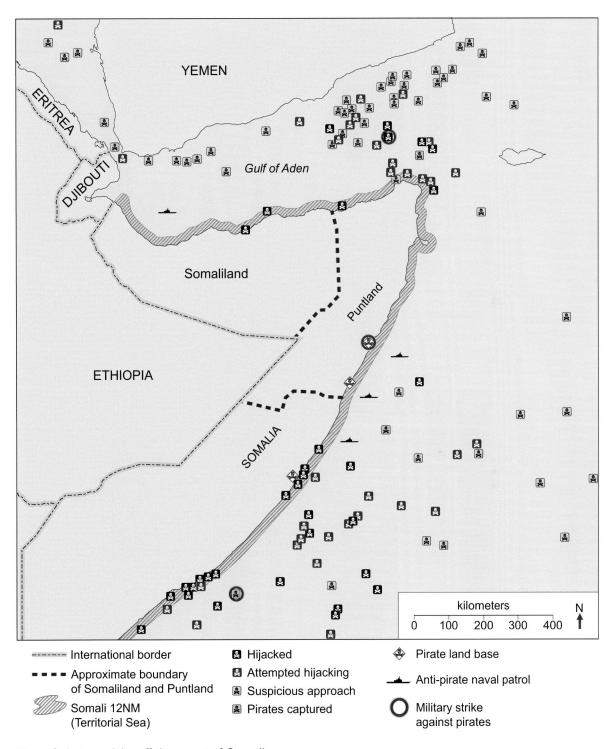

Map of pirate activity off the coast of Somalia

International border	Hijacked	Pirate land base
Approximate boundary of Somaliland and Puntland	Attempted hijacking	Anti-pirate naval patrol
Somali 12NM (Territorial Sea)	Suspicious approach	Military strike against pirates
	Pirates captured	

the Malacca Straits – the 550-mile long waterway separating Malaysia from the island of Sumatra – sees over 50,000 ships per year and one-quarter of the world's oil trade.

Piracy, strictly speaking, is an activity that takes place on the 'high seas' – those that are outside the territorial or jurisdiction of any state. States only have sovereign authority over their territorial waters. But piracy on the high seas requires a base on land and access from there to territorial waters. If piracy has been outlawed by all states – and it has – and if all land is bound by territorial waters – which it is – then how do modern pirates get started? The answer begins on land. As is evident in the case of Somalia, there are places where the authority of the state is so weak or non-existent that groups of individuals can organise pirate activity unmolested by any legitimate authority.

In these cases, pirates organise their own order and governance. In the films of *The Pirates of the Caribbean*, this is referred to as the 'Pirate Code', although almost always with the qualification (like so many sets of rules about social order) that the Code 'is more what you'd call "guidelines"'. Historically, the communities of pirates were understood to have elaborated sets of rules to govern themselves, including ideas of justice. As Cicero pointed out in Roman times:

> not even those who win their bread from evil-doing and crime are able to live without any particle of justice. For if anyone steals or snatches something from one of his fellows in banditry, he leaves no place for himself even within the gang of bandits. And if the one called the pirate chief does not share the booty fairly, he will be killed or abandoned by his comrades. Indeed they say that there are even laws among bandits which they obey and respect.

> (Cicero, 1991, 2.40)

That is to say, where states are unable to order and govern social life people will find alternative ways of ordering themselves. Piracy is one of the ways in which this has happened among groups that seek to make a living by predatory attacks on seaborne trade. In most cases of modern piracy, although the pirates are armed, crews and cargos are ransomed and returned unharmed. The owners and crews of merchant vessels are generally very reluctant to bear arms in self-defence against pirates: first, because they think that this is likely to lead to an escalation as pirates seek more powerful weapons; and second, because except in clear cases of self-defence, the legal basis for the private use of lethal force is unclear.

On the other hand, there are limits to what can be done by the navies of sovereign states who are authorised to use force against piracy on the high seas – that is, outside the territorial waters (generally twelve miles from the shore) of states. This is partly because of the sheer size of the area that would need to be policed and partly because most merchant shipping does not sail under the flags of those states with big navies. In most cases, national maritime fleets have given way to merchant shipping organised as a private economic activity sailing under 'flags of convenience' (where a ship is registered in a country for legal and tax purposes rather than because of having any real connection with the state concerned) from Liberia, Panama or Honduras. Nor are most of the crews that get hijacked citizens of countries with powerful naval forces – in that respect, Captain Richard Phillips was a lucky exception: the *Maersk Alabama* was a US-flagged cargo ship carrying US government food aid for Africa.

NATO forces apprehend Somali pirates, 22 June 2009

For these reasons, analysts of piracy off the coast of Somalia contend that the problem will only be solved when the authority of the Somali state is restored and the Somali authorities are able to police their own territory and territorial waters. General John Craddock, NATO's top commander, stated the point as follows: 'You do not stop piracy on the seas. You stop piracy on the land' (quoted in Charter, 2008).

1.3   Universal jurisdiction

Following the universal outlawing of piracy, other activities have been added to the list of crimes subject to universal jurisdiction.

Activity 2

Can you think of some other activities where states might claim universal jurisdiction?

Activities that are crimes in all or very many countries and which threaten international order as a whole are generally regarded as subject to universal jurisdiction – examples include: the slave trade; hijacking; war crimes; genocide; and, more recently, international terrorism.

To bring the idea of universal jurisdiction into sharper focus and to understand where it might (and might not) apply, let me contrast it with two other kinds of legal principles. First, **territorial jurisdiction** is the idea that states have the right to uphold their own laws in their own territories, whether offences against those laws are committed by nationals or foreigners. The basic idea of territorial jurisdiction is that each country has its own set of laws governing activities that take place on its territory. This is the sort of jurisdiction we might expect the kind of states identified by Weber (e.g. Weber, 1991 [1921]) to claim. Perhaps more importantly, it is the kind of jurisdiction that those travelling to another country on holiday or business need to attend to: what may be legal at 'home' may not be so 'abroad', and when I am abroad it is the law of the country I am in, not my nationality, that matters. For example, certain kinds of drug use that are either legal or carry limited penalties for possession or use in the UK carry mandatory prison sentences, even capital punishment, in some other countries.

Territorial jurisdiction
The legal idea that each state upholds its own laws within its territory.

You read about Weber in Chapter 8 of this book.

A second principle of jurisdiction is that of **national jurisdiction,** under which a state claims the right to apply its laws to its nationals – that is, its citizens – wherever they are located territorially, sometimes independently of the laws that apply in the territories where the nationals are located. For example, UK law has applied this principle of nationality to sex with those under the age of consent. That is to say, UK nationals can be prosecuted for sex with those under the age of consent on their return 'home' whatever the laws governing the activity 'abroad'. To the extent that states claim and uphold the nationality principle, what is 'home' and 'abroad' legally speaking is no longer a clear-cut distinction between what is permissible 'here' and 'there'.

National jurisdiction
The legal idea that states apply their laws to their nationals (or citizens) wherever those nationals are located.

Notice that both the territorial and the nationality principles preserve a close fit between the claims of the state to uphold its order – in this case through laws – and its territory and population. In contrast with both of these principles, universal jurisdiction is the right of a state to prosecute crimes, wherever and by whomever they are committed and without reference to any connection to territory or nationality. Extending the scope of universal jurisdiction is a controversial idea because most states have argued that there is a tension between the territorial and national principles, on the one side, and the principle of universality on the other. Put differently, the principle of universality can only operate when there is widespread agreement on what is to be proscribed and permitted. In the instances referred to above – piracy, the slave trade, hijacking, war crimes, genocide and international terrorism – the breach of widely accepted norms is so strong as to override the concerns of (most) states with their own territorial and national interests. However, in most other areas that are subject to legal regulation, states are extremely reluctant to endorse the principle of universality for fear of undermining their own territorial and national claims.

Summary

- Piracy and pirates are portrayed in fiction as both illicit and attractive, as living adventurous lives outside the law, and as outsiders to the settled and ordered world of government and its laws.

- Pirates, licensed by the rulers of states, were privateers and became a significant source of international violence until their suppression during the nineteenth century.

- Once states decided to outlaw privateering and put an end to piracy, an old doctrine that they were *hostes humani generis* (enemies of all mankind) became widely accepted among states as the basis for universal jurisdiction over their activities and persons.

- The doctrine of universal jurisdiction, which stands in tension with territorial and national ideas about the reach of the state, has since been extended to other categories, including international terrorism.

2   The United Nations and the international community

As the problem of piracy off the coast of Somalia worsened, and in the absence of a stable state and government in Somalia, in 2008 the United Nations Security Council issued a resolution under Chapter VII of its Charter (UN, 1985) which recognised 'the lack of capacity of the Transitional Federal Government (TFG) to interdict, or upon interdiction to prosecute pirates or to patrol and secure the waters off the coast of Somalia, including the international sea lanes and Somalia's territorial waters' (UNSC, 2008, Resolution 1851, p. 1). The resolution determined that 'the incidents of piracy and armed robbery at sea in the waters off the coast of Somalia exacerbate the situation in Somalia which continues to constitute a threat to international peace and security in the region' (p. 2). The resolution then called on 'States, regional and international organizations that have the capacity to do so, to take part actively in the fight against piracy and armed robbery at sea off the coast of Somalia' (p. 2).

At one level, the Security Council was merely reaffirming the principle of universal jurisdiction in relation to piracy. But the resolution contains a key phrase that takes us into the nature of the United Nations (UN) as an organisation that seeks to bring a degree of order to relations among states. The key phrase is the one about the situation in and off the coast of Somalia being 'a threat to international peace and security in the region'. In order to see the significance of this phrase we need to take a brief look at the UN.

2.1   The idea of an international community

The international community
The idea of the international community is that there is a set of agreed rules and institutions, embodied in the United Nations organisation, that govern how states are to act towards one another internationally, and it forms the basis of the liberal approach to international order.

The UN, an organisation that was established after the Second World War and which now includes virtually all the states of the world as its members, claims to speak for **the international community**. The 'international community' refers to the norms and rules developed and practised by the member states of the UN about how they should carry on their relations with one another. There is an important point here about the connection between nations and states: the international order (relations between nations) is in practice organised as a relationship between states (sometimes called the interstate system, or the states-system). This distinction – and some of its implications – will be significant at later points in the chapter. The idea that there is an

The United Nations building in New York, USA

international community of states that enables nations to cooperate with each other according to agreed rules and in shared institutions is known as the liberal approach to international order, or liberal internationalism.

The Charter of the UN attempted to codify a widely shared understanding of how the system of states should seek to order itself, including how the most powerful states should operate. As you will see later in this chapter, there is debate about how far liberal internationalism adequately characterises the actions of the member states of the UN. There are three features of the UN system that I want to draw attention to. First, the purposes of the UN include the promotion of equal rights for all (Article 1(3)). That is to say, although the UN is an international organisation whose members are states, one of its purposes is to promote the rights of all individuals irrespective of territory or nationality – the UN declaration on human rights refers to them explicitly as 'universal'.

The second important aspect of the UN is that it is based on the idea of **sovereign equality**, mentioned in Article 2(1), which refers to a situation in which each state recognises the legitimacy of others to govern and represent their territories and populations as far as international order is concerned. Sovereign equality is a formal notion associated with international law and organisations; it does not imply a substantive equality among states in terms of power or wealth. Still,

Sovereign equality
A formal notion that refers to the equal treatment of each state under international law. It does not mean that all states are equal in substance; for example, some states are richer or more powerful than others.

sovereign equality is important because, when it is recognised and acknowledged by other states, a state partakes of a set of privileges and responsibilities that belong to what diplomats and politicians refer to as the 'international community'. States then have formal equality under international law, are allowed to join international organisations such as the UN and the World Trade Organization, enabled to establish and receive foreign embassies, to have flags and currencies of their own, to send 'national' teams and individuals to international sporting events, and so on. The UK is, of course, typically complicated in this respect.

> You encountered details about the UK's complicated international position in Chapter 5 of this book.

It is important to emphasise the novelty of the idea of sovereign equality – the idea only dates from the founding of the UN in 1945. The reason for this is that, although the European states-system that developed between the seventeenth and twentieth centuries was the first of its kind to develop on the basis that its members recognised one another as sovereign equals – in the formal diplomatic and legal sense of that term – this same system achieved a global ascendancy on the basis of imperialism and colonial rule over most of the non-European world.

Until the end of the Second World War, the European powers did not accept the principle of self-government for the non-European world (or indeed for all groups claiming self-government *within* Europe). The territorial and national states of Europe's 'international community' were also imperial and colonial states. As a universal principle, sovereign equality in international law has been a post-Second World War phenomenon, legitimated by an appeal to racial equality and a right to (national) self-determination. Even then the working out and application of these principles was and remains complex, if only because the question of what constitutes a people with a right to self-determination is both contested and complicated: are all 'nations', however and by whomever defined, equally entitled to self-determination?

Rights and duties of the most powerful states

Primarily, the custom, institutionalised in the Security Council of the United Nations, that the most powerful states decide when force may legitimately be used internationally.

The third feature of the UN that I want to highlight is the way in which it formalised the **rights and duties of the most powerful states** in the UN Security Council. Drafted in the shadow of the Second World War and the advent of nuclear weapons, the UN Charter says that states 'shall refrain in their international relations from the threat or use of force against the territorial integrity or political independence of any state' (Article 2(4)), subject to 'the inherent right of individual or collective self-defence if an armed attack occurs against a Member of the United Nations, until the Security Council has taken measures necessary to maintain international peace and security' (Article 51).

The basic idea was that individual states would foreswear the right to make war because the Security Council would determine when and where force could be used. The UN, through its Charter and the operation of the Security Council, would determine the conditions for international peace and security. As Articles 39, 42 and 2(7) make clear, the Security Council's right to determine the conditions of international peace and security and, as Chapter VII provides, to authorise the use of force to this end supersedes the equality of domestic jurisdiction that is otherwise proclaimed by the Charter. (You can find the entire text of the UN Charter easily online – see UN, 1985.)

Now, the UN Security Council is the highest authority in the organisation and comprises five 'permanent' members and a further ten rotating members. Each of the permanent members – that is, China, France, Russia, the UK and the USA – has a 'veto', so that any one of these states can stop a proposed resolution of the Security Council. So, if Security Council decisions require unanimity among the permanent members, then how much of a change is this from a condition in which each state decides for itself? That depends on the decision making of the Security Council. If the permanent members of the Security Council agree about what measures are necessary to maintain international peace and security, then they can impose decisions on other powers. If, however, there is no unanimity on the Security Council, then there is nothing in the UN Charter that precludes the rights to individual and collective self-defence. So, in the case of Resolution 1851 relating to Somalia, the Security Council was unanimous and the terms of this resolution are binding on all states, and states are authorised to use force to enforce its terms.

2.2   Who speaks for the international community?

Activity 3

Before reading on, make a note of who you think should decide what is a threat to international peace and security and how decisions about these matters should be made. You can then compare your thoughts with the views of the UK Government that you will read about next.

Read the following extract from a speech made by Tony Blair when he was UK Prime Minister:

> Just as within domestic politics, the notion of community – the belief that partnership and co-operation are essential to advance self-interest – is coming into its own; so it needs to find its own international echo. … The principles of international community apply also to international security. … The most pressing foreign policy problem we face is to identify the circumstances in which we should get actively involved in other people's conflicts.

(Blair, 1999)

North Atlantic Treaty Organization (NATO)

According to its own definition, a military alliance of democratic states in Europe and North America. Originally formed as an alliance against the Soviet Union in 1949, it has since evolved into a general military alliance of the West.

At the time Tony Blair gave this speech, the UK and its military allies in the **North Atlantic Treaty Organization (NATO)**, including the USA, were at war with Serbia in order to force a political settlement to a dispute about the international status and government of Kosovo, at the time a predominantly Albanian province of Serbia. Serbia was a state that emerged from the violent break-up of the former state of Yugoslavia after the collapse of communism in Eastern Europe between 1989 and 1991. Prime Minister Blair began his speech by claiming that NATO's war against Serbia was 'a just war, based not on any territorial ambitions but on values' to end 'unspeakable things [that] are happening in Europe. Awful crimes that we never thought we would see again have reappeared – ethnic cleansing, systematic rape, mass murder' (Blair, 1999). These were the kinds of things that justified military intervention in 'other people's conflicts' according to the doctrine the Prime Minister was articulating and attempting to promote. However, in this particular case, many states opposed NATO's war against Serbia and, importantly, NATO was unable to get UN Security Council authorisation for its war because of Russian opposition.

In effect, Prime Minister Blair was arguing for an extension of the notion of universal jurisdiction to include, in certain circumstances, the protection of basic human rights. This was an attempt to build upon earlier statements by the UN Security Council such as the following:

> The absence of war and military conflict amongst states does not in itself ensure international peace and security. The non-military

sources of instability in the economic, social, humanitarian and ecological fields have become threats to peace and security.

(Statement by Security Council Heads of Government and States, January 1992, quoted in Gow, 2005, p. 56)

The Security Council's understanding of what constitutes a threat to peace and security had come to include social and humanitarian questions (among others) and this was reinforced in a statement about the 'responsibility to protect' by the UN Secretary General, Kofi Annan, in 1998, which declared that: 'The Charter protects the sovereignty of peoples. It was never meant as a license for governments to trample on human rights and dignity. Sovereignty implies responsibility, not just power' (Annan, 1999, p. 6). Here a distinction emerges between the sovereignty of states and the sovereignty of peoples – who may not be protected by 'their' states, or at least the states that rule over the territory that they inhabit. The root idea that Prime Minister Blair was attempting to promote as a new rule or norm of international order was that if a state transgresses basic human rights to a sufficient degree, and if domestic sovereignty is fatally compromised, then other states have the right to act without reference to the principles of territoriality or nationality. Blair was seeking to have gross breaches of human rights added to the list of universally outlawed activities that are subject to universal jurisdiction.

Activity 4

Remind yourself of Section 1.3 and think about whether the responsibility to protect basic human rights should be territorial, national or universal in scope.

Now that you have thought about that question, does it change your view if I say that Kosovo was not the first military intervention that could be plausibly classified as 'humanitarian'? For example, Vietnam's invasion of Cambodia brought about an end to the massive suffering of the Cambodian people under the regime of the Khmer Rouge in 1979 and the Uganda–Tanzania war of 1978–79 brought about the end of Idi Amin Dada's murderous regime in Uganda. In both cases, however, these 'interventions' were denounced by the Western powers; and Vietnam, in particular, was subject to punitive sanctions until its forces withdrew from Cambodia. These apparent discrepancies raise the question of who gets to define what is and is not legitimate intervention. As we have seen, the NATO allies have been prepared to intervene without the express sanction of the UN Security Council.

■   Were the actions of Vietnam and Tanzania any less legitimate?

This question is important because it centres on what is being secured and by whom. Who gets to define what is and is not a universal responsibility?

During the period of Cold War rivalry between the Soviet Union and the USA, when international politics was divided into a struggle between two spheres of influence linked to these superpowers and their antagonistic ideological systems, the USA more or less determined what was acceptable in the 'West' and the Soviet Union laid down what might happen in the 'East'. This is a big oversimplification, of course, but there was no basis for an agreement between East and West, and each superpower routinely vetoed resolutions in the Security Council sponsored by the other side. The promise of the UN to provide a set of principles and rules for states based on a framework of international law and respect for human rights and sovereign equality was, to a very large extent, checked by the opposition between the superpowers during the Cold War.

Since the end of the Cold War there have been attempts, led very largely by the Western powers that triumphed in that confrontation, to extend the notion of universal jurisdiction to include the protection of gross breaches of human rights. From the point of view of others this has been less a case of a humanitarian concern with human rights and more a case of Western power and territorial and national interests dressed up in universal language. With the dissolution of communism as an ideological system and the collapse of the Soviet Union as a global superpower, the USA and its NATO allies on the Security Council – France and the UK – have had a greater ability to define the terms on which debates about intervention take place. NATO's war against Serbia over Serbian treatment of its province, Kosovo, was part of this changing approach to international order on the part of some of the great powers. In the specific case of Kosovo, Russia insisted on using its veto against a Chapter VII resolution of the UN Security Council authorising the use of force. The NATO allies went ahead anyway and argued that it was unreasonable for Russia to be able to block what they characterised as an instance of 'humanitarian' intervention; that is, a military intervention 'based not on any territorial ambitions but on values' (Blair, 1999). Unable to get unanimous Security Council agreement that Serbian actions were a threat to 'international peace and security', the NATO allies defined their intervention as an example of universal jurisdiction in defence of human rights.

2.3   The UK and the international community

In 2008, the UK Government drew up for the first time an official, public statement of its national security strategy (NSS). The NSS was published in the wake of a major government review of a whole range of potential challenges to the security of the UK arising from such different things as the effects of climate change, wars in Afghanistan and Iraq, terrorist networks located within the UK, overseas and in-between, threats to IT networks from 'hackers', concerns about global pandemics from varieties of animal flu passing to humans, etc. This was interesting for at least two reasons. In the first instance, the NSS declared that, while a future military challenge to the UK from a hostile state could not be ruled out, there was no such threat at the present time. Rather, the NSS stated that:

> The Cold War threat has been replaced by a diverse but interconnected set of threats and risks, which affect the United Kingdom directly and also have the potential to undermine wider international stability. They include international terrorism, weapons of mass destruction, conflicts and failed states, pandemics, and trans-national crime. These and other threats and risks are driven by a diverse and interconnected set of underlying factors, including climate change, competition for energy, poverty and poor governance, demographic changes and globalisation. ... In the past, the state was the traditional focus of foreign, defence and security policies, and national security was understood as dealing with the protection of the state and its vital interests from attacks by other states. Over recent decades, our view of national security has broadened to include threats to individual citizens and to our way of life, as well as to the integrity and interests of the state.
>
> (Cabinet Office, 2008, pp. 3–4)

Second, the NSS took for granted the expansion of the set of circumstances in which states might intervene in the affairs of other territories and peoples that lay behind NATO's war against Serbia and other 'humanitarian' interventions. The NSS argued that:

> In some circumstances the international community has a responsibility to help countries protect their populations. In most cases, that involves support for the countries' own security forces and agencies; but in some cases, where a government is unwilling or unable to protect its citizens from genocide, war crimes, ethnic cleansing or crimes against humanity, or is perpetrating these acts itself, the international 'Responsibility to Protect' ultimately requires the international community to act.

(Cabinet Office, 2008, p. 48)

Taken together, these doctrines change the understanding of what constitutes a threat to international peace and security and hence what is a threat for a state such as the UK. As the NSS says, traditionally states saw other states, at least hostile states with significant military capabilities, as the chief source of potential insecurity. When threats to international peace and stability were understood in military terms, it was assumed that states had a right, individually and collectively, to self-defence, unless or until the Security Council decided to act. Now, states are redefining what is a potential threat to international peace and security in new ways and are devising new reasons for intervention. This raises an important question: to what extent does an evolution in the notion of what constitutes a threat to international peace and stability imply a corresponding development in the idea of what constitutes legitimate self-defence? Apart from self-defence against an armed attack, under what circumstances can a state legitimately use force? In the next section, I consider whether the only legitimate use of force is that which is authorised by the UN Security Council.

Summary

- The UN was established after the Second World War to embody and speak for the international community, which comprised all the states of the world. It aimed to promote human rights on a universal basis, operate on the basis of the sovereign equality of states, and institutionalise the rights and duties of the great powers to determine the conditions of international peace and security. The idea that the member states can form an international community and operate according to agreed rules and through common institutions is often called the liberal approach to international order, or liberal internationalism.

- Since the end of the Cold War there have been attempts, especially by Western states, to extend the idea of universal jurisdiction to include gross abuses of human rights and to legitimise the idea of humanitarian intervention.

- The national security strategy (NSS) of the UK endorses the idea that, in some circumstances, the UK has a right to get involved in conflicts involving other peoples in other territories and characterises a wide range of issues as potential threats to the security of the state.

- As definitions and understanding of what constitutes a threat to international peace and security change to include other things than an armed attack by one state on another, so the matter of who authorises the use of international force becomes a key question for international affairs.

3   Predators, authority and power

Consider the following statement:

> in accordance with God's will, we pronounce to all Muslims the following judgement: To kill the Americans and their allies – civilians and military – is an individual duty incumbent upon every Muslim in all countries, in order to liberate the al-Aqsa Mosque [in Jerusalem] and the Holy Mosque [Mecca] from their grip, so that their armies leave all the territory of Islam, defeated, broken, and unable to threaten any Muslim. This is in accordance with the words of God Almighty: 'Fight the idolators at any time, if they first fight you;' 'Fight them until there is no more persecution and until worship is devoted to God'.

> (Founding statement of al-Qaeda and the 'World Islamic Front', 23 February 1998, quoted in Lawrence, 2005, p. 61)

Activity 5

Who is authorising the use of force in this case and against whom?

The founding statement of al-Qaeda as well as subsequent fatwas from its leaders sought to authorise the use of force. At that time, al-Qaeda had established the core of its network or organisation in Afghanistan, most of which was then under the government of the Taliban based in Kandahar and led by Mullah Omar. After the attacks of 11 September 2001 (9/11), Mullah Omar refused to hand the leader of al-Qaeda – Osama bin Laden – to the USA. It is not clear that Mullah Omar was in a position to comply with this demand. Christina Lamb reports Mullah Omar's bodyguard as follows:

> We laughed when we heard the Americans asking Mullah Omar to hand over Osama bin Laden … The Americans are crazy. Afghanistan is not a state sponsoring terrorism but a terrorist-sponsored state. It is Osama bin Laden that can hand over Mullah Omar not vice versa.

> (quoted in Lamb, 2002, p. 27)

3.1   Privateers turned pirates?

What is clear is that al-Qaeda was seeking to operate outside the core norms of the international community concerning the use of force. From the point of view of the members of the international community, the international relations theorist Colin Gray (2005, pp. 214–15) notes, 'terrorism is a mode of irregular warfare' and the definition of 'irregularity rests on the legal status of the rival belligerents, not on the character of the fighting'. Clearly, the 9/11 attacks were spectacular and unannounced and they did not involve a formal declaration of war. But what was the 1998 founding statement of al-Qaeda if not a declaration of and call to irregular warfare? The breach of norms supposed to govern 'regular' warfare was further and dramatically symbolised by the fact that the 'weapons' used were civilian aircraft.

Al-Qaeda's attack on the World Trade Center, New York, 11 September 2001

Prior to these attacks, no group had so directly challenged the authority of states to monopolise the means of warfare and no non-state group had inflicted such dramatic and spectacular violence on one of the great powers, indeed the most powerful state of all, militarily speaking. The response of the UN was immediate and clear: the al-Qaeda attacks were interpreted not just as an attack on the USA but also as an attack on the principle that it is states and not other bodies that monopolise the legitimate use of force nationally and internationally. Russia and China, so often the antagonists of the USA on the Security Council, were among the first countries to make clear that they saw the attacks in these terms as a direct challenge to the authority of all states and to the rights and duties of the great powers – now operating through the UN Security Council – to define the terms on which force can and cannot be used.

Consider the language of the following Security Council resolution passed unanimously the day after the attacks.

> *The Security Council,*
>
> *Reaffirming* the principles and purposes of the Charter of the United Nations,
>
> *Determined* to combat by all means threats to international peace and security caused by terrorist acts,
>
> *Recognizing* the inherent right of individual or collective self-defence in accordance with the Charter ...
>
> ...
>
> 3. *Calls* on all States to work together urgently to bring to justice the perpetrators, organizers and sponsors of the terrorist attacks and *stresses* that those responsible for aiding, supporting or harbouring the perpetrators, organizers and sponsors of these acts will be held accountable ...
>
> ...
>
> 5. *Expresses* its readiness to take all necessary steps to respond to the terrorist attacks of 11 September 2001 ...
>
> (UNSC, 2001)

Note that the phrase 'all necessary steps' is the UN's diplomatic euphemism for military force.

One important part of sovereign equality and the mutual recognition involved in a state being a member of the international community is that states hold one another accountable for the violence that is directed from their territories and waters by people in those territories. It was not always like this. As we have seen, in the seventeenth and eighteenth centuries states were not the only bodies that routinely wielded organised force across borders. Mercenaries, pirates and others often deployed considerable force across borders and outside territorial waters on the high seas, sometimes under their own names and sometimes at the behest of emerging sovereign states. But since the end of the nineteenth century, states have suppressed and outlawed the cross-border use of non-state violence. Al-Qaeda challenged this most basic of assumptions, and in its National Security Strategy of 2002 the USA added international terrorism to the list of activities it considered covered by the principle of universal jurisdiction.

Although both piracy on the high seas and international terrorism are subject to the doctrine of universal jurisdiction, they are clearly not the same thing. Piracy is, as we have seen, essentially a predatory economic activity; it thrives in circumstances where the authority of the state is weak or non-existent but it is not a direct challenge to the authority of all states, let alone a form of warfare against the most powerful state. Nevertheless, the potential crossovers between these issues have not gone unremarked. As the US political analyst Robert Kaplan notes:

> Now, counterterrorism experts are worried that al-Qaeda and its affiliates will be inspired by Somali pirates. ... Potentially, piracy is a platform for their activities. ... There are already al-Qaeda affiliates in Somalia. If they can make contact with pirate federations, then al-Qaeda can use piracy as a form of terrorism. ... And, remember, al-Qaeda lives off weakly governed states in an Islamic cultural setting, and that perfectly describes Somalia.
>
> (Kaplan, 2009)

The future of political developments in Somalia will do much to determine whether anything like this develops, but the point is a more general one. Territories and peoples that are outside the reach of states that are active and functioning members of the international community are viewed as a potential threat to that community.

There is another parallel that is worth remarking. In Afghanistan, the rise to power of the pro-Soviet People's Democratic Party of Afghanistan (PDPA) in 1978 provoked a civil war as significant elements of the Muslim society resisted its secularising and socialist measures, specifically its policies of compulsory female education and land reform. Then, in 1979, the Soviet Union invaded the country in order to support a communist government that had seized power in the capital Kabul. The USA and its allies (in this case, including China, Pakistan and Saudi Arabia) then decided to support irregular armed forces, both those in Afghanistan and those that could be recruited from abroad in the Muslim world, to fight the Soviet occupation. The immediate background to the rise of al-Qaeda, then, was the civil war in Afghanistan. As a functioning organisation, al-Qaeda was created during operations backed by the USA, Saudi Arabia and Pakistan to finance and organise the mujahidin's resistance to communism in Afghanistan and to recruit (mainly Arab) Muslims from abroad to fight for that cause. The Arab fighters recruited to this cause were not part of the armed forces of any state, nor part of the national Afghan resistance to Soviet occupation, they were paid for by the USA and Saudi Arabia, armed by these countries and China and Pakistan, and trained by Pakistan.

Activity 6

Do you see any parallels between the Arab fighters who became al-Qaeda and what you have read about in Section 1 of this chapter?

There is a sense in which the Arab fighters in Afghanistan were 'privateers', and there is also a sense in which when they were no longer supported by the states that first recruited and paid for them – principally, Saudi Arabia, the USA and Pakistan – they became 'pirates', if not literally, then at least in their challenge to state-based ideas of legitimate authority. In the period from the 1660s to the 1690s, the British engaged in state-sponsored piracy (privateering) against the Spanish Americas; then they declared piracy illegal again; and from the 1700s to the 1720s pirates were hunted down and executed, and their bases destroyed by military force.

After the Soviet forces withdrew from Afghanistan, the civil war continued and once the Taliban came to power in Kabul (1996) they formed a close alliance with Osama bin Laden's al-Qaeda organisation. Indeed, in some respects al-Qaeda became the military arm of the Taliban. Having helped to evict the Soviets from Afghanistan, al-Qaeda then turned against its erstwhile Western and Saudi Arabian backers. Although al-Qaeda is most widely known for the attacks on the USA of 11 September 2001, they had earlier attacked US embassies in Africa

(7 August 1998) and the USS *Cole*, at sea off the coast of Yemen (12 October 2000). And, like the pirates who declared themselves 'at war with the world' during the early 1700s, al-Qaeda were also hunted down and their bases destroyed.

Looking for parallels – here between privateers and terrorist organisations – is a process of social science reflection. It does not mean that the two examples are the same, or that the analysis should not pay attention to the very different historical contexts. Nevertheless, identifying such parallels can illuminate current phenomena in significant ways. Here, the complicated and shifting relationship between states and 'private' organisations engaging in violence is framed differently by looking at the example of privateers. The example points to how states have both used and repressed forms of 'private' violence.

3.2   International authority – a tale of two wars

Recall that the permanent members of the UN Security Council have the right to determine what is a 'threat to international peace and security' and, through Chapter VII resolutions, to authorise the use of force. Even before the UN was established, the idea of a 'great power' had long been understood as a state that is involved in making decisions about the legitimate use of force. Actions, ideas and discourses that seek to breach or challenge these norms, if unanswered or unpunished, might lead to an erosion of confidence in the ability of the international community and its most powerful states to provide a minimum standard of international order. One consequence of this, as has been powerfully argued by the international relations theorist Oded Löwenheim (2007), is that the response of great powers to attacks or harms inflicted by non-state bodies may have much more to do with the degree to which their *authority* is challenged than with the level of *material* harm caused. Let me elaborate this point a little.

It is at least arguable that the material harm to US society arising from the drug cartels of Central America has been greater than that of the attacks of 11 September 2001. But the actions and people involved in the drugs trade do not pose a challenge to the legitimate authority of the US state and they have not declared war on the USA or the principle of statehood in general. Drug cartels are, in Löwenheim's terms, parasitic on state authority. That is to say, drug cartels need the existence of at least some forms of state authority to assure the conditions of production, circulation and distribution of their products.

Even though the material harm to US society may be very high, it is because the illegal drug trade does not challenge US authority to any substantial degree that no US administration would consider full-blown warfare against, and occupation of, any Central American country in order to stop it. The 'war on drugs' is real and violent, to be sure, and it has involved some US military engagements in Central America, but it does not begin to compare with the war conducted with the Northern Alliance to overthrow the Taliban in Afghanistan in 2001, and the subsequent US and NATO military missions to pacify the country and establish a new Afghan state.

The reason for this, Löwenheim contends, is that al-Qaeda and their hosts – the Taliban government in Afghanistan – represented a direct challenge not only to the principles of state sovereignty and mutual recognition but, even more so, to the authority of the USA as a great power. The breach of the norms had to be punished, and be seen to be punished, if it were not to lead to further questioning of the idea of great power and American authority. By harbouring Osama bin Laden and his al-Qaeda organisation, Afghanistan under the government of the Taliban had put itself outside the basic rules and norms of the international community, a situation that none of that community's members could regard with anything other than deep concern, and which was bound to prompt a substantial response from the target of the attack and the most powerful member of the community.

Notice, however, what subsequently transpired: once the Taliban had been driven from power, the USA sought to put a new state in place and treated it as a legitimate authority with all the rights and duties that this status confers on members of the UN. An attempt was made to bring the territory and people of Afghanistan back into the international community as a people incorporated according to the rules and norms of the club. Whether that attempt will prove to be successful was still in doubt eight years after the fall of Mullah Omar's government in Kandahar.

Let me turn now to the example of the US-led war against Iraq, launched in 2003. On this occasion, the USA persuaded the Security Council to pass a resolution (in November 2002) that brought weapons inspectors back into Iraq and called for Saddam Hussein's regime to complete a disarmament process the UN had called for after the war in 1991, which had ended Iraq's occupation of Kuwait. Saddam Hussein had finally expelled the last of the UN's weapons inspectors in 1998 and the fate of the disarmament process and the state of Iraq's armouries and weapons programmes was not known by the international community. The USA (with the UK and some other allies) maintained that Saddam Hussein's breaches of earlier UN resolutions were a sufficient basis for war. The rest of the Security Council argued that a 'second' resolution, explicitly authorising the use of force, would be needed for any war against Iraq to have UN authority. In the event, the USA (and the others) went to war against Iraq in March 2003 without having been able to get such a second resolution.

The war did not go well for the USA: no weapons of mass destruction were found and while Iraq's conventional forces were rapidly overrun, a guerrilla insurgency soon developed that led to a prolonged occupation, very high levels of Iraqi deaths and US military casualties that soon became politically unpopular in the USA. The point I want to focus on here is the damage that was done to America's international authority. Because many states, including many of America's closest NATO allies (the UK and Poland were exceptions in this respect), believed that the USA should not have gone to war without Security Council authorisation, US international authority was diminished. Practically, this had huge consequences. UN approval for the action in Afghanistan made it possible to mobilise NATO and other international organisations for the post-conflict phase of operations. The case of Iraq was very different. For while the Security Council did pass resolutions authorising the occupation of Iraq after the war, as well as resolutions authorising the elections that established a new state and government, the US effort was unable to establish any significant wider international legitimacy and support.

Activity 7

Did the US-led war against Iraq of 2003 increase or decrease the authority of the USA as a great power?

President George W. Bush may have believed that the war against Saddam Hussein would also shore up the authority of the states-system and bolster America's international authority. But it is equally possible that, because many of the members of the international community thought this was a case of the most powerful state *breaking*, not *enforcing*, the rules, the long-term effect may have been to diminish the USA's authority as a great power. How much this might matter was a subject

US Marines lead away a captured Iraqi man during the battle for Fallujah in 2004

of debate in the US diplomatic community as well as among scholars of international relations. Some argued that the damage to US authority was real and serious, and that it would weaken the ability of the USA to enlist the agency of other states in future international affairs. This was very much the stance take by Barak Obama during his successful presidential campaign in 2008. Others pointed out that the USA was so powerful, militarily speaking, that perhaps it didn't need to worry about questions of authority, just as long as it was feared.

3.3   Power and fear

The idea that *fear* rather than authority might be a basis for international order is not a new one. Indeed, the principle that what provides order in the international arena is fear is probably the oldest and most long-standing claim in theories of international order. Thus far we have been considering a range of ideas – around universal jurisdiction, the role of the UN, the role of UN Security Council resolutions in determining what may legitimately happen internationally, ideas about humanitarian intervention by one state in the affairs of different territories and peoples – that are based, at least in part, on the assumption that it is possible to order relations among states by reference to norms and principles that are widely agreed. That is the core claim and central ideal of the UN as an international organisation.

However, what is called the **realist** tradition of thinking about international order regards this as very largely mythical. 'Realist' in this context names a way of thinking about the states-system and international order that emphasises the absence of legitimate authority at an international level and the centrality of questions of power and especially the zero-sum power involved in the use of coercion and force. Whether realist thinking in this sense is realist in the more conventional sense – that is, realistic or faithful to reality – is a key question for theories of international order.

Realist
The realist tradition of thinking about international order is based on the ideas that there is no legitimate authority internationally and that order is based on power and fear of power, not on legitimate authority.

International order, according to realists, is about fear and power. We have seen that when it is unanimous the UN Security Council, most especially its five permanent members, can determine what constitutes a threat to international peace and security and authorise the use of force. But we have also seen that states have used force in the absence of authorisation by the Security Council. The point here is that states do not always agree on when it is legitimate to use force – as in the case of the invasion of Iraq in 2003. All states can agree that piracy, for example, should be suppressed but not all states agreed in 2003 that bringing down the regime of Saddam Hussein in Iraq was necessary for international peace and security. The USA and its coalition allies did believe that toppling Saddam Hussein was necessary and acted accordingly.

In fact, most uses of force internationally have been regarded as illegitimate by at least some states. In order to analyse this point in more depth, I need to say a bit more about the nature of relations among states in the states-system, and to do this I'm going to discuss a model of the workings of the states-system developed by the prominent theorist of international relations, Kenneth Waltz (1979). Waltz's model, which he uses to develop a wide-ranging theory of the balance of power in international politics, seeks to make clear and precise an understanding of international order found in many other writers. This is a common phenomenon in the social sciences; model builders or theorists take ideas, assumptions and arguments that are perhaps widespread but not very clearly formulated, and seek to give them a more precise account in order to clarify the assumptions involved, to work out the exact logic of the reasoning that connects assumptions to arguments, and to identify ways in which these might be tested against evidence and competing ideas, assumptions and arguments.

Models of this kind always involve degrees of abstraction and idealisation. On the one hand, models abstract from certain features of reality; that is, they pick out some aspects of reality and ignore others in order to simplify and to focus on one thing (or a small number of things) at a time. On the other hand, models add to our partial perceptions of reality by representing the messy, complex, entangled nature of those features they select in general terms. This might all sound, well, rather abstract and idealised, so I'll try to explain what I mean as I outline Waltz's model.

Waltz aims to develop a model of the structure of the states-system. Accounts of social structure are common in the social sciences. Something – in the present case, the system of states – has a structure when it is made up of a number of parts that are arranged together in an orderly way, and an account of structure usually involves specifying both the parts and the relations between them. The parts of the states-system, for Waltz, are just the states that interact with one another, and he defines them in much the same way as Weber. It is the next move that distinguishes Waltz's account – the specification of the relations between the parts. Following Weber, Waltz argues that states, on the whole successfully, maintain a monopoly over the (legitimate) use of force in their own territory. But in relations between states, Waltz contends, there is no such monopoly. On the contrary, each state maintains its own armed forces – forces that may be potentially directed at other states – so that the means of organised violence are distributed across many states. Not only are the means of organised violence distributed across the states-system in this way but also there are no guarantees that states will regard the use of force by other states as legitimate. Each state might regard *its* use of force as legitimate, but that is not the same thing as *other* states seeing it in the same way. This combination of a distribution of the means of force across a range of states and an absence of any generalised legitimacy for the use of force – except perhaps in unambiguous cases of self-defence – is known as international **anarchy**. This is illustrated in Figure 1a.

'Anarchy' does not mean chaos or even disorder in this context; it refers, rather, to an absence of centralised government with state-like characteristics. Whether an anarchical states-system is ordered or disordered depends, according to realist theory, on the workings of the **balance of power**. The realist theory of the balance of power reasons as follows: because all states exist in an anarchical states-system, in which the armed forces of each poses a potential threat to others, each

Anarchy
Anarchy, in international relations, does not refer to disorder or chaos but rather to the absence of legitimate authority. An international anarchy may or may not be ordered, depending on the balance of power.

Political anarchy was briefly discussed in the Conclusion to Chapter 8 of this book.

Balance of power
The principle by which states, fearing the potential threat of other states' military capabilities, balance with and against one another to ensure their security.

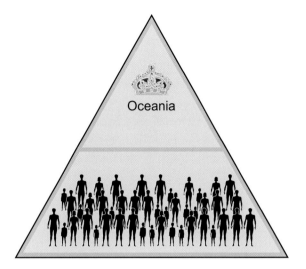

The state claims a monopoly over legitimate violence

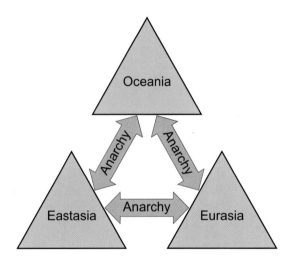

The absence of legitimate authority between states leads to anarchy

Figure 1a Sovereign authority and international anarchy

state must look first to securing the conditions of its own survival, especially as against the more powerful and threatening states in the system. In these circumstances, each state must be aware of the power of other states – especially the coercive power of states to inflict harm on one another – and so calculates its actions accordingly. The basic idea here is that, because each state has to look after itself, it has reason to fear potentially hostile states with significant military capabilities.

The result will be a pattern of interaction characterised by power balancing. This is a long-observed principle of interaction among separate political communities – Thucydides described its working in his history of the Peloponnesian War fought between Athens and Sparta from 431 to 404 BCE and the eighteenth-century philosopher and political theorist David Hume (1994 [1752]), in his essay 'Of the balance of power', described the maxim of preserving the balance of power as 'founded … on common sense and obvious reasoning' (p. 157). The balance of power is preserved when, in a situation where there is a plurality of powerful states, states that seek to maintain their independence align with one another to counteract the power of the strongest or most threatening, since this is the surest way of avoiding subordination – as in Figure 1b.

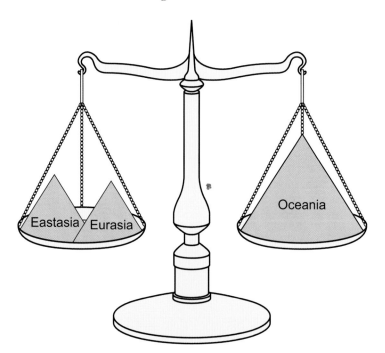

Weaker states can align to balance against a stronger state

Figure 1b   The balance of power

The aim of power balancing is, first, to preserve the political independence of states and, only secondly, to ensure peace. Indeed, war has been one means by which the balance of power has been maintained. Without the threat of war and the possible loss of political independence that might follow from defeat, there would be no need of the balance of power; but, equally, without the potential to check a rising power by (at least the threat of) war, the balance of power is robbed of one of its most important means. Sometimes the only way to balance the power of one state is for another, or others, to fight it. The balance of power, including the threat or reality of conflict, has traditionally been seen – by diplomats and politicians as well as by those scholars seeking to analyse the workings of relations between states – as the principal way in which international affairs are ordered in the states-system. The potentially coercive power of one or more states is ranged against that of others, and order arises from power checking power or from the strong dominating the weak. Mutual fear gives rise to power balancing and power balancing, in turn, produces order.

In reality, not all states have the same power – the very term 'superpower' marks this fact. At any one time, only a small minority of states in the system have commanded the majority of total military power. Since states have very different capabilities, they do not all take part in power balancing. The privilege and responsibility for maintaining the balance of power inevitably falls to the most powerful states. Some states have the power to shape the international arena and other (weaker) states have to adapt and accommodate to the results of the actions of the powerful. Indeed, ever since the conclusion of the Napoleonic Wars in Europe in the early nineteenth century, the special rights and duties of the 'great powers' to manage the balance of power on behalf of the states-system have been more or less explicitly codified. The workings of the UN Security Council are only the latest example of this idea. A great power, internationally speaking, is one that is understood by other states as having, in conjunction with the other great powers of the day, the role of defining and upholding the rules for the use of force in international affairs.

According to this realist analysis of international order, the ultimate determinants of state action, especially action by the major powers, will always be dictated by considerations of power. The advice of realists is always to look for the considerations of power at work in the actions of the most powerful states. Sometimes this is very explicit. The National Security Strategy of the USA, for example, says that it is the policy of the US Government to maintain an unchallengeable military dominance for the future. When the Chinese navy deployed to the Gulf of Aden as part of the campaign against piracy, its commander, Wu Shengli, said: 'It's the first time we go abroad to protect our strategic interests armed with military force' (quoted in Lewis, 2008). By this time, India had already deployed naval forces to the region and, in response to the

Chinese move, the Japanese Prime Minister, Taro Aso, ordered his defence ministry to find ways to deploy naval vessels in the same manner. None of the major powers, it seems, wanted to be left out of the action.

This is not to say that the powerful may not have an interest in promoting rules and norms that all states benefit from and support – after all, the deployments noted above are ostensibly to combat piracy – but it is to ask the question 'Why are they acting as they are?' To return for the last time to our example of piracy off the coast of Somalia: are the warships of some NATO countries, India and China patrolling those waters just because of a concern about the essentially economic crime of piracy or are they there to establish political and military influence in circumstances that might produce international terrorism, or both? Is the international effort to re-establish the authority of the state in Somalia driven by considerations about the welfare and rights of the people of Somalia or by the interests of the great powers in political stability and combating al-Qaeda? Have India and China, which are rising powers and fast-expanding economies, deployed forces to show that NATO and EU forces cannot run the show without taking their interests into account?

Summary

- Al-Qaeda claimed legitimacy to authorise non-state violence on an international basis, most dramatically in its attacks against the USA on 11 September 2001.

- The origins of al-Qaeda as a military organisation can be found in 'privateering' paid for and organised by the USA, Saudi Arabia and Pakistan during the civil war and Soviet invasion of Afghanistan.

- The attacks of 11 September 2001 were a challenge to the authority of states to monopolise the legitimate use of force in the international system, and especially to the authority of the most powerful of the great powers.

- The idea that states exist in a condition of mutual fear, as each worries about the potentially hostile use of other states' military capabilities, is the basis of the realist idea that a balance of power governs order among states.

How do we know?

Evaluating arguments

In this chapter you have studied a range of ideas about international affairs. A central issue in studies of international relations, usually seen as part of the broader study of politics and society, is how far can general understandings of our material lives, our connections to others and the ways in which these are ordered and governed (which we develop by studying a single society such as the UK) be transferred to interactions between societies? In particular, is the international realm, with its considerations of fear and the balance of power, something that raises questions for us as social scientists as well as political leaders about how to understand how and why different states act as they do? Equally, given that questions about legitimacy and who has the authority to act internationally, especially in relation to literally life-and-death issues around the use of force, are much less clear than in the domestic affairs of legitimate states, the question of how do we know when it is right to intervene in other people's conflicts has no easy answers. However, using what you have studied about authority and power in this chapter may help you in addressing these questions.

Conclusion

Pirates (ancient and modern) and predators pose a challenge to both of the main principles of international order. On the one hand, there is the idea – embodied in the United Nations – that international affairs can be governed as an 'international community' in which states operate according to widely agreed rules and norms, even if the most powerful states collectively monopolise key decisions about the legitimate use of force. This is the basis of the liberal idea of international order, or liberal internationalism. On the other hand, there is the much older but still present notion that, in the absence of any legitimate authority to govern the system of states (the UN is *not* a world government), each state must judge for itself what is a threat and so each must worry about its position in the balance of power.

According to the first view, we can understand the international community as a society writ large: that is, we can think of international affairs as being ordered and governed by analogy to the ways we understand what makes up any given society. The second, realist (but don't assume that 'realist' equals 'realistic') view says that there is a fundamental difference between national – that is, *within* any given state – and *inter*national affairs because in the latter there is no final source of legitimate authority. At this point, I want to address an important ambiguity in our ordinary use of the word 'international' that I mentioned briefly earlier. 'International' is derived from 'inter'-'national', which means between or among nations, where 'national' refers to an identity of a population and territory governed by a (nation) state. So 'international' also means or includes relations between and among states. This then is the ambiguity in the word 'international': it can refer *either* to relations among nations, understood as populations inhabiting territories that are governed by states, *or* to relations among the states concerned, *or* to both at the same time.

The questions of international order and disorder, of how international order is made and repaired, and of how attempts to govern it operate are the principal focus of the international relations I have been discussing, but you might want to reflect on the ambiguity in the term 'international' in the light of what you have studied. Finally, you might also want to think about inequalities and differences in international order in the light of the fact that not all states have the same power to shape international order.

References

Annan, K. (1999) 'Reflections on intervention', 35th Ditchley Foundation Lecture, 26 June 1998, in Annan, K., *The Question of Intervention*, New York, UNDPI.

Blair, T. (1999) 'Doctrine of the international community', speech given at the Economic Club, Chicago, IL, April [online], http://www.pbs.org/newshour/bb/international/jan-june99/blair_doctrine4-23.html (Accessed 20 July 2009).

Cabinet Office (2008) *The National Security Strategy of the United Kingdom: Security in an Interdependent World*, Cm 7291, London, TSO.

Charter, D. (2008) 'Royal Navy admiral Phillip Jones heads EU Somali pirate task force', *The Times*, 9 December; also available online at http://www.timesonline.co.uk/tol/news/world/europe/article5309165.ece (Accessed 29 June 2009).

Cicero, Marcus Tullius (1991) *On Duties* (ed. M.T. Griffin and E.M. Atkins, trans. M.T. Griffin), Cambridge, Cambridge University Press.

Colley, L. (2002) *Captives: Britain, Empire and the World, 1600–1850*, London, Jonathan Cape.

Crilly, R. (2009) 'Global piracy levels at a record high as Somali raiders cash in', *The Times*, 16 July [online], http://www.timesonline.co.uk/tol/news/world/africa/article6715399.ece (Accessed 27 July 2009).

Gow, J. (2005) *Defending the West*, Cambridge, Polity Press.

Gray, C.S. (2005) *Another Bloody Century: Future Warfare*, London, Weidenfeld and Nicolson.

Hume, D. (1994 [1752]) 'Of the balance of power' in *Hume: Political Essays* (ed. K. Haakonssen), Cambridge, Cambridge University Press.

Kaplan, R. (2009) 'Experts fear al-Qaeda may turn to piracy', excerpted in *IPRIS Digest*, vol. 2, no. 89.

Konstam, A. (2008) *Piracy: The Complete History*, Oxford, Osprey.

Lamb, C. (2002) *The Sewing Circles of Herat*, London, Penguin.

Lawrence, B. (2005) *Messages to the World: The Statements of Osama Bin Laden* (ed. B. Lawrence, trans. J. Howarth), London, Verso.

Lewis, L. (2008) 'Beijing ends 500 years of tradition as it sends the navy out to attack pirates', *The Times*, 27 December [online], http://www.timesonline.co.uk/tol/news/world/asia/article5400661.ece (accessed 15 October 2009).

Löwenheim, O. (2007) *Predators and Parasites: Persistent Agents of Transnational Harm and Great Power Authority*, Ann Arbor, MI, University of Michigan Press.

Thomson, J. (1994) *Mercenaries, Pirates and Sovereigns*, Princeton, NJ, Princeton University Press.

United Nations (UN) (1985) *Charter of the United Nations and Statute of the International Court of Justice*, Geneva, United Nations, Department of Public Information; also available online at http://www.un.org/en/documents/charter/intro.shtml (Accessed 29 June 2009).

United Nations Security Council (UNSC) (2001) Resolution 1368, 'Threats to international peace and security caused by terrorist acts' [online], http://daccessdds.un.org/doc/UNDOC/GEN/N01/533/82/PDF/N0153382.pdf?OpenElement (Accessed 30 June 2009).

United Nations Security Council (UNSC) (2008) Resolution 1851 'The situation in Somalia' [online], http://daccessdds.un.org/doc/UNDOC/GEN/N08/655/01/PDF/N0865501.pdf?OpenElement (Accessed 30 June 2009).

Waltz, K. (1979) *Theory of International Politics*, Reading, MA, Addison-Wesley.

Weber, M. (1991 [1921]) *From Max Weber* (ed. H.H. Gerth and C. Wright Mills), London, Routledge.

Conclusion: Ordered lives

Simon Bromley and John Clarke

Conclusion: Ordered lives

These three chapters mark the end of your work on new material in the course. There are still things to be done in terms of reviewing the course – but Chapters 7–9 form a sort of end. But what sort of end do they provide? At the most basic level, after reading these last three chapters you should be able to say something about why making and repairing order are such important issues in studying societies. You might also be able to say why these issues are connected with questions about authority and power, not least about the different sorts of authority and power that might be involved in the processes of governing. These different sorts of authority and power point to unequal and different ways of experiencing the processes of governing.

You might also be able to reflect on why the state is a central and controversial institution for these questions of governing and ordering. In these three chapters – as well as elsewhere in the course – you will have come across discussions about the role, power and limitations of states. Why, do you think, is it such a significant institution – and such a central concept in the social sciences?

The three chapters have made important connections between the idea of order and the processes and practices of governing. As you have seen, governing involves claims to *legitimate authority* – made in different settings by different sorts of actors, agents and institutions over different activities, settings and practices: from parents over their children to the international community over 'the enemies of all humanity', such as pirates. But the chapters have also stressed the importance of understanding that legitimacy is always potentially fragile and impermanent – it has to be repaired or renewed in the face of doubt and competing claims.

We want to stress that all three of the chapters have talked about *attempts* to govern and to make order. But social life on small and large scales (parents' authority in the home; the international community and the security of the 'high seas') may outrun attempts to create and sustain order and governing authority. From antisocial behaviour to political dissent; from intractable international dynamics to private choices, the order that governing authorities try to produce is always vulnerable to challenge.

This links to the most fundamental orientation of the course – that society is always in the process of being made, repaired or remade.

What seems to be stable and orderly about social life is the result of the work done by institutions, agencies and actors to make order. But social scientists link this to the constant processes of change that bring new problems to be governed, new threats to the established order and new possible ways of organising and ordering lives in the process. This is what the 'Ordered lives' chapters contribute to the course question about how society is made and repaired.

The chapters also point to some new aspects of the question about how differences and inequalities are made. In Chapter 7, the authors examined inequality as an issue for governing: how does inequality come to be seen as a public issue and what sorts of approaches to dealing with it can be put to work? Chapter 8 pointed to the different ways in which individuals and communities might experience the state, depending on different senses of belonging. In Chapter 9, you saw how making international order might involve both the *formal* equality of nations (or nation states), who each have the right to sovereignty, and the *substantive* inequalities of power between nations (in the discussion of the balance of power). This distinction between formal and substantive is an important one for the social sciences, particularly in relation to issues of equality and inequality. For example, formal equality might involve the equality of one person, one vote in democratic processes, or the principle of equality before the law. Substantive inequality might be differences in income or wealth, or other valued social attributes (health or longevity, for instance), or types of power. How formal equality and substantive inequalities coexist – and interact – is a recurrent concern for the social sciences.

Finally, throughout this book you have been invited to think about and reflect on the question: 'How do we (as social scientists) know?' These chapters have not added anything distinctively new in terms of methods of studying society or types of evidence, but each of them has made use of combinations of evidence and sources. Some of them have been quantitative (from calculations of the threat of global warming to government data on inequalities of income and wealth in the UK). Some have been qualitative (interviews with people about dangers and threats). Some have involved thinking about how symbols or communications work in making and contesting social order – about how issues are framed (Chapter 7), or how artworks such as murals are entwined with politics (Chapter 8), or even how films lead us to think about piracy (Chapter 9). In this way, these chapters exemplify the practices, the problems and the possibilities of *doing* social science. They draw on and make use of diverse sources and types of evidence to make sense of aspects of social life. They have to recognise and deal with the limitations of their sources of evidence. But most of all, they are engaged by the possibilities of enlarging our collective understanding of how social life is possible and of why it is ordered in this way (and not some other way).

Acknowledgements

Grateful acknowledgement is made to the following sources:

Chapter 1

Text

Page 33: BBC News (2007) 'UK "exporting emissions" to China', 5 October 2007, from BBC News at http://bbc.co.uk/news. Copyright © BBC MMVII; Page 42: Campbell, D. (2006) 'Vanuatu tops wellbeing and environment index', The Guardian, 12 July 2006. Copyright © Guardian News & Media Ltd 2006

Tables

Table 1: OECD (2007) OECD Factbook 2007: Economic, Environmental and Social Statistics, Copyright © Table 2: Phillpotts, G. and Causer, P. (eds) (2006) Regional Trends, Office for National Statistics. Crown copyright material is reproduced under Class Licence Number C01W0000065 with the permission of the Controller of HMSO and the Queen's Printer for Scotland

Figures

Figure 2: OECD (2007) OECD Economic Survey: United Kingdom, OECD. Copyright © OECD; Figure 3: Defra (2007) Environment in Your Pocket, Defra. Crown copyright material is reproduced under Class Licence Number C01W0000065 with the permission of the Controller, Office of Public Sector Information (OPSI)

Illustrations

Page 16 left: Copyright © Gideon Mendel/Corbis; Page 16 right: Copyright © Medical-on-Line/Alamy; Page 21 left: Copyright © Ashley Cooper/Corbis; Page 21 centre: Copyright © Howie Twiner; Page 21 right: Copyright © Transtock/Corbis; Page 25 left: Copyright © Hulton-Deutsch Collection/Corbis; Page 25 right: Copyright © Naijah Feanny-Hicks/Corbis; Page 45 left: Copyright © Christophe Boisvieux/Corbis; Page 45 right: Copyright © Neil Farrin/JAI/Corbis

Chapter 2

Figures

Figure 1: Copyright © Tim Jordan; Figure 2: Copyright © Cancer Research UK

Illustrations

Page 58: Copyright © Richard Olivier/Corbis; Page 62: Copyright © UniversalNewsandSport.com/WpN/Photoshot; Page 68: Copyright © The Garden Picture Library/Alamy; Page 78 left: Copyright © Kuoni Travel; Page 72 right: Copyright © Simon Carter; Page 73: Copyright © The Caravan Gallery www.thecaravangallery.co.uk; Page 76: Copyright © Owen Franken/Corbis; Page 79: Copyright © Igor Kostin/Sygma/Corbis; Page 85: Food Standards Agency (2007) Front-of-Pack Traffic Light Signpost Labelling – Technical Guidance, Food Standards Agency, Copyright © Crown Copyright; Page 88: Copyright © British Heart Foundation

Chapter 3

Figures

Figure 2: World Resources Institute (2007) EarthTrends: Environmental Information. Available at http://earthtrends.wri.org. Washington DC: World Resources Institute; Figure 3: Copyright © Ken Avidor

Illustrations

Page 103: Copyright © Chris Madden; Page 104: Copyright © Chris Madden; Page 120: Copyright © Steve Greenberg; Page 132 photo: Copyright © Ashley Cooper/Alamy

Introduction: Connected lives

Illustration

Page 155: Copyright © Isabel Hutchison/Alamy

Chapter 4

Figures

Figure 1: Sriskandarajah, D and Drew, C (2006) Brits Abroad: Mapping the scale and nature of British emigration, Institute for Public Policy Research; Figure 2: Copyright © 2006 SASI Group (University of Sheffield) and Mark Newman (University of Michigan) http://www.worldmapper.org; Figure 4: Copyright © 2007 by The Migration Policy Institute

Illustrations

Page 159 left: Copyright © Mark Campbell/Rex Features; Page 159 right: Copyright © Andrew Fox/Corbis; Page 161 top: Image courtesy of The Advertising Archives; Page 161 bottom: Copyright © Rick Collis/Rex Features; Page 172: The Jewish Museum, London; Page 178: Copyright © Ed Kashi/Corbis; Page 179: Copyright © Hulton-Deutsch Collection/Corbis; Page 182: Courtesy of Daminis; Page 195 left: Copyright © Terrence Spencer/Time & Life Pictures/Getty Images; Page 195 right: Courtesy of Sandhya Suri

Chapter 5

Illustrations

Page 211: Copyright © Justin Kaseztwoz/Alamy; Page 216: Copyright © Kurt Hutton/Hulton-Deutsch Collection/Corbis; Page 218: Copyright © Powered by Light/Alan Spencer/Alamy; Page 220 top left: akg-images; Page 220 top right: akg-images/British Library; Page 220 bottom: The Hay Wain, 1821 (oil on canvas) by Constable, John (1776-1837) National Gallery, London, UK/The Bridgeman Art Library. Nationality/copyright status: English/out of copyright; Page 222 top left: Copyright © Stuart Kelly/Alamy; Page 222 bottom right: Copyright © Nils Jorgensen/Rex Features

Chapter 6

Illustrations

Pages 253 and 256: Courtesy of Jo Hollway; Page 255: Copyright © Ariel Skelley/Blend Images/Getty Images: Page 262: Copyright © Juice Images/Corbis; Page 263: Copyright © Photofusion Picture Library/Alamy; Page 271: Copyright © Neil McAllister/Alamy; Page 272:

Conclusion: Connected lives

Illustration

Chapter 7

Text

Figure

Illustrations

Chapter 8

Figures

Illustrations

Page 357: from http://commons.wikipedia.org, submitted by Amos Wolfe. Reproduced under the terms of the GNU Free Documentation Licence, Version 1.2, www.gnu.org; Page 368: Copyright © Gianni Dagli Orti/The Art Archive

Chapter 9

Text

Page 398: Crilly, R (2009) 'Global piracy levels at a record high as Somali raiders cash in', The Times, 16 July 2009. Copyright © NI Syndication Ltd

Illustrations

Page 395: Copyright © Jerry Bruckheimer Films/Walt Disney Pictures/ The Ronald Grant Archive; Page 400: Copyright © Bob Krist/Corbis; Page 405 left: Copyright © Joao Pedro Fonseca/Corbis; Page 405 right: Copyright © HO/Reuters/Corbis; Page 409: Copyright © Mark Garten/UN Photo Library; Page 419: Copyright © Carmen Taylor/AP/ Press Association Images; Page 426: Copyright © Anja Niedringhaus/ AP/Press Association Images

Index

A

Abshire, Jean 378–9
acid rain 31, 93, 119, 120
Afghanistan 415, 418, 421–2, 424
ageing population, and the costs
  and contributions of migrants 168
air pollution
    and economic growth 46
    reducing in the UK 31
airports
    expansion and the environment 30–1
    risk and antiterrorism measures 61, 62
al-Qaeda 418, 419–23, 424, 432
alcohol consumption, risks of 81
alcoholism, and economic growth 46
allotment soil, scientific testing of 5, 61, 63–70, 80,
  89, 92
Alsace, national identity 237, 238
ambivalence
    and Britishness 213–14, 235
    and national identities 242
    and racial/ethnic identities 231–3
    to the state 386–7, 389
'America', and Britishness 233, 234, 236
American revolution 367
anarchism, and the state 387–8, 389
anarchy, and international order 428–9
Anderson, Benedict 229, 243
animal testing, and PBET soil testing 66
Arctic ice melting 108, 316
arguments, evaluating 433
armed forces, and government 327
Arsenal Football Club, and risk management
  60–1, 92
arsenic in soil, testing for 63, 64
Asian migrants, in East Africa 181–2
Aso, Taro 432
Athenian democracy 367, 368
atmospheric commons 112–18
    and global climate change 6–7, 104–5
    greenhouse gases and economic growth 106–11
    management of 115–18, 147
        Kyoto Protocol 122–7, 128, 139
        market solutions 117–18, 128–36, 138–9

    see also carbon emissions; greenhouse gas
      emissions
Australia
    and the Kyoto Protocol 123
    migrants 172, 173, 177
authority
    of governments 327–30, 439
    see also legitimacy
availability heuristics, and threats to social order
  315–19, 320

B

balance of power, and international order 427–31,
  440
Baltic states, national identities 240
banal nationalism 229, 230, 242
Barnes, Peter 117
Barrie, James, *Peter Pan* 395
Bauman, Zygmunt 338
the Beatles, mural paintings of 384
Beck, Ulrich, on risk society 61, 79–80, 81, 86, 92,
  110, 145
Beetham, David 366
Bevan, Aneurin 190
Bhutan 17, 39, 45, 46
    GNH (gross national happiness) 41–2
Billig, Michael 229, 230, 242, 274
bin Laden, Osama 418, 422, 424
bioaccessibility testing (PBET) 65–6
    and risk assessment 68, 69
biological reductionism
    and ethnicity 232
    and identities 277
Birmingham, St Patrick's Day Parade
  159, 163
black skin, identities and social meaning 251,
  277–85, 286–7
Blair, Tony 329, 332, 334
    and the international community 412, 413
Blunkett, David 221, 223, 224, 225
bodies and identity
    black skin and social meaning 277–85

identity change 251, 253–4, 287–8
    new mothers 261, 262, 266
Brazil, economy and well-being 39
British Empire 221, 235
Britishness 153, 209–30, 243–4
    and culture 153, 215, 219–25
    and history 215
    and imagined communities 229–30
    as a national identity 209–14, 237
        consequences of 212–14
        discovering 210–12
    and Others 231–6, 243
        'America' 233, 234, 236
        'Empire' 233, 234, 235, 236
        'Europe' 233, 234–5, 236
        race/ethnicity 215, 231–3
    and personal identity 212
    and place 215, 216–19
Brown, Gordon 190, 332, 363
Bulgaria, migrant workers from 20
Bush, George W. 308, 425
business connections, and migration 181–2
Byron, Lord, *The Corsair* 395

C

Cambodia, invasion of 413–14
Canada
    economy and well-being 26, 39
    and sulphur trading 119–22
car industry, takeovers and the UK economy 19, 21
carbon emissions 102
    cumulative effect of 106–7
    and the Kyoto Protocol 122–7, 128, 139
    mechanisms for combating 101, 138–9
    regulation of 117
    social organisation of 102–5
    sources of 108–10
    trading schemes 128–35
        cap and trade 123–4
        CDM 123, 124, 125, 126, 128–33
        JI mechanism 123, 124–5, 126, 128
    UK target to reduce 36
carbon footprints 104, 134
cars
    and antiterrorist measures 61
    and risks for cyclists 57–8, 59

Catholic Church, and Spain 237
CDM (Clean Development Mechanism) 123, 124, 125, 126, 128–33
census (UK) 294, 358–9
CFCs (chlorofluorocarbons) 116
Chamberlain, Joseph 339
Channel Islands 218
Chernobyl disaster 79–80, 93, 145
child abuse, as a public issue 323, 324, 343–4
childcare
    as a public issue 323–4
    and the state 353, 354
children
    and identity change 252
    migrants
        costs and contributions of 165–6, 168
        defining 164
China
    and Afghanistan 422
    and al-Qaeda 420
    campaign against piracy 431–2
    carbon footprint 104
    cross-border money flows 186, 187
    and greenhouse gas emissions, UK 'exporting' to 33–5
    and the UN Security Council 411
Chinese diaspora 183
choice, and risk assessment 67–70
Cicero, *De Officis* 399, 404
citizenship
    and migration 164, 171
    and national identities 207–8, 219
        Britishness 210, 212, 213, 214
    and the state 364
citizenship ceremonies 361, 362, 366, 372, 384
    and pledges of allegiance 363–4
class, and migration 185
Clean Development Mechanism *see* CDM (Clean Development Mechanism)
climate change 6–7, 93, 101–39, 145
    and economic growth 4–5, 7, 14, 16, 30–7, 101, 102–4
    threat of 305, 306, 307–11, 343
        and risk assessment 311–15
    vulnerability to 109–10
    and the weightless economy 33–6
    see also carbon emissions; greenhouse gas emissions

choropleth world map, of money flows
    186–7, 294
closed economies 17–18
clothes
    migration and women entrepreneurs 181–5,
        184–5
    new mothers and identity change 270–2
Coarse, Ronald 121, 122
coercion
    and government 328
    and the state 373
Coke, Sir Edward 399
Cold War, and the international community 414
Colley, Linda 401
colonialism
    and carbon trading 130
    and racial thinking 231–2
common world
    and the environment 101, 104–5
    Hardin's tragedy of the commons argument
        112–15, 136
    see also atmospheric commons
the commons, and global climate change 6–7
conflict
    and identity change 252–3
        new mothers 260, 267, 269, 269–70, 272,
        273, 275–6
        school–work transitions 280, 284–5
connected lives 3, 147, 151–4, 293–5
    see also identities; migration
consent, government by 328
Conservative governments (UK), economic
    policies 24–5
Conservative Party policy, maternity services 262
consumer choice
    and happiness 42, 45
    and holidaymakers 74
consumption 15
    and diasporic origins 183, 185
    and economic growth 30
    and national identities 241
    and the weightless economy 33
contraceptive pill, and epidemiological
    knowledge 86
Cooper, Diana 322–3
coronary heart disease, research into the
    prevention paradox 87–9
Corus 21
costs of migration

and definitions of migrants 165–6
    and migrant numbers 168–70
country of birth, defining migrants by 164, 165
Craddock, General John 405
crime
    and the availability heuristic 317–18
    and universal jurisdiction 405–7
critical awareness, and social science 135–6
CSM (Committee on the Safety of Medicine), and
    epidemiological knowledge 86
culture
    and Britishness 153, 215, 219–25
        everyday cultural practices 221–3
        high culture 219–21
        and other places 235, 236
    consumption and national identities 241
    cultural meanings and identity change 271–2
    and migration 168
    and racial thinking 231–2
cycling helmets, and risk 57–8, 59, 92

D

danger, and risk 59
data analysis
    research on identities 285
        black youth 282–5
        new mothers 267–76
data collection, and research on identities 259,
    263–5
Davison, Charlie, research into the prevention
    paradox 87–9
deaths
    and epidemiological knowledge 83, 87
    from terrorism and climate change 315
deliberative democracy 369
demand *see* supply and demand
democracy 366–70
    defining 369
    lived experience of 369–70
    'minimalist' and 'maximalist' approaches to 369
Department for International Development, on
    economic growth 30
Depp, Johnny 395, 396
depression
    and economic growth 46
    post-natal 261
deregulation, and the UK economy 24–5
determinism, and probability 84

developed economies 4, 17
   GDP per capita 25–6, 38, 40–1, 45, 47
   location of 18
   pollution and economic growth 30–1
   weightless 31–6
   see also UK economy
developing countries
   defining 30
   and economic growth 30
development psychology, and identity change 252
Devenny, Danny 379, 384
devolution, and state renewal and repair 372
diasporas
   and connections between places 152, 183–6
   and ethnic identities 232–3
   and money flows 186–7
differences 3, 7
   of identities 153–4
digestive system, and PBET soil testing 65–6
digital information, and the weightless economy
  32–3
direct democracy 367, 369
disidentification 274, 276
distribution, and economies 15
diversity
   and Britishness 224–9
   defining 225
doctors, migration to the UK 190–5
domestic violence, as a public issue 343–4
Drake, Sir Francis 400
drug cartels, and the United States 423–4
Dufferin Fund, and medical migration 194

E

East Africa, Asian migrants in 181–2
Eastern European migrants, in the UK 160,
  171, 179
ecological effects, of carbon trading 130–1
economic crisis (2008/9) 17
economic globalisation, and the UK economy
  19–20, 24, 26
economic growth 4–5, 13–49
   and carbon emissions 101, 102, 104–5
   defining 30
   and environmental change 4–5, 7, 10, 14, 30–7
   and happiness 5, 13–14, 41–7, 49
   and risk 57
   see also UK economy

economic interdependence, and national
  identities 241
Economic and Social Research Council, Identities
  and Social Action (research programme) 258–9
economies 4, 15–17
   defining 15
   weightless 31–6, 57, 145
   see also developed economies; UK economy
educational qualifications, and the value of
  migrants 173–5
Edward II, King of England 218
elections, and state legitimacy 366
Elizabethan England, piracy in 399–400
'Empire', and Britishness 233, 234, 235, 236
empirical research 293
   on happiness and economic growth 45–7
   on identities 258–66, 286, 294–5
      project design 259–66
     in the UK 258–9
energy efficiency, and economic growth 31
entrepreneurship and migration
   business connections 181–2
   diasporas 183
Environmental Agency (EA), and scientific testing
  of soil 68
environmental interdependence, and national
  identities 241
environmental problems 146
   and economic growth 4–5, 7, 14, 30–7, 101
   and the Happy Planet Index 43–4
   see also climate change; greenhouse gas
    emissions
environmental risks 5, 93, 101
epidemiology 83–91, 93
   and government policies 84–5
   and infectious disease 83
   lay 89–90
   and the probabilistic approach 83–4
   uses of epidemiological knowledge 85–90
equality
   and democracy 369
   formal 440
   sovereign equality 408–9, 420, 440
   see also inequalities
Erikson, Erik 252–3, 260, 273, 279, 287
Ervine, Mark 384
ethnic cleansing 239
ethnicity *see* race/ethnicity
'Europe', and Britishness 233, 234–5, 236

Europe, and state renewal and repair 371, 372
European countries, migration and national
  identities 240–1
European Economic Area (EEA) 171
European Union (EU) 326
  and Britishness 234
  citizenship 364
  and Eastern European migrants 160
  and the Kyoto Protocol 123
evidence
  framing of 342
  and qualitative data 242
  and quantitative data 47–8, 146
exchange, economic 15
expatriate communities 177, 178, 186, 193, 219
expert knowledge 147
  and lay knowledge 5–6, 61, 81, 83–91, 90–1, 93
    attitudes to sun exposure 73–8
    availability heuristic 318–19
    climate change 311
    mediation of 321
  mediated 321, 343
  and the risk society 79–80, 81
  and scientific testing 61, 63–70, 80
  see also epidemiology

F

Fairbanks, Douglas 395
family photographs, new mothers and
  identification 255–7
Fanon, Frantz 277, 281, 285, 287
  Black Skin, White Mask 278–9
FDI (foreign direct investment), and the UK
  economy 20, 24
fear, and international order 427, 431
films, Pirates of the Caribbean trilogy 395–6, 404
financial crisis (2008/9) 17
financial services
  and the Scottish economy 28–9
  and the UK economy 4, 20, 25, 26
finite resources, demand for 103–4
firms, economies of 16
First World War, and the state 355–6
flags
  and British national identities 211
  of convenience 405
flat view of social inequality 338
flooding, threats of 308, 309–10, 314, 315, 316

flow maps, and diasporic connections 184
flows
  and economic globalisation 19, 20
  and identity change 286
  of migration 152, 184
    money flows 186–7, 294
focus group research 91, 146–7
  holidaymakers and sun exposure 61, 71–8, 85,
    89–90
food labelling, and epidemiology 84, 85
food risks
  and epidemiological knowledge 85, 89
  and scientific testing 5, 61, 63–70, 89
football stadiums, and risk management 60–1
foreign direct investment see FDI (foreign direct
  investment)
formal equality 440
fossil fuels
  and carbon trading 131–2
  and climate change 101–2, 104, 134, 309
Foucault, Michel 198
framing devices, and public issues 321
France
  and Alsace 237, 238
  and climate change 309
  economy 19, 20, 26
    and well-being 39, 41
  racism and black identity in 278–9
    and the UN Security Council 411
Franklin, Benjamin 358
free trade, and wasteful trade 34–5
freedom, and democracy 369
French language, and national identity 237, 240
French Revolution 367
Freud, Sigmund 274–5

G

G7 (Group of 7) developed economies, measures
  of economic development 26, 38
gated communities 341
GDP (gross domestic product)
  contribution of migrants to 169, 186
  and economic growth 30
  and the HDI (human development index) 42
  per head/per capita 25–6, 38, 40–1, 45, 47
  and the UK economy 21–3, 25–6
  and well-being 44, 46
gender, and Britishness 213

generational identity, and new mothers 270, 272–3, 275, 286

geography, and the weightless economy 32

Germany, economy and well-being 26, 39

Glasgow Airport, attempted car bomb attack on 61, 62

Glasgow, holidaymakers from, attitudes to sun exposure 73–8, 85, 89–90, 91, 92, 93

global climate change *see* climate change

global economy 16–17

    measuring economic growth and well-being 25–6, 27, 38–41, 45–7

    and the UK economy 17–24

global North

    and carbon emissions 102–3, 136

    CDM carbon trading schemes 128–35

    and citizenship 208

    and climate change 7

    defining 102

    and the Kyoto Protocol 125–7

global South

    CDM carbon trading schemes 128–35

    and climate change 7

    defining 102

    and greenhouse gas emissions 136

    and the Kyoto Protocol 125–7

global warming *see* climate change

globalisation, and the UK economy 19–20, 24, 26

Glynn, Seimon 167, 168, 171, 172, 173, 293

GNI (gross national income) per head 38, 39, 40–1

Goklany, Indur 46

Goodhart, David, on Britishness 225–6, 228, 229–30, 241

governing, and government 326

governing social order 299, 305–44, 439

    public issues

        governing 322–30, 343

        making 319–21, 343

    social inequality 305, 331–41

    and the state 299, 305

    threats to

        climate change 305, 306, 307–15, 343

        identifying 315–19

government policies

    and epidemiology 84–5

    and maternity services 261–2

governments 326–30

    authority of 327–30

and the state 357–8

and the UK economy 15–16, 24–5, 31

Greece, economy and well-being 39

green consumers 134

greenhouse gas emissions

    and the atmospheric commons 106–11, 138–9

    and climate change 104–5

    Kyoto Protocol and targets for 35–6

    sources of 108–10

    sulphur trading 119–22

    and the UK economy 14, 31, 33–5

    and the weightless economy 33

    see also carbon emissions

Gulf Stream, and climate change 108

Gupta, Akhil 354, 358

GVA (gross value added), and the UK economy 27–9, 38

H

Haiti, cross-border money flows 186

happiness

    and economic growth 5, 13–14, 41–7, 49

    and inequality 331

    and risk 57

Happy Planet Index 43–4

Hardin, Garrett, tragedy of the commons model 112–15, 136

hate crimes, and Britishness 223

Hayter, Teresa, *Open Borders: The Case Against Immigration Controls* 170

HDI (human development index) 42

health

    cycling and risk 59

    and suntans 78

health education 6, 78, 146

    and epidemiological knowledge 85–90, 93

health risks 5

    and the availability heuristic 318–19

    and sun exposure 61, 71–8, 80, 81

    see also epidemiology

health visitors, and maternity services 262

heart disease, research into the prevention paradox 87–9

hierarchical view of social inequality 338

high culture, and Britishness 219–21

historical–structural theory of migration 193–5, 196

history, and Britishness 215

Hobbes, Thomas, *Leviathan* 358, 359

Hoffman, John 373

holidaymakers, assessing risks of sun exposure 61, 71–8, 85, 89–90, 92, 93

Home Office, guide to British citizenship 210, 212, 217–18, 224

Hood, Christopher 356

hoodies, stereotypes of 283–4, 287

household economies 16, 17

human capital, and migrants 173–5, 293

human digestive system, and PBET soil testing 65–6

human rights, and the international community 409, 412–13

Hume, David, *Of the balance of power* 430

hunting bans, as a public issue 322–3

Huntington, Samuel P., *Who are We? Challenges to America's National Identity* 240

I

ICT (information and communication technologies), and the UK economy 24, 32

identification
  and identity change 286
    new mothers 255–7, 269–70, 272–3, 275–6
  theories of 274–6

identities
  black skin and social meaning 251, 277–85, 286–7
  consequences of 212–14
  empirical research on 258–66, 286, 294–5
  political debates about 152
  see also national identities

identity changes 152, 153, 251–7
  bodies 153
  new motherhood 153, 251, 255–7, 286
    empirical research on 259–76
  through the life course 252–3, 260, 273
  uneven pace of 253–4

identity crises 252

illegal migrants 171–2

imagined communities, and Britishness 229–30, 243

immigration, politics of 160, 161

improvement systems, and governments 327

incomes
  inequalities 331–7

measuring economic growth and well-being 25–6, 27, 38–41, 45–7
  and the UK economy 13, 26–7, 29

India
  campaign against piracy 431–2
  cross-border money flows 186, 187
  economy and well-being 39
  flooding in 309
  medical migration from the UK to 194–5
  partition and national identities 239

Indian diaspora in the UK, and ethnic identities 232–3

indigenous knowledge, and market solutions to pollution 138–9

individuals
  and anarchism 387–8
  and epidemiological knowledge 87–9, 93
  green consumers 134
  and the state in everyday life 266, 351–4, 354–5, 361, 386

industrialisation, and greenhouse gas emissions 106

inequalities
  and Britishness 223
  and carbon trading 131–2
  defining inequality 331
  economic 5, 26
    measures of 41
  and global climate change 7
  and identities 153–4
  in material lives 145–6
  as a public issue 320
  and risk 57
  substantive 440
  see also social inequality

infant mortality, global comparisons 39

infectious diseases, and epidemiology 83

insurance, and epidemiology 85

international community 408–17, 434, 439
  defining 408
  and human rights 409
  and liberal internationalism 408
  and the rights and duties of the most powerful states 410–11
  and sovereign equality 408–9
  and the UK 415–16

international law, definition of piracy in 399, 402

international migration 167–8

international order, organisation of 426–32, 434, 440
International Passenger Survey 164, 294
international trade, and the UK economy 18–19
internet
    global access to the 39, 40
    Mumsnet site 317
    and the weightless economy 32
interviews, research on identities 259, 263–4
IRA (Irish Republican Army) 377
Iraq war 424–6, 427
Ireland
    and Britishness 217, 218
    partition of 374, 375
    and the St Patrick's Day Parade in
      Birmingham 159
    see also Northern Ireland
Italy, economy and well-being 26, 39

J

Japan
    carbon trading 131–3
    economy 19, 26
        and well-being 39, 40
    migration 177, 178
Jews
    diasporas 183, 185
    migration to the UK 171
JI (Joint Implementation) mechanism 123, 124–5, 126, 128
Joseph Rowntree Foundation 338

K

Kahneman, D. 315–16
Kaplan, Robert 421
Kennedy, Donald 121
Kenya, Asian migrants in 182, 185
Kimbrell, Andrew 118
King, Sir David, on the problem of climate change 307–11, 312, 314, 329
knowledge, and power 198
knowledge economy, and migrants 174
knowledge-intensive services, and the UK economy 24, 32
Konstam, Angus 399–400
Kosovo, and the UN Security Council 412–13, 414–15

Kuhn, Thomas, The Structure of Scientific Revolutions 197
Kyoto Protocol 35–6, 122–7, 128, 139

L

Labour Force Survey, data on migrants 165
Labour government (UK)
    economic policies 25
    and income inequalities 332–5
    and maternity services 261–2
labour market
    and the UK economy
        liberalisation 24–5
        migrant workers 20
Lancaster, John 139
language
    and migration 168
    and national identities 208, 209, 237, 240, 243
the 'last person', and lay epidemiology 89, 90
Latvia, national identity in 240
laws, and governments 327
lay epidemiology 89–90
lay knowledge
    availability heuristic 315–19
    and expert knowledge 81, 83–91, 90–1, 93
        attitudes to sun exposure 61, 73–8
        climate change 311
    and government 329
    mediation of 321, 343
Layard, Richard 45–6, 47
legitimacy 439
    and international order 426–32
    and sovereign equality 408–9
    of states 300, 366–70, 384–5, 389
Lesotho, cross-border money flows 186
liberal internationalism 408
liberalisation
    and the UK economy 24–5
    see also markets
life course
    and identity changes 252–3, 260, 273
        school–work transitions and black youth 279–80, 282–5, 287
life expectancy
    and economic growth 39, 40
    and the Happy Planet Index 43, 44
    in the UK 13
lifestyle, and epidemiological knowledge 88–9

Lister, Ruth 338
literature
  and Britishness 219, 220, 222
  pirates in 395
Lithuania, migrant workers from 20
Liverpool, as Capital of Culture (2008) 384
living standards
  inequalities in 332
  and the UK economy 13–14, 25–6
local commons 115
  management of 117
local communities, and carbon trading 130–1, 132–3
local economies 16
Lohmann, L. 124, 125, 134, 135
London
  Borough of Hackney (LBH), allotment soil and food risk 63–70
  Docklands and nineteenth-century migration 179
  Heathrow Airport expansion 30–1
  Thames Barrier and flooding 308, 312
  Tower Hamlets, empirical research on identities 259, 263–76
  and the UK economy 27, 28
Löwenheim, Oded 423–4
Luxembourg, economy and well-being 39, 40, 42

M

MacKenzie, Donald 120, 136
Madison, James 367–8
Maersk Alabama (merchant ship) 398, 405
Major, John 24, 25
Malacca Straits, and piracy 404
Man, Isle of 218
manufacturing, and the UK economy 23, 31
markets
  and the atmospheric commons 1, 110–11, 117–18, 119, 138–9
  and carbon emissions 102, 110–11, 133–5
    CDM schemes 16, 123, 124, 126, 128–33
    Kyoto Protocol 122–7, 128
  and climate change 101
  and the environment 7
  and household economies 17
  and social inequalities 337
  and the UK economy 15, 16, 24–5, 26
material lives 3–7, 145–7

as controversial and political 146
inequalities in 145–6
see also climate change; economic growth; risk
'maximalist' approaches to democracy 369
media reports
  and the availability heuristic 317–18
  on migration 160, 165
  on pirates 398
  on risks 80–1
    and epidemiological knowledge 86
  and the state 354
mediated knowledge, of public issues 320–1
mental health, and inequality 339
merchant shipping, and pirates 398, 404–5
migration 152–3, 159–99
  celebrations of migrant communities 159, 163
  connections established by 181–9
    business connections 181–2
    diasporas 152, 183–6
    translocalism 152, 187–9
  costs and contributions of migrants 165–6, 168–70, 172–5, 293
  and 'Empire' 235
  histories 185–6
  history of 193–4
  inter-company transfers 177–8
  migrant workers in the UK 20, 160, 173–5
  and nation 162
  and national identities 207, 240–1
  and the NHS 152, 162, 190–5
  nineteenth century 178–9, 193
  and open borders 160, 170
  politics of 160, 161
  questions for social scientists 160–2
  stories 162, 163–80
    of arrival 166–7
    categorising and valuing migrants 171–5
    defining migrants 163–6
    departure and circulation 175–80
    numbers of migrants 167–9
  theories of 193–6, 197
  UK expatriates 176–7, 186
Migration Watch, on the costs of migrants 165–6
military forces, and governments 327
'minimalist' approaches to democracy 369
Mitchell, Timothy 358
mobile phone use, risks of 81
money flows, and migration 186–7, 294
motherhood

identity changes and new mothers 153, 251,
  255–7, 286
    research project on 259–76
  social mothering 266
movement, defining migrants by 164
moving picture of society 151–2, 295
multiple identities
  and Britishness 214, 225–9
  positions of 254
multiplicity, and identity change 257
mural painting in Northern Ireland 373, 374–84,
  385
  Nationalist/Republican 376–7, 378–80, 381,
    382, 383
  Painting from the Same Palette 383, 384
  Unionist/Loyalist 375–6, 379–80, 381–3

N

nation states, and governments 326–7
National Health Service *see* NHS (National Health
  Service)
national identities 153, 199, 207–44
  Alsace 237, 238
  Baltic states 240
  India 239
  making 237–42
  and pirates 402
  and race/ethnicity 231–3
  reasons for focusing on 207–8
  Scotland 386
  Spain 237, 238–9
  Wales 386
  Yugoslavia (former) 239
  see also Britishness
national jurisdiction 406–7
national territory 215, 229
nationalism, banal 229, 230, 242
nations
  as imagined communities 229–30, 243
  and national identity 241
  and states 362
NATO (North Atlantic Treaty Organization)
  and the Iraq war 425
  and the UN Security Council 412, 414, 416
negative externalities, and the atmospheric
  commons 110, 111, 113–14
NHS (National Health Service)
  maternity services 261–2

and migration 152, 162, 174, 190–5
nineteenth-century migration 178–9, 193
  and translocalism 188–9
nineteenth-century piracy 401–2
non-governmental organisations (NGOs), making
  public issues 320
North Korea 17, 367
Northern Ireland
  Assembly 372
  and Britishness 217, 218–19
  economy 27, 28, 29
  Good Friday Agreement 379, 380–2, 383–4
  hunger strike by Republican prisoners 378
  policing 377
  and political legitimacy 384–5
  state renewal and repair 373, 374–84,
    386, 389
  and mural painting 373, 374–84, 385
  the 'Troubles' 377–8
  and the United Kingdom 362, 371
Norway, carbon trading 129–31
NSS (national security strategy), and the
  international community 415–16

O

Obama, Barak 426
observation
  and research on identities 259, 264–5
    researcher reflexivity 280–2
    'role play' data 277, 279–80, 282–5
occupations, and contributions of immigrants 173
OECD (Organisation for Economic
  Co-operation and Development), and),
  and FDI 22–3
off-shoring, and the UK economy 24
Office for National Statistics, data on income and
  wealth distribution 335–7
open economies 17, 18, 26
  and FDI 23
  and risk 57
The Open University, and the state 356–7
ordered lives 299–300, 439–41
  see also governing social order; international
    community; the state
Others and Britishness 231–6
  racial and ethnic identities 231–3
outsourcing, and the UK economy 24
Owain Glyndwr/Owen Glendower 218

P

Painter, Joe 354
Painting from the Same Palette 383, 384
Paisley, women workers and translocalism 188–9, 293
Pakistan
    and Afghanistan 422
    economy and well-being 39
paradigms, and theories 197
Parekh, Bhikhu, on diversity and Britishness 226–7, 228–9
Paris, Treaty of (1865) 401
participant numbers, in research on identities 265–6
participative democracy 369
PBET (physiologically based extraction test) 65–6, 68, 69
Peloponnesian War 430
pensions, and UK expatriates 176, 186
personal identity, and Britishness 212
Phillips, Captain Richard 398, 405
Phillips, Trevor 223, 224, 225
pirates 395–7, 398–407, 421, 434
    in film and literature 395–6
    history of 399–402
    and international order 431–2
    modern 402–5
    order and governance 396, 404
    resurgence of 398
    self-defence against 404–5
    and universal jurisdiction 396–7, 402, 405–7, 408
    see also Somali pirates
Pirates of the Caribbean trilogy 395–6, 404
place
    of Britishness 215, 216–19
    and race/ethnicity 231–3
Poland
    economy and well-being 39
    migrant workers from 20
police force, and government 327
political authority, of governments 327
political legitimacy, of the state 300, 366–70, 384–5
political order 300, 351–89
    defining 352
    see also the state
political parties, making public issues 320

politics
    of migration 160, 161
    and national identities 207–8, 209
    and the public/private divide 322–5
polluter pays principle 34
pollution
    and economic growth 30–1, 41, 46
    and management of the commons 115–18, 138–9
    see also greenhouse gas emissions
Pompey the Great 399
positive externalities, and the atmospheric commons 110, 111
positive-sum power, in Northern Ireland 374–5
post-natal depression, and identity change 261
postcolonial melancholia 235
poverty, and inequality 332–5, 338–9
power
    and international order 427–32
    and knowledge 198
practices
    and identity change 254, 287–8
        new mothers 260–1, 267, 268–9, 269–70, 272–3, 275
    and the state 354–5
Pratchett, Terry, *Discworld* novels 357
pregnant women, and alcohol consumption 81
prevention paradox, and epidemiological knowledge 87–9, 90, 93
price mechanism 135, 136
    and environmental problems 110–11, 114, 117
        sulphur trading 122
    and the UK economy 15–16
privateers 399–401
    and terrorist organisations 422–3
privatisation
    of the commons 114–15, 117–18
    and the UK economy 24, 25
probabilities
    and epidemiology 83–4
    and threat of climate change 312, 313
production 15, 16
productivity, of the UK economy 24, 26, 27–9, 38
professional networks, and migration 193
professional organisations, making public issues 320
projection, and identification 275, 276

property rights
and carbon emissions 134
and the commons 117
and sulphur trading 121–2
Proudhon, J.-P., *General Idea of the Revolution in the Nineteenth Century* 387–8
proxy measures, of national income 41
psychoanalysis, and identification 274–5
public issues
governing 322–30
making 319–20
public/private divide 322–5
push–pull theory of migration 193, 196

Q

qualitative data 293, 440
and research on identities 259, 263, 264, 265–6, 295
speaking and writing as 242
quantitative data 293–4, 440
on the economy and well-being 40, 49
interpretation of 48
on migration 169, 293–4
questioning evidence using 47–8, 146
and research on identities 263, 264, 295

R

race/ethnicity
and Britishness 213–14, 215
ethnic diversity 225–6, 228–9
identities of 231–3, 243, 277
black skin and social meaning 277–85
and medical migration 192
researching racial difference 279–80
racial thinking 231–2
racism
and black identity 278–9
and Britishness 227, 228–9
radioactive material, risk from 79–80
realist tradition, of international order 427–32, 434
referendums, and democracy 369
reflexivity of researchers 280–2
regimes of truth 198
regional differences, and the UK economy 4, 16, 27–9
regulation of the commons 114, 115–17
trading in sulphur dioxide permits 119–22

relationships
and identity change 254, 287–8
new mothers 260, 267, 269, 269–70, 273
religions, and government 329–30
renewable energy sources 134
representative democracy 367
researcher reflexivity 280–2
resources, and economies 15
risk 5–6, 57–93
and cycling helmets 57–8, 59, 92
defining 58–9
economic risks 57
environmental risks 101
and epidemiology 83–91
evaluating threat of climate change 311–15
focus group research on 91
food risk and scientific testing 5, 61, 63–70, 80
holidaymakers and sun exposure 61, 71–8, 85, 89–90
media reports on risks 80–1
sun exposure 71–8
and uncertainty 59, 91, 92
see also expert knowledge
risk society 5–6, 79–81, 92, 145, 312
and environmental problems 103, 110
and epidemiological knowledge 86
'role play' data, on black skin and social meaning 277, 279–80, 282–5, 287
Roman Empire, and piracy 399
Romania, migrant workers from 20
Rose, Geoffrey 87
Runnymede Trust, Commission on the Future of Multi-Ethnic Britain 226–7, 228–9
Russia
and al-Qaeda 420
economy and well-being 39, 40
and the UN Security Council 411, 412, 414–15

S

Sabatini, Rafael 395
Saddam Hussein 424–5, 427
St Lucia 134
Sands, Bobby 378, 379
Sartori, Giovanni 369
Saudi Arabia, and Afghanistan 422
school–work transitions, black teenagers and identity change 279–80, 282–5

scientific authority, and government 329
scientific evidence, and threat of climate change
  308, 310–11, 311–12
scientific testing
    soil and food risk 61, 63–70, 80, 89 92, 89
        choice and risk assessment 67–70
        laboratory processes 64–7
Scotland
    and Britishness 217, 218, 219
    economy 27, 28–9
    migration and translocalism 188–9, 293
    national identity 386
    and the United Kingdom 362, 372
Scott, Sir Walter, *The Pirate* 395
sea level rises, and flooding 308
Second World War, and the state 355–6
selective tradition, British culture as 219–21
Sen, Amartya 367
separatist movements, and national identities
  238–9
Serbia, and the international community 412–13,
  414–15, 416
services, and the UK economy 17, 23–4, 31–6
sex
    and national jurisdiction 406
    as a public issue 322, 323
SGVs (soil guidance values), and scientific testing
  64, 67
Shakespeare, William 215
    Richard III 216–17
Sharma, Aradhana 354, 358
single status, and Britishness 213
Sinn Féin 378–9
skin cancer, and sun exposure 61, 72, 77, 81
smoking risks
    and the availability heuristic 319
    and epidemiological knowledge 84, 86
social exclusion 337–8
social identification 274
social identities 153–4
social inequality 305, 331–41
    governing 340–1
    incomes 331–7
    problem of 337–40
social mothering 266
social networks theory of migration 193, 196
social order *see* governing social order
solidarity, and Britishness 225–6, 228
Somali pirates 398, 402, 403, 404, 405

and international order 432
and terrorism 421
UN Resolution on 408
South Africa
    apartheid 229
    economy and well-being 39
sovereign equality 408–9, 420, 440
Soviet Union (former)
    and the Baltic states 240
    invasion of Afghanistan 421–2
Spain
    national identity 237, 238–9
    UK expatriates in 177, 178, 186, 193, 219
spatial segregation, and inequality 340–1
the state 299–300, 351–89, 439, 440
    abstract quality of 356–7
    and anarchism 387–8, 389
    authority of 329–30
    defining 354–9
    encounters with 351–60
    in everyday life 266, 351–60, 354–5, 361, 386,
      388
    and government 357–8
    legitimacy of 300, 366–70, 384–5, 389
    limits of state authority 300
    making and remaking 361–5
    and nations 362
    permanence and continuity of 357–8
    repairing 371–84
    size and complexity of 355–6
    see also international community; political order;
      universal jurisdiction
state institutions 353
states governing social order 299, 305
states-system, and international order 428–31
status anxiety, incomes and happiness 46
stereotypes
    of hoodies 283–4, 287
    and national identities 207
Stevenson, B. 46–7
Stevenson, Robert Louis, *Treasure Island* 395
Stiglitz, Joseph 26
structured interviews 263, 264
sulphur dioxide emissions
    regulations to reduce 31
    tradable permits 119–22
sun exposure
    assessing risks of 61, 71–8, 80, 81, 85, 89–90
    and epidemiological knowledge 83, 85, 89–90

supply and demand
  and the atmospheric commons 110–11, 117, 147
  changes in 15–16
  and global climate change 7
symbolic risk, and material risk 76–7, 76–8
symbols, holidaymakers and suntans 76–8
systemic view of social inequality 338

T

takeovers, and the UK economy 19–20
Tanzania, economy and well-being 39, 40
Tata Group 20–1
taxation
  of the commons 114, 116
  and governments 327
  and the state 354
  and the UK economy 15–16, 31
Taylor, A.J.P. 355–6
technological change, and environmental change 31
territorial jurisdiction 406–7
territory
  and Britishness 215
  and states 364
terrorism
  al-Qaeda 418, 419–23, 424
  car bombs and antiterrorist measures 61
  threat of compared with climate change 307–11, 312, 314–15
  and universal jurisdiction 406
Tesco 21
Thailand, carbon trading 131–3
Thatcher, Margaret 24, 25
theory as method 197–8
Thucydides 430
time, and the weightless economy 32
TNCs (transnational corporations), and the UK economy 20–1
Tonge, John 377
tourist industry, holidaymakers and sun exposure 72, 74
toxins in soil, scientific testing for 63–70
trade
  international trade and the UK economy 18–19
  wasteful 34–5
traffic risks for cyclists 57–8, 59
translocalism 152, 187–9

transnational corporations see TNCs (transnational corporations)
Tversky, A. 315–16

U

Uganda, carbon trading 129–31
UK economy 4–5, 13–49
  and the environment 4–5, 30–7, 101–2, 104
  and global comparisons 38–40
  and governments 15–16
  and the Happy Planet Index 43
  overview of 17–26
  regional differences 4, 27–9
uncertainty
  and the availability heuristic 315–19
  and risk 59, 67, 91, 92
'Uncle Norman', and lay epidemiology 89, 90
United Kingdom (UK) 3–4
  and the international community 411, 415–16
  legislation
    Aliens Act (1905) 171, 172
    Climate Change Act (2008) 35
    Commonwealth Immigrants Act (1962) 171
    Government of Ireland Act (1920) 374
    Special Powers Act (1922) 377
  and state renewal and repair 371–4
  use of the term 217–18, 362
United Nations 326
  Development Programme, human development index (HDI) 42
  Framework Convention on Climate Change (UNFCCC) 122
  and the international community 397, 408–17, 434
  Security Council 410, 411, 423
    and al-Qaeda 419–21
    and international order 426–7
    and the Iraq war 425
    and war with Serbia 412–13, 414–15, 416
  statement on race/ethnicity 232
United States
  and Afghanistan 422
  and democracy 367–8
  and drug cartels of Central America 423–4
  economy 19, 21, 22
    and measures of well-being 26, 39, 41, 46
  governing inequality 340–1

and the international community 414
and the Iraq war 424–6, 427
and the Kyoto Protocol 123, 124–5
migration 177, 178
national identity 240
National Security Strategy 431
and piracy 401
and sulphur trading 119–22
and terrorism 419–21, 424
and the UN Security Council 411
universal jurisdiction, and piracy 396–7, 402,
405–7, 408
unstructured interviews 263, 264

V

vaccinations, and epidemiological knowledge 87–8
value diversity, and Britishness 225, 228
values
Britishness and common values 221–3
happiness and well-being 44, 46
and identities 152
value-laden categories of immigrants 172–5
Vannais, Judy 375, 379
Vanuatu, economy and well-being 39, 40, 42–4, 45
Vietnam, invasion of Cambodia 413–14
visual consumption, holidaymakers and suntans
76–7
vitamin D, and sun exposure 81
vulnerability, to climate change 109–10

W

Wales
and Britishness 217, 218, 219
migration to from England 167, 168
national identity 386
and the UK economy 27, 28, 29
and the United Kingdom 362, 372
Waltz, Kenneth, model of the international order
427–8
Ware, Vron, on Britishness 210–11, 212, 213–14,
224, 233
wasteful trade 34–5
'we'
and Britishness 229–30, 236, 244

and threats to social order 308, 310–11,
319–20
wealth distribution, inequalities in 335–7
Weber, Max 232, 233, 373, 428
Weeks, Jeffrey 322
weightless economies 57, 145
and environmental change 31–6
welfare state 354, 356
well-being
and economic growth 13–14, 49, 57
measures of 39–44
and happiness 5, 13–14, 41–5, 57
William of Orange, and mural painting in
Northern Ireland 376, 379–80
Williams, Raymond 219
win-win situations
and carbon trading 126, 129–30
and trade 19
Winnicott, Donald 265
Wolfers, J. 46–7
women
entrepreneurs and migration 181–2, 183–5
and medical migration 194–5
migrant workers 160, 174, 175
and translocalism 188–9, 293
world cities, London and the UK economy 28
World Health Organization, report on inequality
339
World Resources Institute, map of carbon dioxide
emissions 108–9

Y

young people
value as migrants 173, 175
and the Youth Mobility Scheme 178
Youth Mobility Scheme 178
Yugoslavia (former) 357
and national identities 239

Z

zero-sum power
and international order 427
in Northern Ireland 374–5, 380
Zimbabwe 43